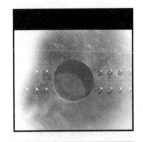

Succeeding with Object Databases

A Practical Look at Today's Implementations with Java™ and XML

Akmal B. Chaudhri
Roberto Zicari

Wiley Computer Publishing

John Wiley & Sons, Inc.

NEW YORK · CHICHESTER · WEINHEIM · BRISBANE · SINGAPORE · TORONTO

Publisher: Robert Ipsen
Editor: Theresa Hudson
Developmental Editor: Kathryn A. Malm
Managing Editor: Angela Smith
Text Design & Composition: Benchmark Productions, Inc.

Designations used by companies to distinguish their products are often claimed as trademarks. In all instances where John Wiley & Sons, Inc., is aware of a claim, the product names appear in initial capital or ALL CAPITAL LETTERS. Readers, however, should contact the appropriate companies for more complete information regarding trademarks and registration.

This publication is designed to provide accurate and authoritative information in regard to the subject matter covered. It is sold with the understanding that the publisher is not engaged in professional services. If professional advice or other expert assistance is required, the services of a competent professional person should be sought.

Library of Congress Cataloging-in-Publication Data:

Chaudhri, Akmal B.
    Succeeding with Object databases : a practical look at today's implementations with Java and XML / Akmal B. Chaudhri, Roberto Zicari
        p. cm.
    Includes bibliographical references and index.
    ISBN 0-471-38384-8 (cloth : alk. paper)
    1. Object-oriented databases. 2. Java (Computer program language) 3. XML (Document markup language) I. Zicari, Roberto. II. Title.

QA76.9.D3 C3848 2000
005.75'7--dc21   00-043455

Printed in the United States of America.
10 9 8 7 6 5 4 3 2 1

Per Aldo.

—RZ

Contents

Acknowledgments

Special thanks are due to Michael Tjahjadi for his initial work in this area, defining the mapping between EXPRESS and object-relational schemas in engineering design applications. We also thank Nilan Yang for her help with refinement of the School Database example in Chapter 2.

The Penguin project described in Chapter 4 was the thesis work of Thierry Barsalou at the Stanford Section for Medical Informatics. Subsequent developments addressed issues in Civil Engineering and Integrated Circuit Manufacturing. Julie Basu developed and evaluated caching algorithms with Meikel Poess as part of her thesis work while supported by Oracle Corporation. Many other students at Stanford contributed to these projects. The effort leading to this paper was supported in part by the Microelectronics Manufacturing Science and Technology project as a subcontract to Texas Instruments on DARPA contract number F33615-88-C-5448 task number 9, and the Center for Integrated Systems. Earlier work leading to these concepts was supported by The National Library of Medicine (NLM) and by ARPA funding for Knowledge-based Management Systems (KBMS) (N039-84-C-0211).

Thanks to Aurélie Bridault for her active contribution to the XML application and Timothy Pullman for his precious re-reading and advice in Chapter 5.

Thanks to Joan Nordbotten for her guidance and support with the research that made Chapter 8 possible. GeoKnowlege also deserves thanks for placing their application at the disposal of this work and for providing useful ideas and additional information on how RDBMSs can be used with an OO application. Thanks also to Akmal B. Chaudhri for the inspiration to enjoy benchmarking and the help he gave in the process of creating the benchmarks. Last, but not least, thanks to the dear friend Karla Clark for her encouragement and proofreading Chapter 8.

The work reported in Chapter 10 was conducted over an 18-month period by the members of the UPSIDE research group of the Cooperative Research Center for Advanced Computational Systems (ACSys). The authors would like to thank members of the UPSIDE group including John Zigman, Gavin Mercer, Luke Kirby, and Zhen He for their part in the development of PSI, OPJ, OVJ, and ABS-BR demonstrator. We are also indebted to the Australian Bureau of Statistics for working with us on this project. We would particularly like to thank those on the ABS-BR team who gave their time to assist us with our research.

We would like to thank the Marine Corps Warfighting Laboratory (MCWL) for sponsoring the work in Chapter 17 as a part of the Urban Warrior Advanced Warfighting Experiment under Program Element 63640M. We would like to thank our program managers at the MCWL, Lt. Cols. Bott, Durham, and Stewart. We would also like to thank the National Imagery and Mapping Agency under the direction of Mr. Steve Hall and Mr. Gary Rogan.

The design and implementation of the DaRT system described in Chapter 18 could not be undertaken without the help of many people. Special thanks are due to the colleagues of Deutsche Bahn AG, TLC and sd&m for their efforts during the last years. Without their creativity and dedication DaRT would not be deployed and this chapter would not exist.

Special thanks to all our contributors. Without them, this book would not have been possible. Thanks, also, to the people at Wiley who worked on this book: Terri Hudson, Kathryn Malm, Angela Smith, and Gerrie Cho.

Introduction

There is a definite need by many users and practitioners for documented case studies and examples that demonstrate the first-hand use of Object Data Management in real-world applications and systems. During the past few years, we have seen tremendous interest in Java. There has been an important shift from using Java just on the client-side to the middle and backend tiers and, additionally, many vendors have begun offering application servers and database products that support Enterprise JavaBeans (EJB) and XML.

In the past, many organizations would wait until an emerging technology had settled and there was an established base before adopting it for use in their enterprise. This is no longer true and many companies post-Y2K appear eager to embrace new Java- and XML-based technologies to achieve a competitive edge. However, any new technology carries with it a number of risks and pitfalls. There are several ways to mitigate these risks. One method is to undertake detailed product evaluations, which may include paper evaluations as well as building prototypes or undertaking small-scale pilot projects. A second approach is to read documented case studies that describe the experiences of others. Both of these approaches can be used together. For example, an organization may have selected a number of potential products and undertaken paper evaluations. To save time, they may find that documented examples help to eliminate some of the candidate products. It is the goal of this book to provide such examples.

This book brings together a collection of chapters principally on Object Databases, but also some chapters covering Object-Relational Databases. Some of the chapters have a strong focus on Java and XML in keeping with new advances in technology.

How This Book Is Organized

This book consists of 18 chapters, grouped into 6 major parts. Each part contains a number of chapters that cover broadly similar topics. These Parts are:

Part One: Introduction (1 chapter)

Part Two: Object-Relational Systems (3 chapters)

Part Three: XML (3 chapters)

Part Four: Benchmarks and Performance (3 chapters)

Part Five: Database Development (4 chapters)

Part Six: Case Studies (4 chapters)

Readers not familiar with the history of Object or Object-Relational Databases may find the Introduction (Part One) a useful starting point, before proceeding to read other parts of this book. Readers already familiar with the history of these database technologies may wish to skip the Introduction. Each of the remaining five Parts is self-contained and can be read in any order.

Part One: Introduction

Part One, Introduction contains Chapter 1, "OODBMS History and Concepts," by Bertino and Guerrini, which provides a good historical perspective on how Object and Object-Relational Databases evolved and some of the current trends in database technology. The roots of Object Databases can be traced back to many different domains, such as the work in persistent programming languages, the growth and popularity of C++ and Smalltalk during the late 1980s and early 1990s, as well as limitations in Relational Database implementations for managing richer data types and complex graph structures. The engineering community also fueled the growth and development of Object Databases during the early days and use of the technology was found in many engineering applications, such as the ubiquitous and often-cited CAD/CAM, and so forth. As the technology matured and became a less risky choice for users, it also became more popular within other vertical markets, including Financial Modeling and Telecommunications Network Management.

Part Two: Object-Relational Systems

Pure Object Databases provide one of a number of possible alternatives to managing persistent objects. During the past few years, there has been a steady growth in the development and use of Object-Relational Databases. These products attempt to build upon the strengths of Relational technology, while providing better support for richer data types. Designing database schemas for such products, however, is still an area that is not well-understood. With Relational Databases, the common techniques of Normalization and Entity-Relationship Modeling are well-known. Extending Relational products with OO features, such as inheritance, is a two-edged sword as it brings both flexibility and complications, since design choices will be greater and ensuring that the best design has been used for a particular problem could be difficult. One part of that problem is how to map a particular modeling language to a database. Chapter 2, "Mapping UML Diagrams to Object-Relational Schemas in Oracle 8," by Urban, Dietrich, and Tapia addresses this issue. It shows, through the use of examples, how the popular Unified Modeling Language (UML) can be mapped to Oracle 8 schemas.

Today, Java is increasingly being used for building applications in multi-tier systems. Many of these applications require persistence and will typically use a Relational Database on the backend. Therefore, the need arises to store and retrieve Java objects from Relational tables. Sun Microsystems developed JDBC a few years ago to meet this requirement. JDBC is modeled on the popular ODBC. It is also a low-level API and drivers are available for most major Relational Database products. Another interesting development has been a way to directly embed SQL within Java, as is possible with many other popular programming languages. The result of this work has been SQLj, and some of the major Object-Relational Database vendors are beginning to offer this capability in their products. Chapter 3, "SQLJ and JDBC: Database Access in Java," by Basu provides a comparison and discussion of SQLj and JDBC. It is interesting that the two technologies actually complement one another.

For many organizations, moving to Object-Relational Databases may not be possible or may be inappropriate. However, new requirements may still arise that use data in existing Relational Databases. If this is coupled with the need to access that data using an OO Programming Language, such as C++ or Java, then one possibility is to use a mapping tool. Hand coding is also possible, but if the mapping is complex, it may be better to buy rather than build. Today, there are many Object-to-Relational mapping tools vendors. In fact, the focus of many of these vendors is specifically Java-to-Relational mapping. Some of the early and pioneering work in Object-to-Relational mapping and Object Mediators was undertaken by Keller and Wiederhold and in Chapter 4, "Penguin: Objects for Programs, Relations for Persistence," they discuss some of the practical and pragmatic reasons why it is necessary as well as providing a tutorial on the subject.

Part Three: XML

It is difficult to find detailed evaluations of Object Database products for real-world systems. One reason for this is that many companies view this technology as giving them a competitive edge and so are reluctant to divulge their findings, whether positive or negative. Chapter 5, "A New Stage in ODBMS Normalization: Myth or Reality?" by Guennou is, therefore, a valuable contribution, particularly as it is from the financial domain. The chapter provides a discussion of the current state of the Object Database market and first-hand evaluation of ODMG support in several products. The use of XML for managing corporate data with an Object Database is also discussed and shows that this database technology is well-suited to this type of application. Finally, the chapter compares O2 and Versant along a number of dimensions and the performance results show the importance of the choice of hardware platform.

One area that offers tremendous potential is to use Java and XML with some kind of persistence mechanism or database system. Chapter 6, "PDOM: Lightweight Persistency Support," by Huck, Macherius, and Fankhauser provides details of some research that investigates a Persistent Document Object Model (PDOM) system. In this chapter, they discuss a number of thorny issues and their solutions to them. In particular, managing schema-less systems, the impedance mismatch between the DOM and the underlying storage system, and support for caching mechanisms.

Today, many organizations that work with object technology are using modeling languages, such as UML, to capture their designs in ways that can be communicated more easily between developers and design teams. However, the features and capabilities of some languages are so extensive that they can be difficult to use in practice. Chapter 7, "The Model of Object Primitives (MOP)," by Georgalas describes an approach, called the Model of Object Primitives (MOP), that provides expressive power through simplicity. In this chapter, MOP is compared against three technologies that are very relevant to database systems, namely XML, ODMG, and the Relational model. The comparison shows that MOP can represent the semantics of any of these models. Two short case studies then demonstrate MOP in practice.

Part Four: Benchmarks and Performance

Database performance is an area where the Relational vendors have often competed fiercely with each other on the well-known TPC benchmarks. Within the Object Database world, there has been no equivalent organization to TPC, but a few well-known benchmarks, such as OO1 and OO7 with their roots in the engineering world, continue to be used by many researchers. In commercial evaluations, such benchmarks tend to have little value, since they are not representative of many Object Database applications today. There are even fewer public benchmarks that attempt to compare both Object and Relational Databases. Chapter 8, "A Performance Comparison of Object and Relational Databases for Complex Objects," by Bjørge is, therefore, particularly interesting. He uses part of a live system and describes his experiments in detail. The results show that an Object Database is not always faster than a Relational Database, which can in fact provide good performance in some cases. Bjørge concludes that it is important to undertake application-specific tests and pay care and attention to implementation details with any products under test, as such considerations may have noticeable performance implications.

Many database vendors from both the Object and Relational worlds have begun to offer strong Java support in their products. For Object Database vendors this would appear to be a natural extension of their previous offerings that supported C++ and Smalltalk. The Java language binding of the ODMG standard also appears to be the best supported by the pure Object Database vendors. However, we still do not understand many issues about the performance of such database systems using Java, and the language may bring with it its own special problems. Chapter 9, "Object Databases and Java Architectural Issues," by Danielsen provides a good insight into some architectural issues, based on his evaluation of the Java language binding of a full-featured Object Database System. He discusses a number of general architectural issues as well as some more specific to Java, highlighting potential areas of concern and interest.

In any large-scale system development, questions of managing complexity and system scalability are perhaps uppermost in the minds of many developers, architects, and managers. Marquez and Blackburn describe one large-scale implementation that uses an Object Database in Chapter 10, "Addressing Complexity and Scale in a High Performance Object Server." The chapter is also a very good example of Academia and Industry working together to develop answers to modern-day problems in using new technology. The discussion centers on how to tackle the issues of complexity and scale. One way to reduce complexity is to improve abstraction. Through the development of a prototype system, based upon Orthogonally Persistent Java (OPJ), the authors successfully show how complexity can be better managed. Furthermore, while scalability was not directly tested, their work looks very promising for the future.

Part Five: Database Development

Chapter 11, "The Unified Modeling Process in Web-Deployed Object-Oriented Data Base Systems," by Janssen, Rine, and Damiani begins with an overview of the issues in designing object-oriented applications, using a methodology that they have been developing for several years to improve team productivity and quality. They pay particular attention to the design and development of those aspects that include a persistent common object model. Next, they describe their experiences with development using the Unified Modeling Language (UML) in Rational Rose and an Object-Oriented Database for an application called B2C_Sys. Finally, they discuss some future directions.

Many universities and colleges have been offering courses in Object Databases for a number of years now but we are not aware of any published papers that describe experiences that lecturers have had with this technology or the successes/problems their students have encountered using Object Databases for practical assignment work. Chapter 12, "Teaching Object-Oriented Database Concepts," by Tari, Bukhres, and Craske is, therefore, a very useful contribution. The chapter provides a discussion of the teaching methods used, some of the practical assignments that were set, and some of the issues and problems that students encountered. This chapter also provides some details about the teaching material used and should serve as a good reference to many lecturers and students.

Sometimes when dealing with a new technology, it can be useful to have a "quick start" guide that provides some useful information for developers to get them up to speed quickly. Furthermore, any pitfalls to avoid or "gotchas" to use can also be very valuable. Chapter 13, "Building a Jasmine Database," by Fallon falls into this category. Based upon his experiences using Jasmine over a period of time, he uses his knowledge to good effect by describing some examples using particular product features. Although the chapter is obviously focused on one particular Object Database, you should become more alert to product-specific issues when evaluating different Object Databases. Furthermore, the number of Jasmine developers is growing and many of them are still using the current GA version of Jasmine and may find the ideas presented in this chapter to be helpful.

One of the major benefits that Object Databases claim over Relational Databases is that they use existing programming languages and manage both transient and persistent (database) objects in a similar way, overcoming the often-quoted "impedance mismatch" problem. This should make the task of the developer easier, since the language used for application development is the same language that the database understands. In reality, some extensions to existing languages are typically needed to manage database operations, such as opening/closing a database, and transactions. Chapter 14, "Seamlessness and Transparency in Object-Oriented Databases," by Kaplan and Wileden shows that for products that follow the ODMG standard, seamless persistence is not possible, since transient and persistent objects are treated differently, with the result that transparency is lost. Furthermore, the problem is greater for multiple language bindings. Through their research work, the authors also report upon their experiences with multiple language bindings.

Part Six: Case Studies

A common argument for using Object Databases instead of Relational Databases for some applications is that they provide better capabilities to capture the structure and behavior of objects from the problem domain. There are many examples from the Financial and Telecommunications industries that show this to be the case. Another domain where this technology appears to have proved itself useful is in Genetics. Today, there exist many research laboratories and academic institutions that are actively undertaking important research into the Human Genome Project and some have published their experiences with Object Databases recently. To determine whether advances in Object Databases over the past few years have led to improved support for genetics work, we have included Chapters 15 and 16. Chapter 15, "Experiences Using the ODMG Standard in Bioinformatics Applications," by Paton provides a discussion and evaluation of a product that claims ODMG compliance, for modeling and analyses of the yeast genome, while Chapter 16, "An Object-Oriented Database for Managing Genetic Sequences," by Bellahsene and Ripoche provides a discussion of Object and Relational Databases for genomic data and how some of the limitations in a prototype using an Object Database were overcome.

Another area that has attracted strong interest in the use of Object Databases is for modeling Geospatial information. Such data consist of features, such as lines and points, which can be awkward to model in a Relational Database, as they may contain many relationships, which incur a performance overhead when trying to reconstruct topological features. Chapter 17, "The Geospatial Information Distribution System (GIDS)," by Chung et al. discusses the use of an Object Database for modeling multi-dimensional spatial data in a three-tier system, consisting of thin Java clients, CORBA in the middle-tier, and an Object Database on the backend. The three technologies worked very successfully together as demonstrated by a warfare simulator that is also described.

Mergers and acquisitions between organisations are commonplace today. This can be problematic when integrating their Information Technology (IT) systems as companies may use different hardware and software platforms. Chapter 18, "Architecture of the Distributed, Multi-Tier Railway Application DaRT," by Zimmermann et al. describes a multi-tier distributed system that was used to integrate the two different parts of the German railway company Deutsche Bahn AG (from East and West Germany). To improve performance for users, caching was used on the various tiers of their architecture and they evaluate a number of caching policies with database clustering in mind. The experiences reported also demonstrate the benefits of using object technology, although the learning curve for those unfamiliar with this approach can be steep. The lessons reported should be very beneficial to others facing similar system integration problems.

Who Should Read This Book

This book can be read by anyone interested in how Object Data Management can be effectively used. It is, therefore, aimed at a very broad readership and should appeal to anyone ranging from a seasoned professional to a university or college student. Readers should be familiar with Object Technology, Database Management Systems, and Software Development Techniques. Readers familiar with the history and background of Object and Object-Relational Databases can skip the Introduction (Part One). Each of the other five Parts is self-contained and can be read in any particular order.

What's on the Web Site

Additional resources for this book are available at the following Web site:
   http://www.wiley.com/compbooks/chaudhri/
   These resources will include links to relevant Web sites and other related publications. Contributions from readers are welcome to help make the Web site a useful resource for all interested parties.

Summary

In putting together this collection of chapters we wanted to provide some examples of how Object Data Management was being used by users and practitioners. We hope that this book will serve a useful role in bringing to the wider community a collection of papers that also give useful insights into some of the new and emerging technologies, such as Java, XML, and Object-Relational Systems.

PART

One

Introduction

In this section, Chapter 1, "OODBMS History and Concepts" by Bertino and Guerrini, provides a good historical perspective on how object databases evolved and discusses some of the current trends in database technology.

The roots of object databases can be traced back to many different domains, such as the work in persistent programming languages, the growth and popularity of C++ and Smalltalk during the late 1980s and early 1990s, as well as limitations in relational database implementations for managing richer data types and complex graph structures. During the early days, the growth and development of object databases was also fuelled by the engineering community, and use of the technology was found in many engineering applications, such as the ubiquitous and often-cited CAD/CAM. As the technology matured and became a less risky choice for users, it also became more popular within other vertical markets, including Financial Modelling and Telecommunications Network Management.

However, several trends have prevented the more widespread use of object databases. First, many of the relational vendors announced that they would provide support for object-orientation in their products, so loyal relational customers waited for these capabilities. Second, many organizations already had made a considerable investment in relational databases, so it was not easy switching to another database technology. Third, the Y2K problem over the past few years focused the attention and resources of many companies, so new investment and developments were put on the back burner until this issue was resolved. Fourth, the rate of change of technology has accelerated, and Java has become very popular in just a few short years. This has led to the tremendous growth in Java-to-relational mapping tools; companies can keep their investment in existing relational technology while being able to develop new applications with Java. Fifth, multitier architectures are now common practice and many former relational database vendors have begun offering application servers, which build upon their existing customer base. Finally, internal politics and preferences within an organization can sometimes be the deciding factor on the use of a particular database technology, and managers may stick with something with which they are familiar rather than risk a new technology—something that is less of an issue with programming languages and development tools.

Despite these setbacks, many object database vendors, because of their small size, have responded quickly to market forces. For example, one of the major object database vendors switched its positioning to become an application server vendor a few years ago. Also, some of the other vendors now are marketing their products as containers for EJB servers.

OODBMS History and Concepts

The first and most important database applications were used in business and administration, typically for banking applications to maintain information about customers and accounts, and also for applications that stored record-oriented data, such as an inventory system. This influenced the organization and use of data into database management systems (DBMSs). In the 1980s, as a result of hardware innovations, new data intensive applications emerged, for which traditional DBMSs, based on the relational data model, were inadequate. Examples of such applications include design and manufacturing systems (CAD/CAM, CIM), scientific and medical databases, geographic information systems, and multimedia databases. These applications have requirements and characteristics, such as highly structured data, long transactions, multimedia data, and nonstandard, application-specific operations, which are different from those typical of traditional database applications.

Object-oriented database management systems (OODBMSs) have been developed in order to meet the requirements imposed by those applications. The object-oriented approach provides the required flexibility because it is not limited to the data types and query languages available in traditional database systems. One of the most important features of OODBMSs is the ability to specify both the structure of complex application objects and the operations to manipulate those structures.

OODBMSs result from the integration of database technology with the object-oriented paradigm developed in the programming language and software engineering areas. The basic principle of the object-oriented approach in programming is to consider the program as a collection of independent objects grouped in classes, which communicate with each other through messages. The same concepts, however, have also been introduced in other computer science areas, such as knowledge representation languages, and have often been interpreted in different ways.

In an object-oriented programming language, objects exist only during the execution of the program that creates them. In an object-oriented database, by contrast, objects can be created that persist and can be shared by several programs. Thus, object-oriented databases store persistent objects in secondary storage and support object sharing between different applications. Support for persistent objects requires integration of the object-oriented paradigm with typical DBMS mechanisms such as indexing, concurrency control, and transaction management.

Commercial OODBMS products appeared more than a decade ago. Since then, although OODBMSs were improving significantly from their earliest releases and the object-oriented paradigm was establishing itself in many contexts (e.g., programming languages and software engineering), many changes have occurred in computer science. For example, the emergence and quick increase in use of the Internet and the World Wide Web (WWW) have significantly changed the way applications are developed. These changes have strongly impacted both object-oriented technology and OODBMSs.

In this chapter we provide a brief historical overview of OODBMSs and a short introduction to the basic concepts of the OODBMS data model and query language. We first discuss the most relevant phases in OODBMS history and then focus on specific systems that most relevantly influenced the field.

Historical Perspective

Strong experimental work and the development of several prototype systems have characterized research in the area of object-oriented databases; however, only later were theoretical foundations investigated and standards developed. These trends represent, in some way, the reverse of what happened for relational DBMSs (RDBMSs), for which the development of systems began after the formal definition of the data model. The first OODBMSs appeared on the market in 1986, and since then not only the systems but also the computer science and application scenarios have changed considerably. In this section, we provide a brief overview of what happened in those years.

The Beginning

The late 1980s saw the birth of OODBMSs and, since then, this type of system has undergone intense industrial development. In the space of a few years, different generations of OODBMSs were developed.

The first generation of OODBMSs dates back to 1986, when the French company Graphael introduced G-Base on the market. In 1987, an American company, Servio Corporation, introduced GemStone. In 1988, Ontologic (later to become Ontos, Inc.) introduced Vbase and Symbolics introduced Statice. The common goal of this group of products was to support persistence for object languages, in particular those languages related to artificial intelligence. The distinguishing features of these systems were that they were stand-alone, were based on proprietary languages, and did not use standard industrial platforms. In 1990, the total number of systems installed by those companies was perhaps between 400 and 500, and the systems were located mainly in the research departments of large companies.

The release of Ontos from the company of the same name in 1989 marked the beginning of the second generation in the development of OODBMSs. Products from Object

Design, Objectivity, and Versant Object Technology (ObjectStore, Objectivity/DB, and Versant ODBMS, respectively) followed soon after. Compared to the first generation of OODBMSs, all the second-generation systems used a client/server architecture and a common platform: C++, X Windows, and UNIX workstations.

The first product of the third generation, Itasca, was released in August 1990, only a few months after the release of second-generation OODBMSs. Itasca was a commercial version of Orion, a project developed by the Microelectronics and Computer Corporation (MCC), a research institute based in Austin, Texas, and financed by a number of American hardware manufacturers. The other third-generation OODBMSs were O2, produced by the French company Altaïr, and Zeitgeist, a system developed internally by Texas Instruments.

Though first-generation OODBMSs can be considered as extensions of object-oriented languages—that is, they typically extend such languages with database capabilities, adding things like transactions, for example—third-generation systems can be defined as DBMSs with advanced characteristics (e.g., version support) and with data definition and data manipulation languages that are object-oriented and computationally complete. Beyond the technical differences in architectures and functionalities, third-generation DBMSs are the result of long-term research projects run by large organizations who sought to capitalize on their investments. Therefore, they are very advanced systems from the viewpoint of both database technology and software development environments.

The beginning of OODBMSs was thus characterized by the development of a large number of systems, most of which were produced by small vendors. These systems were revolutionary with respect to previous DBMSs in that they were built from scratch with a different code base and a different data model. In this initial period, the research community felt the need to at least define what an OODBMS was. Thus, in 1989, the Object-Oriented Database System Manifesto [Atkinson 1989] was published. This document describes the main features and characteristics that a system must have to qualify as an OODBMS.

Standardization

The OODBMS panorama at the beginning of the 1990s was characterized by a quite a large number of systems that lacked a common data model, and whose use in applications was still at the experimental stage. One of the reasons for the slow growth in OODBMSs was the resistance by customers and companies to migrate to new technologies. However, a common feeling within the OODBMS community was that the lack of an object database standard was the major limitation that prevented their widespread use. The success of RDBMSs did not simply result from a higher level of data independence and a simpler data model than previous systems, but also from the standardization they offered. The SQL standard offers a high degree of portability and interoperability between systems, simplifies learning new RDBMSs, and represents a wide endorsement of the relational approach. All these factors are important for OODBMSs as well. Actually, these factors are even more important for OODBMSs, because companies that develop most products in this area are young, small companies; portability and endorsement of the approach are thus essential to customers. In addition, the scope of OODBMSs is more far-reaching than that of RDBMSs, because

OODBMSs integrate the programming language and the database system, and encompass all of an application's operations and data.

The ODMG (Object Database Management Group) consortium was formed the summer of 1991 in response to the lack of an existing standards body working on OODB standards, and as a way to help the small OODB vendors gain a foothold in the competitive database marketplace. The primary role of this group was to develop a set of standards that would allow an OODBMS customer to write portable applications; that is, applications that could run on more than one OODBMS. ODMG member companies represented almost the entire OODBMS industry. This standardization effort falls within the common effort of promoting the definition of standards for the object-oriented world. ODMG is affiliated with the Object Management Group (OMG), established in 1989, and tried to benefit as much as possible from the work developed by that group. The main contribution of OMG has been the definition of the CORBA architecture for distributed object systems interoperability.

Since OODBMSs provide an architecture for developing applications that is significantly different from RDBMSs, the nature of the standard is also substantially different. Rather than providing only a high-level language such as SQL for data manipulation, an OODBMS transparently integrates database capability with an application programming language. Thus, in contrast to RDBMSs, OODBMSs require standards based on integration with existing programming languages. OODBMSs have been integrated with C++, C, Smalltalk, and LISP. Overlap with the RDBMS standard only concerns the query language component of the standard.

The ODMG standard was first released in 1993, followed by release 1.2 of the standard, published in a book [Cattell 1996]. The ODMG standard included a reference Object Model (ODMG Object Model), an Object Definition Language (ODL), and an Object Query Language (OQL). Moreover, it defined the C++ and Smalltalk programming language bindings for ODL and data manipulation. The ODMG Object Model specifies the standard data model for object-oriented databases, and ODL is the Data Definition Language (DDL) that is provided to define an object database schema according to that model. OQL is a declarative query language, strongly inspired by the SQL query language, whereas the language bindings specify how the object model concepts are mapped into the considered languages, and how ODMG objects can be accessed and manipulated by the languages. The ODMG object model was defined as a superset of the OMG object model, and ODL extended the OMG IDL (Interface Definition Language).

Object-Relational DBMSs

Object-relational DBMSs (ORDBMSs) provide an alternative approach to using objects with a database system. Whereas OODBMSs represented a revolutionary approach in that they turned object-oriented programming languages into DBMSs, object-relational DBMSs took an evolutionary approach, integrating objects with the relational data model and extending existing RDBMSs with object-oriented features. The two approaches strongly conflicted in the early 1990s: one group proposed extensions to object-oriented languages (the pure OODB approach) and the other stated that we should start with relational databases and add OO extensions (the hybrid approach). Now they seem much more convergent.

The idea of object-relational DBMSs dates back to 1990 when the Third Generation Database System Manifesto [Stonebraker 1990] was published as a response to the Object-Oriented Database System Manifesto. The basic premise of the Manifesto was that new (third) generation DBMSs must be able to handle objects and rules, and must be compatible with second-generation (that is, relational) DBMSs. In the same year that the Manifesto was published, UniSQL, Inc. was founded by Won Kim, one of the designers of the Orion OODBMS. UniSQL produced the UniSQL Object-Relational DBMS, which used SQL/X, an extension of SQL-92, as the database language. In the 1990s there was intense research and experimentation with object-relational DBMSs. The early object-relational vendors were start-up companies that included, in addition to UniSQL, Illustra and Omniscience. In 1996 Informix acquired Illustra, and all the other major database vendors (Sybase, IBM, and Oracle) began moving toward object-relational products. Then, a consensus on the object-relational data model features emerged in the SQL-3 standard [Mattos 1996] and all the major database vendors (Informix, Sybase, IBM, and Oracle) have released object-relational products that reflect this consensus.

Object-relational DBMSs extend the traditional relational database model to include the object-oriented benefits of encapsulation, polymorphism, and inheritance. These systems are relational because they support SQL; they are object-oriented because they support complex data. In some sense they represent a marriage between SQL from the relational world and the modeling primitives from the object world. The main motivation that has pushed the development of these systems is the feeling that RDBMSs satisfy the requirements only of applications that handle "simple data with complex queries." Object-relational DBMSs offer good performance, support concurrent access to data, and provide access control and reliability. OODBMSs, by contrast, allow you to manage complex data, but they do not offer adequate associative query support ("complex data with simple queries") and they do not provide, at the same level of adequacy, many of the data management functions provided by RDBMSs, such as authorization, concurrency control, and recovery. The goal of object-relational systems was thus to support RDBMS functions efficiently with respect to traditional data handling, and at the same time to extend the data model so that complex data can be handled as well. Moreover, users of object-relational DBMSs will not suffer migration problems, since backward compatibility and handling of legacy data is ensured.

During the 1990s, both the quality of DBMS functions offered by OODBMS products and their support for declarative query facilities improved, and this is the reason why OODBMSs and ORDBMSs converged. For example, the OQL query language is very similar to the SQL-3 query language. In addition to their different beginnings, some strong differences also persist between the two database technologies. First, OODBMSs provide persistence to objects created in languages such as Java, C++, and Smalltalk. Programmers define new types or classes of objects in these languages (employing any data structures they care to code) and create instances of these classes. Using the DBMS mechanisms, these objects can be stored and shared. As a result, OODBMSs are highly flexible, supporting a wide range of structures and types. They can be thought of as an extension of an object-oriented programming environment, since the integration with the programming language is almost seamless. This approach differs from object-relational DBMSs, which introduce a separate API (based on SQL) to work with stored data. When using ORDBMSs, class definitions must be mapped into data types supported by the database system. Second, OODBMSs often feature a highly client-centric architecture, managing a cache of objects on the client machine and providing the means to navigate through interrelated objects. This architecture is highly suitable for certain applications, such as iterative design work. Object-relational DBMSs, by contrast, typically adopt a server-centric approach, which is more suitable for a large number of arbitrary concurrent queries.

Java

A big revolution in the object-oriented world occurred in the mid-1990s with the development of the Java programming language, which very quickly established itself as the programming language for Web applications. The increasingly wider use of Web-related technologies, together with the fact that Java is the synthesis of good experiences gained from other object-oriented languages such as C++ and Smalltalk, has made Java the most common object-oriented programming language. Today, many companies are making an expensive shift to object technology, and currently the language of choice appears to be Java. Moreover, Java technology has become the standard platform for both distributed and intranet applications.

Different alternatives have been devised to add persistence to Java. The simplest method relies on the serialization facility provided by the language, which allows objects to be flattened into a stream of bytes that, when read later, can recreate objects equivalent to those that were written into the stream. This approach, however, is viable only for a small amount of data for which reliability and other typical DBMS features are not required.

A second solution is represented by the use of RDBMSs to store Java data, connecting Java applications to an RDBMS through a set of Java database connectivity (JDBC) classes. These classes were introduced by JavaSoft, and represent a standard SQL database interface. Storing Java data in a relational database actually requires much more work than enabling only access to an RDBMS; Java objects must be mapped to the relational schema. Mapping can be performed with the help of available commercial tools that provide support for obtaining a relational database to store a set of objects, relying on mapping mechanisms between the object and the relational data model. The work of the SQLJ consortium [Shaw 1999] also falls in this direction. SQLJ is the SQL relational language with the ability to be embedded in Java. This follows the approach used with other languages, such as C, C++, and Pascal, where SQL code can be "hosted" within another language to provide database access. This consortium is developing a Java-relational database technology that consists of SQLJ Embedded SQL (specifying how to embed SQL in Java), SQLJ Procedure (specifying how to use Java static methods as SQL stored procedures and functions), and SQLJ Data Types (specifying how to use pure Java classes as SQL Abstract Data Types (ADTs), as an alternative to SQL3 ADTs).

Orthogonally Persistent Java (OPJ) provides a third solution. This is the goal of the Forest project at Sun Microsystems Laboratories. Persistent Object Systems that rely on the notion of orthogonal persistence automate data management tasks and provide a single model for both short-term and long-term data. This means, for instance, that there is no visible or separate database from the perspective of the programmer. In the OPJ approach, the Java Virtual Machine (JVM) is responsible for managing the entire storage hierarchy; the programmer simply views the Java platform as a database. Note that in this approach persistence is provided, but many database features such as querying, data sharing, and durability are missing.

Finally, Java objects can be stored in an OODBMS. The impact of Java on the OODBMS world has been considerable, and most commercial OODBMSs have been extended to offer native support for storing Java objects. OODBMSs such as POET and ObjectStore, which initially were developed to store persistent C++ objects, now provide versions to store persistent Java objects. This can be achieved with minimal modifications to the Java code in applications. The extensions are based on the use of a pre-processor that automatically prepares objects for storage in an object database. The development effort to use an OODBMS with native support for Java is significantly lower than the effort required to use an RDBMS, since the modifications required to Java applications in order to add persistence-related operations are very small.

As a result of the development and increasing popularity of Java, the second version of the ODMG standard (ODMG 2.0 [Cattell 1997], released in 1997) has added a Java programming language binding to the C++ and Smalltalk bindings that were defined in the first version. Moreover, the influence of Java is also reflected in many changes to the object model, such as the notion of an interface and the introduction of two different inheritance hierarchies. The latest published version of the ODMG standard (release 3.0 [Cattell 2000]) has further enhanced the Java binding.

OODBMS Products and Their Evolution

In this section we discuss the object-oriented database management systems that, in our opinion, most heavily influenced the field. For each system, we highlight the aspects that have been investigated prominently, and the peculiar characteristics that impacted the ODMG standard as well as other OODBMSs. This is not an exhaustive and detailed survey; for each system we discuss its most relevant and noteworthy features, and its main evolution from earliest releases.

ORION/Itasca

The ORION next-generation databases project in the Advanced Computer Technology (ACT) Program at the Microelectronics and Computer Technology Corporation (MCC) in Austin, Texas, started at the end of 1985 and completed at the end of 1989, under the direction of Dr. Won Kim. The ORION system was developed to provide direct support to the object-oriented paradigm, as well as innovating features to CAD/CAM and artificial intelligence (AI) applications. In particular, it has been used to provide persistence to the Proteus expert system developed in the same project.

The ORION project prototyped a family of three next-generation database systems. MCC released the first prototype, ORION-1 (implemented in Common Lisp), in May 1987, as a single-user system. MCC extended ORION-1 to the ORION-1SX prototype system and released it to the shareholder companies in April 1988. ORION-1SX was a multi-user system with a multiclient, single-server architecture. The third prototype, ORION-2, introduced a distributed, object-oriented architecture for a multi-user environment. MCC released the third prototype to shareholder companies in July 1989.

ORION-2 has a multiclient, multiserver architecture. Having met its objectives, MCC stopped all work on ORION at that time. Over five million dollars was spent for the three generations of prototypes. Most of the results achieved in the project are reported in "Introduction to Object-Oriented Databases" [Kim 1990].

A peculiar feature of the distributed architecture of ORION-2 is the distinction between shared and private databases. The shared database is distributed across workstations (sites) in a network. An ORION-2 server controls the partition of the shared database at each site. ORION-2 clients provide transparent access to the various partitions of the shared database. The architecture allows any number of private databases at each distributed database site, and data can move between private and shared databases. Private databases store private data that is not shared with other users of the database.

The architectural issues for object-oriented databases that the ORION project has addressed include dynamic schema evolution, versions and change notification, composite objects, query model, automatic query optimization, indexing, transaction management and concurrency control, authorization, and multimedia data management. The ORION project was the first to publish detailed foundational papers on many of these topics.

Since August 1990, an extension and commercialization of the ORION-2 prototype from MCC is sold as the product Itasca. Itasca Systems has added major enhancements and features, improved the performance, and strengthened the code. It now runs on UNIX systems from multiple vendors and is an industrial-strength, documented product, for which several tools have been developed. Itasca is now distributed by IBEX Knowledge Systems S.A. IBEX has joined the ODMG consortium after the first release of the standard, and has been a voting member of ODMG since the release 2.0 of ODMG in 1997.

O2

The Altaïr consortium developed O2 as a result of a five-year project that began in September 1986. Its goal was to implement a next-generation database system. The five-year period was divided into two phases: a three-year prototyping period and a two-year development phase. A first throwaway prototype was demonstrated in December 1987, and a second working prototype was completed in March 1989, although work continued to improve upon it until September 1989, when it was released to a set of selected partners for evaluation. O2 Technology released O2 as a product in 1991.

The focus of the project, whose history and main results are collected in "Building an Object-Oriented Database System: The Story of O2" [Bancilhon 1992] was on programming languages and environments, rather than on architectural issues. Programming tools as well as a user interface generator have been developed as part of the project. Considerable research results have been achieved concerning the formal definition of the data model and the specification of a declarative, SQL-like algebraic query language.

From September 1992 until November 1995, the European Project GOODSTEP had investigated the use of O2 as the basis for a Software Engineering Environment, with the goal to enhance and improve the product. In the context of the GOODSTEP project the following issues have been investigated for O2: schema evolution, versions, view mechanisms, triggers, and concurrency control (in particular, the extension of the original page-based mechanism to an object-level mechanism). The first two features have been integrated in the product since version 4.6, released in 1995.

O2 Technology has been part of the ODMG consortium since its conception, and its members have acted as OQL editors for the standard. O2 Technology then became Ardent Software, which is now selling the two object-relational products UniData and UniVerse.

GemStone

First introduced in 1987, GemStone [Bretl 1989] is the oldest commercial OODBMS available today. GemStone extends the object-oriented programming language Smalltalk-80 into a database system. Servio Logic Development Corp., involved in research and development of object-oriented data management systems since 1983, developed GemStone with the goal to produce a DBMS with a very powerful data model that would reduce development time for complex applications.

GemStone initially was implemented in Pascal and then reimplemented in C. From its early versions, it provides a C interface, a C++ interface, and a Smalltalk interface for applications written in C, C++, and Smalltalk, respectively, to access GemStone. The programmatic interface to Smalltalk is called OPAL. This proprietary interface is a database extension to Smalltalk; that is, it extends Smalltalk with data definition and data manipulation capabilities.

GemStone has been one of the most visible OODBMS both in terms of database features provided and contributions to the field. It has been one of the first OODBMSs to support concurrency control (through a very interesting mechanism that combines pessimistic and optimistic approaches), recovery (through a shadowing mechanism), dynamic schema modifications, transaction management, authorization (but in a much more limited form than in ORION), indexing, and queries (though through a much more limited language than O2).

The GemStone data model has some peculiar characteristics due to its Smalltalk origins. Everything is an object (that is, literals are not supported), the specification of attribute domains is not mandatory, extents are separated from classes, and no explicit object deletion operation is provided; rather, objects are garbage collected when no longer referred to by other objects.

GemStone Systems, Inc. now distributes GemStone, and is an active member of the Object Management Group and of ODMG since their constitution. Two different versions are currently available: GemStone/S (Smalltalk version) and GemStone/J (Java version). GemStone/J is targeted in particular to Internet commerce and supports the generation and storage of XML documents.

IRIS/OpenODB

The IRIS database management system [Fishman 1989] is a research prototype developed at Hewlett-Packard (HP) Laboratories. It has been developed with the aim of providing object-management services to C programs and LISP programs through a C-interface and a LISP-interface. The users may access IRIS through an object-oriented extension of SQL, called OSQL, or a graphical editor. The IRIS object manager was based on a relational storage system called HP-SQL.

The IRIS data model is based on the DAPLEX functional model. One elegant aspect of IRIS is the consistent use of a function formalism in its data modeling. It has been one of the first object-oriented data models that support the notion of relationship and of inverse property. Other interesting aspects of the data model are object migration, multiple class direct membership, and support for referential integrity. It moreover supports (a limited form of) rules. IRIS also supported a healthy list of database features, including limited schema evolution, versions, a query language, and query optimization. It further supported transactions, concurrency control, and recovery via HP-SQL.

The IRIS project resulted in the OpenODB DBMS, whose features include multimedia data handling, indexing, clustering, transaction management, and multi-user support. OpenODB is the combination of HP's object/relational adapter Odapter and HP's ALLBASE/SQL relational DBMS.

Vbase/Ontos

Ontologic Inc. launched Vbase [Andrews 1987] in 1988 as an object-oriented development environment that combined a procedural environment with persistent data management. Vbase was based on two proprietary languages: TDL (Type Definition Language), which was used as data definition language, and COP (C Object Processor), a C superset used as method definition language and to write applications. Interesting aspects of Vbase were the support of an exception mechanism, the support for inverse attributes, and the possibility of customizing accessor and mutator functions provided by the system. Vbase provided only a basic set of database features, including programmer-controlled clustering of objects, recovery, an SQL interface, and limited support for concurrency control and access control.

Both TDL and COP are proprietary languages and, for this reason, despite various interesting aspects of the languages, Ontologic has decided to abandon the languages and adopt C++ as the programmatic interface of its OODBMS (whose name has been changed to Ontos). Ontos has evolved into a fully distributed OODBMS. Ontologic became ONTOS, Inc., and has participated as a reviewer member in the ODMG consortium since its constitution.

ObjectStore

ObjectStore [Object Design 1999] was launched by Object Design in 1989. ObjectStore has been designed to simplify the conversion of existing applications and it is targeted to applications areas such as interactive modeling and computer-aided analysis and design. ObjectStore provides persistence to C++ objects, supporting a tightly integrated interface to achieve an easy migration path for existing C and C++. Thus, transparent interfaces for popular C++ programming environments are provided. No declarative SQL-like query language is provided. ObjectStore more recently has been extended to provide persistence to Java objects, exactly in the same spirit of the C++ version of ObjectStore.

Access to ObjectStore is provided through a library-based application interface that is compatible with popular C and C++ (respectively, Java) compilers and programming environments. The application interface provides powerful high-level function calls that enable the programmer to create multi-user applications that share large amount of data. These functions include collection management, object iteration, storage management, relationship management, version management, transaction management, index management, and clustering. In addition to persistence, ObjectStore supports a set of traditional DBMS features such as transaction management (concurrency control and recovery), distributed access, and indexing.

One of the specific goals of the system was that of achieving good performance. To achieve this goal, an architecture based on virtual memory with page-faults has been employed. When an application refers to data that are not in main memory, a page-fault occurs. The page-fault is handled by ObjectStore, which loads in main memory the database segment containing the requested data.

Object Design has been part of the ODMG consortium since its constitution, and participated as a voting member to both releases of the standard. ObjectStore is now distributed by eXcelon Corporation, which also distributes eXcelon [Object Design 1999], an ObjectStore-based tool for storing, indexing, and retrieving XML documents.

POET

The POET Software Corporation, created in 1992 and a voting member and C++ workgroup chair of ODMG since its constitution, produces the POET OODBMS [Poet 1999]. Initially conceived to provide persistence transparently to C++ objects, POET later extended to provide persistence to Java objects in such a way that database objects are referred exactly as application objects and all database definition is done through a small extension to C++/Java declaration syntax. In addition to persistence, POET provides the following database features: indexes, navigation, multi-user operations using a client/server architecture, flexible locking for objects and sets, associative queries, and nested transactions.

In addition to the OODBMS POET OSS (version 6.0), POET Software currently distributes POET CMS (Content Management Suite) to manage XML and SGML document repositories, targeted to the requirements of XML and SGML publishers.

Data Model Concepts

In this section we provide a short overview of the basic object data model concepts: objects, classes, and inheritance. We mainly refer to these notions as adopted in the ODMG Object Model.

Objects

An object-oriented database is a collection of objects. In object-oriented systems, an object represents each real-world entity. Each object is identified by an *object identifier* (OID), has a *state* and a *behavior*. The state consists of the values of the object *properties*; the behavior is specified by the *operations* that can be executed on or by the object, possibly acting on the object state. Properties can be either *attributes* of the object itself or *relationships* among the object and one or more objects. Typically, the value of an object property can change over time.

OODBMSs do not actually require each entity to be represented as an object. They distinguish between objects and *literals* (or values). The main difference between an object and a literal is that an object has an identity (OID) that is independent from its state, whereas a literal has no identifier, and is identified by its value. Literals are described as being constant or immutable since their values cannot change. By contrast, objects are described as being mutable. Changes to the values of an object's properties do not affect its identity. Literals are universally known abstractions, and they have the same meaning for each user; objects, by contrast, correspond to abstractions whose meaning is specified in the context of the application. Literals are elements of built-in domains, whereas objects are elements of uninterpreted domains. Typical examples of literal are integers, reals, and strings.

Object Identity

One of the most important properties of an object is that of having an *identity*, different from the identity of any other object, and immutable during the object's lifetime. Object identifiers usually are not directly visible and accessible by database users; they are internally used by the system. In addition to the object identifier, an object can be characterized by one or more names that are meaningful to the programmer or end-user. Object names are used for convenience, especially to refer to root objects, which provide entry points into the database.

The notion of an object identifier is quite different from the notion of a key used in the relational model to uniquely identify each tuple in a relation. A key is defined as the value of one or more attributes, which can be modified, whereas an OID is independent from the value of an object's state. In particular, two different objects have different OIDs even when their states are identical. Moreover, a key is unique with respect to a relation, whereas an OID is unique within the entire database. The use of OIDs, as an identification mechanism, has a number of advantages with respect to the use of keys. First of all, because the OIDs are implemented by the system, the application programmer does not have to select the appropriate keys for the various sets of objects. Moreover, because the OIDs are implemented at a low level by the system, better performance is achieved. A disadvantage in the use of OIDs with respect to keys could be the fact that no semantic meaning is associated with them. Note, however, that very often in relational systems, for efficiency reasons, users adopt semantically meaningless codes as keys, especially when foreign keys need to be used.

The ODMG Object Model supports the notion of a key, but only as a semantic integrity constraint, which is not used to identify objects. An important difference between the object and relational model is represented by the fact that the object model is identity-based, whereas the relational model is value-based. Thus, keys in the relational model, besides establishing integrity constraints, are also used to refer tuples through the foreign key mechanism. Although the first use of keys is meaningful in the object context, the second is not, since objects are always referred through their identity.

OIDs are used in OODBMSs to identify objects and to support object references through object property values. Objects can thus be interconnected and can share components. The notion of object identity introduces at least two different notions of object equality:

Equality by identity. Two objects are identical if they are the same object; that is, if they have the same identifier.

Equality by value. Two objects are equal if their states are recursively equal.

Obviously, two identical objects are also equal, whereas the converse does not hold. Some object-oriented data models also provide a third kind of equality, known as shallow value equality, where two objects are equal, though not identical, if they share all attributes.

Object State

In an object-oriented database the value associated with an object (its state) consists of its values for a number of attributes and of its relationships with other objects. Attribute values can be complex; that is, they can be values built from other objects and values, using some type constructors. Complex (or structured) values are obtained by applying those constructors to simpler objects and literals. The minimal set of constructors that a system should provide includes sets, lists, and tuples (records). Constructors can be arbitrarily nested. A complex value can contain, as components, references to objects.

Many OODBMSs support storage and retrieval of nonstructured values of a large size, such as character strings or bit strings. Those values are passed "as is" to the application program for interpretation, and are commonly known as BLOBs (binary large objects). Those values are not structured in that the DBMS does not know their semantic structure. The application using them knows how to interpret them. For example, the application may contain some functions to display an image or to search for some keywords in a text.

Relationships hold between objects. Object models support only binary relationships; that is, relationships between two object types, and literals cannot participate in relationships. One-to-many and many-to-many relationships can be represented using set or list collection constructors.

Object Behavior

Objects in an object-oriented database are manipulated through methods. A method definition usually consists of two components: a signature and an implementation. The signature specifies the method name, the names and types of method arguments, and the type of the result, for methods returning a result value. The method implementation consists of a set of instructions expressed in a programming language.

The use of a general-purpose, computationally complete programming language to code methods allows the whole application to be expressed in terms of objects. There is therefore no longer the need, typical of RDBMSs, of embedding the query language (e.g., SQL) in a programming language. In a RDBMS, queries and application programs acting on relations are usually expressed in an imperative language that incorporates statements of the data manipulation language (DML), and are stored in a traditional file system rather than in the database. In such an approach, therefore, there is a sharp distinction between programs and data and between query language and programming language.

This distinction has led to the problem known as *impedance mismatch,* related to the fact that a considerable effort is devoted to the proper communication between the database and the programming language through which the database is manipulated. This communication is not trivial since the database system and the programming language are based on different types and on different units of computation.

In an object-oriented database, by contrast, data and operations manipulating them are *encapsulated* in a single structure: the object. Data and operations are thus designed together and are stored in the same system. The notion of encapsulation in programming languages derives from the concept of an abstract data type. In this view, an object consists of an interface and an implementation. The interface is the specification of the operations that can be executed on the object, and are the only part of the object that can be seen from outside. Implementation, by contrast, contains data—the representation or state of the object—and operation implementations. Encapsulation provides a type of "logical data independence," which allows the data to be modified without having to modify the applications using them.

An important consequence of encapsulation is logical data extensibility: The user can extend the set of types and there is no difference between the types provided as built-ins in the system and those added by the user. Most OODBMSs provide rich class libraries to deal with most common types of data, such as dates, currencies, and geometric shapes, which can be extended depending on application needs.

The encapsulation principle, in the database context, is reflected in the fact that an object contains both programs and data. However, in the database context it is not clear whether or not the data structure defining the type of an object (and thus the object state) is part of the interface. In the database context, direct access to the object's attributes, and references made through them to other objects, is often useful (e.g., to formulate queries). This can be supported through *private* (i.e., encapsulated, and not accessible from outside) and *public* properties.

Classes

In an object model, both objects and values are categorized according to their types. All objects of a given type have the same set of properties and the same set of operations. An object type is defined through a class. The notion of a class is the basis for instantiation. A class is a template, specifying structure (the set of instance properties) and behavior (the set of instance operations).

Object types (class names) can be used as domains for properties as well as for types of operation arguments. Object-oriented databases provide an extensible type system that enables users to define new types, according to the requirements of the applications. The types provided by the system and those defined by the users can be used exactly in the same way.

An aggregation relationship is established between two classes, C and C' (whenever C' is specified as domain of a property of C). Such a relationship specifies that C is defined in terms of C'. Since C' can in turn be defined in terms of other classes, the set of classes in the schema is organized into an *aggregation hierarchy.*

The following is an example of a class declaration, in which the properties and the operations of the class instances are declared (we adopt the syntax of ODMG Object Definition Language ODL). Note that relationships are declared by specifying a pair of *traversal paths*, one for each direction of traversal of the relationship. In this particular case, relationship `is_married_to` is its own inverse.

```
class Person:Object {
    attribute short age;
    attribute string name;
    attribute enum gender {male, female};
    attribute Address home_address;
    attribute set<Phone_no> phones;
    attribute Department dept;

    relationship Person is_married_to
        inverse Person::is_married_to;

    void get_married(in Person p);
};
```

Some OODBMSs allow the specification of class features that cannot be seen as attributes of its instances, such as the number of class instances present in each moment in the database or the average value of an attribute. An example of an operation that is invoked on classes rather than on objects is the *new* operation for creating new instances. In those systems, properties and methods characterizing the class as an object can be defined, which are not inherited by the class instances. These features usually are referred to as *class properties* and *class methods*.

In the object model, different notions are related to the description of the common features of a set of objects: types, classes, and interfaces. The differences among those concepts are confusing and the terms are employed with different meanings in different contexts and systems. The *type* is a programming language concept, and provides the specification of a set of objects and values; that is, the operations that can be invoked on them. This specification is used (usually at compile time) to check program correctness. A *class*, by contrast, provides the implementation (i.e., the definition of object properties and the implementations of operations) for a set of objects of the same type. It also provides primitives for object creation. An *interface* provides the specification of the external behavior of a set of objects; a class can implement an interface but it cannot be instantiated directly. Both classes and interfaces are supported by the ODMG object model. Classes include the specification of object properties and operations; however, they do not include the implementation of operations, which is supposed to be given through a language for which the model provides a binding, whereas interfaces include only the specification of object operations.

Extents and Persistence Mechanisms

Besides being a template, a class also acts as an object factory since it has the capability of generating instances (usually through a *new* operation). The collection of all instances generated from a class is referred to as a class *extent*. Extents are the basis on which queries are formulated. In some OODBMSs extents automatically are associated with each class, whereas in others they must be maintained by applications. In those systems in which a class defines only the specification and the implementation of objects, such as ObjectStore, GemStone, and O2, explicit collections of objects of the corresponding types must be defined. Objects must be inserted in those collections upon creation, queries issued against those collections, and indexes built on those collections. The automatic association of an extent with each class has the advantage of simplifying the management of classes and their instances. By contrast, systems in which extents are handled manually provide greater flexibility at the price of increased complexity in managing class extents.

An important issue concerns the persistence of class instances, and the mechanisms by which objects are made persistent (inserted into the database) or deleted (removed from the database). In relational databases, explicit statements (INSERT and DELETE in SQL) are provided to insert and delete data from the database. In OODBMSs, two different approaches can be adopted with respect to object persistence:

- Persistence is an implicit property of all class instances; the creation (through the *new* operation) of an instance also has the effect of inserting the instance in the database, thus the creation of an instance automatically implies its persistence. This approach usually is adopted in systems in which classes also have an extensional function. Some systems provide two different new operations: one for creating persistent instances of a class, the other one for creating temporary instances of that class.

- Persistence is an orthogonal property of objects; the creation of an instance does not have the effect of inserting the instance in the database. Rather, if an instance has to survive the program that created it, it must explicitly be made persistent for example, by assigning it a name, or by inserting it in a persistent collection of objects. This approach usually is adopted in systems in which classes do not have the extensional function.

With respect to object deletion, two different approaches are possible:

- The system provides an explicit *delete* operation. Explicitly deleting objects poses the problem of referential integrity; if an object is deleted and there are other objects referring to it, these references are no longer valid (such references are called dangling references).

- The system does not provide an explicit *delete* operation. A persistent object is deleted only if all references to it have been removed (a periodic garbage collection is performed). This approach ensures referential integrity.

Migration

Because objects represent real-world entities, they must be able to reflect the evolution in time of those entities. A typical example is that of a person who is first of all a student, then an employee, then a retired employee. This situation can be modeled only if an object can become an instance of a class different from the one from which it has been created. This evolution, known as object *migration*, allows an object to modify its features—attributes and operations—by still retaining its identity.

Object migration among classes introduces, however, semantic integrity problems. If the value for an attribute A of an object O is another object O' (instance of the class domain of A), and O' changes class, if the new class of O' is no more compatible with the class domain of A, the migration of O' will result in O containing an illegal value for A. For this reason migration is not currently supported in most existing systems.

Inheritance

Inheritance allows a class, called a subclass, to be defined starting from the definition of another class, called a superclass. The subclass inherits attributes and operations of its superclass; in addition, a subclass may have some specific, noninherited features. Inheritance is a powerful reuse mechanism. By using such a mechanism when defining two classes, their common properties, if any, can be identified and factorized in a common superclass. The definitions of the two classes will, by contrast, specify only the distinguishing specific properties of those classes. This approach not only reduces the quantity of code to be written, but it also has the advantage of giving a more precise, concise, and rich description of the world being represented.

Inheritance Hierarchies

Some systems allow a class to have several direct superclasses, referred to as *multiple inheritance*, whereas other systems impose the restriction to a single superclass, referred to as *single inheritance*. Defining a class starting from several superclasses simplifies the task of class definition. However, conflicts may arise. Conflicts can be solved according to different strategies. An ordering can be imposed on the superclasses so that conflicting features are inherited from the superclass preceding the others in the ordering. Alternatively, an explicit qualification mechanism can be provided by which the user explicitly specifies from which superclass each conflicting feature must be inherited.

Different inheritance notions can be considered, corresponding to at least three different hierarchies that can be distinguished:

Subtype hierarchy. Expresses the consistency among type specifications, by specifying subtype relationships that support the substitutability of a subtype instance in each context where a supertype instance is expected.

Implementation hierarchy. Supports code sharing among classes.

Classification hierarchy. Expresses inclusion relationships among object collections (extents).

Each hierarchy refers to different properties of the type/class system; those hierarchies are, however, generally merged in a single inheritance mechanism.

The ODMG Object Model supports two inheritance relationships: the *ISA* relationship and the *EXTENDS* relationship. Subtyping through the ISA relationship pertains to the inheritance of behavior only. Thus interfaces may inherit from other interfaces and classes may also inherit from interfaces. By contrast, interfaces may not inherit from classes, nor may classes inherit from other classes through the ISA relationship. Because the ODMG object model supports multiple inheritance of object behavior, it could happen that a type inherits operations with the same name from two different interfaces. The model precludes such a possibility by disallowing name overloading along the ISA hierarchy.

In addition to the ISA relationship that defines the inheritance of behavior between object types, the ODMG object model provides the EXTENDS relationship for the inheritance of state and behavior. The EXTENDS relationship is a single inheritance relationship between two classes, whereby the subordinate class inherits all properties and operations of the class that it extends.

Overriding and Late Binding

Inheritance provides a very powerful behavior specialization mechanism, because of the notions of overloading, overriding, and late binding. In an object-oriented system, an operation can be defined in a class and inherited by all of its subclasses. Thus, the operation has a single name and can be used indifferently on various objects. The operation implementation can be redefined for each class; this redefinition is known as *overriding*. As a result, a single name denotes different programs and the system manages the selection of the appropriate one (i.e., the most specific with respect to the inheritance hierarchy) during execution.

A fundamental property of inheritance is substitutability. An instance of a subclass can be used whenever an instance of a superclass is expected. Each program variable has a static type, that is, the type declared for it, and a dynamic type, that is, the class to which the object denoted by the variable belongs.

To support the selection of the most specific code to execute—the one corresponding to the variable dynamic type—the system is no longer able to bind operation names to corresponding code at compile time. It must perform such binding at run time. This late translation is known as *late binding*.

Let us discuss these notions on a classical example [Atkinson 1989]. As a case in which it is very useful to adopt the same name for different operations (overloading), consider a display operation that receives as input an object and displays it. Depending on the object type, different display mechanisms are exploited. If the object is a figure, it should appear on the screen; if the object is a person, its data should be printed in some way; if the object is a graph, a graphical representation of it should be produced. Another problem occurs when displaying a set of objects without knowing the type of its members at compile time.

In an application developed in a conventional system, three different operations *display_graph*, *display_person*, and *display_figure* would be defined. This requires the programmer to be aware of all possible object types and all the associated display operations, and to use them properly. Under a conventional approach, the application code performing the display of a set of objects on the screen would be organized as follows:

```
for x in X do
begin
case of type(x)
person: display_person(x);
figure: display_figure(x);
graph: display_graph(x);
end;
end;
```

In an object-oriented system, by contrast, the *display* operation can be defined in a more general class in the class hierarchy. Thus, the operation has a single name and can be used indifferently on various objects. The operation implementation is redefined for each class; this redefinition is known as overriding. As a result, a single name denotes different programs and the system takes care of selecting the appropriate one at each time during execution. Thus the preceding code is compacted as:

```
for x in X do display(x)
```

This approach to design application code provides several advantages. The application programmers implementing the classes write the same number of methods, but the application designers do not have to take care of that. The resulting code is simpler and easier to maintain, since the introduction of a new class does not require the modification of applications. At any moment, objects of other classes, for example information on some products, can be added to the application and displayed by simply defining a class—for example, product—providing a proper (re)definition of the *display* operation. The important advantage is that this compact application code would not require any modification. By contrast, the traditional application code would require modifications to deal with the new object classes.

Note that while most systems allow arbitrary overriding of method implementations, most systems impose some constraints on signature redefinition. These constraints are needed to ensure type safety (i.e., the property that each program that was ensured to be type correct at compile time cannot cause a type error at run time). In particular, property domain refinement (i.e., the modification of the domain of a property in a subclass by replacing it with a more specific domain), though useful from the modeling viewpoint in some cases, is not type safe, and is thus disallowed in most systems (and in the ODMG Object Model). For what concerns method signatures, type safety is ensured by the covariant for output-contravariant for input redefinition: In the subclass signature, subtypes replace the types of output parameters, whereas supertypes replace the types of input parameters. The contravariant rule is counterintuitive and is not very useful in practice, thus most systems (and the ODMG Object Model) simply disallow method signature overriding.

An Example

The following is an example of database schema, defined according to ODL syntax, concerning projects, the tasks in which they consist, publications related to them, and employees involved in them. Note that in the example, we have arbitrarily chosen to represent some links between classes as object-valued attributes (e.g., attribute coordinator in class Task) and some others as relationships (e.g., traversal paths project in class Employee and participants in class Project). The main difference between representing a link between objects as a relationship rather than as a reference (i.e., attribute value) is in the nondirectionality of the relationship. If, however, only one direction of the link is interesting, the link can be represented as an attribute. In this second case, the system does not ensure referential integrity, which is by contrast ensured if the link is represented as a relationship. Referring to class Employee, note that ODMG allows expressions of one-to-one (e.g., leads-leader), one-to-many (e.g., project-participants), and many-to-many (e.g., tasks-participants) binary relationships.

```
class Employee
(   extent Employees
    key name)
{
    attribute string name;
    attribute unsigned short salary;
    attribute unsigned short phone_nbr[4];
    attribute Employee manager;

    relationship Project project
        inverse Project::participants;
    relationship Project leads
        inverse Project::leader;
    relationship Set<Task> tasks
        inverse Task::participants;

    int bonus();
}

class Document
(   extent Documents
    key title)
{
    attribute string title;
    attribute List<Employee> authors;
    attribute string state;
    attribute string content;
}

class Article EXTENDS Document
(   extent Articles)
{
    attribute string journal;
    attribute date publ_date;
}

class Project
(   extent Projects
    key name)
{
    attribute string name;
    attribute Set<Document> documents;
    attribute Set<Task> tasks;

    relationship Set<Employee> participants
        inverse Employee::project;
    relationship Employee leader
        inverse Employee::leads;
```

```
   }

   class Task
   (   extent Tasks)
   {
       attribute unsigned short man_month;
       attribute date start_date;
       attribute date end_date;
       attribute Employee coordinator;

       relationship Set<Employee> participants
           inverse Employee::tasks;
   }
```

Query Language

Query languages are an important functionality of any DBMS. A query language allows users to retrieve data by simply specifying some conditions on the content of those data. In RDBMSs, query languages are the only way to access data, whereas OODBMSs usually provide two different methods to access data. The first one is called navigational and is based on object identifiers and on the aggregation hierarchies into which objects are organized. Given a certain OID, the system is able to directly and efficiently access the object referred by it and can navigate through objects referred by the components of this object. The second access method is called associative and it is based on SQL-like query languages. These two different access methods can be used in a complementary way: A query is evaluated to select a set of objects that are then accessed and manipulated by applications through the navigational mechanism.

Navigational access is crucial in many applications that involve graph traversal. Such type of access is inefficient in relational systems because it requires the execution of a large number of join operations. Associative access, by contrast, has the advantage of supporting the expression of declarative queries, and of reducing application development time. Some of the success of RDBMSs can be attributed to their support for declarative query languages. Early OODBMSs did not provide any declarative query languages—they provided navigational access to data. This was because many applications that motivated the development of OODBMSs required navigational access. It is now quite well accepted that declarative query languages and associative access are among the DBMS features that an OODBMS should provide. The ODMG standard includes a declarative query language (OQL), which has been inspired by SQL. In the paragraphs that follow, we briefly outline the main characteristics of object-oriented query languages, and their main differences with respect to relational ones. To discuss some concrete examples of object-oriented queries, we consider the query language of the ODMG standard OQL, and refer to the database schema introduced in the previous section.

The first feature of object-oriented query languages is the ability to impose conditions on nested attributes of an object aggregation hierarchy through *path expressions*, to express joins to retrieve the values of the attributes of an object's components. In object-oriented query languages, two different kinds of joins can be distinguished:

Implicit join. Deriving from the hierarchical structure of objects.

Explicit join. Comparing two objects (as found in relational query languages).

As an example of implicit join expressed through the use of path expressions, consider the query returning all tasks with manpower greater than 20 months, whose coordinator earns more than 20000, expressed in OQL as follows:

```
select t
from Tasks t
where t.man_month > 20 and
      t.coordinator.salary > 20000
```

As an example of a query involving an explicit join, consider the query "retrieve the technical reports having the same title of an article," which is expressed in OQL as:

```
select tr
from Technical_Reports tr, Articles a
where tr.title = a.title
```

Other important aspects are related to inheritance hierarchies and methods. A query can be issued against a class or against a class and all of its subclasses. Most existing languages support both these possibilities. Methods can be used as derived attributes or as predicate methods. A method used as a derived attribute is similar to an attribute; however, whereas an attribute stores a value, the method computes a value starting from data values stored in the database. A predicate method is similar, but it returns the Boolean constants True or False. A predicate method evaluates some conditions on objects and thus can be part of the Boolean expressions determining which objects satisfy the query. As an example of query containing a method invocation, consider the query "retrieve the name and the bonus of employees having a salary greater than 20000 and a bonus greater than 5000", which is expressed in OQL as:

```
select distinct struct(n: e.name, b: e.bonus)
from Employees e
where e.salary > 20000 and e.bonus > 5000
```

The equality notion also influences query semantics. The adopted equality notion determines the semantics and the execution strategy of operations like union, difference, intersection, and duplicate elimination. External names that can be associated with objects provide some semantically meaningful handles that can be used in queries.

A relevant issue for object-oriented query languages is related to the language closure. One of the most relevant characteristics of relational query languages is that the results of a query are relations. The result of a query can be used as an operand in another query. In the object-oriented context, by contrast, the result of a query is often a set of objects whose class does not exist in the database schema. The approach adopted in OQL is that the result of a query is seen in those cases as a set of literals (tuples). This issue has been intensively debated, and some previously proposed object query languages imposed severe restrictions on queries to ensure closure: Either all the object attributes are returned by the query, or only a single attribute, and no explicit joins are supported. In this way the result of a query is always either a set of literals of a set of already existing objects, or instances of an already existing class.

OQL operators can be composed freely, as a consequence of the fact that query results have a type that belongs to the ODMG type system. Thus, queries can be nested. As a stand-alone language, OQL allows query objects to be denotable through their names. A name can denote an object of any type (e.g., atomic, collection, structure, literal). The query result is an object whose type is inferred from the operators in the query expression. The result of the query "retrieve the starting date of tasks with a manpower greater than 20 months," expressed in OQL as:

```
select distinct t.start_date
from Tasks t
where t.man_month > 20
```

is a literal of type Set<date>, whereas the result of the query "retrieve the starting and ending dates of tasks with a manpower greater than 20 months," expressed in OQL as:

```
select distinct struct(sd: t.start_date, ed: t.end_date)
from Tasks t
where t.man_month > 20
```

is a literal of type Set<struct(sd:date, ed:date)>.

A query can return structured objects having objects as components, as it can combine attributes of different objects. Consider as an example the query "retrieve the starting date and the coordinator of tasks with a manpower greater than 20 months," expressed in OQL as:

```
select distinct struct(st: t.start_date, c: coordinator)
from Tasks t
where t.man_month > 20
```

produces as result a literal with type Set<struct(st:date, c:Employee)>.

Conclusion

OODBMSs appeared on the market more than a decade ago, as revolutionary systems with respect to existing (mainly relational) DBMSs. They offer several advantages over RDBMSs, such as directly storing complex data and representing both data and behavior. Another important advantage of OODBMSs, related to the increasing usage of object technology, is represented by the fact that a single paradigm (the object-oriented one) is employed in all phases of software development, from analysis to coding, and at all levels. Thus, there is no need to design the database structure separately, and there are no communication problems between the DBMS and the programming language. The object paradigm (and thus OODBMSs) also offers great potential for heterogeneous systems integration.

Since the early years, OODBMSs certainly have improved as products, and today represent a mature technology that has been able to evolve and adapt itself to the technological innovations that have continued during the recent past. At the same time, some competitor systems have emerged, such as Persistent Object Systems and object-relational DBMSs. The application requirements met by these kinds of systems, however, are different from those of OODBMSs. Thus, it seems that these technologies can coexist. For example, OODBMSs offer a number of advantages over object-relational DBMSs for applications that require seamless integration with a specific object-oriented programming language, and use a navigational approach to data access.

To overcome the difficulties due to the presence of several different systems, each with some distinctive characteristics, a standard for OODBMSs has been defined. However, although a consortium comprising almost all OODBMS vendors has defined the standard, much work still needs to be done to make existing systems compliant. For example, the standard defines a declarative query language (OQL), but only a few OODBMSs claim to support it. This gives the impression that the companies participating in ODMG do not actively support the standard, and it seems to have gained more attention from academia than from industry.

OODBMSs, far from having reached a level of use similar to that of RDBMSs after a comparable period from their birth, currently enjoy success only in a number of vertical markets, such as telecommunications and finance. However, they seem to be a promising technology for handling Web-related semistructured data, and several OODBMS vendors are already offering tools and facilities for storing and querying XML data. Some of the other chapters in this book discuss this and other issues in more detail.

PART
Two

Object-Relational Systems

Pure object databases provide one of a number of possible alternatives to managing persistent objects. During the past few years, there has been a steady growth in the development and use of object-relational databases. These products attempt to build upon the strengths of relational technology, while providing better support for richer data types. Designing database schemas for such products, however, is still an area that is not well understood. With relational databases, the common techniques of normalization and entity-relationship modeling are well known. Extending relational products with object-oriented (OO) features (such as inheritance) is a two-edged sword as it brings both flexibility and complications. Design choices will be greater, and ensuring that the best design has been used for a particular problem could be difficult. One part of that problem is how to map a particular modeling language to a database. Chapter 2, "Mapping UML Diagrams to Object-Relational Schemas in Oracle 8" by Urban, Dietrich, and Tapia, addresses this issue. It shows, through the use of examples, how the popular Unified Modeling Language (UML) can be mapped to Oracle 8 schemas.

Today, Java is being used increasingly for building applications in multitier systems. Many of these applications require persistence and typically will use a relational database on the backend. Therefore, the need arises to store and retrieve Java objects from relational tables. A few years ago, Sun Microsystems developed JDBC to meet this requirement. JDBC is modeled on the popular Object Database Connectivity (ODBC). It is also a low-level API, and drivers are available for most major relational database products. Another interesting development has been a way to embed SQL directly within Java, as is possible with many other popular programming languages. The result of this work within ANSI has been SQLJ, and some of the major object-relational database vendors are beginning to offer this capability in their products. Chapter 3, "SQLJ and JDBC: Database Access in Java" by Basu, provides a comparison and discussion of SQLJ and JDBC. It is interesting that the two technologies actually complement one another and can be used together.

For many organizations, moving to object-relational databases may not be possible or appropriate. However, new requirements may still arise that use data in existing relational databases. If this is coupled with the need to access that data using an OO programming language such as C++ or Java, then one possibility is to use a mapping tool. Hand coding is also possible, but if the mapping is complex, it may be better to buy rather than build. Today, there are many object-to-relational mapping tool vendors. In fact, the focus of many of these vendors is specifically Java-to-relational mapping, for reasons mentioned earlier. Some of the early pioneering work in object-to-relational mapping and object mediators was undertaken by Keller and Wiederhold. In Chapter 4, "Penguin: Objects for Programs, Relations for Persistence," they discuss some of the practical and pragmatic reasons why it is necessary, and give a good tutorial on the subject.

Mapping UML Diagrams to Object-Relational Schemas in Oracle 8

The recent emergence of object-oriented design tools and object-relational database technology into the commercial market has caused new challenges for the implementation of conceptual database designs. The process of database design typically involves the development of a conceptual schema that uses a high-level conceptual modeling language, such as the Extended Entity-Relationship (EER) model [Elmasri 2000]. The conceptual design is then mapped to the model of the target database system that is to be used for implementation of the application. Although well-defined mapping procedures exist for mapping EER and EER-like schemas into relational database designs, very little work has been done to define the mapping of object-oriented schemas, such as class diagrams in UML [Fowler 1997], into object-relational database schemas.

The Unified Modeling Language (UML) is a standard modeling language that provides a graphical notation to represent the design of object-oriented software. UML is the integration of popular object-oriented analysis and design methods, resulting from a wealth of research in this area in the late 1980s and early 1990s. The Object Management Group (OMG) is the organization that is leading the standardization process [OMG 1999]. Object-relational technology [Stonebraker 1996], on the other hand, extends the traditional notion of the relational table with the notion of object tables, where the tuples of an object table generate object identifiers as in the instances of classes in object-oriented database systems. Relationships between tables are then established through the use of object references. Path expressions can be also incorporated into SQL queries to provide a more concise, object-oriented approach to query expression. Furthermore, object-relational models incorporate the notion of user-defined types, or abstract data types, in addition to providing built-in support for large objects and aggregate types such as sets, arrays, and nested tables. As a result, attributes within an object table or traditional relational table are no longer limited to atomic values. The presence of these features requires a new look at how to use object-relational concepts effectively in the implementation of object-oriented conceptual designs.

This chapter presents our experience with using the Oracle 8 object-relational model [Oracle 1999] in the implementation of UML class diagrams. The results presented are based on our initial work with using object-relational database concepts within an engineering application [Tjahjadi 1997]; [Urban 2000]. In particular, the work in "The Design and Implementation of an EXPRESS to Oracle 8 Mapping" and "A Case Study in Mapping Conceptual Designs to Object-Relational Schemas" provides a detailed description of mapping EXPRESS conceptual schemas into object-relational schemas in Oracle 8, where EXPRESS is a standard for conceptual modeling within the engineering design domain [Schenck 1994]. Since UML has become an industry standard for expressing object-oriented designs, this chapter revisits many of these mapping issues in the context of UML to address a broader audience of database designers. Although there are differences between the object-relational models that are currently available by different database vendors, the mappings should provide a model of mapping techniques that can be modified for use in systems other than Oracle 8. We are currently teaching these mapping issues in an advanced undergraduate database course at Arizona State University that covers object-relational database technology [CSE494DB 2000].

The work presented in this chapter, together with the original work in "The Design and Implementation of an EXPRESS to Oracle 8 Mapping" on which it is based, provides one of the first descriptions of conceptual-to-object-relational mapping procedures. In "Object Database Development: Concepts and Principles" [Embley 1997], Embley provides a brief overview of a case study that maps a database application designed using the Object-Oriented Systems Model into the UniSQL object-relational system. Specific details of how to use object-relational features, however, are not provided. Grimes [Grimes 1998] also provides an overview of commercial tools that support the generation of object-relational schemas for systems such as Oracle 8, the IBM DB2 Universal Database, and the Informix-Dynamic Server. As described in "Modeling Object/Relational Databases," however, most of these tools are still immature and functionally incomplete. Furthermore, a significant problem with these existing tools is that they do not provide sufficient methodological support to help the user understand how to use object-relational features. Rational Software Corporation, for example, provides a tool for generating Oracle 8 schemas from UML diagrams [Rational 1998]. The user, however, must already understand how object-oriented modeling concepts map to object-relational features in order to construct UML diagrams with appropriate Oracle 8 class stereotypes. The stereotypes provide Rational Rose with instructions on how to generate the Oracle 8 schema. In fact, Grimes states [Grimes 1998] that object-relational database systems have not yet entered the mainstream and, at this point, are more likely to be used by advanced users that are willing to skip conceptual modeling. The mapping procedures described in this chapter represent an initial step towards defining a methodology for generating object-relational schemas from object-oriented designs such as those provided by UML.

The following sections provide an overview of UML notation as well as a comparison of UML to EER notation. A sample application is also presented to support examples of mapping issues. After providing an overview of the object-relational features supported by Oracle 8, we then elaborate on the generation of object-relational schemas from UML class diagrams. The chapter concludes with a summary and dis-cussion of future work.

Overview of UML

UML has become an industry standard for expressing object-oriented designs. Model-ing object-oriented software is complex and UML provides the capability to express various relationships within an object-oriented software system. The *conceptual class diagrams* (also called static view diagrams) of UML describe the types of objects and the relationships between objects. Although the UML methodology was developed for software designs, UML conceptual class diagrams are similar to that of EER diagrams [Elmasri 2000], which are used for conceptual database design. Table 2.1 compares the terminology of the EER and the UML graphical models.

To support the comparison, Figure 2.1 presents an EER diagram of a School enter-prise application [Tapia 1999], and Figure 2.2 presents the same enterprise in UML notation. The School enterprise provides an example that will be used throughout the rest of this chapter to illustrate UML-to-object-relational mapping issues. As shown in Figure 2.1, the School database has five entities that are enclosed in rectangles: Person, Faculty, Student, Department, and Campus Club. Attributes in the EER diagram are enclosed in ovals and attached to the entities that they describe. Since Student and Fac-ulty are disjoint specializations of Person, as indicated by the letter "d" in the special-ization circle, Student and Faculty inherit the attributes of the class Person. The double edge of the specialization of Person into its subclasses represents a total specialization constraint, which requires a Person to belong to one of its subclasses. The diamonds in an EER diagram represent relationships between entities. The numeric annotations on the edges linking relationships to the entities to which they relate are cardinality ratios, indicating the number of entities that can be involved in the relationship. For example, the Clubs relationship specifies that a Student can be a member of several Campus Clubs and a Campus Club can have several student members. The Advises relation-ship indicates that a Campus Club can have a Faculty member as an advisor and a Fac-ulty member can advise many Campus Clubs. A double edge linking an entity to a relationship indicates a total participation constraint and requires that an entity be

Table 2.1   Comparison of EER and UML Terminology

EER	UML
Entity	Class
Relationship	Association
Attributes	Attributes
Roles	Roles
Structural Constraints	Multiplicity
Generalization & Specialization	Generalization & Classification

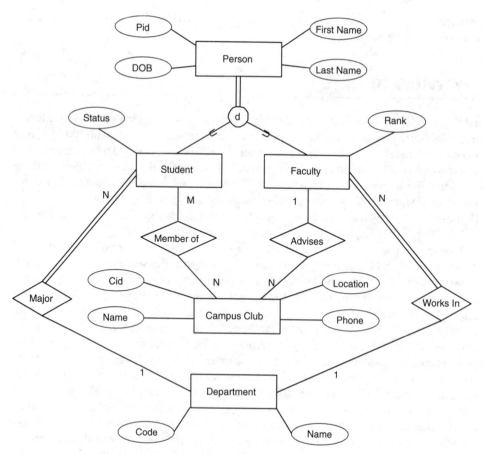

Figure 2.1   EER diagram of the School Database.

involved in at least one relationship instance. For example, each Student and Faculty member must be associated with a Department through its Major and WorksIn relationships, respectively. These relationships also relate a Department to the Students majoring in the Department and the Faculty working in the Department.

In UML, a class is an entity that is described by its attributes and operations. Graphically, a class is enclosed in a rectangle and its attributes and operations are shown in compartments listed after the name of the class, as shown in Figure 2.2. An attribute definition optionally can include a type and default value, in the format *attributeName:type=defaultValue*. Operations on a UML class are listed in a compartment following the attribute specifications. For brevity of presentation, Figure 2.2 shows the names of two operations for the Department class: GetStudents and GetFaculty. These operations return the students majoring in the department and the faculty working in the department, respectively. The operations for the other classes are omitted. An operation optionally can be specified in the format *methodName (parameterList) : returnTypeExpression*. From a database perspective, the operations on a conceptual class diagram should correspond to the public interface of the class to facilitate schema definition.

An association in UML is a binary relationship. Graphically, an association is indicated by an undirected edge between the two classes that it associates. Figure 2.2 provides the Advises association name for the relationship between Faculty and CampusClub. In a similar manner, the relationship between Student and CampusClub is labeled with the Club's association name. Association names correspond to relationship names in Figure 2.1. Both the EER model and UML provide for naming the role of an entity or class in the association. For example, in Figure 2.2, Faculty has the role of advisor in the Advises association and CampusClub has the role of advisorOf. Although not shown in Figure 2.1, the same role names can be added to the EER diagram to describe the role of the entities in the Advises relationship. For example, the edge between Faculty and Advises can be labeled with the role advisor, and the edge between CampusClub and Advises can be labeled with the role advisorOf.

A UML diagram, unlike an EER diagram, includes the concept of navigability. An undirected edge is a bidirectional association, which assumes that an inverse binary relationship is maintained between the classes. Navigability is denoted by a directed edge, which indicates a unidirectional association. Navigability is therefore a reference between two classes that is only maintained in one direction. In Figure 2.2, the Clubs and Advises associations are bidirectional, whereas the associations between Faculty and Department and between Student and Department are unidirectional. As a result, since the association between Faculty and Department is indicated by an association arrow that points to Department and is labeled with the worksIn role name, a Faculty object will maintain information about the Department in which the faculty member works. The inverse direction is not automatically maintained but can be derived by the GetFaculty method of Department.

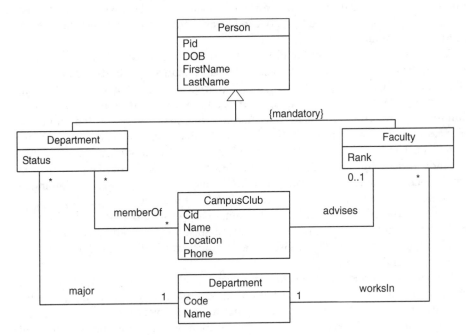

Figure 2.2   UML diagram of the School Database.

A database designer specifies the structural constraints of an enterprise in the EER conceptual model by using cardinality ratios in conjunction with partial/total participation constraints or by using min-max pairs. Figure 2.1 specifies structural constraints using cardinality ratios (1:1, 1:N, M:N) and participation constraints. Cardinality ratios on the edges of a relationship indicate the number of times an entity is related to another entity in the relationship. For example, the WorksIn relationship in Figure 2.1 has a 1:N cardinality ratio since a Faculty member works in one Department and a Department has many Faculty members working in it. Participation constraints are given by the edges; a single edge represents partial participation in the relationship and a double edge represents total participation. For example, a Faculty member must work in a Department but a Department does not have to have Faculty members working in it.

Min-max pairs can be used in the EER model to provide an alternative specification to the structural constraints shown in Figure 2.1. A min-max pair, denoted as "(min,max)", labels the edge between an entity and the relationship, indicating the minimum and maximum times that an entity participates in a relationship instance. For example, consider the participation of the Faculty entity in the WorksIn relationship of Figure 2.1. Since Faculty has total participation in WorksIn, a Faculty entity must be related to a Department. Furthermore, the cardinality ratio indicates that a Faculty entity can be related to only one Department. Therefore, the edge between Faculty and WorksIn can alternatively be labeled with the min-max pair (1,1). Since a Department does not have to participate in the WorksIn relationship, but it can participate many times, the edge between Department and WorksIn can be labeled by the min-max pair (0,n). In this example, adding the min-max pairs to the diagram of Figure 2.1 would be redundant since no additional semantics is provided beyond the participation and cardinality constraints. However, if the enterprise were changed to require that a department have a minimum of 6 faculty members working in it, then the min-max pair (6,n) on the edge between Department and WorksIn would provide additional information.

The structural constraints of the EER model are referred to as multiplicity in UML, indicating the number of times an object participates in an association. The placement of the multiplicity constraints on the UML diagram is similar to that of the placement of cardinality ratios in the EER diagram, although multiplicity is more closely related to min-max pairs. The multiplicity, specified as "min..max", indicates the minimum and maximum number of times that an object participates in an association. There are several shorthand notations available for multiplicity. A 1 indicates a 1..1 multiplicity, and * indicates a 0..infinity multiplicity. A minimum of 0 indicates partial participation in the association, where a minimum of at least 1 indicates a total participation in the association. As shown in Figure 2.2, CampusClub has a multiplicity of 1 in the Advises association, indicating that a CampusClub must have exactly one advisor. However, Faculty has a multiplicity of * in the Advises association, indicating that a Faculty entity does not have to be the advisor of a CampusClub, but potentially can be the advisor of several CampusClubs.

The goal of conceptual design is to capture graphically the constraints of the enterprise being modeled. Both EER diagrams and conceptual class diagrams are useful for representing many constraints, but they cannot represent every constraint. Therefore, a conceptual class diagram allows for the specification of constraint rules. A constraint rule is specified in a free-form syntax within curly braces. For example, for multivalued roles, the default collection type is assumed to be a set. A designer can use the constraint {ordered} to indicate a list or {bag} to indicate an unordered collection possibly containing duplicates. Since a constraint rule does not have a strict syntax, the constraint specification can range from an informal English statement to a formal statement in predicate calculus.

An important feature of UML is its support of generalization and classification. This concept is similar to generalization and specialization in the EER conceptual data model. Diagrammatically, a classification is specified by linking the subclasses of a classification to one triangle, which points to the superclass. In Figure 2.2, Person is classified into the subclasses of Student and Faculty. This notation is similar to the EER model where the subclasses of the specialization are linked to a small circle, which is linked to the superclass. Recall that an "o" inside a circle within an EER diagram indicates possibly overlapping subclasses, and a "d" indicates a disjoint specialization. In UML, a generalization link may be labeled with a discriminator. A discriminator is an attribute of the superclass that indicates the basis for the subtyping. The subtypes that have the same discriminator are assumed to be disjoint. A constraint rule of {mandatory} can also be used to indicate a total specialization. As shown in Figure 2.2, the Person hierarchy has the {mandatory} constraint, indicating that a Person must be either a Student or a Faculty. Although not shown in Figures 2.1 or 2.2, both the EER and UML allow for multiple classifications, such as an additional specialization of Person into Male and Female subclasses.

Figure 2.3 demonstrates the use of attributes on relationships in the EER and UML notations. To illustrate this feature, assume that the example in Figure 2.1 is extended to capture the date that a student joins a club. In the EER notation of Figure 2.3, the attribute is attached to the diamond that represents the relationship. In UML, this feature is supported through the use of association classes. As shown in Figure 2.3, ClubsInformation is an association class that lists the attribute of the association. The association class is connected to the association with a dashed line.

UML class diagrams provide additional advanced concepts that are beyond the scope of this overview. For example, UML allows for the specification of aggregation, commonly referred to as the part-of relationship, which is not inherently supported by the EER conceptual model. The mappings presented in the following sections describe the fundamental concepts needed to support class definitions, class hierarchies, and relationships between objects. Advanced concepts of UML, such as aggregation and other features that are not described here, build on these fundamental mapping procedures through the implementation of constraints in application code. (Refer to *UML Toolkit* by Hans-Erik Eriksson and Magnus Penker [Wiley] for information on more complex UML features.)

Overview of Oracle 8

The Oracle 8.03 (O8) DBMS represents an object-relational extension of its predecessor Oracle 7 [Oracle 1999]. In O8, *object types* (also known as abstract data types, or ADTs) can be used as abstractions of real-world objects. Object types consist of two main components:

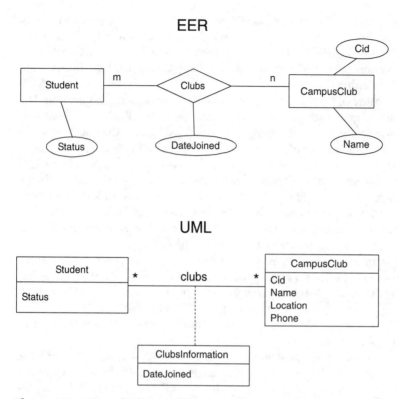

Figure 2.3   EER and UML notations for attributes on relationships.

Attributes. Contain built-in types or other object types as values. Attributes model the structure of the real world entity.

Methods. Functions or procedures written in PL/SQL or an external language like C that are stored in the database. Methods implement the operations the application can perform on the real world entity.

Object types can be used to create *object tables* and/or to define *embedded objects*. In object tables, the tuple instances have object identifiers. Object types that are used to create object tables can be used as the attribute types of attributes in other relational or object tables to create object references between tables. Embedded objects do not have object identifiers, and are used to define complex record structures as attribute values within relational or object tables. The current release of O8 does not support object type hierarchies. O8 does, however, support a feature that allows traditional relational schemas to be transformed into *object views*. By using object views, a user can retrieve, update, insert, and delete relational data as if they were stored as object entities.

O8 supports a number of new types in addition to the scalar types already supported by Oracle 7:

- *VARRAYs* and *nested tables* are two new types that allow a structured collection of data to be the type of a table column.
- REFs (or object references) are used to store logical pointers to objects.
- *LOBs* are large arrays of bytes with additional system-defined properties.

The following section elaborates on the use of the object-relational features of O8 in the generation of O8 schemas from UML conceptual class diagrams.

Mapping Issues

At a high level, mapping UML conceptual diagrams to object-relational schemas in O8 can be summarized as follows:

- Classes map to object tables, where the type of an object table must first be defined as an object type.
- Single-valued relationships between objects (i.e., the 1 side of a 1:1 or 1:M relationship) map to either:
  - References between objects using REFs.
  - Derived attributes that are calculated through the use of functions. A derived attribute can be used only on one side of the relationship.
- Multivalued relationships between objects (i.e., the M side of a 1:M relationship or either side of a N:M relationship) map to the use of either:
  - Structured collections such as VARRAYS or nested tables.
  - Derived attributes that are calculated through the use of functions. A derived attribute can be used only on one side of the relationship.
- Superclass/subclass relationships can be mapped to the use of either:
  - A superclass variable that appears in subclasses to establish class hierarchy relationships.
  - An object type that represents the flatten class hierarchy with relational views established to simulate the subclass structure.
- If object reference information is explicitly maintained on both sides of a relationship, triggers can be generated to maintain inverse relationships automatically.
- Object types can be created to represent user-defined structures, enumeration types, or other complex types that may be needed within an application. Such types can then be used to create embedded objects within relational and object tables.

The following subsections present examples of these mapping procedures and address some of the mapping issues of which a designer must be aware in the mapping process. In the text that follows, Oracle schema components are shown in italics, and UML schema components are shown in normal text, with classes and attributes capitalized and relationships in lowercase.

Objects and Relationships between Objects

To illustrate the mapping of classes to object tables, consider the Department class in Figure 2.2. Listing 2.1 illustrates that the object type *department* is created and then used to create the *departments* object table. Each row in the *departments* object table is referred to as a row object and will have an object identifier (OID). Columns in the table correspond to the attributes of the object type definition, which in this case are *Code* and *Name*.

The navigability notation in Figure 2.2 defines that *department* objects do not maintain attributes that contain the faculty working in the department or the students majoring in the department. Instead, the GetFaculty and GetStudents operations are specified in Figure 2.2. These operations are implemented as functions in Listing 2.1. Each function returns a *persons_array* type, which is a VARRAY of references to *person* objects. We will discuss the *persons_array* definition in more detail in a later section.

The type definition for *department* includes a type body, which defines the code for each of the member functions defined in Listing 2.1. Since we are interested primarily in structural mapping issues in this chapter, the code for the member functions is not shown. This feature of O8, however, readily supports the implementation of methods that are associated with UML class definitions. Since each UML class corresponds to an O8 object type, each method signature in a UML class should have a corresponding function or procedure specification in the object type definition, with an implementa-

```
CREATE OR REPLACE TYPE department AS OBJECT (
    Code    VARCHAR(20),
    Name    VARCHAR(40),
    MEMBER FUNCTION get_students    RETURN persons_array,
    MEMBER FUNCTION get_faculty     RETURN persons_array,
);
/
CREATE OR REPLACE TYPE BODY department IS
    MEMBER FUNCTION get_students RETURN persons_array IS
        — declarations go here
    BEGIN
        — function definition goes here
    END;

    MEMBER FUNCTION get_faculty RETURN persons_array IS
        — declarations go here
    BEGIN
        — function definition goes here
    END;

    END;
/
CREATE TABLE departments OF department;
```

Listing 2.1   Department object type and object table definition.

tion in the type body. Although not shown here, an object type in O8 also requires the definition of a *map member function*, which defines the relative position of a given instance in the ordering of all instances of the object type. Map member functions are used implicitly by O8 in object type comparisons.

As an example of a more complex object table definition that contains attributes that define relationships with other objects, consider the CampusClub class from Figure 2.2. The CampusClub class is implemented in O8 using the *campus_club* object type and the *clubs* object table shown in Listing 2.2. Attributes such as *Cid, Name, Location*, and *Phone* are implemented as in traditional relational mappings. Since each Club has one advisor through a relationship in the UML diagram to Faculty objects, the *Advisor* attribute is implemented as a REF to a *person* object. In Listing 2.2, *person* is assumed to be an object type associated with the Person hierarchy from the UML diagram. The complete definition of the *person* object follows in the next section, in which we address mappings for superclass/subclass hierarchies. By defining *Advisor* as a REF of type *person*, the *Advisor* attribute will contain references to OIDs of *person* objects. This representation is similar to object references used in object-oriented databases and replaces the use of foreign keys in the pure relational model. As we will illustrate later, SQL queries can navigate through object relationships that are represented as REFs. In addition to the *Advisor* attribute, the *Members* attribute, representing the membership relationship between Campus Clubs and Students, is represented as a VARRAY that contains REFs of *person* objects. Additional functions and procedures associated with the CampusClub UML class definition can be defined within the *campus_club* object type as needed.

Object Hierarchies

Given that O8 does not support the concept of object hierarchies, a hierarchical structure can be simulated through the use of hierarchy flattening. As discussed in "The

```
CREATE OR REPLACE TYPE campus_club AS OBJECT (
    Cid         INTEGER(2, 10),
    Name        VARCHAR(25),
    Location    VARCHAR(25),
    Phone       VARCHAR(25),
    Advisor     REF person,      — RELATION Advised by
    Members     persons_array,   — RELATION Member of
    MEMBER FUNCTION get_advisor_fname    RETURN VARCHAR,
    MEMBER FUNCTION get_advisor_lname    RETURN VARCHAR,
    MEMBER PROCEDURE print_members,
    MEMBER PROCEDURE add_member(member_to_add IN REF person),
    MEMBER PROCEDURE delete_member(member_to_delete IN REF person));
CREATE OR REPLACE TYPE BODY campus_clubs IS
    — code for the type body goes here
/
CREATE TABLE clubs OF campus_club
```

Listing 2.2   CampusClub object type and object table definition.

Design and Implementation of an EXPRESS to Oracle 8 Mapping" and "A Case Study in Mapping Conceptual Designs to Object-Relational Schemas" [Tjahjadi 1997]; [Urban 2000], the flattening approach implements the superclass at the top of the hierarchy together with all of the attributes of its subclasses. Views for each of the subclasses are then constructed to show the attributes that belong to each subclass. In Listing 2.3, the flattened object type is *person*, which contains attributes of the Person class as well as attributes of the Student and Faculty subclasses. The attributes *Is_person*, *Is_student*, and *Is_faculty* are attributes included in the flattened object type to identify the subclass membership of a *person* object instance.

Relational views allow the flattened hierarchical structure to simulate the class hierarchy from Figure 2.2. Listing 2.4 shows derived views of the Student and Faculty classes. The information returned for the *student* and *faculty* views includes the REF of the *person* object, the inherited attributes from the Person class, and the immediate attributes of either the Student or Faculty class, respectively. O8 *instead of* triggers can then be used to allow the user to modify the relational views and redirect the changes to the flattened *persons* object table. Relational views are used instead of using the object view feature of O8. Object views allow a user to build virtual objects from relational data. If used on top of object tables, however, object views do not return the same object identifier as in the original object table, thus generating multiple OIDs for the same object.

```
CREATE OR REPLACE TYPE clubs_table AS TABLE OF REF campus_club;
/
CREATE OR REPLACE TYPE person AS OBJECT (
    DOB            date_t,
    Pid            VARCHAR(20),
    FirstName      VARCHAR(20),
    LastName       VARCHAR(20),
    Status         current_year,
    Member_of      clubs_array,        —  RELATION Member of
    Advisor_of     clubs_table,
    Major          REF department,     —  RELATION Major
    Works_in       REF department,     —  RELATION Works_in
    Is_person      NUMBER(1),
    Is_student     NUMBER(1),
    Is_faculty     NUMBER(1),
    MEMBER FUNCTION ivalidation             RETURN BOOLEAN,
    MEMBER FUNCTION get_department_name     RETURN VARCHAR,
    MEMBER FUNCTION is_associated_club
        (candidate_club IN REF campus_club)RETURN BOOLEAN,
    MEMBER PROCEDURE add_club(club_to_add IN REF campus_club),
    MEMBER PROCEDURE delete_club(club_to_delete IN REF campus_club)
/
CREATE TABLE persons of person
    NESTED TABLE "ADVISOR_OF" STORE AS advised_clubs
```

Listing 2.3 Person object type and object table definition.

Listing 2.5 provides an example of an *instead of* trigger that is used to insert objects into the *persons* object table through the use of the Faculty view. The trigger first verifies that the department *Code* is valid and that there is no other person in the database with the same identifier. A tuple is then inserted into the *persons* object table. Note that the attributes of Person and Faculty are set to appropriate values and attributes associated with Student are set to null. In addition, the *Is_person* and *Is_faculty* flags are set to one and the *Is_student* flag is set to zero. Similar triggers can be created to allow modification and deletion of objects from the views in Listing 2.4. These triggers should be developed to enforce all class hierarchy and membership constraints as specified in the UML schema. For example, in Figure 2.2, a Person is required to be either a Student or a Faculty object, and Student and Faculty objects must be disjoint.

Object-relational systems other than O8 may directly support class hierarchies, and as a result will not require the approach described in this section. In such systems, mapping superclasses and subclasses to object definitions will more closely parallel class definitions that typically are found in object-oriented database systems, where support for inherited attributes and methods is provided automatically. The obvious disadvantage of the hierarchy flattening approach in O8 is that it requires significant overhead in the specification of class views and in the coding of *instead of* triggers associated with each view. On the other hand, hierarchy flattening can be a flexible approach for dealing with conceptual models such as UML, which allow objects to be instances of multiple subclasses and support constraints on subclass membership. The work in "The Design and Implementation of an EXPRESS to Oracle 8 Mapping" [Tjahjadi 1997] compares the flexibility of the hierarchy flattening approach to class hierarchies in object-oriented database systems, where objects are only allowed to be an instance of one class, and membership constraints on subclasses are not supported.

An alternative translation option for class hierarchies in O8 is to create a separate object type and table for each class in the hierarchy. Object references can then be used to link together the classes that belong to the hierarchy. The problem with this approach is that an object will have multiple OIDs, one for each class to which it belongs in the hierarchy. Inherited attributes must also be referenced explicitly through the use of the REF attributes.

```
CREATE OR REPLACE VIEW student (obj_ref, DOB, Pid, FirstName,
      LastName, Status, Member_of, Major) AS
   SELECT REF(p), p.DOB, p.Pid, p.FirstName, p.LastName, p.Status,
         p.Member_of, p.Major
   FROM    persons p
   WHERE   p.Is_person = 1 AND p.Is_student = 1;

CREATE OR REPLACE VIEW faculty (obj_ref, DOB, Pid, FirstName,
      LastName, AdvisorRnk, Advisor_of, Works_In) AS
   SELECT REF(p), p.DOB, p.Pid, p.FirstName, p.LastName,
         p.AdvisorRnk, p.Advisor_of, p.Works_in
   FROM    persons p
   WHERE   p.Is_person = 1 AND p.Is_faculty = 1;
```

Listing 2.4   Student and Faculty views derived from the person object table.

VARRAYS and Nested Tables

In the previous sections, Listings 2.1 and 2.2 introduced the use of the *persons_array* VARRAY. Listing 2.3 also introduces the use of the *clubs_array* VARRAY and the nested table *clubs_table*. This section elaborates on some of the issues associated with the use of the VARRAY and nested table collection types for representing multivalued attributes and multivalued relationships between objects.

The VARRAY and nested table collection types are similar in that:

- The data types of all elements in each collection must be the same (i.e., each collection must be of a homogeneous type).

- A VARRAY or nested table can be used as the data type of a column in a relational or object table, or as a PL/SQL variable, parameter, or function return type.

```
CREATE OR REPLACE TRIGGER faculty_insert
    INSTEAD OF INSERT ON faculty
    FOR EACH ROW
DECLARE
    p_ref       REF person;
    counter     INTEGER;
    depts       INTEGER;
BEGIN
    SELECT COUNT(*) INTO depts
    FROM departments d
    WHERE ref(d) = :new.Works_In;
    SELECT COUNT(*) INTO counter
    FROM persons p
    WHERE p.Pid = :new.Pid;
    IF (counter = 0) THEN
        IF (depts  = 1) THEN
            INSERT INTO persons p VALUES
                (:new.DOB, :new.Pid, :new.FirstName, :new.LastName,
                    NULL, :new.AdvisorRnk, NULL, NULL, NULL,
                    :new.Works_In, 1, 0, 1)
                RETURNING REF(p) INTO p_ref;
        ELSE
            RAISE_APPLICATION_ERROR(-20001,
                'Error - not a valid department code');
        END IF;
    ELSE
        RAISE_APPLICATION_ERROR(-20001,
            'Error - a person already exists with this Pid');
    END IF;
END;
```

Listing 2.5   INSTEAD OF trigger for the faculty view.

The differences between the two are primarily due to the manner in which they are internally managed by O8. A VARRAY must always have a specific size limit. If the size of the ARRAY is smaller than 4000 bytes, O8 stores the VARRAY directly inside the table in which it is defined. Otherwise, O8 will create a binary large object for separate storage of the VARRAY. VARRAYs are also ordered and the contents are dense. This means that all elements from the beginning to the end of the VARRAY must be filled. Individual elements of a VARRAY cannot be deleted. To update a VARRAY, the entire collection must be replaced with a new collection.

Nested tables do not have an upper bound on the size limit. Nested tables are sparse, allowing individual elements to be deleted and inserted at any point in the table. A nested table is always stored as a table separate from the table in which it is defined. Unlike VARRAYS, a nested table can be indexed. The choice of using a VARRAY or nested table therefore depends on application needs. VARRAYS are better for smaller, ordered collections that do not require frequent changes. Nested tables are better for larger collections that are more volatile in nature. In the School Database example, VARRAYS and nested tables are used to illustrate the way in which each collection type is defined and accessed.

To illustrate the use of a nested table, return to the definition of the *persons* table in Listing 2.3. A nested table is used in this example to store the clubs that a faculty member advises. Initially, *clubs_table* is defined as a table of REFs to *campus_club* objects. The *clubs_table* type is then used in the *person* type definition to define the type of the *Advisor_of* attribute. In the table definition statement for the *persons* table, the phrase *"NESTED TABLE "ADVISOR_OF" STORE AS advised_clubs"* is included to create the internal name of the table space that will be used to store the actual nested table.

Definition of the *persons_array* and *clubs_array* VARRAYS is complicated by the fact that recursive references exist. For example, Figure 2.2 shows that Students are members of CampusClubs and CampusClubs have Students as members. Since we want a *person* type to have a VARRAY of REFs to *campus_club* and we want *campus_club* to have a VARRAY of REFs to the *person* type, the types have to be incrementally introduced and refined. In particular, we must create the types *campus_club* and *person* as incomplete object types, allowing the creation of the VARRAYs of REFs for each type. The sequence of definitions is shown in Listing 2.6.

As shown previously in Listing 2.3, the full definition of the object type *person* includes the *Member_of* attribute of type *clubs_array*. The full definition of the object type *campus_club* in Listing 2.2 includes the *Members* attribute of type *persons_array*. Because of the VARRAY definitions, there can be at most 50 members in a given club, and there can be

```
CREATE OR REPLACE TYPE campus_club
/
CREATE OR REPLACE TYPE clubs_array as VARRAY(15) of REF campus_club
/
CREATE OR REPLACE TYPE person
/
CREATE OR REPLACE TYPE persons_array as VARRAY(50) of REF person
```

Listing 2.6   Recursive VARRAY definitions.

at most 15 clubs to which a person belongs. After the recursive definitions in Listing 2.6, *clubs_array* and *persons_array* are holding types that have not yet been declared as objects. After the necessary array types have been created as in Listing 2.6, we can define the *campus_club* and *person* object types as shown in Listings 2.1 and 2.2, respectively.

To illustrate the use of VARRAYS and nested tables, Listing 2.7 shows a function that, given a specific person and club object, determines if the person is associated with the club. The use of DEREF transforms the *to_person* object reference into a tuple of type *person*, thus allowing access to the attributes of a *person* object rather than just the object identifier. If the *person* is a Student, then the code iterates through the *Member_of* VARRAY to determine if the student is a member of the club. If the *person* is a Faculty member, then the code iterates through the *Advisor_of* nested table to determine if the faculty member is an advisor of the club. O8 provides features such as COUNT, FIRST, and LAST for accessing the elements of VARRAYS and nested tables.

Triggers for Maintaining Inverses

We have already illustrated the use of triggers for creating views of an object hierarchy. Triggers can also be used to maintain inverses. As an example, there is an inverse rela-

```
CREATE OR REPLACE FUNCTION is_associated_with_club
    (candidate_club IN REF campus_club,to_person IN REF person)
    RETURN BOOLEAN IS
        is_associated      BOOLEAN;
        prsn               person;
BEGIN
    select DEREF(to_person) into prsn from dual;
    is_associated := false;
    IF (prsnIis_student = 1) THEN
        FOR i IN 1..prsn.Member_of.COUNT LOOP
            IF (candidate_club = prsn.Member_of(i)) THEN
                is_associated:= TRUE;
            END IF;
        END LOOP;
    END IF;
    IF (prsn.Is_faculty = 1) THEN
        FOR i IN prsn.Advisor_of.FIRST..prsn.Advisor_of.LAST LOOP
            IF (candidate_club = prsn.Advisor_of(i)) THEN
                is_associated:= TRUE;
            END IF;
        END LOOP;
    END IF;
    RETURN is_associated;
END;
```

Listing 2.7 Traversal through VARRAYS and nested tables.

tionship between Faculty and CampusClubs through the Advises relationship. The application has been designed so that triggers are used to maintain this relationship. In particular, the advisor of a CampusClub is specified through modification of the *Advisor* attribute of a *campus_clubs* object. The list of clubs that a Faculty member advises is updated automatically through the use of a trigger associated with modification of a *campus_clubs* object. In a similar manner, modification of the relationship from the Faculty side will cause the appropriate *campus_clubs* objects to be modified. Listing 2.8 illustrates a trigger defined for deletion of a *faculty* object. For all clubs advised by the deleted *faculty* object, the trigger sets the *Advisor* attribute to null. Application code for maintaining inverses should enforce all minimum and maximum bounds on the relationship as specified in the UML diagram.

As with the hierarchy flattening approach, the specification of triggers for maintaining inverses represents additional overhead in the schema generation process. Most object-oriented database systems automatically maintain inverse relationships. If the designer of an object-relational schema chooses to explicitly maintain inverse relationships between objects, the designer must be prepared to fill in the appropriate trigger code, potentially iterating through VARRAYS and nested tables in the case of 1:N and N:M relationships.

Derived Attributes

An alternative to explicitly storing both sides of an inverse relationship is to use a function to derive one side of the inverse relationship. In the School Database application, the major and worksIn relationships are expressed using navigability in Figure 2.2, which indicates that only one side of the relationship should be explicitly maintained. As a result, the *person* type in Listing 2.3 was defined to support the *Major* and *WorksIn* attributes, containing REFs to the department that a Student or Faculty member majors in or works in, respectively. As specified in the department class of Figure 2.2, the *department* object type in Listing 2.1 defines the *get_students* function to return the students majoring in a department and the *get_faculty* function to return the faculty that work in a department.

```
CREATE OR REPLACE TRIGGER faculty_delete
    INSTEAD OF DELETE ON faculty
    FOR EACH ROW
DECLARE
    p_ref    REF person;
BEGIN
    SELECT REF(p) into p_ref FROM persons p WHERE p.PID = :old.Pid;
    UPDATE clubs c SET c.Advisor = NULL WHERE p_ref = c.Advisor;
    DELETE FROM persons p WHERE p.PID = :old.Pid;
END;
```

Listing 2.8   Trigger for updating the clubs advised by a faculty member.

```
MEMBER FUNCTION get_faculty RETURN persons_array IS
    temp_array persons_array;
BEGIN
    SELECT CAST(MULTISET
                (SELECT REF(p)
                 FROM persons p
                 WHERE p.Is_faculty = 1 and deref(p.Works_in) = SELF)
           AS persons_array)
    INTO temp_array
    FROM dual;
    RETURN(temp_array);
END;
```

Listing 2.9 Function for deriving the faculty members of a department.

The *get_faculty* function is shown in Listing 2.9, which returns a *persons_array* of *faculty* objects (i.e., *person* objects with *Is_faculty* = 1) that have a *WorksIn* attribute set to a specific *department* object. The DEREF function is used to transform the *department* object reference within the *works_in* attribute into a tuple of type *department* for comparison with SELF, where SELF is the specific department object that is executing the *get_faculty* function.

Embedded Objects

In addition to supporting the creation of object tables, object types can also be used to create *embedded objects*. Embedded objects are used to support user-defined types that do not need to be represented as independent objects with object identifiers. Embedded objects are stored directly inside of other objects and are created by using the object type definition as an attribute type rather than using a REF to an object type. In the definition of the *person* object type in Listing 2.3, the type *date_t* is used as an embedded object to define the *DOB* (date of birth) attribute of a *person* object. The definition of *date_t* is shown in Listing 2.10, where a date is defined to consist of *day*, *month*, and *year* attributes together with functions for validating a date value. The *date_t* object type therefore encapsulates the semantics of date values. A *person* object *p* can then refer to *p.DOB.year*, for example, to return the year in which the person was born. Using this approach, a date does not have an object identifier but exists as a complex object inside of another object type. Embedded objects can also be used as attribute values in relational tables.

In the School Database example, we have also used user-defined object types to implement enumeration types that serve as embedded objects. For example, the *month* attribute in Listing 2.10 is defined using another object type *months_t*, where *months_t* is used to define valid month values. The *current_year* and *persons_rank* types are also used as embedded objects for enumeration values in the *person* object type definition of Listing 2.3. The *current_year* type defines the enumeration values of freshman, sophomore,

```
CREATE OR REPLACE TYPE date_t AS OBJECT (
    day          INTEGER,
    month        months_t,
    year         INTEGER,
    MEMBER FUNCTION ivalidation                    RETURN BOOLEAN,
    MEMBER FUNCTION valid_date (par IN date_t)     RETURN BOOLEAN,
    MEMBER FUNCTION leap_year (year IN INTEGER)    RETURN BOOLEAN,);
```

Listing 2.10   The date_t object type definition for use as an embedded object.

junior, senior, and graduate. The *persons_rank* type defines enumeration values that are used to identify a faculty member as being either an assistant, associate, or full professor.

Listing 2.11 shows the object type definition for *months_t*, together with the table definition that enumerates the valid month values and also associates each value with an internal numeric index. The implementations of the functions and procedures associated

```
CREATE OR REPLACE TYPE months_t AS OBJECT (
    current_choice INTEGER,
    MAP MEMBER FUNCTION type_value RETURN INTEGER,
    MEMBER FUNCTION ivalidation RETURN BOOLEAN,
    MEMBER FUNCTION ivalidation(choice IN INTEGER) RETURN BOOLEAN,
    MEMBER FUNCTION ivalidation(choice IN VARCHAR2) RETURN BOOLEAN,
    MEMBER FUNCTION get_value RETURN INTEGER,
    MEMBER FUNCTION get_enumerated RETURN VARCHAR2,
    MEMBER PROCEDURE set_value (new_choice IN INTEGER),
    MEMBER PROCEDURE set_enumerated (new_choice IN VARCHAR2));

CREATE TABLE months_choices (
    elem_id INTEGER PRIMARY KEY,
    element VARCHAR2(200) UNIQUE);

INSERT INTO months_choices VALUES ( 0, 'January');
INSERT INTO months_choices VALUES ( 1, 'February');
INSERT INTO months_choices VALUES ( 2, 'March');
INSERT INTO months_choices VALUES ( 3, 'April');
INSERT INTO months_choices VALUES ( 4, 'May');
INSERT INTO months_choices VALUES ( 5, 'June');
INSERT INTO months_choices VALUES ( 6, 'July');
INSERT INTO months_choices VALUES ( 7, 'August');
INSERT INTO months_choices VALUES ( 8, 'September');
INSERT INTO months_choices VALUES ( 9, 'October');
INSERT INTO months_choices VALUES (10, 'November');
INSERT INTO months_choices VALUES (11, 'December');
```

Listing 2.11   The month_t object type definition for defining enumeration types.

with *months_t* (not shown in Listing 2.11) use the table *months_choices* to ensure that only valid month values are assigned to the *current_choice* attribute of *months_t*. The technique for defining enumeration types used in the School Database example is based on the technique described by Tjahjadi in [Tjahjadi 1997].

Embedded objects are especially useful in support of mappings from UML schemas. UML class diagrams provide the user with flexibility in specifying the types of attribute values. Using embedded objects in O8, a developer can implement user-defined types that correspond to the types used in the UML specification. Unlike other object-relational systems, object types in O8 fully support encapsulation, where function and procedure definitions can be associated explicitly with type definitions.

Queries over Objects

One of the advantages of using object REFs and collections of object REFs in an object-relational schema design is that REFs allow a more direct representation of object-oriented conceptual schemas. As a result, queries can make use of REFs to navigate through object relationships instead of explicitly specifying join conditions. As an example, suppose that we want to return the name of the department of a club's advisor. The following select statement uses object references to traverse through the single-valued relationships that exist from a club to its advisor and from an advisor to the department in which the advisor works:

```
select    c.Advisor.WorksIn.Name
from      clubs c
where     c.name = "Epsilon Sigma";
```

This query returns a string value representing the name of the appropriate department.

Queries that return objects must be written either to return the object REF or to return the tuple that represents the object type. The DEREF function is provided to access the actual type of an object reference. As an example, the following query retrieves the code and name of the department in which Pablo is a major:

```
DECLARE
    d department;
BEGIN
    select DEREF(p.Major) into d
    from persons p
    where p.FirstName = "Pablo";
END;
```

In this query, *p.Major* returns a REF to a *department* object. *DEREF(p.Major)* returns a tuple of type *department*, which contains the *Code* and *Name* attributes as defined in Listing 2.1.

Comparison to Other Systems

As part of our study, we performed comparisons of the mappings described in the previous sections to:

- The relational model
- A different object-relational model
- An object-oriented database model

Due to its object-oriented nature, UML obviously provides a smoother mapping to an object-relational model than to a traditional relational model. Object tables, nested tables, VARRAYS, and object references have provided a more natural representation of UML data than relational tables. The object extensions to SQL also provided a more concise expression of queries compared to traditional relational queries. Class definitions and user-defined types, however, require the generation of the appropriate methods and triggers that subsequently can be used to access objects and complex types as well as to check the appropriate constraints associated with such types. As a result, the translation of conceptual schemas from a model such as UML to an object-relational schema is more complex than traditional ER-to-relational mapping techniques. The mappings that we have defined not only identify the object types, relational tables, and object tables of the target schema, but also define the manner in which the methods and triggers associated with types and tables should be used.

PostgreSQL was the first database management system that utilized object-relational database concepts. The system is public-domain software that supports a subset of SQL92 and some extended features of object-relational systems. Illustra Information Technology (a wholly owned subsidiary of Informix Software, Inc.) also provides a commercial object-relational database system called *Data Blade,* which was originally based on Postgres (Stonebraker 1996). Since *Data Blade* was not freely available at the time of this study, PostgreSQL is used for comparison in this subsection.

Although PostgreSQL also has a *CREATE TYPE* statement, the way it is used is different from the Oracle 8 *CREATE TYPE* statement. The approach in Oracle 8 for defining object types is to create a composite type with its associated member functions (like creating a *class* in C++) that can be used as attribute types or to create object tables. In PostgreSQL, the *CREATE TYPE* statement will create a new base (primitive) type that is stored as a TEXT type internally, except for the base type that is used as an array. The new base type, which is referred to as a *user-defined type,* can have a name at most 15 characters long. A PostgreSQL user-defined type must have *input* and *output* functions. These functions are used to determine how the new type appears in string form for input by and output to the user, and how the new type is stored in memory. Contrary to Oracle 8, the PostgreSQL user-defined type cannot specify any encapsulated member functions. Global functions are used to access and manipulate the type. PostgreSQL also does not have strong procedural language support as with Oracle's PL/SQL. As a result, PostgreSQL requires the use of *native calls implementation* for most of the PostgreSQL functions.

A table in PostgreSQL is the same as an object table in Oracle 8. Every instance in PostgreSQL has a unique object identifier, which is stored implicitly in a special attribute called *oid.* A PostgreSQL table can also be used as a user-defined type for arguments in PostgreSQL functions or as an attribute type. Because of the PostgreSQL table properties, a UML class would be mapped using a PostgreSQL table. Forward relationships between objects are implemented using the OID built-in type (or an array of OIDs for multivalued relationships). A PostgreSQL OID can be viewed as a generic OID that stores only the persistent object logical address. To retrieve the object instance that owns the OID, an SQL join operation has to be performed.

UML inverse relationship mappings in PostgreSQL use the same UML-to-O8 mapping principles. The first alternative is to use a function to determine the inverse relationship. This approach could face function name conflicts caused by the same inverse attribute names for different tables since all PostgreSQL functions have to be defined globally and are not encapsulated as in Oracle 8 member functions. The other approach is to have an attribute of OID type to store the inverse relationship information. This approach needs the PostgreSQL rule system to maintain the integrity of the OID. UML derived attributes would also be mapped using PostgreSQL functions, which can cause name conflicts between derived attributes with the same name but used for different tables. The advantage of PostgreSQL over Oracle 8, however, is its support for inheritance. In PostgreSQL, there is no need to create multiple table views as in the O8 mapping scheme, since object tables in PostgreSQL can be organized into inheritance hierarchies.

For mapping comparisons to object-oriented database technology, we used Objectivity/DB [Objectivity 1995], a commercial object-oriented database system that is compliant with the ODMG-93 standard [ODMG 1996]. A UML class is represented in Objectivity/DB using a class that inherits from *ooObj* class. UML inheritance hierarchies can be mapped directly to Objectivity inheritance hierarchies. To support persistent inheritance, only the supertype of the type hierarchy needs to be inherited from the *ooObj* class. Creation of Objectivity classes that represent multiple inheritance are required to enforce overlapping subclasses in UML. The ability to redefine the default constructor for Objectivity classes can be utilized to enforce UML subclass constraints. By default, every Objectivity persistent class inherits a virtual function called *ooValidate* from *ooObj* class. The *ooValidate* function can be overridden to do any necessary constraint checking that can be called from the persistent class constructors.

Object instances that inherit from *ooObj* can have *to-one* or *to-many* relationships to other *ooObj* instances. Objectivity supports both unidirectional relationships and bidirectional relationships that can be maintained automatically by the database system. Bidirectional relationships can be viewed as inverse relationships. These *ooObj* features can be used directly for the UML forward and inverse relationships without any triggers or member function simulations as in O8 and PostgreSQL. Expressing a derived attribute in Objectivity is implemented simply by using the class public member function. Collection types can be represented using the Objectivity array called *ooVArray*, a generic variable array that can contain elements of the same type.

The primary advantage of an object-relational system such as Oracle 8 over the use of an object-oriented database is found in the use of SQL. Most object-oriented databases do not yet support the advanced query facilities found in object-relational systems.

Conclusion

This chapter has described the fundamental issues associated with mapping UML class diagrams to object-relational schemas using the Oracle 8 object-relational system as a framework to define the basic mapping issues. The mapping defined in this research has been targeted to utilize most of the object features within Oracle 8. In particular:

- Object types support the creation of abstract data types that correspond to class definitions in UML and to other, user-defined complex types that are needed for attribute definitions.

- Object tables are created from object types and used to hold persistent instances with object identifiers that correspond to UML class objects.

- Embedded objects are used to define complex attribute values from user-defined object types.

- Object references (REFs) are used to define relationships between objects.

- VARRAYS and nested tables are used to implement multivalued attributes and multivalued relationships between objects.

- Triggers are used to maintain inverse relationships between objects.

- Relational views and instead of triggers are used to simulate the functionality of UML class hierarchies.

Our work with mapping UML to an object-relational model demonstrates several important results about the use of object-relational concepts. As with the relational model, designing an application directly through the creation of an object-relational schema can be a difficult task; it is still more desirable to design an application at a higher level using a modeling language such as UML. The generation of the underlying implementation schema, however, is complicated by the advanced features of the object-relational model. More alternatives must be considered in the translation process to exploit fully the use of object-relational features. As a result, the designer may need to be more involved in decisions about the final mapping solutions and in filling in the details associated with views, triggers, and user-defined types. Ideally, automatic schema translation tools are needed that understand the different mapping options and interact with the designer in the effective use of object-relational technology.

CHAPTER 3

SQLJ and JDBC: Database Access in Java

In this chapter we will look at SQLJ and JDBC, the two standard ways of using object-relational databases in Java programs. Java is the language of choice for writing Internet applications, and SQL is the prime language for programming databases. SQLJ and JDBC are important technologies that provide the bridge between front-end Java applications and back-end SQL databases.

The first question that comes to mind is: Why do we need two ways? Why is one, just SQLJ or only JDBC, not enough? The answer is that JDBC and SQLJ are meant to serve distinct but complementary purposes—SQLJ supports *embedded SQL* whereas JDBC is an *application program interface*, and SQLJ typically uses JDBC under the covers to execute SQL operations. But before we dive into their differences, let us first look at when and why these database programming frameworks came into existence.

A Bit of Background

Java is an object-oriented language. Object-oriented programming is based on the concept of *objects* and *classes*. A class is used to group logically related data into a modular unit and to provide *methods* that encapsulate the behavior associated with this data. An object is an instance of a class. Object-oriented languages such as Smalltalk and C++ have been widely used for a number of years. Java combines their good features but eliminates much of the complexity of C++. It also emphasizes robustness and portability across different platforms. Java is strongly typed; that is, each Java object has a specific type that defines its attributes and methods. Most type errors are caught while compiling Java programs, thus promoting robustness. Additionally, only safe memory operations are permitted in Java. Unlike a C or C++ program, a Java program cannot perform unsafe and arbitrary pointer operations on data residing in memory. Java also provides automatic garbage collection that reclaims memory of objects no longer used in a program, as in Smalltalk.

As the use of Java took off among the programming community in the mid-1990s, designers at Sun Microsystems saw the need to support database access from Java programs. Working with the major database vendors, in 1996 they specified a proposal for JDBC. The JDBC specification [JDBC Spec] defines a set of interfaces for SQL-based database access from Java. JDBC is an application program interface (API), which means that SQL statements are executed on a database by calling methods in the JDBC library from Java code. The JDBC programming model is based on ODBC, which is an earlier standard for database programming.

The JDBC API soon became the de-facto standard for database programming in Java. Shortly after, the major database companies initiated a joint effort to design and standardize embedded SQL support in Java. This language is known as SQLJ. The open-source SQLJ Reference Implementation was made publicly available by Oracle in early 1998, and around that time the SQLJ language was also submitted to ANSI for standardization. It was formally accepted as an ANSI standard in December 1998.

Now let's get back to our original question—What is the goal of SQLJ? Why do we need SQLJ if we already have JDBC? Here's why: In contrast to the library calls in JDBC, SQLJ allows SQL statements to be written directly inside Java code using the compact and convenient #sql notation, as in the code snippet shown in Listing 3.1. The intent of the code should be intuitively obvious, but let us look into the details to better understand how it actually works.

SQLJ Basics

SQLJ consists of several different aspects:

- The SQLJ language with special syntax for embedding SQL statements
- A translator that converts SQLJ code to Java
- The SQLJ runtime/execution model

We will examine each of these topics briefly in the sections that follow.

```
String name = "Joe Doe";
String phone = "(650)123-4567";
#sql { INSERT INTO PHONES (name, phnumber)
     VALUES (:name, :phone)
   };
```

Listing 3.1   An SQL INSERT operation written in SQLJ.

Embedded SQL Syntax

The #sql prefix denotes the start of an SQLJ construct in a source file. A static SQL operation may follow within curly braces and can span multiple lines, ending with a semicolon. The embedded SQL statement must be *static*; that is, known at the time the program is written. The SQL text can include comments that conform to ANSI SQL-92 convention. Arguments may be passed to the SQL statement using colon-prefixed Java *host variables*. In fact, SQLJ supports general Java *host expressions* as long as they appear within parentheses. All standard JDBC types are valid host expression types in the SQLJ standard (we will discuss datatypes later in this chapter). Apart from executable SQL operations, #sql statements can also be used to declare special SQL-related Java classes; for example, for iterating through query results. We look at declarative #sql statements later in the chapter.

Going back to the code snippet in Listing 3.1, the first two lines are Java declarations of two host variables: name and phone. Following this Java code is a #sql statement with an embedded SQL command, which in our case is an INSERT operation on an SQL table named PHONES. The colon-prefixed quantities name and phone in the VALUES clause are Java *host variables*—they are first evaluated and then passed as arguments to the SQL operation. Notice that we have omitted the important step of connecting to the database, but we will get back to that shortly.

SQLJ Translator

The mixed SQLJ source is converted to pure Java code by the SQLJ translator, with the #sql statements resulting in calls to the SQLJ run-time library. This generated code can be compiled with a standard Java compiler. For ease of use, the sqlj command-line tool integrates the SQLJ translation and Java compilation steps. The Java compiler used is javac by default, but can be specified explicitly if different.

A very useful feature of the SQLJ translator is that it can optionally connect to a database and check SQL statements for syntax errors as well as potential Java-to-SQL type mismatch errors. This compile-time SQL checking greatly reduces the risk of run time exceptions, making SQLJ programs more robust compared to JDBC (more on this shortly). Of course, to realize the benefits of compile-time checking, the structure of the SQL tables and stored programs should remain the same at run time.

The SQLJ translator places the embedded SQL statements in Java binary resource files known as *profiles*. These profiles can be *customized* before execution without altering source code for the application, thus promoting *binary portability* across databases. Profile customization is a powerful technique with many uses; for example, it can be employed for vendor-specific database features or for performance optimizations such as caching and precompilation of SQL statements.

The architecture of the SQLJ translator is open and extensible so that each vendor can provide its own SQL checkers and profile customizers as plug-in modules while sharing the same code base for other functions. The translator also supports a call interface for easy integration into development tools.

Execution Model

After the SQLJ code is compiled into Java binary, the application can be run against a database using the SQLJ run-time library, which executes the SQL commands via an underlying API to the database. This API is most commonly JDBC, although other implementations are possible. The SQLJ execution model is shown in Figure 3.1.

The SQLJ run time is written in pure Java. An important benefit is that we can deploy an SQLJ application in any configuration supported by Java; for example, as an applet, servlet, or stand-alone application.

The SQLJ Standard

The vendor-neutral SQLJ language specification was produced jointly by major database companies including Oracle, IBM, Sybase, Informix, Tandem (now owned by Compaq), and others who form the SQLJ Consortium (see [SQLJ Home] for details). This effort is supported by Sun Microsystems, which is the primary body that controls the development of Java and related languages.

The SQLJ language and the run-time API have been standardized by ANSI as the specification X3.135.10-1998, Information Technology—Database Languages—SQL—Part 10—Object Language Bindings (see www.ansi.org/). This specification is also

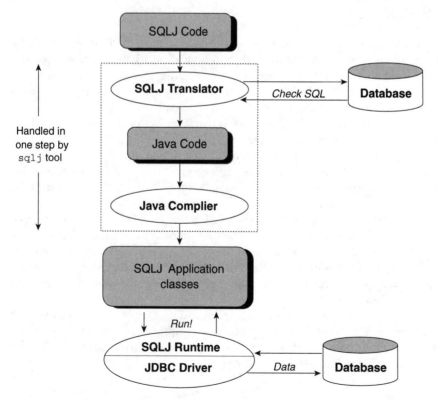

Figure 3.1   The SQLJ programming framework.

known informally as the *SQLJ Part 0* specification. The SQLJ Consortium additionally has drafted the *SQLJ Part 1* and *Part 2* proposals, which deal with SQLJ stored procedures and stored classes in the database server. SQLJ Part 1 is already an ANSI standard, and SQLJ Part 2 is expected to be submitted for standardization shortly. In this chapter we will look at SQLJ Part 0 issues only.

JDBC Basics

As we mentioned earlier in this chapter, JDBC is the call-level API for executing SQL operations on a database. An essential distinction between JDBC and SQLJ is that JDBC has an inherently dynamic execution model—SQL statements may be constructed on the fly and executed via method calls. The programmer has greater flexibility in this case, the cost being that (unlike SQLJ) there is no notion of compile-time SQL checking in JDBC—all errors are necessarily detected at run time. Hence more code paths may need to be tested in a JDBC program in order to achieve the same degree of robustness as an SQLJ program. Besides this difference, JDBC programs are also less compact—the #sql syntax of SQLJ corresponds to a sequence of JDBC calls and provides a higher level of abstraction. A key concept in JDBC that is hidden in SQLJ (i.e., automatically managed by the SQLJ run time) is the statement object. We briefly review its function in the next section; refer to the JDBC 1.2 API Specification [JDBC Spec] for details.

Statements

The JDBC statement corresponds to a single unit of SQL execution. It is represented by the Statement type (an interface) in the java.sql package. Given a JDBC connection object (which is an instance of the java.sql.Connection type) a Statement object can be created using the method createStatement() on the connection, and then executed with a SQL command string.

As a warm-up exercise, let us rewrite the SQLJ code snippet of Listing 3.1 using a JDBC Statement.

Here are some points to observe in the piece of code shown in Listing 3.2:

```
public static void insertRow (java.sql.Connection conn)
                throws java.sql.SQLException
  { // create a JDBC statement on the connection
    java.sql.Statement s = conn.createStatement();
    String name = "Joe Doe";
    String phone = "(650)123-4567";
    s.execute("INSERT INTO PHONES (name, phnumber) VALUES " +
            "('" + name + "','" + phone + "')");
    s.close();  // release the statement
  }
```

Listing 3.2   An SQL Insert operation written in JDBC.

- The insertRow() method throws a java.sql.SQLException. This type of exception represents an error in execution of the SQL statement and is thrown by most method calls in JDBC. The same type of exception is also thrown by executable #sql statements in SQLJ.

- We have built up the SQL command dynamically using Java string concatenation—the name and phone values that are to be added to the PHONES table are placed as constants in the VALUES clause of the INSERT. A limitation of the basic statement object is that it cannot have bind parameters or arguments for the SQL operation. A common programming scenario is that the same query or update is executed in a loop with changes in just the parameter values; in this case it does not make sense to reparse and reoptimize the invariant SQL command each time. JDBC provides the type called PreparedStatement exactly for this purpose. We discuss prepared statements in the section dealing with performance issues.

- An issue that we have glossed over is the database connection setup. In the JDBC program the method has an explicit argument of type java.sql.Connection on which the statement is created. But where is the connection in our SQLJ code? This apparent mystery has a simple explanation—SQLJ has the notion of a default connection and we assumed that it has been initialized before. We will look into database connections shortly, but first a short note on the deployment of database programs.

A Note on Deployment

Database vendors provide different implementations of the JDBC interfaces for their specific databases. These implementations are known as JDBC *drivers.* Some JDBC drivers may use Java Native Interface methods to call underlying C libraries (the *Type 2* drivers in JDBC parlance), whereas others may be written completely in Java (such as the *Type 4* drivers). Oracle, for example, provides three different types of JDBC drivers:

JDBC-OCI driver. Uses the client-side Oracle Call Interface C libraries.

JDBC thin driver. Written purely in Java.

JDBC server-side driver. Used for executing Java stored programs in the Oracle 8*i* database.

We will use the JDBC-OCI driver in our next examples. Which JDBC driver is appropriate for a particular application depends upon deployment requirements; for example, a pure-Java driver is needed to run a JDBC program as an applet within a browser. The important point is that all JDBC drivers support the same standard set of interfaces, thereby promoting portability across different JDBC drivers as well as different vendors' databases.

Connecting to the Database

Database connections in SQLJ are represented and handled somewhat differently than in JDBC. For SQLJ, database connections come into the picture at translation time for

SQL checking as well as at run time. SQLJ uses the concept of a *connection context* to represent a database connection. It is analogous to the JDBC notion of java.sql.Connection, with the important difference that a certain connection context type can be used to represent the particular structure of a database schema (e.g., what tables and stored procedures are accessible in it).

Connecting at Run Time in SQLJ

To make programming easier for the common cases, the SQLJ run time supports the notion of a default connection context. Setting up the default connection in SQLJ requires two steps:

1. Register a JDBC Driver.
2. Establish a connection as the default.

The first step is done by calling the registerDriver() method in the DriverManager class of the JDBC libraries, with the name of a JDBC driver class as the argument. Next, the SQLJ default connection context is initialized by calling the static method setDefaultContext() in the sqlj.runtime.ref.DefaultContext class. In Listing 3.3 we show these connection steps using the JDBC-OCI driver for an Oracle database.

As shown in the code of Listing 3.3, the setDefaultContext() method takes an instance of the DefaultContext class, which has four parameters in its constructor (the constructor is the method that actually connects to the database). The first parameter is the *Universal Resource Locator* (URL) for a database, in the format required by a JDBC driver. The second and third arguments are the name of the user schema and password for the database. The fourth and last parameter is a Boolean flag for auto-commit mode, which is set to true if updates are to be committed automatically to the database without requiring an explicit COMMIT operation in SQL. We recommend that this flag be set to false to have greater control over commits.

All #sql operations that do not specify a connection context implicitly use the default one. Note, however, that for some programs such as multithreaded applications and SQLJ applets an implicit default connection is inherently unsafe as it relies on static variables in the SQLJ run time. Explicit connections must be used in these cases, and also for multiple database connections in the same SQLJ program. A special syntax is provided

```
public static void dbConnect() throws SQLException
{ java.sql.DriverManager.registerDriver(  // register JDBC driver
    new oracle.jdbc.driver.OracleDriver()); // JDBC driver class
  sqlj.runtime.ref.DefaultContext.setDefaultContext(
    new sqlj.runtime.ref.DefaultContext(
              "jdbc:oracle:oci8:@", // database URL
              "scott", "tiger",  // schema logon info
              false // auto-commit flag
    ));
}
```

Listing 3.3   Connecting at run time in SQLJ.

in SQLJ for this purpose—a connection context instance may be specified in brackets after the #sql token to indicate the connection on which the SQL is to be executed.

Connecting to the Database for SQLJ Translation

Database connections come into the picture at SQLJ translation time as well. To enable SQL checking at translation time, database connection information can be specified on the SQLJ command line, or in a Java *properties file*. The following line is an example of SQLJ command-line invocation that uses the JDBC/OCI driver during translation to check static SQL operations on the default connection context by logging on to the scott/tiger schema:

```
sqlj -user=scott/tiger -url=jdbc:oracle:oci8:@   Foo.sqlj
```

For flexibility, the SQLJ translator supports many other options, including the JDBC driver class to be used at translation time. Most options have reasonable default values—for example, for Oracle the JDBC driver is preset to the class oracle.jdbc .driver.OracleDriver. The SQLJ translator also supports SQL checking on multiple connection contexts at translation time, through command-line options that are (optionally) *tagged* with the connection context type name.

Connecting in JDBC

In the case of JDBC, the first step in the connection setup is the same as in SQLJ—that is, registering the name of the JDBC driver class. The second step is slightly different from SQLJ—initializing a variable of type java.sql.Connection instead of a connection context (which is a purely SQLJ concept) by calling the getConnection() method on the JDBC DriverManager class. The arguments of this method are the database URL, the userID and password for the schema. An example of this step is:

```
java.sql.Connection conn = java.sql.DriverManager.getConnection(
                    "jdbc:oracle:oci8:@","scott", "tiger");
```

Mix and Match SQLJ and JDBC

In some cases it is necessary to use both SQLJ and JDBC in a program. For example, if the SQL statement is dynamic and not known until run time, then JDBC must be used. To allow this, SQLJ has been designed to interoperate nicely with JDBC. We can easily convert JDBC connections to SQLJ connection contexts and vice-versa. Here is how we can initialize the SQLJ default connection context with a JDBC connection:

```
java.sql.Connection conn = ...; // Create JDBC connection
sqlj.runtime.ref.DefaultContext.setDefaultContext( // use it in SQLJ
        new sqlj.runtime.ref.DefaultContext(conn));
```

It is also possible to get a JDBC connection object from an SQLJ connection context instance:

```
java.sql.Connection conn =
    sqlj.runtime.ref.DefaultContext.getDefaultContext().getConnection();
```

Similar conversions are also supported between JDBC result sets and SQLJ iterators, discussed in the following sections.

Interfacing SQL and Java

Most object-relational databases speak the SQL language, which is different from Java not only in syntax but also in the programming paradigm and datatypes supported. One area of impedance mismatch is that SQL is set-oriented; for example, the result of a query is returned as a set of rows. In contrast, procedural programming languages like Java are sequential in nature, with iterative constructs such as for and while to loop over data sets. This difference manifests itself in the processing of SQL query results. A special Java interface known as a ResultSet is provided in JDBC to process the rows returned by an SQL query. Another a central issue in interfacing to SQL databases from Java code is how to map Java datatypes to SQL types and vice-versa. We now look into these two aspects: query result processing and datatype mapping in SQLJ and JDBC.

Retrieving Data through an SQL Query

Let us look at the query processing schemes in the two programming frameworks, starting with SQLJ.

Single-Row SQLJ Queries

The simplest query in SQLJ consists of fetching columns from a single row into a group of Java variables. For example, assuming our PHONES table also has a column for address, we can search the table to look up the name and address for a certain phone number corresponding to a single row in the table. Listing 3.4 shows such a single-row query written in SQLJ.

In this example, the SELECT list contains the name and address columns of the row matching the WHERE clause, and the INTO clause lists the Java variables name and address to hold the selected values. In the last two lines we print out the retrieved information.

The SELECT..INTO construct in SQLJ is very convenient for queries that are guaranteed to return a single row of data, such as when querying via a primary key or some other unique column value. It cannot, however, be used for queries that return no rows or more than one row—a run-time exception of type SQLException is thrown in these cases. In our example this exception is being thrown out of the lookupNameAddr() method, to be handled by its caller.

```
public static void lookupNameAddr (String ph_number)
        throws java.sql.SQLException {
    String name, address ;
    #sql { SELECT NAME, ADDRESS
      INTO :name, :address
      FROM PHONES
      WHERE PHNUMBER = :ph_number
        };
    System.out.println("Name: " + name + ", Address: " + address);
}
```

Listing 3.4   A single-row query in SQLJ.

SQLJ Iterators for Multirow Queries

Suppose that we wish to list the names and addresses of all the people in our PHONES table. In this case, we need to use a SQLJ *iterator* to fetch multiple rows in the result and to examine each row in turn. SQLJ iterators come in two flavors—*named* and *positional*. Named iterators retrieve column values by using the names of SQL query columns, whereas positional iterators use the column positions in the SQL query. We will illustrate the use of named iterators; we leave positional iterators as an exercise for you.

Iterators are declared as Java types using the #sql iterator syntax. An example of a named iterator declaration is shown in Listing 3.5. Class access modifiers such as public are allowed in the declaration.

When the SQLJ translator finds such an iterator declaration it generates a Java class with methods for accessing data. In our case a public Java class named NameAddrIter is generated with built-in methods for result set processing, such as next() to move to the next row, close() to release the result set, etc. Additionally, this class has two *accessor* methods, name() and address(), which return java.lang.String values. These accessor methods read data from the matching columns in the query—the method name() returns the value of the name field and the method address() returns the value of the address field. Since the names of the accessor methods match the SQL column names, the iterator is called a *named* iterator. Here are some things to keep in mind about SQLJ iterator declarations:

- Iterator declarations may be placed wherever a Java class declaration is legal, for example, as a nested class.
- The SQL query may require column aliases for the accessors names to match the SQL column names. Also, return types of the accessor methods must be datatypes supported by SQLJ.

```
#sql public iterator NameAddrIter (String name, String address);
```

Listing 3.5   A named SQLJ iterator.

```
public static void allNameAddrs() throws SQLException {
    NameAddrIter na = null; // declare an iterator instance
    try { #sql na = // populate it with a SQL query result
            { SELECT NAME, ADDRESS
                FROM PHONES ORDER BY NAME
            };
        // Loop through the rows, printing name and address
        while (na.next()) {
            System.out.println(na.name() + ", " + na.address());
        }
    } catch (java.sql.SQLException se) {
        System.out.println("SQL error : " + se);
    } finally {
        na.close();  // close the iterator
    }
}
```

Listing 3.6   Using an SQLJ named iterator.

An instance of the iterator can be initialized with a SQL query using #sql syntax, as shown in Listing 3.6. This example shows a method allNameAddr() that lists all the names and addresses in our PHONES table. The method first declares a variable na of the iterator type NameAddrIter defined earlier. Next, the iterator instance na is populated with a SQL query result in the #sql statement. The query selects the two columns name and address (matching the accessor names) and sorts the rows by name using an ORDER BY clause.

Successive rows in the result set are examined using the next() method of the iterator. Each call to this method fetches the next row if one exists, or returns false otherwise. So the while loop terminates when all selected rows have been listed. Inside the while loop we print out the name and address for each row using the accessor methods name() and address() of the iterator. In the finally block the resources of the iterator are released by calling close().

JDBC ResultSets

Let us now implement a similar program using JDBC routines. JDBC does not distinguish between single-row and multirow results—both types of queries have to be coded using the JDBC ResultSet. We will first need to create a JDBC statement using a JDBC connection. Once we have a statement handle we can set up the query string and execute the query. This sequence of operations is shown in the code example of Listing 3.7.

In this example, the conn variable represents the JDBC connection to the database, and the condition variable denotes a dynamic search condition; for example, name LIKE 'A%', that is entered by the user. The query text is built up by appending the input condition to the WHERE clause of the general SQL query on the PHONES table. Execution of the query returns a result set named rs. The while loop calls rs.next() to fetch successive rows. The column values for each row are retrieved using the method

```
    public void matchNameAddrs(java.sql.Connection c, String condition)
            throws java.sql.SQLException {
    java.sql.Statement s = null;
    java.sql.ResultSet rs = null;
    try { s = c.createStatement();  // get a statement
        String query = "select name, address from PHONES where " +
                    condition;  // add input condition to query
        rs = s.executeQuery(query);
        while (rs.next()) { // print name,address for each row
            System.out.print(rs.getString(1)); //name from 1st column
            System.out.println("," + rs.getString(2)); //address 2nd
        }
    } catch (java.sql.SQLException se) {
        System.out.println("SQL Error: " + se);
    } finally {
        rs.close(); s.close(); // close the result set and statement
    }
    }
```

Listing 3.7   Using a JDBC ResultSet.

getString() which takes an integer argument for the column position (or alternatively, a string argument for the column name). Before exit, the result set and statement objects are closed in the finally block.

In addition to sequential forward-only result sets, the recent JDBC 2.0 specification also defines *scrollable* result sets to support moving forward and backward through a set of rows, as well as arbitrary positioning. Iterative processing in the forward direction is done through the next() method, and backward processing is through the previous()method. A scrollable result set provides relative positioning through the relative() method as well as absolute positioning through methods such as absolute(), first(), and last().Note that scrollable result sets are an optional feature of JDBC 2.0; other optional features include *updateable* result sets and *disconnected* rowsets. For details, refer to the JDBC 2.0 specification [JDBC20 Ext].

We will now use a scrollable updateable result set in JDBC 2.0 to change the data in a row of the PHONES table. Listing 3.8 gives an example of this functionality, and an explanation of the code follows.

The first thing to notice is the different way in which the statement is created for a scrollable result set. In the createStatement() call there are two additional parameters:

The *scrollability* and *sensitivity* of the result set. This parameter controls whether the result set can be scrolled backward and forward, and whether it is sensitive; that is, if it can see updates made to the database while the result set is open. The parameter can have one of three static constant values defined in the java.sql.ResultSet class: java.sql.ResultSet.TYPE_FORWARD_ONLY, java.sql .ResultSet.TYPE_SCROLL_INSENSITIVE, or java.sql.ResultSet.TYPE_SCROLL

```
public static void updatePhone(java.sql.Connection c,
                             String condition)
            throws java.sql.SQLException {
  java.sql.Statement s = null;
  java.sql.ResultSet rs = null;
  try { // Get a statement for scrollable, updateable result set
      s = c.createStatement
              (java.sql.ResultSet.TYPE_SCROLL_INSENSITIVE,
               java.sql.ResultSet.CONCUR_UPDATEABLE);
      String query = "select phnumber, address from PHONES where "
+
                      condition;  // add input condition to query
      rs = s.executeQuery(query);  // execute the query as usual
      rs.last();
      rs.updateString(1, "(123)456-7890");  // new phone
      rs.updateString(2, "Latest Address"); // new address
      rs.updateRow();

      // Update will be made permanent in the database at the
      // next COMMIT operation

  } catch (java.sql.SQLException se) {
      System.out.println("SQL Error: " + se);
  } finally {
      rs.close(); s.close(); // close the resultset and statement
  }
}
```

Listing 3.8 Using a scrollable and updateable JDBC ResultSet.

_SENSITIVE. If the type is forward-only, the result set is not scrollable and not sensitive to updates (JDBC 1.0 functionality). A scroll-sensitive result set is both scrollable and sensitive to changes in the underlying column values, and the scroll-insensitive result set is scrollable but not sensitive to changes once the query is executed.

The *concurrency type* of the result set. This parameter determines whether the result set can be used to perform updates, including inserting new rows or deleting existing rows. It can have one of two static constant values defined in the java.sql.ResultSet class: java.sql.ResultSet.CONCUR_READ_ONLY, java.sql .ResultSet.CONCUR_UPDATABLE. A read-only result set does not allow data in the rows to be modified. For an updateable result set, updates, inserts, and deletes can be performed on the rows in the result set and copied to the database.

Coming back to the example in Listing 3.8, once the JDBC statement has been created with the desired scrollability/sensitivity type, the query can be executed in the usual way. This creates a result set of the specified type, which in our example is scroll-insensitive and updateable.

Let us assume that we just want to update the last row in the result set. In this case the scrollable result set is positioned to the last row by calling the last() method for absolute positioning. The data in this row is then modified through updateXXX() calls (available only for updateable result sets) that change the column values, where XXX stands for the column type such as String or Int. Each of these updateXXX() methods takes two arguments: an integer value denoting the column number or a string for the column name, and then the new value of the appropriate type. After all the columns have been updated, in our case the phone number and address, the updateRow() method is called to copy the changes to the database. These changes are made permanent with the next COMMIT operation. The changes can be undone and the columns reverted to their original data values by calling the cancelRowUpdates() method instead of updateRow().

SQLJ Iterators versus JDBC ResultSets

Now that we have learned about both SQLJ iterators and JDBC result sets, a natural question that comes to mind is: *What is the crucial difference between the two?* Is it just syntactic, using accessor methods instead of JDBC get calls to fetch column values? No, the difference is not merely syntactic, although it may appear at first glance to be so. Unlike a JDBC ResultSet, an iterator represents the shape of the result rows. In our example, the NameAddrIter declaration specifies that the row has two columns, name and address, both of type String. This additional information supports early error detection through compile-time type-checking. If we pass an instance of this iterator as an argument to a method elsewhere in our code, the argument type must be of type NameAddrIter for the Java code to compile successfully. That is, static type-checking by the Java compiler prevents a wrong type of iterator from being passed to a method and causing run-time errors, say by accessing an invalid column position. The same compile-time checking does not apply for a JDBC ResultSet object, since it is a generic type representing any query result with no information about the query shape. Of course, SQLJ iterators are implemented using JDBC result sets, but they additionally provide the safer type-checking functionality through explicit declarations of the query shape.

SQLJ iterators and JDBC result sets are designed to interoperate well with each other. Given a SQLJ iterator, the underlying JDBC result set can be retrieved by calling the getResultSet() method on the iterator. It is also possible to construct a SQLJ iterator instance from a JDBC result set (refer to the SQLJ documentation for details).

Datatype Mapping

The other central issue in interfacing Java to SQL is datatype mapping. Consider an SQL table with a column of type NUMBER. To be handled in a Java program, this quantity must first be mapped to a Java datatype such as int, long, or float. More precisely, the Java arguments to SQL operations must have compatible datatypes that can be correctly mapped to SQL types, and vice-versa. For example, an SQL DATE type cannot be fetched into a Java int or float type in a JDBC or SQLJ program. The set of allowed datatype mappings is defined by JDBC and the same set is also supported by SQLJ. Table 3.1 lists some commonly used scalar SQL types and their compatible Java types. This list is not exhaustive—other mappings are also possible.

JDBC drivers from leading database vendors such as Oracle support additional datatypes that are specific to their own databases. We give a brief overview of Oracle extensions toward the end of this chapter.

The LOB (Large Object) datatypes are new in JDBC 2.0 and are useful for storing and retrieving large amounts of binary or character data in SQL columns, such as a picture or audio/video. The LOB data type is represented in Java as a java.sql.Blob or java.sql.Clob depending on the type of the LOB data. Java variables of these data types can be used in the get and set methods of a JDBC result set to pass LOB arguments, and JDBC methods can be used to read and write the LOB data.

Mapping User-Defined Types

Java is an object-oriented programming language, and a Java programmer typically uses Java classes to model real-world entities such as an employee. The SQL-99 standard also allows the definition of SQL object types in an object-relational database. Hence the question arises, can we use Java classes corresponding to SQL Object types? The answer is yes, and there are two options:

- By default, JDBC maps SQL objects and object references to the generic type java.sql.Struct. This type has methods to get the attributes present in the SQL object.

- Alternatively, SQL object types can be mapped to custom Java classes that implement the standard interface java.sql.SQLData. This interface has methods read-

Table 3.1 Compatible Mappings between SQL Types and Java Types

SQL TYPES	COMPATIBLE JAVA TYPES
CHAR, VARCHAR, LONG	java.lang.String, java.sql.Date, java.lang.Integer, int, long, float, double, etc.
DATE	java.sql.Date, java.sql.Time, java.sql.Timestamp, java.lang.String, etc.
NUMBER	java.math.BigDecimal, java.lang.Integer, short, int, long, float, double, etc.
RAW, LONGRAW	byte[]
BINARY LOB (BLOB)	java.sql.Blob (JDBC 2.0 only)
CHARACTER LOB (CLOB)	java.sql.Clob (JDBC 2.0 only)

SQL() and writeSQL() that specify how to read data from a SQL object into the Java class, and how to write the object back to the database. Let us look at this scheme in a bit more detail.

The JDBC 2.0 specification [JDBC20 Ext] defines the notion of a *type map*, which is a hash table for mapping SQL object types to their corresponding Java classes. A type map may be associated with a database connection or specified in the getObject() and setObject() JDBC calls. When fetching an SQL object type through getObject(), the JDBC driver automatically looks up the type map (the one provided in the method call or the type map set on the connection) and invokes the readSQL() method on the appropriate Java class. This method populates the attributes of the Java class in the correct order from the SQL data input stream (of type java.sql.SQLInput). Likewise, the writeSQL() method is called by JDBC when setObject() is called for data update. The following example illustrates the use of a custom Java class for an SQL object type.

Let us assume an SQL object type named EMPLOYEE_TYPE that has two attributes: EMP_NAME and EMP_ID. We will first have to define a Java class called Employee that is intended for this SQL type. The Java class must implement the java.sql.SQLData interface, as shown in the code fragment of Listing 3.9.

Our Java class Employee has two attributes—empName and empId—corresponding to the attributes in a SQL EMPLOYEE_TYPE object. The code in Listing 3.10 uses the Employee class to fetch these SQL objects.

In this example, we define a method called getEmployees(). This method first calls the put() method on the type map object for the input connection to associate the SQL object type EMPLOYEE_TYPE with the Java class Employee. Then a set of employee objects is selected through an SQL query, and fetched into this Java class using the getObject() method call on the result set. The empName and empId fields of the Java class are printed out for each employee object that is read.

```
public class Employee implements java.sql.SQLData
{
  public String empName; public int empId; public String sql_type;
  public Employee(){}
  // implement methods in the SQLData interface
  public String getSQLTypeName() throws java.sql.SQLException {
    return sql_type; }
  public void readSQL(java.sql.SQLInput inStream, String typeName)
    throws java.sql.SQLException {
    empName = inStream.readString(); empId = inStream.readInt();
    sql_type = typeName;
  }
  public void writeSQL(java.sql.SQLOutput outStream)
    throws java.sql.SQLException {
    outStream.writeString(empName); outStream.writeInt(empId); }
}
```

Listing 3.9   A custom Java class for an SQL object.

```
public static void getEmployees(java.sql.Connection conn)
  throws Exception {
    // First set up the type map on the connection
    java.util.Map map = conn.getTypeMap();
    map.put("EMPLOYEE_TYPE", Class.forName("Employee"));
    java.sql.Statement s = conn.createStatement();
    java.sql.ResultSet rs = s.executeQuery( // select employee objects
                           "select * from employee_table");
    while (rs.next()) {
       Employee ee = (Employee) rs.getObject(1); //populate Java class
       System.out.println("EmpName: " + ee.empName +
                          " EmpId: " + ee.empId); }
    rs.close();  s.close();
}
```

Listing 3.10   Using a custom Java class for an SQL object type.

Performance, Performance

Databases are intended to manage large quantities of data efficiently. Programming languages used to interact with the database must necessarily also be concerned with performance and efficiency issues. Here we consider some of the important performance-related features in JDBC and SQLJ.

JDBC Prepared Statements

For example, suppose that an SQL statement to insert a new row in a table is to be executed 1000 times in a loop with different data values. It is inefficient to reparse and reoptimize the same SQL statement over and over again, since the execution plan of an SQL statement will not change depending on the data values (or *bind variables*) being inserted. The JDBC specification addresses this issue with the notion of *prepared* statements—the java.sql.PreparedStatement type is a subtype of Statement and extends it with parameter binding routines for repeated execution. The SQLJ run time also makes use of JDBC prepared statements—they are cached and reused for execution in a loop. The code fragment in Listing 3.11 demonstrates the use of JDBC prepared statements.

Notice in this example that the prepared statement object is created only once by calling the method prepareStatement() on the JDBC connection with the SQL command as the argument. The "?" in the SQL text represents the bind parameter. The SQL INSERT operation is executed in a loop to add 10,000 rows into the table. Each insert uses a different data value, represented by the variable i in the for loop. This data value is bound to the "?" placeholder in the prepared statement through the setInt() call. The PreparedStatement type provides such set calls for all datatypes supported by JDBC.

```
public static void insertPreparedRows(java.sql.Connection conn)
        throws java.sql.SQLException  {
   java.sql.PreparedStatement ps = conn.prepareStatement( //prepare once
          "INSERT INTO MY_TABLE (AN_INTEGER) VALUES(?)");
   for (int i=1; i<=10000; i++) { // execute in a loop
     pstmt.setInt(1,i);              // bind the parameter value
     pstmt.executeUpdate();          // insert the row
   }
   pstmt.close();
}
```

Listing 3.11   Using JDBC prepared statements.

After binding the parameter(s), the prepared statement is executed. No reparsing of the SQL command is necessary on successive iterations, only parameter rebinding.

Batching of Updates

DML operations in SQL, such as INSERT, DELETE, and UPDATE statements, may be *batched* in JDBC 2.0 and SQLJ. Batching is a performance optimization that works as follows: If we are inserting or updating data through the same DML statement in a loop, then the parameter bindings can be collected locally on the client side until explicitly sent to the server via the executeBatch() method call, when the DML statement is executed with an array bind of the collected set of parameter values. Thus, batching saves round trips to the database. The JDBC 2.0 code for batching looks as follows:

```
stmt.setString(1, "Data 1");  stmt.addBatch(); //add to local batch
... // repeat adding to batch on client side
stmt.setString(1, "Data N");  stmt.addBatch(); //add to local batch
stmt.executeBatch();  // now send batch to server and execute
```

SQLJ also supports batching of updates through *execution contexts*. A #sql statement may specify a certain execution context that determines its environment, such as batching and other execution characteristics. Methods can be called on an execution context instance to set the environment, and in particular to turn on batching and to set a batch size limit. A pending batch may be flushed explicitly by calling the executeBatch() method of the execution context, or implicitly flushed by the SQLJ run time when the specified batch size is reached or a different SQLJ statement is executed.

Connection Pooling

Connection pooling is a framework for multiple database applications to share connections from a common cache. This supports reuse of *physical* connections and reduces the cost of creating and closing them. A *logical* connection serves as a tempo-rary handle to the underlying physical connection of a *pooled connection* object, and closing the logical connection returns the physical connection to the pool without actu-ally terminating it. Thus, a single physical database connection can be reused by a series of logical connection instances. Managing the cache of physical connections typ-ically is done by middle tier software that operates between the applications and the database server. JDBC 2.0 introduces the concept of *data sources* for connecting to data-bases (as an alternative to the JDBC DriverManager facility that we discussed earlier) and defines a connection pooling framework through the javax.sql.ConnectionPool-DataSource and related interfaces. Please refer to the JDBC documentation for further details on data sources and connection pooling.

SQLJ and JDBC in Oracle 8i

Oracle has not only led the development of the SQLJ standard and made an open-source Reference Implementation available for it (see www.sqlj.org/), but has also adopted it fully. Oracle SQLJ provides its own SQL checker plug-in module for trans-late-time verification of static SQL statements. The SQLJ translator is also well inte-grated with Oracle's JDeveloper IDE, which is a GUI tool for Java development. It allows SQLJ translation, Java compilation, and profile customization to be performed in one step, and provides debugging support at SQLJ source code level.

   The Oracle 8*i* database has comprehensive support for Java, including SQLJ and JDBC. In addition to implementing the JDBC 2.0 specification and the SQLJ ANSI standard, Ora-cle provides support for its own extended set of datatypes and features. For example, the oracle.sql package includes datatypes such as oracle.sql.CHAR and oracle.sql.NUMBER, which are direct representations of the corresponding SQL datatypes in SQL format. These datatypes can be used as input and output parameters in Oracle SQL statements to avoid conversion overhead and information loss in mapping data between SQL and Java (as from a SQL NUMBER to a Java double). Among other Oracle extensions are the REF CURSOR and ROWID datatypes, and the CustomDatum interface for programming with object types. The oracle.sql.CustomDatum interface is an alternative to the JDBC 2.0 java.sql.SqlData interface that we have discussed, and provides more flexibility in fetch-ing Oracle objects into custom Java classes via SQLJ and JDBC (but at the cost of less portable and vendor-specific code). To facilitate programming with object types, the JPub-lisher tool [Oracle JPub Doc] generates Java class definitions for SQL objects, either for the SQLData or for the CustomDatum interface. The CustomDatum interface is quite power-ful in that it can also be used for special processing of any datatype.

   Both SQLJ and JDBC are tightly integrated with the JavaVM embedded in the Ora-cle8*i JServer*. Stored programs and triggers written in SQLJ and JDBC can be compiled and executed inside the database, thus supporting a uniform programming style at the client and the server. Oracle provides a special server-side JDBC driver for the execu-tion of SQL statements in stored Java programs running inside the database. This JDBC driver is also used for execution of SQLJ stored programs, and is optimized for fast access to SQL data on the server. Refer to Oracle documentation for further details on Oracle JServer and its SQLJ and JDBC support [Oracle SQLJ Doc]; [Oracle JDBC Doc].

SQLJ versus JDBC

We conclude with a comparison of SQLJ and JDBC.

SQLJ provides compact syntax and a higher level of abstraction for static SQL statements by hiding some details of SQL execution, such as JDBC statement handles and parameter binding calls. Writing SQLJ programs is therefore easier and quicker than writing JDBC code, and they are easier to maintain too! Additionally, SQLJ promotes robust programming—static SQL statements can be verified during translation by logging on to a database schema. This helps detect errors during the program development phase, rather than at run time (as for JDBC). Programmer productivity is thus higher for SQLJ.

An important note is that the embedded SQL statements are *static*; that is, they are known at the time we are writing the program. In a majority of database applications the SQL operations are indeed known a priori and do not change during program execution, making SQLJ a better programming choice. On the other hand, if SQL statements are to be constructed dynamically, say from user input in a GUI application, then the more flexible JDBC API must be used. Table 3.2 summarizes the differences between SQLJ and JDBC.

Conclusion

In this chapter we have provided a brief introduction to SQLJ and JDBC, the standard mechanisms for database access in Java. The two frameworks are closely related—a JDBC driver typically is used to run translated SQLJ code—but at the same time they have

Table 3.2   Comparison of SQLJ and JDBC

FEATURE	SQLJ	JDBC
Compact embedded syntax	Yes, e.g., via host expressions	No, e.g., get/set calls for data
Early checking of static SQL	Yes, by SQLJ translator	No, runtime checking only
Typed iterators and connection contexts	Yes, for query shapes and schema structures	No, has generic result sets and connections
Profile customization	Yes, for binary portability	No
Dynamic SQL	No, but interoperates with JDBC	Yes, fully dynamic API
Statement handles	Managed by SQLJ runtime	Managed by programmer
Object type support	Yes	Yes
Portable source code	Yes, ANSI standard	Yes, JavaSoft specification

different programming models. The JDBC library is an API, whereas SQLJ supports embedded SQL—it hides many underlying details to provide a simpler model for static SQL.

We have given an overview of the basic concepts in SQLJ and JDBC: single-row queries via the convenient SELECT..INTO construct in SQLJ, multirow queries through SQLJ iterators that encode query shapes or through JDBC result sets, and JDBC statements and prepared statements. Both frameworks support efficient SQL execution through powerful datatypes such as LOBs and object types, and performance features such as batching of updates and connection pooling.

It is worth repeating here that SQLJ and JDBC are complementary approaches. SQLJ does not preclude the use of JDBC or vice-versa. In fact, we can easily mix and match SQLJ and JDBC code in the same source file, depending on whether the SQL operation is static or dynamic. SQLJ is designed to interoperate nicely with the JDBC API—for example, they can share a single database connection—so we can easily switch between the two styles of programming as per the requirements of our application.

Penguin: Objects for Programs, Relations for Persistence

Penguin is designed to support object-orientation for application programs while using relational databases as the persistent backing store. Objects are attractive to customers and programmers of applications because they structure information into a relevant and effective view. The use of relational databases that store large amounts of base data for long periods of time enables Penguin to take advantage of mature solutions for sharing information, concurrency, transactions, and recovery. We expect that application programs will be designed best with their own object schemata, so each object schema is supported as a series of views of the underlying relational databases. Penguin provides for multiple mappings to diverse object configurations, enhancing interapplication interoperation. This approach supports coexistence and sharing data among programs using relational technology with diverse application programs using object technology, as well as facilitating a migration to object technology.

Penguin is an object data management system that relies on relational databases for persistent storage. Object views of the relational databases allow each application to have its own object schema rather than requiring all applications to share the same object schema [Wiederhold 1986]. In this chapter, we discuss the principles, architecture, and implementation of the Penguin approach to sharing persistent objects.

The primary motivation for using a database management system (DBMS) is to allow sharing of data among multiple customers and multiple applications. To support sharing among independent transactions, DBMSs have evolved services including transaction independence, persistence, and concurrency control. When a database is shared among multiple applications, these applications typically have differing requirements for data access and representation. Such differences are supported by having views, which present diverse subsets of the base data [Chamberlin 1975].

The primary motivation for defining objects is to include shareable semantics and structure in the information. Must all applications sharing objects use the same object schema, or is it better to give each application its own object schema and somehow to integrate them? If multiple applications differ in view, the needed compromise reduces the relevance and effectiveness of the object representation [Abiteboul 1991]. For instance, `customers` will have an orthogonal view of an `inventory` versus the `suppliers`.

When combining independently developed applications, we do not have the luxury of choosing a common object schema. Many legacy databases and legacy data are still being used. We must retain the investment in existing application software and databases while building new software using the object approach. When creating a federation of heterogeneous (preexisting) databases, we must support a degree of interoperation among these databases and their schemas. Consider also that current projects will become legacy in a few years hence, but their semantics will remain. Whatever solutions we create in shared settings must support evolution and maintenance.

Object-oriented database management systems (OODBMSs) define an object schema that is used to support all information for its applications. Typically, that object schema is designed for one initial application, and other applications that want to share the information will have their needs *grafted on* [Tsichritzis 1989]. To us, it appears preferable for each application to use the object schema most convenient for it. Typical OODBMSs do not support mappings between object schemas. Encapsulation provides data independence only from outsiders, but does not support integrating new applications.

Database development was greatly influenced by the three-level data modeling architecture from the ANSI/SPARC committee [Steel 1980]. Their model partitions the concerns of information management into a view level, conceptual level, and physical level. The view level is composed of multiple user data models, one for each application, which cover only part of the database and provide for logical data independence. The conceptual level describes a common data model for the entire database and provides for physical data independence. Today, in a distributed environment, there may not be a single conceptual model, but rather one for each configuration of databases used in a set of applications. The physical level describes the implementation of the database at an abstract level, including distribution, data structures, and access paths. Most RDBMSs support the view level, and many views may be defined corresponding to various user roles. In contrast, OODBMSs typically do not support the view level; there is only one view corresponding to the conceptual level [Shilling 1989].

The Penguin approach builds on mature relational database management system (RDBMS) technology by creating object views. Our techniques could be used to create object views of alternate object databases, but we have not yet done this work, so it is beyond the scope of this chapter.

Mapping from the Object Model to the Relational Model

An object schema defines data elements as well as its structure. Object classes may have single or multiple inheritance. Object instances within an object class may have internal structure, such as object classes that are composed of other object classes by reference or embedding.

Let us consider a database design approach, in which multiple object schemas and schemas of legacy databases are mapped into the relational model, and then integrated into a common database schema. Figure 4.1 illustrates this approach.

Object schemata have semantics. Inheritance and composition hierarchies organize elements so that they are convenient for the current task. Object methods contain further semantics but these are not needed for mapping to the relational model or for integration. Relational structures have few semantics: there is no defined hierarchy. Rather, the elements are composed as needed by the application through views and queries.

To perform a mapping from object schemata to a relational model, we integrate the object hierarchies into a semantic model network, which is more general than a hierarchy. The semantic model we use is the Structural Model, which only describes systematic relationships, and does not require separate instance storage over that in the relational database [Wiederhold 1980]. Additional classes can be defined within this framework by augmenting the model. Storage of data elements from the object is accomplished by creating base relations as needed. If appropriate relations exist they can be augmented and connected.

Once the base relations are populated, instances of links can be computed from the model and the stored base relations. The Structural Model can reconstruct component object classes as well as new potential object classes by recognizing hierarchies within its network. New classes can be created as well, by connecting them to each other and to relevant existing relations.

For each of the input object schemata, the Penguin approach converts the inheritance (IS-A) and composition (PART-OF) structures into directed graphs. To handle inheritance, horizontal and vertical partitioning are supported. Also supported is the option

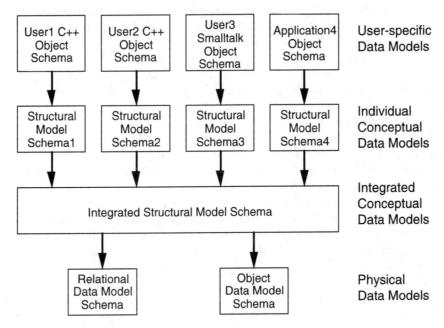

Figure 4.1   Database mapping and integration.

where (part of) an inheritance hierarchy is stored in a *universal relation* containing all attributes in the hierarchy along with an attribute indicating the type of the object instance [Ullman 1988]. We normalize object nodes into Third Normal Form (3NF) using standard relational database design techniques. The result is a network representation.

The Structural model recognizes various types of relationships, formalized into three types of *connections*. A Structural model is a graph where each node represents a relation and each edge represents a connection (or relationship) between two relations. This model is comparable to the Entity-Relationship (E-R) model, but uses the Relational model as a base. Connections require a feasible join path. Penguin also defines an information metric that assigns strengths to each combination of each direction of the three connections types. The types are:

1. *Ownership connection*, which links instances that depend on the owner. The linked instances disappear when the owner is removed. For example, `Equipment` owns its `Maintenance` records. Its cardinality is *n:1*. This connection type is also used to represent part-of semantics, as `vehicle` has `engine, wheels`, etc. Penguin considers ownership a strong relationship (0.9), and being owned weak (0.3).

2. *Reference connection*, which links to abstract entities. The referenced entities must exist while there are references to them. For example, Hazard refers to Hazard Codes. Its cardinality is 1:n. Reference connections are weak (0.3, 0.5).

3. *Subset connection*, which links a generalization to a subtype. The subtype instance disappears when its generalization instance is deleted. For example, `Resource` is linked to `Equipment` (because `Equipment IS-A Resource`). Its cardinality is *1:1 partial*. The selection may be based on a predicate. Subset connections have strengths weaker than full ownership (0.75, 0.2).

The *m:n* relationship of an E-R model is modeled by pairing two structural connections, since in relational implementations the instances of *m:n* links are represented explicitly in a joining relation. For example, a relation `Equipment-location` is needed to represent such a relationship, and may use an ownership connection from `Equipment` and a reference connection to a `Location` relation [Wiederhold 1980].

Once we have a Structural model for each input schema (object, relational, or legacy), we can proceed to integrate these schemata. There has been extensive research on integrating relational database schemata or E-R schemata [Navathe 1986], and little work in integrating object database schemata [Saltor 1997]. Using the Penguin approach, research results on integrating relational and E-R schemata become applicable to integrating object schemata. In addition, there is even some work on integrating Structural models that is directly applicable.

An integrator identifies and coalesces common elements (relations and connections). Problems occur due to semantic heterogeneity among the input schemata, such as differences in naming, value representation, schema, and data semantics. To solve these, it may be necessary to add mediating services, creating intermediate connections and relations. Such research is being undertaken at many sites, for example, "Semistructured Data: The TSIMMIS Experience" at Stanford University [Hammer 1997a].

Warehouses provide high performance through physical integration and replication of data [Quass 1997]. However, physical integration of the component databases is not needed, as long as access paths to data instances, direct or mediated, can be provided.

Relational Database Storage and Semantic Modeling

The relations of the integrated structural model are ordinary 3NF relations representing entities. Actual data instances are stored as tuples in a relational database system. Connections in the structural model are relationships among those relations to which formal semantics have been attached. Connections instances are represented as matching values in the connected relations, they are not stored as instances. View instances can be created by joining sets of tuples along these connections.

We will discuss concurrency control and transaction processing after we discuss caching for Penguin. Note that data partitioning and replication approaches to handling multiple persistent data stores is orthogonal to the issues of having an object layer above the DBMS.

Defining Object Views of Relational Databases

In this section, we describe the definition of object classes (view-objects) in Penguin as object views of the underlying persistent data store [Barsalou 1990]. The input is the integrated structural model. We will refer to the person controlling this process as the object base administrator (OBA), corresponding to the term database administrator (DBA), the definer of database models and schemas.

Choosing a Pivot Relation

The entities that define the root for the desired object class are identified by determining a *pivot* relation (R). The pivot relation will have a one-to-one correspondence between tuples in the relation and object instances in the desired object class. The key of the pivot relation becomes the *semantic key* of the object class.

Once the OBA selects the pivot relation, the Penguin system computes the closeness from the pivot to all connected relations, using the information metric values sketched earlier. The closeness is computed by computing the product of strength values associated with the connections along the paths. It then displays those relations that are *closer* in terms of the path than an OBA-defined threshold to the pivot relation. The *candidate set* consists of these semantically *nearby* relations. Figure 4.2 shows a structural model with pivot relation marked with R and the candidate set shaded. The ODB can eliminate relations containing irrelevant data from the candidate set, keeping the objects trim. Figure 4.3 shows the names of the relations in the candidate set.

The Penguin system then converts the candidate set to a *candidate bag*. The candidate bag is a *covering tree* of the candidate set; that is, nodes creating cycles in the graph are replicated so that there is a copy of node for each acyclic path from the pivot relation. Edges typically are not replicated. Figure 4.4 shows the candidate bag.

Structural Model

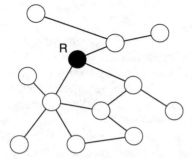

Figure 4.2   Structural model and candidate set.

Candidate Set

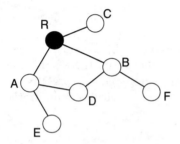

Figure 4.3   Candidate set labeled.

Candidate Bag

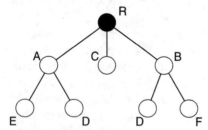

Figure 4.4   Candidate bag.

Choosing Instance Variables

The tree now represents the object structure, containing all attributes from the candidate bag. Now the ODB can select or deselect variables for the object class. Attributes values can refer to object subclasses that have their pivot relations in the candidate bag, to support PART-OF hierarchies. Attributes can be inherited from other object classes to support IS-A hierarchies. Figure 4.5 shows the object class.

Object Class

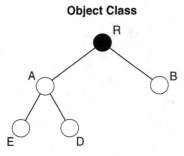

Figure 4.5   Object class.

Specify Inheritance

Next the ODB can indicate the object class(es) pivoted on the same relation from which this new object class should inherit. This approach can support multiple inheritance if the programming language does. (For example, in C++ we instantiate the object instance of the right type and populate it with the data from the database.) This approach is compiler independent. Figure 4.6 illustrates how a new object class inherits from object classes R1 and R2. Attributes in relations A and E are inherited from R1. A reference to an object class pivoted on B is inherited from R2. Any new instance variables from relation D are added.

Updating Base Relations from Objects

We have also developed methods that validate potential updates from the defined object types [Barsalou 1991]. Here the ODB is informed of all possible update ambiguities, which typically involves understanding relations beyond those included in the object view [Blakeley 1989]. The ODB selects one of the alternatives, which is then recorded in the object schema [Keller 1986]. End-users then are not faced with update ambiguities at execution type. These methods have not been integrated into Penguin systems at this time, since implementations have focused on distributed resources and read-only object retrieval [Law 1990]. All updates then originated at the sources. When the ODB has completed the definition of a Penguin object schema it can be made available to users and their applications. We have created only C++ object definitions, although the process is language independent.

Heterogeneous Data Sources

This data mapping is straightforward if the persistent store's schema is described by the Structural model. However, we must handle legacy data as well. We handle legacy data by describing it as a Structural model and wrapping the source to provide adequate access [Hammer 1997]. The result is included as one of the constituent schemata input to the integration phase.

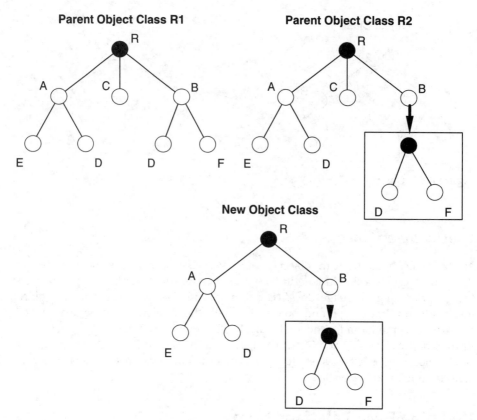

Figure 4.6   Inheritance example.

Wrapping source objects is relatively simple. Internal object semantics focus on ownership connections, whereas linkages between objects are commonly references. Multiple inheritance could require *m:n* relationships. Any Penguin objects that match one-to-one should be able to be copied directly from the sources, but we have not developed such a shortcut. Instead, applications may prefer to retain direct access, which is not a problem if update is constrained to one of the access mechanisms.

Methods

Penguin generates basic methods for fetch, store, and update automatically based on declarative descriptions of the object classes. Navigation methods are generated for navigating among object instances using object class references. Query methods are generated that support path expressions on each object class. Update methods are generated that support changing a cached object, making the change persistent, and committing or aborting change transactions.

Databases also support updates to sets of tuples and relations. Penguin could support such an approach, which will allow changes to be made to multiple objects, and the corresponding changes could be made as one SQL statement to the base relations. Providing a method that can update more than one object at a time would require generation of additional C++ code.

Penguin also supports methods defined by the user. The object classes defined by Penguin are object classes that obey the normal inheritance mechanism of the object programming language (e.g., C++), so user object methods are inherited correctly. Unfortunately, user methods defined for one application's object schema are not applicable to another application's object schema, even if they share the same data.

Concurrency Control

We need to coordinate concurrency control and transaction processing of the object layer and conceptual layer with the persistent data store. Thus transactions of the object layer are based on transactions of the persistent data store. Concurrency control in the object layer is based on concurrency control on the underlying data in the persistent data store. For example, the object layer can implement optimistic concurrency control on objects in an in-memory cache. When the object layer transaction commits, the transaction is validated, and a (distributed) transaction is invoked to commit the changes to the (multiple) underlying persistent data store(s).

Performance Issues

The conversion of relational base data into objects incurs a performance penalty. There are two aspects to reduced performance versus direct use of an OODBMS. First of all, the single application focus of the object paradigm allows substantial user control at the physical level [Wiederhold 1987]. An RDBMS, focused on sharing, must compromise, and tries to overcome that compromise by extensive query optimization. Since Penguin supports sharing, that aspect is intrinsic.

The second aspect is the additional cost of dynamic object creation. Here, many well-known techniques can be adapted, of which caching is the primary one. Since we expect to operate in a client/server environment, some data-shipping improvements can also make a significant difference [Delis 1992].

Caching Structure

Navigating a relational database tuple-at-a-time is very inefficient. In contrast, issuing a query to a relational database and then loading the result into a cache provides for much more efficient navigation [Franklin 1993]. Penguin improves performance in navigation by using a cache [Wang 1991]. We first discuss the organization of the cache, and then we discuss concurrency control and transactions.

Penguin uses a two-level cache. The lower level of the cache is a network representation that corresponds to the structural model. The upper level of the cache corresponds to the object classes of the ODB-defined object schema. In a server/client architecture the caches would be distributed physically. There is also a virtual level of the cache that is language-specific.

The lower level of the cache contains a network representation that matches the structural model. In the cache, tuples are linked together according to the joins based on the connections of their relations. We use *semantic pointer swizzling* to turn semantic key references (foreign key to primary key) into pointers in memory [White 1992]. Data in this level of the cache are stored nonredundantly. The lower level of the cache is shared among all applications on the same computer. Figure 4.7 illustrates the network level of the cache.

The upper level of the cache corresponds to the object classes of the user object schema. Data is stored in hierarchical form according to the object classes of the application. References to other object instances are also swizzled. Data in the object cache is stored redundantly if necessary. The object cache is for a single application client and lives in the application's address space. Figure 4.8 illustrates the object cache.

The virtual level of the cache is language-specific. For C++, we need to specify the type of each object instance when there is multiple inheritance [Stroustrup 1986]. To make an object accessible in C++, Penguin copies the data, if necessary, from the source data or the network cache into the object cache and determines the type based on the data contents. To determine the matching application type, a user-supplied method is required that refers to the data contents. Penguin then creates an object instance of the correct type and links the C++ object root to the corresponding data in the object cache [Keller 1993]. Figure 4.9 illustrates the virtual level of the cache. The ovals represent the C++ object of the correct type, which refers to the data in the object cache. The virtual cache is maintained in the application's address space.

Cache Management

To improve performance, Penguin loads the cache using relational, set-based queries and then navigates the cached data [DeWitt 1990]. Data in the cache is reused when issuing queries through the technique of predicate-based cache descriptions [Keller 1996]. These descriptions address two questions. First, do we know whether the

Network Cache

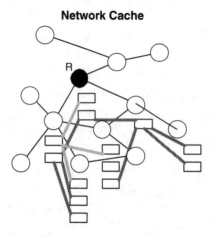

Figure 4.7   Network cache.

Object Cache

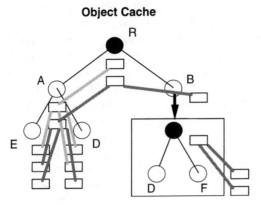

Figure 4.8   Object cache.

desired query is entirely contained in the cache? Second, do we know whether we have the latest data in our cache [Gupta 1993]?

If we know that the desired query is entirely contained within the cache, then the Penguin client can avoid going to the persistent data store for data. We use a *conservative cache description*. That is, everything in the description is found in the cache, but the description can omit objects that are in the cache. If an object really in the cache is omitted from the conservative cache description, its processing will be nonoptimal, but not wrong. The conservative cache description is based on queries used to load the cache. It is used instead of the exact cache description because it can be simpler to use, although it requires some extra effort to maintain this cache description in a simple form. Queries contained in the cache can be processed (in memory) locally. Such processing requires that local indexes be built on the fly. That is, server data indexes are not used, so contention is reduced among multiple clients. If the query is not entirely contained in the cache, then the query must go to the server (persistent data store). If only part of the

Virtual Cache

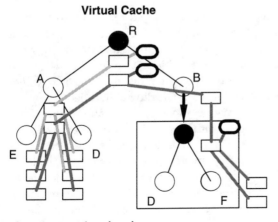

Figure 4.9   Virtual cache.

query is contained in the cache, the query may be trimmed to omit the part already cached if trimming speeds up server query processing or data transmission.

To support serializability, it is important to know that the cache contains the latest data [Gray 1993]. If a client is the only client performing updates (or perhaps only to this part of the data), then the client has the latest data. The client can lock data at the server to ensure that no other client updates the data. If we choose to use optimistic concurrency control, when a transaction commits the updates are propagated to the server (the persistent store). The server uses a *liberal cache description* to determine which clients to notify. The description includes everything in a client's cache, but it can include objects not actually found in the cache. If an updated object is in the liberal cache description but not actually in the cache, processing will be nonoptimal but not wrong. The liberal cache description is based on queries used to load the cache, and notifications of cache cleanup or flush.

We call our in-memory caching approach *associative caching*. From simulation results [Basu 1997a]; [Basu 1997b], our associative caching algorithms have performance exceeding that of the no-caching approach under these conditions:

- When there are no updates, unless cache containment reasoning is too expensive

- When updates are few

- When there are many updates (e.g., 40 percent of transactions perform updates) except when there is very high contention on a small portion of the database by all clients

In this last case, if the small portion of the database with high contention fits in the server buffer memory, then associative caching does not perform as well as server buffer caching. Note that contention is on the data, as each client maintains its own indexes.

Our findings have shown that indexes should be maintained and distributed independently (as in associative caching) or centrally (as in typical client-server architectures), but not distributed and unified (as in some object-oriented database architectures) [Basu 1997c];[Basu 1997d].

Data Transfer

In object-oriented client/server systems, the overhead required for data transmission from server to client and the control of such transmissions is significant. As users of protocols such as CORBA have noticed, fetching and updating data from many small objects kept at a remote object store is costly. Larger objects also incur costs due to pointer swizzling [Carey 1991]. The Penguin approach can move the relational, value-based linkage references to the client, and perform all swizzling at the client.

We have analyzed three data transfer alternatives: objects, views, and relation fragments, and concluded that for a wide range of situations relation fragments are best [Lee 1994]. Relation fragments are the selected and projected subsets of the base relations needed to construct the object view. They avoid the redundancy in relational views when owner tuples are replicated by the join operations that create views. Although foreign and base keys are replicated, this cost is close to the information needed for swizzling. At the same time, the number of instances is much smaller, determined by the complexity of the query, than the number of object instances typically needed, which is determined by the cardinality of the pivot. A low cardinality greatly reduces transmission overhead.

Future Directions

The concepts developed in Penguin lead to many further alternatives. Object-oriented access is direct and fast. The generality of an RDBMS requires more accesses and processing, reducing performance, which gives a significant incentive to using an OODBMS. But our navigation in the structural model generalizes to navigation among object classes, allowing object-oriented storage as well. For instance, if one object model dominates, then mapping costs can be reduced by storage of the data in a primary object database, while keeping the integrated structural model available for mapping to secondary object configurations, or even back to relations. A mapping to object instances would require that the object store supports a powerful query language, such as that of ODMG-93 [Cattell 1991].

As RDBMSs move to hybrid configurations, they should evolve to provide more control over an increased variety of data structures. Then the performance advantage over OODBMSs will diminish. Unless OODBMSs provide increased view support, they will find it increasingly difficult to compete with enhanced RDBMSs.

The Penguin approach does not allow persistent object-identifiers. Cross-references are hence always resolved with content-based queries. It is unclear to what extent this is a liability and to what extent it should be addressed [Kato 1992].

As with all independently defined objects, methods defined for one application's object schema are not applicable to another application's object schema, even if they share the same data. To increase sharing to more general methods than the access methods provided in Penguin, we propose that these methods be described declaratively. When the data schemata are integrated, the declarative method descriptions should also be integrated. When object classes are defined, the declarative method descriptions should be carried with them. Then, user methods could be generated. This process would mitigate maintenance costs incurred by sharing data among multiple applications. However, we have not explored these ideas in detail.

The interaction of storage granularity, data transfer approaches, and caching is complex and will be subject to ongoing analysis as the relationships of latency, bandwidth, and user patterns changes. The development of data warehouses encourages much larger views to be transmitted for analysis, although much of the processing may be statistical, so that object concepts are less relevant, whereas data transpositions (i.e., storage by columns of tables) will again become important [Batory 1979]. Similar mapping notions as used in Penguin may be applicable.

Conclusion

The Penguin system supports multiple object views for multiple applications sharing data. All data are currently stored in a relational DBMS, but our approach extends to storing data also in an object DBMS. Our approach is based on a formal model of object views on relational databases. We propose an approach to object schema integration that takes advantage of the large body of work on relational and entity-relationship schema integration.

There is an operational prototype for Penguin. Some of the concepts have been developed and tested outside of that prototype. Furthermore, some of the ideas used in Penguin are reflected in commercial products [Keller 1993a]; [Agarwal 1995]; [Keller 1995]; [Turner 1995].

PART

Three

XML

It is difficult to find detailed evaluations of object database products for real-world systems. One reason for this is that many companies view this technology as giving them a competitive edge and so are reluctant to divulge their findings, whether positive or negative. Chapter 5, "A New Stage in ODBMS Normalization: Myth or Reality?" by Guennou is, therefore, a valuable contribution, particularly as it is from the financial domain. The chapter provides a discussion of the current state of the object database market, and first-hand evaluation of ODMG support in several products. The use of XML for managing corporate data with an object database is also discussed and shows that this database technology is well suited to this type of application. Finally, the chapter compares O2 and Versant along a number of dimensions, and the performance results show how important the choice of hardware platform is.

One area that offers tremendous potential is using Java and XML with some kind of persistence mechanism or database system. Chapter 6, "PDOM: Lightweight Persistency Support" by Huck, Macherius, and Fankhauser, provides details of research that investigates a Persistent Document Object Model (PDOM) system. In their chapter, the authors discuss a number of thorny issues and their solutions to them; in particular, managing schema-less systems, the impedance mismatch between the DOM and the underlying storage system, and support for caching mechanisms.

Today, many organizations working with object technology are using modeling languages such as UML to capture their designs in ways that can be communicated more easily between developers and design teams. However, the features and capabilities of some languages are so extensive that they can be difficult to use in practice. Chapter 7, "The Model of Object Primitives (MOP)" by Georgalas describes an approach that provides expressive power through simplicity. In this chapter, MOP is compared against three technologies that are very relevant to database systems—XML, ODMG, and the Relational model—and the comparison shows that MOP can represent the semantics of any of these models. Two short case studies then demonstrate MOP in practice.

CHAPTER 5

A New Stage in ODBMS Normalization: Myth or Reality?

Object database management systems (ODBMSs) result from two radically different approaches:

- Language-oriented ODBMSs, where a programming language, generally C++, is extended with persistence capabilities
- Model-oriented ODBMSs, where a specific object model is the foundation of the database development process

Until two years ago, in spite of the Object Database Management Group (ODMG) standards initiative, this duality really had not yet evolved.

With the emergence of ODMG 2.0 and Java, the editors of the ODMG standard claim that they have achieved a new level of maturity, trying to add new members concerned with object storage to their organization.

This chapter summarizes our recent investigations of the ODMG standard through ODBMS technology. First, our personal concerns on ODMG are presented, particularly against SQL3. We then present the main results of a project we undertook to experiment with O2 and Versant for an internal XML document management system with fine-grained information storage and retrieval features.

State of the ODBMS Market

Object DBMSs have existed for more than 10 years. During this time, although we have seen increasing acceptance and deployment of object technologies in software development, ODBMS vendors have not crossed the chasm of the market maturation model presented by [Loomis 1995]; namely to enlarge their typical users' profile (innovators and early adopters of high-technology products) to a broader majority. Furthermore, their relative share of the total DBMS market is still very small. This observation is confirmed by the current reorientation of most ODBMS vendors toward the middleware market (or even more recently in the XML and e-commerce arenas), promoting their products as fast cache object servers, rather than DBMSs.

Three major reasons may explain this state of the ODBMS market:

- Relational DBMSs represent the second DBMS generation and the great data management revolution of the 1980s. Many companies invested massively in this technology during the late 1980s, just before the commercialization of ODBMS products. Legacy systems rebuilt during that time are still recent, so that most customers expect evolution from database management technologies rather than a new revolution. In that sense, current narrow ODBMS market niches are not a surprise. Deductive DBMSs, a still-active research domain and initially a very promising one (these systems were the potential legitimate successors to RDBMSs, even according to the RDBMS research community), also faced this reality at a previous step of maturation.

- Standards are even more important for ODBMSs than for RDBMSs, because vendors are relatively small companies (except for Computer Associates with its recent Jasmine product) and object technology is much more complex than relational technology (due to the underlying model). However, ODBMS vendors have delayed on standards issues. Furthermore, the great differences between products (theoretical foundations, language- or model-oriented DBMSs, active or passive database, unique query language or not, etc.) didn't favor the idea of a cohesive and safe-buy technology. It is only since ODMG 2.0 and the Java wave that many of the ODBMS vendors have really manifested their endorsement of a standard. As a comparison to the RDBMS world, Sybase was in a similar position to ODBMS vendors just prior to gaining popularity, in view of its financial market niche, but it implemented and promoted SQL from the very beginning.

- Many object developers of the early 1990s didn't have a "databasey" culture [Maier 1998]; they did everything as much as possible by hand or with a basic library to store and retrieve objects on disk: an ODBMS was hardly considered more than yet another library. On the other hand, RDBMS users were not fond of languages like C++ and favored *fourth-generation languages*, especially those directly integrated in RDBMS engines (e.g., Transact SQL in Sybase or Pro SQL in Oracle).

Technical factors, such as performance, tuning, durability or confidentiality had their own effect upon this market but, it seems, to a lesser extent and in a way that is more open to controversy. And yet other current techniques for describing, storing, and retrieving large volumes of complex objects are far from ideal:

- Object/relational mapping products (such as Persistence or DBTools from Roguewave) are specific approaches with no standard interface.

- Object extensions to RDBMSs are late; SQL3 as the replacement for the current SQL standard (ISO 1992) has been delayed, although most extensions were specified in

1993. In any case, SQL3 will provide a restricted number of collection types: nested table and varying array. Well-known collection types in object programming languages, such as set, list, and bag, have been left out of SQL3 and may be re-addressed only in a future SQL4 [Fortier 1999]. Furthermore, it is not clear to what extent vendors will implement this future standard; that is, the minimum Core SQL3 or a more advanced implementation, business dictating standard support, as usual. For example, in Oracle 8i, subtyping, one major object design contribution to express generalization/specialization properties, doesn't even exist. Finally, a very important point with SQL3 is its position, as another computationally complete object-oriented language, relative to object languages like Java. At present with the SQL3 Bindings, there is currently nothing more specified than the usual embedded facilities, with their well-known *impedance mismatch* problem. The question facing developers today when writing an application with SQL3 and Java is: "What is the right breakdown and cooperation of programs, respectively, written in these two languages?"

Our department develops and manages information systems for *Caisse des Dépôts Group*, a large French financial and savings group. The role of our department is to federate common interest research and recommend suitable technologies for the group. ODBMSs belong to a category of technology in which we became interested in 1995. In our group we are large-scale users of DBMSs, with hundreds of applications and thousands of users. The reason for our interest was that we observed that the object-programming paradigm was increasingly becoming a reality. At that time and after two successive experiments in 1995 and 1996, we concluded that existing ODBMS products were immature and too dissimilar. But in 1998, with the new ODMG version 2.0, we wanted to reexamine this point of view since we thought this event was the sign of a potential new rise of ODBMS technology.

Why a Standard Like ODMG?

Relational databases have become progressively pervasive in our company. No new application that produces and stores data does not envision using an RDBMS: DB2, Oracle, or Sybase environments exist and are administrated by experienced teams. Furthermore, the development cycle is organized with well-established rules.

Another common point of these applications using RDBMSs is that more and more often they use "standard" object programming languages: financial market or credit risk calculation is implemented in C++, project activity management uses Java for middle tier and client sides.

Our experiences in classical object/relational mapping techniques used for these kinds of applications is that they provide very disparate levels of satisfaction and are without common solid foundations: Long-standing operational projects that originally invested in object/relational mapping products have progressively given them up because of performance and control difficulties, and as far as we know, there is no new project trying to use any of them.

Manual object/relational mapping, with ODBC, JDBC, or RDBMS vendor interfaces, represents a 30 percent average share of the development process [Barry 1998].

In practice, each developer has his or her own "art of programming" to address this topic. These range from a generic approach—in which interactions between the program and the database are clearly specified and implemented at an interface level, with a view to reusability and program/database schema independence—to a hard-coded one, in which interactions are fully explicit in each program, including low-level conversions between a column of a tuple and its corresponding object attribute. There isn't really any methodology, and whatever approach is used, the developer generally has to deal with difficult and physical details like cache or transaction management at the object level. Moreover, since the only information exchange unit is the table, the developer always has to arbitrate between atomic queries to instantiate program objects when needed, and complex queries (with complex transformation programs) to reduce the number of query executions and network traffic (see Figure 5.1).

In the previous example, the developer can instantiate a document program object by hand in different ways, two of which are as follows:

- Load the document with all its paragraphs directly through one query:

```
select * from document d, paragraph p
where d.title = $1 and d.paragraph = a.parid
// $1 is the parameter giving the name of the searched document
```

- Load the document surface properties in a first step and later, if needed, successively load its different paragraph properties:

```
select * from document where title = $1  // run once
select * from paragraph where parid = $2 // run as many times as there
are document paragraphs, $2 being one of them
```

In view of this situation, we are interested in ODMG in a broader way than a strict ODBMS standard. More precisely, we expect a common interface specification

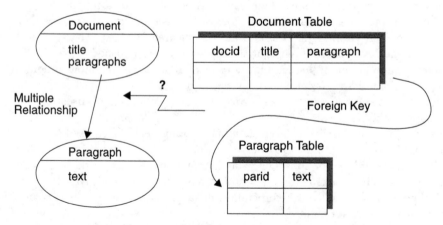

Figure 5.1   The developer's headache: atomic or complex queries?

between the most widely used object programming languages and DBMSs (whatever DBMS is used, either an ODBMS or even an RDBMS), as well as a pragmatic and powerful relational extension approach. Recent ODMG developments have moved in this direction, as discussed in the following sections.

ODMG: A Reconciliation between Programming Languages and DBMSs

ODBMS vendors, manifesting their desire for product standardization, formed ODMG. This has been presented and debated in different texts [Cattell 1994]; [Cooper 1997]; [Jordan 1997]; [Loomis 1995] or publications [Alagic 1997]. Whatever the product's compliance, this consortium has largely contributed to a better common understanding of the respective concepts.

Initially ODBMS vendors were the only ones likely to implement this standard, either on top of their own DBMS or even on top of an existing RDBMS (e.g., O2 with its CRB for C++ and JRB for Java relational binding modules). But with version 2.0 in 1997 and its more recent transformation in 1998, ODMG has embraced the wider domain of object data management, trying to add new members to strengthen and extend its standard. It is currently the only initiative that has the potential to satisfy our need to harmonize OPL (object programming language) bindings with DBMSs in a transparent and independent way. The only alternative, SQL3, is language dependent and, as we already mentioned, there is no seamless OPL binding specified. Some recent efforts in the research community support this opinion:

- INRIA (the *French National Institute for Research in Computer Science and Control*) should commercialize its recent ObjectDriver product [INRIA 1999], a new ODMG compliant *Open Object Wrapper dedicated to Relational Databases* and supporting the ODMG C++ and Java bindings, as well as OQL. This is the first object/relational mapping product showing a concern for standards.

- The University of Wisconsin has recently announced its new ODMG compliant ODBMS, called lambda-DB [Wisconsin 1999] and built on top of SHORE (a persistent object system from the same university).

One fundamental and much appreciated characteristic introduced by RDBMSs, namely that a DBMS should be accessible by different programming languages in an independent way (embedded SQL being the current standard one for SQL), is enhanced by ODMG to a bidirectional way (see Figure 5.2). This is achieved with the underlying ODMG Object Model, which clearly separates interface from implementation, and ODL (Object Definition Language) usage, which enables multilanguage and multi-DBMS access. It is this separation that makes it possible to build ODMG-compliant object/relational mapping products.

Nevertheless, most ODBMS products haven't completed this separation, and no vendor has implemented ODL at present. They take advantage of what is a rather confusing point in ODMG—that is, the schema being directly defined with the object programming language (ODMG defines an equivalent ODL binding language for each OPL, called for instance C++ ODL for C++). This process binds together the specifica-

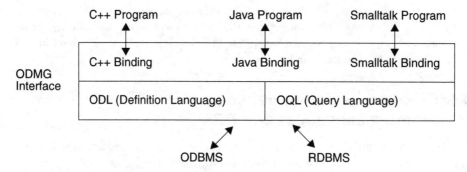

Figure 5.2   A portable and seamless OPL/DBMS interface.

tion and implementation levels, whereas ODL is the interface specification level which achieves a degree of the desired separation [Loomis 1995].

An RDBMS Evolution toward Object Paradigm

Compared to SQL3, ODMG presents different advantages and drawbacks, relative to our need for object extensions to RDBMSs (see Figure 5.3). On the one hand, we know that ODMG does not support some major and famous SQL characteristics [Kim 1994]:

- There is no DCL (Data Control Language) equivalent, including views, dynamic schema changes, or even access authorization concepts.

- OML (Object Manipulation Language) does not provide any query-based facilities to insert, delete, or update objects, in the way that SQL does with its INSERT, DELETE, and UPDATE clauses. The OML imperative instructions (provided for each OPL binding) are the only way to manipulate objects, just as the declarative SQL clauses do with tables.

User-defined active constraints (SQL triggers) at the database schema level for enforcing database integrity is not an issue addressed in ODMG. On this point, most ODBMS products provide event notification facilities, but at the programming language level, so there is no safe way of implementing integrity constraints.

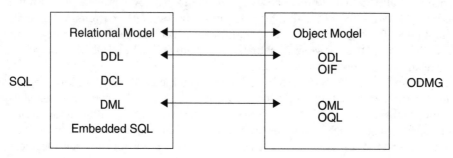

Figure 5.3   An SQL/ODMG analogy.

On the other hand, ODMG has many advantages over SQL3, with true SQL extensions [ODMG 1994]:

- The ODMG object model is a pure object model, which subsumes the relational model (consider the Table type, semantically equivalent to a collection of structs) and the Java model (consider the interface and single inheritance relationship choices, which are exactly the same in the models).

- OQL is a functional language subsuming SQL-92 (for that purpose, OQL even accepts SQL constructions which are not functional). Its OPL embedding is seamless.

- ODMG is far more concise than SQL3 and easier to present (the ODMG specification takes up just 250 readable pages, whereas it requires more than 1500 pages in SQL3).

- OQL query optimization, contrary to generally accepted ideas, does not need techniques fundamentally different to SQL ones; an OQL parser should be even quicker than an SQL one, due to the more compact OQL syntax [Moerkotte 1999].

Including some object orientation, SQL3 looks more like a patchwork with strong support for previous versions of SQL to preserve table-minded backwards compliance. To our knowledge, few developers know and use current SQL expressiveness (for instance, powerful outer joins or complex chained/enclosed queries). How will SQL3 be able to have an influence on changing habits while it is offering much more advanced features?

XML Application Founded on OQL

Document management applications belong in the complex applications category that drove the initial research and development of ODBMSs. Particularly in the area of structured documents, using SGML or more recently XML as the document representation format, ODBMS potential and suitability are well-known [Futtersack 1997], a natural basic approximation of a document being an object tree. Furthermore, the first well-known ODBMS benchmark, OO1 (Object Operations Version 1), demonstrated that ODBMSs could provide better performance than RDBMSs for complex (network/tree-like) applications.

In our ODMG investigations, we chose this domain to experiment with O2 and Versant (and a financial application not discussed here), the two ODBMS products that seemed to us to provide the best compromise, considering their respective local expertise and standards work endorsement. After initial promising experiences, we progressively developed different prototypes that lead to an operational application: Our platform now manages all our documents published in an XML format and these documents are consulted on our intranet site through advanced navigation and query facilities. OQL is used as the basis for this service, which explains why we chose O2, as Versant doesn't implement OQL. Indeed, after an increasing and satisfying use of this language for querying our XML database, its qualities revealed it to be a very useful component for wider purposes [Abiteboul 1998].

In late summer 1999, Ardent announced that it was giving up commercialization of O2. At the time this chapter was written, we didn't yet have opportunities to experiment alternatives to O2 for this kind of application. Poet seems an interesting ODBMS candidate for its OQL implementation (though incomplete) and its background in document management (regarding SGML and more recently XML); eXcelon (Object Design, built on top of ObjectStore ODBMS) and Tamino (Software AG) could be other interesting alternatives, as native XML DBMSs (implementing dedicated XML facilities like an XML query language).

System Motivations

Our initial intranet site consisted of static Web pages and a classical search engine, to provide online information access about the main domains of our work and expertise, publications, projects, presentations, technical data sheets, persons, and so on. Site administration was difficult (e.g., a new document would require updates to all static Web pages to which it would refer). We also wanted to make our information base more attractive with more relevant and integrated information retrieval features.

Actually, most commercial search engines that we used gave priority to the volume/response time ratio, as they were designed to index any indeterminate information in advance. For a restricted production and publishing system like ours, this priority was no longer necessary as information content was humanly known; an exact full-text indexing technique with a preliminary document classification by topic provided better results (even a huge site like Yahoo! manually classifies documents).

Another major aspect concerns the document publishing process. Our user environments are very heterogeneous, therefore HTML is the inevitable publishing format for document consultation (PDF as well, but for document printing). UNIX workstations cannot display a Microsoft Word or Microsoft PowerPoint document, and most PCs cannot display a FrameMaker document (our publications make significant use of this product). In our first intranet version, we developed HTML converters for these formats, with a view to having a common presentation style. But we still had to maintain separately two kinds of information for each document—its HTML content and its description (e.g., authors, document type, dates, topics, PDF file addresses, etc.). Moreover, the search engine restrictions were inescapable.

Why XML?

XML is a convenient way to describe different kinds of information, either numerical or textual, in a structured, single, and eventually self-described content (a DTD—Document Type Definition, the information description—being associated in this case to the information itself).

Like HTML, XML tags and attributes identify information parts. But more than HTML and in an easiest way than its ancestor SGML, XML (eXtensible Markup Language) enables applications to define their own markups: from this point of view, XML is a set (infinite) of information representation languages, HTML being one of them (XHTML 1.0, defined by the World Wide Web Consortium (W3C), is the present XML version of HTML 4.0).

In our application, gathering each document content and its description in only one XML content facilitated system development, as documents' content and properties became easily manipulated in a common, efficient, and cohesive way (see Figure 5.4). Unlike HTML, which is a display format, this achieves one major XML design goal (like SGML), to ensure easy information processing by programs.

Furthermore, HTML contents generally don't conform to any DTD (though HTML is specified formally by W3C as an SGML application; in particular through a DTD). XML nonvalidating mode, where documents need only to be well-formed (by start- and end-tags nested properly within each others, without complying with the constraints expressed in a DTD), greatly simplified our XML migration. We just had to adapt our HTML converters to replace the previous HTML output by a well-formed XML expression, enhanced with the document description part. Even for nonaddressed format cases, where the HTML content is badly formed (like most Web page editors), it is feasible "to XML" the document, using, for instance, Microsoft Internet Explorer HTML parser, which produces a well-formed tree for any HTML document.

```xml
<?xml version="1.0" encoding="ISO-8859-1"?>
<DOCUMENT>
  <DESCRIPTION>
    <AUTHOR SEX="M" FIRSTNAME="Sylvain" LASTNAME="Guennou" ENAME="sguennou"/>
    <TOPICS>
      <TOPIC NAME="DATABASES ">
        <TOPIC NAME="ODMG"/>
        <TOPIC NAME="SQL"/>
      </TOPIC>
      <TOPIC NAME="LANGUAGES">
        <TOPIC NAME="XML"/>
      </TOPIC>
    </TOPICS>
    <TYPE>PUBLICATION</TYPE>
    <DATE YEAR="1999" MONTH="11"/>
  </DESCRIPTION>
  <HTML>
    HEAD>
      <TITLE>A new stage in ODBMS normalization: myth or reality?</TITLE>
      <LINK HREF="publications.css" REL="stylesheet" TYPE="text/css"></LINK>
    </HEAD>
    <BODY>
      <DIV class="Header">
        <H1 class="Title">A new stage in ODBMS normalization: myth or
        reality?</H1>
      </DIV>
      <DIV class="Abstract">
        <P>Object database management systems are issued from two radically
        different approaches:</P>
        <UL TYPE="circle">
          <LI>Language oriented ODBMSs, where a programming language,
          generally C++, is extended with persistence capablilties; </LI>
          <LI>Model oriented ODBMSs, where a specific object model is the
          foundation of the database development process. </LI>
        </UL>
```

Figure 5.4 An XML encapsulation approach.

The Database Model

There are two main approaches for coupling an object model with XML. The first one, qualified as generic, considers all document information like tags, attributes, or textual contents as objects of predefined classes, interconnected between each other with links that preserve XML structure: for instance, there is only one class for any kind of XML tag of any document type. The Document Object Model (DOM) [W3C 1998] uses such an approach, as it addresses any XML document, even those well-formed documents (without any DTD) that may present more or less variable structures for a same type of document.

The other approach, strong-typed and qualified as specific, describes a new class for each new kind of information: for instance, a "DATE" tag could lead to a "Date" class with three attributes "day," "month," and "year." This approach suits especially valid XML documents (with a DTD), matching semantically the document structure, which is an invariant specified by the DTD. But mapping only well-formed documents is quite another matter, as any new document potentially may require a new model: This issue is a present research topic.

To store and manage our XML documents, we used the generic approach since our documents are only well formed (see the previous section). Furthermore, implementing full text retrieval features requires a generic way to associate any relevant document word with any kind of XML information where it is referenced [Burkowski 1991]. In any case, the technique is very basic and straightforward to implement, and it gave us some typical advantages (in addition to the easiness of development) over the specific-approach well-known ones (performances, volumes, and software quality). For instance, any structure modification appearing in some new documents (adding a sub-type tag in the description part) is without any impact on the current database (neither the model nor the data); also, our query generator (see later), though not optimized for a specific type of document, was developed only once.

We enhanced the traditional tree-like representation of a document to implement the full text retrieval features by representing and storing for each word its relative document occurrences, and for each of these occurrences the relative document elements where it appears (including its position in the text). We preferred this solution since a classical full text engine couldn't store our useful word/element link.

The description that follows is a specification extract of our database schema, expressed in ODL. The document node type is defined by an interface (a document has no node instances), whereas other node types are defined by classes. As we need entry points into the database only for document, word, element and attribute objects, we declare extents (instances of a type) only for the classes concerned.

Our model is somewhat different from the DOM, for storage optimization reasons. For instance, only an element object (there is one such object for each tag occurrence) can know on which nodes it depends, as storing this information for other node types would be useless and space consuming for any database like ours.

```
Interface Node
{
    attribute string getTextContent(); // returns the textual content
(recursively for nodes of type Element)
```

```
        attribute string getEnhancedContent(in list (unsigned long start, end)
    l); // returns the textual content by underlining text segments specified
    }
Class Element : Node
(    extent TheElements)
{
    attribute string tagname;
    relationship list<Node> children inverse Element::father;
    attribute list<Attribute> attributes inverse Attribute::element;
    Document getDocument();
}
Class Text : Node
(
    attribute string content;
)
Class Word
(    extent TheWords)
{
    attribute string name;
    relationship bag<IndexedDocument> ids;
}
Class IndexedDocument
{
    attribute Document document;
    relationship bag<IndexedElement> ies;
}
Class IndexedElement
{
    attribute Element element;
    attribute unsigned long start, end;
}
```

Database Management Using O2 versus Versant

To populate an XML database conforming to the model, we chose C++—at the time we were experimenting, XML parsers for this language were more mature than those for Java. First, we experimented with Versant and its ODMG C++ binding for this purpose. Then, the code developed was reused with O2, which was full of lessons for us in terms of the level of ODMG compliance of these products.

Schema Independence

Neither O2 nor Versant support ODL. Using the C++ binding part for ODL, a portable database schema in the ODMG sense was still implemented, needing minor syntactic changes to switch from Versant to O2. On the other hand, object sharing between different languages isn't fully achieved for either of these products:

- Versant allows object sharing between Java and C++ in only one way; that is to say, a Java program can access and update C++ objects (i.e., objects designed and created with C++; certainly, the most useful way).

- An O2 schema is, in theory, language independent so that any program written in O2C (O2's own OPL), C++, or Java should be able to manipulate any O2 object database. This is true between O2C and C++ (we manipulated C++ objects from O2C programs). But implementing bidirectional object sharing between Java and C++ was much more difficult than Ardent (the vendor of O2) expected.

Population in C++

Both O2 and Versant provide a very reliable and ODMG-93 compliant C++ binding, which constitutes the main part of the most recent ODMG 2.0 version (ODMG 2.0 specifies a few new features like a schema access interface, not implemented yet in these products).

The populating program is written in a pure ODMG style, without any specific product optimization (ODBMS index usage is specified outside the code). It reads any XML document, creates its corresponding tree in the database, and updates word links for full text retrieval features (any document word that doesn't exist yet in the database is created at this occasion). Thus, the program for Versant was a straightforward adaptation for O2, using some transformation rules presented in Table 5.1, and from the fact that these products provide class library header files with their own naming conventions. Such an adaptation is easier in this way than it would be from O2 to Versant, because an OQL query generally needs to be rewritten for Versant in a procedural form (the Versant query language is much less expressive than OQL).

We benchmarked the populating program execution on Sun Solaris (Sparc 20) and Windows PC/NT (Pentium 300Mhz) machines, for both O2 and Versant. The graph in Figure 5.5 shows response times obtained through successive insertions of the same XML document. The used document contained about 15,000 nodes (200 A4 pages),

Table 5.1 O2 and Versant ODMG Differences

O2	VERSANT
No d_Dictionary class	One dictionary class, but non-ODMG compliant
No class extent (planned in V5.1)	No naming object mechanism, only class extent
Global transient ODMG collection impossible	No d_Error class (specific exceptions handling)
Mandatory non-ODMG d_Session class	Non compliant OQL access
	d_String class: append method without ODMG equivalent!

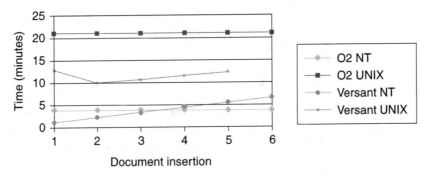

Figure 5.5   Population benchmark.

generating about 40,000 objects, and 3MB in the database (O2 and Versant, including database indexes).

It is interesting to note that we obtained better results on a UNIX platform with Versant (even the compilation process was much faster), but better results on a PC platform with O2 (debugging was easier as well, as Versant didn't provide an ODMG library in debug mode).

For our production site using O2, we then drastically improved performance by replacing critical OQL queries with low-level API calls (OQL precompilation in C++ appearing in O2 release 5.1).

The Information Retrieval Technique

In this section, we will present some of the techniques that we used for Information Retrieval.

An OQL Query Generator

Since populating our XML database, we have found that OQL has been powerful enough to retrieve and structure any information in a declarative way, due to its extensibility (by implementing, for instance, a new class method when needed). Of course, OQL is not dedicated to XML but, from experience, our model genericity makes it easier to understand and quicker to learn than XQL or XML-QL, a current XML query language submission to the W3C, for people who already know SQL.

In our system, any user request is analyzed and submitted to O2 via an OQL query. There are two request types, one asking for documents matching specific criteria (e.g., a topic and a full-text expression), and the other asking for the textual content of one of the relative documents found. The following examples illustrate query typology of the first type.

Full Text Queries

Suppose that the user wants to search for the documents containing the word "XML". We want to return these documents in the descending order of the number of occurrences of this word (see the previous database model):

```
select docname: id->document, count: count(select e from partition p, e
in p->id->ies)
from w in TheWords, id in w->ids
where w->name = "XML"
group by id->document
order by count(select e from partition p, e in p->id->ies) desc
```

Here, we query the word collection to find occurrences of "XML" directly. OQL partitioning (with "group by" and "order by" clauses) is used intensively for ranking results. We extended this query structure to full text expressions including "and", "or", and "exact phrase" retrieval operators.

Structured Queries

Suppose now that the user wants to search for documents about "ODBMS". We want to return these documents in descending order of their relative publication date:

```
select e->getDocument()->name
from a in TheAttributes, e in bag(a->element)
where a->value = "ODBMS" and e->tagname = "TOPIC"
order by e->getDocument()->getDate() desc
```

This query shows OQL's flexibility and the diversity of possible strategies to solve the same problem. Here, we chose to query the attribute collection (rather than the document or element ones), as we know that looking first for "ODBMS" attributes is more selective than looking first for "TOPIC" elements. This might be different with someone interested in documents having no topic at all! The method getDate is a specific one we developed to deal with document dates.

Mixed Queries

Suppose, finally, that the user wants to search for documents satisfying the two previous constraints. We merge the two previous queries with an additional join constraint (a pure navigational strategy may be more efficient in certain cases, but we haven't optimized that part yet). We give more importance to the order by clause with the number of occurrences rather than to the one with the date (see earlier). The where clause becomes (the rest of the query now being trivial):

```
where w->name = "XML" and a->value = "ODBMS" and e->tagname = "TOPIC"
and id->document = e->getDocument()
```

The Navigation Interface

From an OQL query, O2Web is a convenient tool to interact with users. Far richer than the SQL view concept, the OQL class constructor makes it possible to process and present any query result in any desired form. For example, we add for each document found its related topics and for each of these topics a link to other documents about the same topic, each link being in turn a new generated OQL query. Formally, if Q is a query, it means creating a class C with the same structure as Q's result, implementing its reserved HTML presentation methods ("html_header", "html_report", etc.) in C++ or the O2C language and submitting C(Q) to O2Web.

The following query illustrates our most difficult process to enhance the textual content of a document:

```
EnhancedContent(element(select r:d->getElementByTagName("HTML"),
l:(select struct(e->start,e->end)from w in TheWords, id in w->ids,
e in id->ies
where w->name = "XML" and id->document = d)
from d in TheDocuments where d->name = "D"))
```

EnhancedContent is a class whose presentation method executes a getEnhanced-Content method on the retrieved document tree root. getEnhancedContent recursively reconstitutes the document content with additional links between successive relevant text occurrences ("XML" in the preceding example), from its list argument of relevant positions. With this process, we also can retrieve and reconstitute just the relevant fragments of document such as titles, paragraphs, tables, etc. (see Figure 5.6).

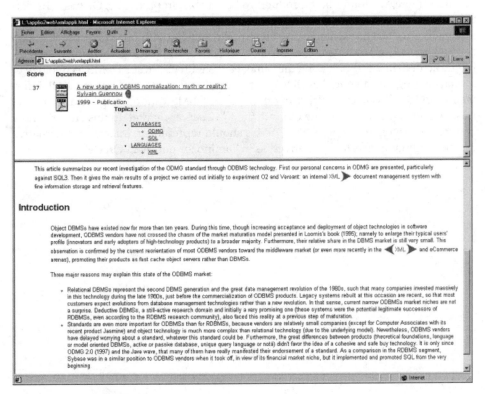

Figure 5.6 Highlighted reconstitution of a document.

Conclusion

The two ODBMSs that we experimented with do not support the new features of ODMG 2.0, except for the Java binding, which was logically introduced in this version. Versant provides only an ODMG-93 compliant C++ binding, whereas O2 implements a full ODMG-93 compliant OQL. These products' recent reorientations are not moving towards a standardization process, which is in any case largely uncompleted. Our overall impressions are that, despite the unified approach created by ODMG, the standard is somewhat illusory.

On the other hand, from our experiences we observe that portability between such products is not an illusion. We were able to adapt a program developed in Versant to O2 without any difficulty. This process was greatly simplified by the use of the ODMG C++ binding, to such an extent that it was almost automatic. This represents a radical difference from the problems we would have faced if we had tried the same transformation between an ODBMS and a RDBMS, or even between two RDBMSs. For a company like ours, this degree of portability represents a critical factor that ensures the durability of the applications developed by Object programming.

Furthermore, we found both products to be reliable. In particular, O2 has considerably improved its robustness in comparison to several years ago; it has been more than a year since we last encountered any abnormal problems with our O2 server. The ease of development and the overall performance of our XML application also impressed us. It is difficult to imagine obtaining the same results with classical RDBMS technology.

Considering this potential of ODBMSs to store, manipulate, and retrieve XML information, indeed it is hardly surprising that most ODBMS vendors (e.g., Ardent, Object Design, and Poet) are launching out into the XML server market. In this area, the now mature underlying technology of ODBMSs should represent an interesting alternative to other emerging ones (either natives, as in Tamino, or not, as in Oracle).

CHAPTER 6

PDOM: Lightweight Persistency Support

Java is the prevailing implementation platform for XML-based systems. Several high-quality, in-memory implementations for the standardized XML-DOM API are available. Persistency support for the Document Object Model (DOM) poses the following challenges:

No schema. The DOM can model schema-less XML documents, for which it is difficult to design a fixed database schema.

Impedance mismatch. The DOM is an object-oriented API with navigational methods, which cannot easily be mapped to the data-only APIs of database or file systems.

Live objects. Java DOM implementations use Java garbage collection to control the lifecycle of objects, which needs to be synchronized with any persistent medium.

This chapter introduces PDOM (persistent DOM), a lightweight persistency solution for the DOM, which is implemented in pure Java. To deal with schema-less data, it employs a compact, self-describing file format. Impedance mismatch is avoided by making all file access fully transparent. Finally, a caching object manager synchronizes the persistent images of objects with their main memory counterparts, which are controlled by the Java garbage collection.

Introduction to DOM

A growing share of electronic information is exchanged and managed in XML. For just-in-time information in distributed environments it is the data format of choice. Also, a growing number of legacy systems are adapted to output data in the form of XML documents.

The Document Object Model (DOM) is a platform- and language-neutral interface for XML. It provides a standard set of objects for representing XML documents, a standard model of how these objects can be combined, and a standard interface for accessing and manipulating them. Vendors can support the DOM as an interface to their proprietary data structures and APIs, and programmers can utilize the standard DOM interfaces rather than product-specific APIs, thus increasing interoperability.

There are a half-dozen DOM implementations available for Java from several vendors such as IBM, Sun Microsystems, and Oracle. However, all these implementations are designed to work in main memory only. Traditional databases are of limited use for realizing persistency support for the DOM, because (well-formed) XML documents do not adhere to a fixed document type, from which an efficient database schema could be derived.

The persistent DOM (PDOM) implements a lightweight, transparent persistency layer below in-memory DOM objects, which does not require the burdensome design of a fixed schema. Great care has been taken to hide implementation details from the application level. As a result, it is possible to plug in a PDOM wherever an in-memory DOM was used before. Thus a PDOM can replace proprietary database solutions and greatly simplify software design.

The following sections introduce the overall architecture, which will subsequently be detailed in a bottom-up fashion; describe the physical file organization; detail the object management approach, the caching strategy used, and give some performance figures; and discuss related work.

Architecture

The PDOM mediates between in-memory DOM object trees and their physical representation in binary random access files. The central component is the persistent object manager. It controls the lifecycle of objects, serializes multithreaded method invocations, and synchronizes objects with their file representation. Two additional subsystems may be enabled at user control: a cache to improve performance and a commit control to mark recovery points in case of system crashes. Figure 6.1 shows the overall architecture.

The standard DOM API methods for object tree manipulation are transparently mapped to physical file operations (read, write, and update). The system aims to hide the storage layer from an application programmer's view to the greatest possible extent. Thus for most applications it is sufficient to use only standard DOM methods. The only exception is document creation, which deliberately is left application-specific by the W3C DOM standard.

The specific API allows applications aware of the PDOM to tune system parameters, for the persistent object manager and its subsystems cache and commit control. A third

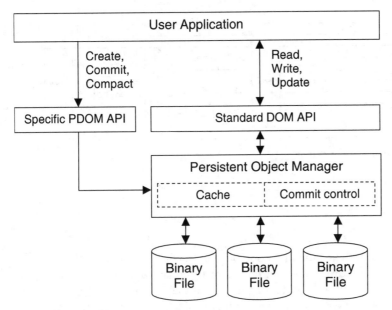

Figure 6.1 Architecture overview.

subcomponent, a structural index for hierarchical tree relations, is implemented but is beyond the scope of this chapter. Although the specific API allows for fine-grained control of the PDOM, it is not intended for the casual programmer; rather, it is the place to experiment with ideas and proof concepts.

Binary File Organization

The PDOM binary file format is depicted in Figure 6.2. It is organized in node pages, each of which contains 128 DOM serialized objects. Thus a page does not have a fixed length in terms of bytes, but in terms of the number of (variable size) objects it holds. At the head of the file there are two pointers, the first pointing to the node page index (NPI), the second pointing to a dictionary maintaining a mapping between element names e_i and attribute names a_i, respectively, and numeric values used for compact storage. The NPI holds an array of pointers to the start of each node page.

Each object is serialized. A type flag encodes its DOM-type. Then comes its content, for example, PCDATA, which is encoded as UTF, or its element name, which is encoded as a numerical value. Finally, the identifiers of the objects related in the DOM are stored, or OID. This serialization is self-describing; that is, depending on the type flag, serialization structure and length of the remaining segments can be determined.

On this basis, the mapping between object identities in memory (OID) and their physical file location is given by the equation

$$OID = PI * 128 + I$$

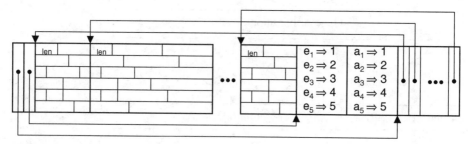

Figure 6.2   PDOM file organization.

where PI is the index of the containing node page in the NPI, and I is the object index within that page. This address does not refer directly to any byte offset in the file or page (which may both change over time). Because of this it can be used as a unique, immutable object identity within a single document.

The file format was designed with three main objectives in mind:

- Compactness
- Fast random access
- Recoverability

Compactness is of great importance, as the most costly operation in data management systems is file access. Because bytes not present in the file do not need to be transferred, we trade file space for computation time wherever possible. Thus, for each of the fifteen DOM classes an individual binary file image is used, keeping only the minimal information needed to restore the respective object.

Fast random access is achieved by organizing the file in pages of 128 DOM objects each. A page is the atomic transfer unit for I/O operations; access to single objects is always done in main memory. Pages can have variable length, depending on the size of their objects. Due to this it is also possible to compress pages with varying compression ratios. We have experimented with the gzip algorithm, available as a standard Java library. This leads to a disk space reduction to about 60 percent, and costs only a few percent read performance, because decompression overhead is outbalanced by decreased disk I/O.

The page layout does not need to be aligned with the tree structure in a fixed fashion. Thus, the objects stored in each page do not need to have specific relationships such as parent/child. This allows the composition of pages with regard to application semantics; for example, keeping element objects with a common name in the same physical page. However, the default clustering policy groups objects along preorder traversal of the document tree.

Recoverability is eased by the "pointered" file organization, which minimizes the time period a file is in an inconsistent state during update operations (see the section "Safe File Updates").

Persistent Object Manager

The most widely employed technique for database APIs is the cursor concept, where only one data item is in focus at a time. Cursors also can traverse data items only in sequence. The DOM offers a larger (but still limited) number of tree navigation operators: parent, document root, next sibling, previous sibling, first child, and last child. Every DOM node offers these methods, not just a single dedicated cursor. In addition, all navigations could be carried out in parallel from different threads.

In terms of database concepts, a persistent DOM needs to maintain an arbitrary large number of cursors in a tree data structure while enforcing consistency with a serialized file, memory constraints, and thread safety.

Object Serialization and Deserialization

At the core of the PDOM implementation is the object serialization and deserialization component. It is responsible to map sequences of bytes in the file to objects and back again. In addition, tight control of object creation and destruction by Java's garbage collection is needed to handle object collections potentially orders of magnitude larger than the main memory available.

Figure 6.3 illustrates the architecture for pages of eight objects and a cache of three rows (the actual implementation uses 128 objects per page and a user-defined number of cache rows).

When an existing PDOM file is opened, its NPI is loaded and kept in main memory. The application is handed the document object, which always has OID zero and thus is the first object in the first node page. Starting here, all objects of a PDOM can be accessed by navigations to child nodes. Assume that we want to visit the document

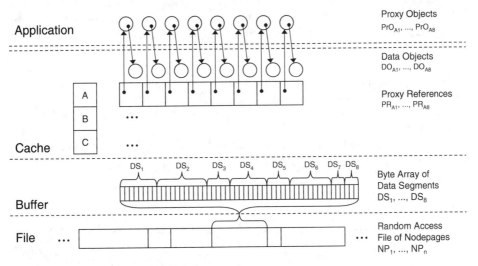

Figure 6.3   Object serialization and cache.

object's first child. Using the addressing scheme given in the section "Binary File Organization," the child's node page is calculated and read into the decoding buffer.

The page fetched is deserialized into data sections, and for each of them a proxy object PO_{Xi} and a data object DO_{Xi} are created. The proxy object is very lightweight, holding only its OID, a reference to its owner document, and a reference to DO_{Xi}. This heavyweight object contains the real data; for example, for PCDATA nodes a string, and for element nodes the OIDs of neighbor objects, necessary for DOM navigation. The pointers to all 128 proxy objects created for a fetched node page are stored in a cache row (labeled A, B, C in Figure 6.3). Finally, the requested proxy object is passed to the user application. A proxy object implements the DOM method interface of its class by querying its corresponding data object.

The reason for using two objects to represent a single DOM node is simple: Whenever an object is passed to the application, the cache can no longer control the number of references to it. As a result, it possibly can no longer be disposed by Java's garbage collection because of references existing in the user application. However, to enforce a configurable memory footprint, document data has to be discardable from main memory when necessary. Clearing the reference to data objects within the proxy objects whenever a page is removed from the cache does this.

Consider now the case that the page is no longer in the cache, but the user application still references the proxy object. Any DOM method call to this proxy object that needs data from the data object results in a reload of the required node page. A fresh data object is created, and reregistered with the proxy. This proxy object now shares the same data object as the new proxy created by default every time a page is loaded. This requires node identity to be based on OIDs and owner documents rather than Java's default object identity. However, as proxy objects are designed to have minimal space requirement (12 bytes), this compromise is tolerable. If two threads manipulate a data object shared by different proxy objects, serialization is ensured by Java's built-in thread synchronization.

Update operations set a dirty flag associated for each cache row whenever a data object is modified by the user application. When a dirty page is discarded from the cache, its data is reserialized to disk using the strategy described in the section, "Safe File Updates." To guarantee consistency of parallel read and write accesses, the PDOM also utilizes Java's built-in thread synchronization. More complex operations can enforce atomic execution by synchronizing the critical code section on the PDOM document object itself.

For new objects produced by the document's factory methods a new OID is allocated. Either it refers to a free place in the last node page found in the NPI, or, if this page is already filled, a new node page is created and added at the end of the NPI.

Whenever nodes are deleted, the proxy object reference is nullified in the corresponding node page and the node page is marked dirty. Nullified references are serialized as a single byte containing an illegal type flag.

Cache Strategy

The page cache employs the novel "lucky loser" caching strategy, which is based on the well-known LRU caching algorithm. As central data structure it uses a queue of pages sorted by the timestamps of the last cache hit of any node in a page.

With a pure LRU strategy, always the least recently used page in the tail of the queue is discarded when a new page needs to be loaded. But the main access pattern to the PDOM is (repeated) traversal of a portion of the document in pre-order. When the size of this portion exceeds the cache size, the *most* recently used page in the head of the queue is in fact the page that is *least* likely to be needed in the near future. An obvious brute-force strategy that takes this into account would simply always throw out the most recently used page, and in effect maintain a fixed cache. But this cache cannot adapt to changing access patterns. In the worst case a new access pattern that would fit completely into the cache would need lots of reloads, because most of the cache is occupied by pages for some previous access pattern.

The lucky loser strategy is a compromise: Whenever a node page is discarded from the tail of the queue, a small random number of pages, normally 1..3, of the remaining pages at the tail of the queue are explicitly touched. These are the lucky losers, which move up to the first positions in the queue. In effect, pages in the back of the queue survive more likely to serve some fixed access pattern, but the most recently used pages are still prioritized to serve changing access patterns, and access patterns that do not exceed the cache size.

Figure 6.4 compares the lucky loser strategy with a pure LRU strategy. We performed ten complete traversals of the complete Shakespeare plays (about 8MB of XML) in pre-order, with a varied cache-size to document-size ratio, and with varying maximum numbers of lucky losers (0 to 8, where 0 corresponds to a pure LRU strategy). The figures reveal that the lucky loser strategy never performs worse than pure LRU, and with increasing cache-size clearly outperforms LRU, leading, for example, to performance gains of about 25 percent for a cache to a document ratio of 0.6. Naturally, pure LRU performs worst for a cache just slightly smaller than the document, because with increasing cache-size the overhead of loading and discarding node pages is maximum.

Safe File Updates

The PDOM aims to ensure consistency of the binary file even in case of unexpected termination, for example, caused by power failure. To this end it employs a conservative log file strategy, which trades disk space for safe and speedy file updates.

A typical sequence of update operations is illustrated in Figure 6.5. Immediately after creation all pages of a PDOM file are in strict order, and the NPI and the dictionary reside at the end of the file (Figure 6.5(a)).

During programmatic DOM manipulation, pages are loaded into the cache and possibly modified while in main memory. Whenever modified pages are supplanted from the cache, they are completely reserialized. In a log file manner, pages are always appended at the end of the file (Figure 6.5(b)). There are several advantages of this strategy. First, because the size of a page may be changed by update operations, it cannot be guaranteed that the modified page will fit into its former position. Second, just appending pages does not invalidate the file organization, because they are not yet pointed to by the NPI. Third, the writeback can be done quickly, since positioning to the end of a file is a cheap I/O operation. Fourth, appending to the end of the file can never destroy any data. An obvious drawback of this strategy is that unused file sections (gaps) remain after reserialization of pages (shown as white blocks in Figure 6.5(b)).

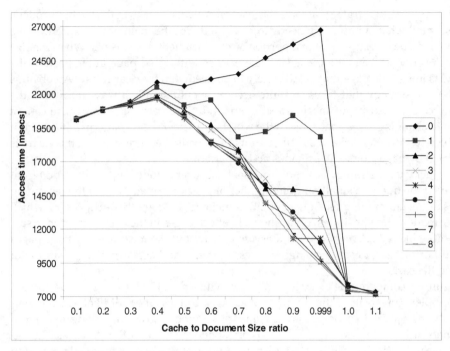

Figure 6.4 (a)   Absolute performance of the lucky loser cache.

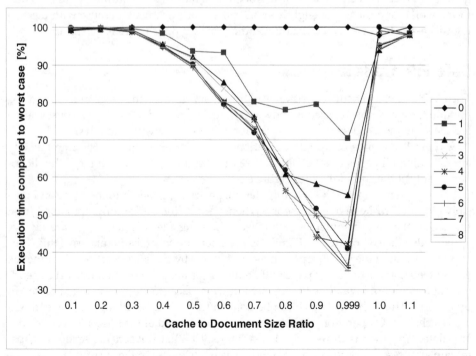

Figure 6.4 (b)   Relative performance of the lucky loser cache.

At any time the user chooses, or automatically when a PDOM document object is garbage collected, changes are committed permanently (Figure 6.5(c)). A commit operation appends the current in-memory NPI' to the end of the file, updating pointers to include pages appended since the last successful commit. The pointer at the beginning of the PDOM file is changed only after the new NPI' has been completely built. This is the only time a crash may invalidate the file. Crashes at any other moment will leave the file accessible in the state of the last successful commit operation. In a similar manner the dictionary is refreshed whenever new element types or attributes are either introduced or removed from the document (Figure 6.5(d)).

To reclaim unused file sections two compaction methods are available, operating at either the page (shallow compact) or node level (deep compact). Both methods first create a new file for writing and then start traversing the PDOM to be compacted (Figure 6.5(e)). A shallow compact just reads pages in the order found in the NPI and copies them to the new file byte by byte. Gaps within a page, resulting from the deletion of single objects, are not detected. To also reclaim this space, deep compaction traverses the PDOM object tree and rewrites it object by object. In the course of this operation objects may be placed in a new page, so in addition all OIDs are recalculated. Finally the copy is moved, and it replaces the fragmented original.

Compaction is never started automatically. Instead, the user application may at any time request the ratio of file size versus actually used bytes. Based on this figure a compaction may be started, for example, when surpassing a threshold value, or in periods of low workload.

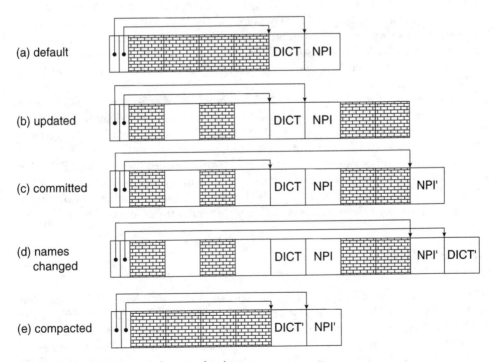

Figure 6.5 PDOM file update mechanism.

Performance Evaluation

As Java benchmarks may vary in the order of one magnitude even on the same machine, we give the exact setup of our Java environment: IBM Java JDK 1.1.8 JVM with a fixed heap size of 60MB on a 233MHz Pentium-II, IBM xml4j parser 2.0.14, and OpenXML 1.0.6 in-memory DOM. All tests were executed twice with only the second run measured to ensure the JVM has warmed up; for example, JIT compiled all the code and loaded all classes.

As a test document we used the concatenation of 37 Shakespeare plays, an XML document of 7.712KB, which parses to 327,145 DOM objects. In PDOM file representation it requires 8.922KB (including structural indices), 6.366KB (excluding structural indices), or 4.620KB (with gzip page compression) of disk space. The PDOM binary representation is computed from the textual XML document in 33s.

The operation tested is a simple left-to-right preorder traversal of all DOM nodes. Two scenarios were timed: a one-shot run typical for client side operations, for example, for reading or writing XML bookmark lists; and repeated traversal typical for server applications such as query processors. For the in-memory DOM in the one-shot scenario, the time necessary for parsing the textual XML is included. In the test for the median-of-ten runs, the in-memory DOM started fully instantiated and the cached PDOM started with all objects already loaded into the cache. Results for partially cached documents can be taken from Figure 6.4(a).

In the one-shot case, uncached PDOM traversal is 450 percent faster than the in-memory DOM because no overhead is required for parsing textual XML at startup. Most strikingly, the PDOM only uses 2.2 percent of the main memory required by the in-memory DOM. These figures clearly point out the main advantages of the PDOM approach: short startup time and minimal space requirements. Thus, for the one-shot case using the PDOM cache results in performance loss. Due to increased memory usage and garbage collection the overall gain compared to the in-memory DOM is reduced to 275 percent.

In the median-of-10-runs scenario, the in-memory DOM is 75 percent faster than a fully cached PDOM. This figure reflects the overhead introduced by synchronized method calls, indirection through proxy objects, cache lookups, and cache management. The memory overhead for caching is less significant, adding only 15 percent for file buffers, indices, and cache data structures. For obvious reasons the uncached PDOM is an order of magnitude slower then both the main memory competitors. However the figure shows that an uncached PDOM still has an XML throughput of 3.5MB/s, or in other words 160,000 objects per second. Complete results are shown in Table 6.1.

Related Work

Currently, there exist only few Java-based, persistent DOM implementations. Excelon [Object Design 1999] from Object Design realizes a persistent Java DOM on top of the OODBMS ObjectStore. It thus requires installation of a complete DBMS server and is available only from within DBMS server extensions written in Java. Other commercial DBMS vendors like Software AG (Tamino) [Software AG 1999] and Oracle (Oracle 8i)

Table 6.1 Comparison of PDOM and In-Memory DOM Performance

	ONE-SHOT TRAVERSAL		MEDIAN OF 10 TRAVERSALS	
	TIME [MS]	MEMORY [KB]	TIME [MS]	MEMORY [KB]
1. IDOM, in memory	17115	38219	412	38219
2. PDOM, full cache	6208	43176	705	43176
3. PDOM, no cache	3065	839	2133	840

[Oracle 1999] are developing XML storage support as well, but it is not yet known whether they plan to support a Java-based access API.

MIRO-WEB [Florescu] is a European research project, which, among other components, provides a generic storage component for XML documents on top of relational tables. A Java API, based on the semistructured, self-descriptive OEM (Object Exchange Model) data model [McHugh 1997], is used to access and navigate transparently the document trees stored in the relational tables.

Though not Java based, several research prototypes and technologies address structured document storage. Lore [McHugh 1997]; [Quass 1996] is a fully fledged, native DBMS for OEM, which is also used for storing structured documents [Goldman 1999]. Both "A Structured Text ADT for Object-Relational Databases" [Brown 1998] and "Text /Relational Database Management Systems: Harmonizing SQL and SGML" [Blake 1994] describe a system and data model based on object-oriented extensions (ADTs) to relational DBMS (SQL3). They allow storage of SGML-based data in relations, using existing element type information for creating appropriate entries in tables. HyperStorM [Böhm 1997] extends an object-oriented DBMS with support for SGML documents, using a hybrid (OO/text) approach. Here, specifications describe which elements are mapped onto object types and which are stored as flat text objects. Lore is a generic storage system as it allows inserting directly any structured document, whereas "A Structured Text ADT for Object-Relational Databases" [Brown 1998], "Text/Relational Database Management Systems: Harmonizing SQL and SGML" [Blake 1994], and HyperStorM need knowledge about the document structure in order to be able to instantiate tables or objects correctly.

Beside these high-level storage systems, which exploit the capabilities of existing systems and their models, there exists some work that addresses efficient low-level storage of and access to document trees. Several clustering policies have been proposed for small variable-sized data objects or tree structures [Kanne 1999]; [Zou 1998] that aim to find a good grouping of objects in clusters such that given access patterns can refer repeatedly to the objects in one cluster. These are accompanied by mechanisms for cluster management and organization; for example, VClusters [McAulliffe 1998]. Our approach provides for an initial clustering of nodes in document order, which fits especially to the navigation operations provided by the DOM that always refer to a node's direct neighborhood.

Good clustering policies and cluster organization maximize the utility of buffer caches by minimizing the number of relevant clusters that need to be kept in the cache for given access patterns. Dozens of caching strategies have been proposed that utilize buffer ranking schemes that differ from LRU or LFU; for example, based on buffer size or buffer fetching costs [Young 1994]; [Cao 1997], access time history [O'Neil 1993], or request priority [Brown 1996]. These ranking schemes are complemented by predictive strategies; for example, prefetching buffers [Griffioen 1994] based on cache access history. The lucky loser strategy presented in this chapter results in a dynamic ranking scheme, which adapts itself to particular repetitive access patterns.

Conclusion

In this chapter we have described an efficient and lightweight persistency component for DOM objects. Unlike database solutions, the PDOM requires no fixed schema, but can deal with arbitrarily structured documents consisting of variable sized objects. A carefully compacted file format and adaptive caching policy minimizes costly file access operations.

The persistency support is completely hidden from the application programmers. Thus they do not need to load objects from disk by means of explicit cursors within transaction boundaries, but can completely rely on the DOM interface. Check in and check out of objects occurs on demand and is synchronized with Java's garbage collection.

At GMD, the PDOM has been used in a number of projects with varying demands with respect to size of data, heterogeneity, and complexity of structure, and typical access patterns. The XML Broker project integrates information from several Web sites with weather information, routing information, and golfing information using the PDOM as an XML data warehouse containing approximately 2MB of data. The Relimo project uses a similar approach with much larger sources to integrate several bio-informatics databases, materializing a warehouse of about 30MB. Finally, the AMetaCar project utilizes the PDOM in combination with a relational database to store irregularly structured information on used cars taken from various sources. For more information on these projects and a free download of the PDOM see www.xml.darmstadt.gmd.de/xql/ [Huck 1999].

Currently we are working on the following issues. We will experiment with refined caching strategies, which take the tree structure of documents and predominant access patterns into account. Along the same lines we will experiment with more flexible page layouts to deal with objects of highly varying size. Furthermore, we are working on generalizing the addressing scheme to support full multidocument identifiers valid across document boundaries and extensibility for special purpose indices; for example, to realize efficient full-text search on content.

The Model of Object Primitives (MOP)

In contemporary business environments, different problems and a variety of diverse requirements compel designers to adopt numerous modeling methodologies that use semantics customized to suit ad-hoc needs. This fact hinders the unanimous acceptance of one modeling paradigm and lays the groundwork for the adoption of customized versions of some. Based on this principle, we devised and present the Model of Object Primitives (MOP), which aims at providing a minimum as well as generic set of semantics without compromising expressive capability. It is a class-based model that accommodates the representation of static and dynamic characteristics—state and behavior—of objects acting within the problem domain. It uses *classes* and *policies* to represent object state and behavior and *collections* to collate them into complex structures.

In this chapter we introduce MOP and provide an insight into its semantics. We examine three case studies that use MOP to represent the XML, ODMG, and Relational data–models, and also schemata that are defined in these models. Subsequently, another two case studies illustrate practically how MOP can be used in distributed software environments to customize the behavior or construct new components based on the powerful tool of behavior policies.

Adequate and precise modeling is key for the successful development of information systems. It is common practice, at present, to model information and system behavior using object-orientated (OO) languages such as the Unified Modeling Language (UML) standard [UML]. It is evident, however, that designers pick and choose parts of languages to produce a customized modeling paradigm that best suits their current requirements. Such paradigms, however, constitute an amalgamation of semantic constructs and notations. Hence, although a standard such as UML generalizes concepts and semantic constructs encountered in different paradigms in order to establish a broadly accepted modeling approach, practice works conversely; that is, designers specialize and adopt extensions to the standard in order to achieve their ad hoc objectives [Vauttier 1999].

In this chapter we introduce MOP, the Model of Object Primitives. It is used as a means to represent complex object structures while maintaining the set of semantic constructs simple and rich in expressive capability. MOP is based on four main dimensions:

Classification. Everything in MOP is modeled as a class. MOP classes can instantiate other MOP classes; hence schemata can be organized at different levels according to their abstraction.

Unified representation of object state and behavior. Both are uniformly treated since MOP has *class* as its basic representation mechanism. This is a unique feature, which contrasts with traditional OO approaches where object state and behavior are described as part of a class.

Aggregation. MOP provides an explicit mechanism to define complex aggregated objects.

Minimum set of representation mechanisms. MOP supports a small number of mechanisms capable of representing very complex concepts. Hence, simplicity does not compromise modeling flexibility. Several case studies examined in following sections show how flexible MOP modeling mechanisms are.

MOP is a blend of modeling features and ideas encountered in different fields. There is a lot of influence gained from knowledge representation languages such as TELOS [Mylopoulos 1990]; semantic and information models like UML [UML], CDIF [Flatscher 2000], CIM [CIM], XML [W3C 1998] and OEM [Garcia-Mollina 1997]; object-orientated languages like Java and ODMG [ODMG 1998]; modeling of distributed systems [Cheung 1994] and software components [Maier 1997]. It also draws upon approaches for information integration [McBrien 1998]; [Poulovassilis 1998]; [Frederiks 1997]. Rather than extensively examine these fields here, we will present similarities and differences to existing technologies and approaches along the way where they arise.

The chapter is structured as follows. First, we briefly introduce MOP, presenting a short overview of its semantics. Then, MOP semantics is described more analytically. Subsequently, we examine three conceptual case studies in order to show that MOP can be used to model information that is represented in different languages, hence it can become the conceptual integrating element for a variety of modeling approaches. Special focus is given to XML, ODMG, and the relational data model, which at present emerge as standards with large potential for dominance. Following that, we briefly report on two practical case studies in order to demonstrate MOP's applicability and effective influence in building and customizing distributed service components. Finally, the chapter ends with a discussion about MOP features and some concluding observations.

Model of Object Primitives

Object-orientated methods attempt to analyze and model entities relevant to a problem domain as objects of a specific class. An object has *state*, which can change in the course of time, and presents certain behavior. State is reflected in the values of the object attributes and behavior is determined by the methods the object implements. Additionally, a class is perceived to be the abstraction that describes state and behavior characteristics for objects of the same type. In other words, a class acts as a template that packages together data variables and methods. Hence, inevitably, state and behavior become concepts that are tightly associated with the objects of a certain class.

The Model of Object Primitives aims at looking deeper into the structure of objects. Objects are analyzed in their founding constituents, data, and methods; that is, state and behavior. It is these primitive constructs that are of importance in MOP and not the whole objects. Each primitive construct is modeled as a separate class. *MOPClass* is the main modeling mechanism of MOP. Object primitives are modeled as *State Classes* and *Behavior Classes*[1], which are special forms of MOPClass. A State Class models the state/data variables encountered in objects and a Behavior Class models object methods. Another form of MOPClass is *Collection Class*. This packages together other MOP-Classes—for example, State, Behavior, or other Collection Classes—to construct more complex structures. This point is where MOP meets the classic OO paradigms, since a designer can use Collections to assemble the appropriate data variables and methods and build a construct similar to a class in the traditional sense; that is, a Java or UML class. *Relationship* is another MOP mechanism that indicates an association between two MOPClasses. MOP supports *Constraints*, which specify certain limitations a designer wants to apply on MOPClasses. For instance, relationship cardinality ratio, ownership, isA relationships, and weak entities can be modeled as plain relationships or classes augmented with a constraint appropriately defined to capture the restrictive properties for each case. Finally, *Policies* are used as the means to specify behavior in MOP. They get associated with Behavior Classes and aim at describing the way the latter deliver their services. Figure 7.1 illustrates the meta-model for MOP.

MOP Semantics

In this section, we examine the basic modeling mechanisms of MOP, namely MOPClass, State Class, Behavior Class, Collection Class, Relationship, Constraint, and Policy.

MOPClass

A *MOPClass* is the cornerstone of MOP. It is never used directly when building a schema in MOP. It only constitutes the root construct that is extended in order to implement each one of the primary MOP classes—state, behavior, collection, and relationship. Hence, it accumulates the features that commonly are encountered among those. Everything in MOP is modeled as a class that is generally of type state, behavior,

---

[1] In the sequel, a Behavior Class will alternatively be referred to as method.

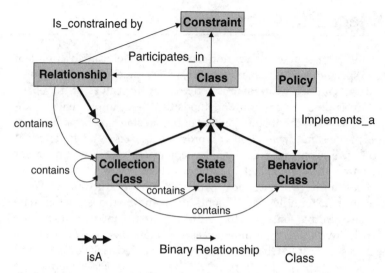

Figure 7.1   Meta-model for MOP.

collection, or relationship. Since the latter types inherit from the root, any class can be considered as an instance of MOPClass.

An instance of MOPClass is characterized by the structure *<id, name, description, MOPClass[] type>*. *id* is a non-null and unique integer that identifies different classes. The *name* attribute indicates the name of the class. More than one name can be given at the definition of a class, serving as alternative aliases. An optional attribute, *description* is a free-text description of what the class represents. The *type* feature specifies classes that the current one instantiates. As mentioned in the introduction, MOP supports *classification*; that is, a MOPClass can be an instance of other, more abstract classes. Additionally, MOP supports *multiple instantiation*; that is, a class can be an instance of more than one abstract class, hence, a MOPClass can have more than one type. This is the reason for representing the type feature as an array.

Classification is a property encountered in several semantic models, such as the TELOS knowledge representation language [Mylopoulos 1990]. It introduces the principle of meta-modeling, where someone can build "models that describe models" [Flatscher 2000]. More specifically, classification allows classes to be considered as instances of others. This feature manifests in MOP through the typing mechanism, which considers that each MOPClass has a type; that is, it instantiates other classes. This arrangement organizes MOPClasses in conceptual/abstract planes, which construct a bottom-up hierarchy. A similarly layered architecture is adopted by the EIF/CDIF standard [Flatscher 2000], which is, however, restricted to only four levels. Classification in MOP is unlimited; therefore, the number of abstraction layers is also unlimited. The lowest layer, $M0^2$, is occupied by MOPClasses that cannot be further instantiated because they represent concrete values such as integers and strings. Levels M1, M2, and above host instantiable MOPClasses. To show that a MOPClass A instantiates a MOPClass B we may use the keyword *instanceOf* and write *A instanceOf B*.

---

[2] The layer names M0, M1, M2 are chosen to be compatible with the names adopted by the EIF/CDIF standard.

Generally, a MOPClass is modeled with one exclusive type of primitive; for instance, State Class or Collection Class. However, a MOPClass could have some instances represented as State Classes and others as Collections. Such a case is encountered in Table 7.2 (later), which describes the mappings of ODMG into MOP. Table 7.2 shows that an Attribute can be represented in MOP as a State Class or a Collection. To avoid modeling inconsistencies, it is necessary that MOP capture the concept of Attribute in a way that facilitates its instantiation by State Classes and Collections. This generally is achieved by defining the concept as a MOPClass and declaring in its type feature the primitive types expected to be encountered among the concept instances. In the particular example, the Attribute should be defined as MOPClass with its type feature set to StateClass and CollectionClass, as shown:

```
MOPClass ODMGAttribute {
type: StateClass, CollectionClass
}
```

Constraint

A constraint applies to MOP classes and relationships in order to enforce restrictions on their characteristics or instances. Constraints are related with their restricted parties through the keyword *constrainedBy*. A class or relationship can establish an association with a constraint either at the time of definition or when included as part of another construct such as a Collection. In the former case the constraint will always apply, wherever and whenever the class occurs. In the latter case, the constraint will be enforced only within the local/special boundaries of the declaration. A useful keyword when expressing a constraint is *this*, which identifies the class to which the constraint applies. If the constraint applies to an embedded class, that is, a class included within another, *this* refers to the embedded and not the overall class. In all other cases, *this* refers to the MOPClass wherein it is used. Examples of constraints are given in the section, "Mapping Data-Models to MOP," where MOP is used to represent the XML, ODMG, and Relational data models.

State Class

A *State Class* inherits all features of the root MOPClass and is modeled with an almost similar structure: *<id, name, description, type, contentType>*. The only additional property is *contentType*, which is introduced for usage merely by M1 State Classes. It indicates the type that the M0 instances of a M1 State Class should have. Consequently, the *content-Type* feature can be regarded as equivalent to applying a constraint that forces all instances of the current State Class to be simultaneously instances of the contentType-specified MOPClass. Generally, however, and in the interest of simplicity, it is preferable to use the *contentType* feature, which implies a constraint, rather than explicitly applying the constraint *per se*.

An example follows, where *Name* is defined in two equivalent ways: as a State Class with *contentType* String and as a State Class with a *constraint* that forces all instances of *Name* to be of type String. Both declarations would dictate that State Class *Aris* should be a string. The same can be achieved if, instead of *Name* setting its contentType feature, *Aris* sets its type to *Name* and *String*. This way of modeling, however, would not seem practical. In general, constructing a schema that models a problem domain (classes that reside on level M1) happens before populating the schema with real world entities (classes that reside on level M0). Hence, for completeness, each M1 class should specify all properties including those that the M0 instances should satisfy. The *contentType* feature is such a property, aiming to specify in advance—at the definition of the M1 State Class—the additional type the M0 instances should have.

```
StateClass Name{              StateClass Name{              StateClass Name {
type: ODMGAttribute          type: ODMGAttribute          type: ODMGAttribute
contentType: String          constrainedBy:               }
}                            TypeOfContent                StateClass Aris {
StateClass Aris {            }                            type: Name, String
type: Name                                                }
}
Constraint TypeOfContent: ∀ i instanceOf this, i instanceOf  String
```

The *contentType* feature should refer to types that are represented as either State Classes or Collections of State Classes.

MOP is a purely class-based model. Therefore, it does not support any atomic data types, such as int, short, char, and so on, which typically are used in data definition languages. Instead, these literals are wrapped up in MOPClasses in order for these to become the built-in types of MOP and for MOP to persist its class-based profile. The idea of wrapping literals into classes is also encountered in Java. MOP supports a default set of built-in types that includes *Character, String, Integer, Long, Float, Double,* and *Boolean*. These types are considered to be State Classes and resemble the set of Java classes that wrap up Java literals. The set of MOP built-in types can be enriched if requirements so dictate. For example, this may need to happen when integrating a new model that supports literals not included in or not bound to the MOP literals of the built-in set. These additional literals can be similarly wrapped up as MOPClasses, and comprise part of the built-in MOP types.

Behavior Class

A Behavior Class is a primitive MOPClass that is modeled as a structure of the form *<id, name, description, type, MOPClass[] argumentTypes, MOPClass[] argumentValues, MOPClass resultType, MOPClass[] resultValues>*. The first features are inherited from the root MOPClass. *argumentTypes* is an array of MOPClasses that represent the types of arguments input in the Behavior Class. *argumentValues* is an array of MOPClasses that represent the argument values input in the method. These values should comply with the respective types stated in *argumentTypes*; that is, each member of *argumentValues* should be an instance of the respective member of *argumentTypes*. *returnType* designates the MOPClass that represents the type of output of the Behavior Class. Finally, *resultValues* is an array of MOPClasses that represent discrete values of type *resultType* and are potential outputs of the class.

We distinguish two categories: the *predetermined results Behavior Class* and the *non-predetermined results Behavior Class* category. The former includes Behavior Classes that return results from an *a priori* determined finite set of discrete values, which is generally a subset of the set[3] of all possible results. Here, the *resultValues* array depicts the values of the finite set. For instance, in this category fall methods with *resultType* Boolean, since their *resultValues* is [True, False]. The latter category includes Behavior Classes whose outcomes are not *a priori* known. This holds mainly because the values such methods return depend on results reached at run time. Here, the *resultValues* feature remains null.

An example is presented next to demonstrate the way a MOP Behavior Class is defined. The example assumes concepts of an ODMG schema mapped to MOP according to Table 7.2 (later).

```
StateClass Name {            BehaviorClass isMale {
type: ODMGClass             type: ODMGMethod
contentType: String         argmumentTypes: Name
}                            resultType: Boolean
                             resultValues: True, False
                             }
```

The main contribution of a Behavior Class is that it separates the implementation and focuses on the description of method properties. This makes a Behavior Class similar to the concept of an interface, such as a Java interface, which contains signatures of methods and omits their implementations. There is, however, a significant difference. Basically, a MOP Behavior Class refers directly to *one* behavior atom, that is, one method. A Java interface may contain more than one method description, hence it acts as a package of behavior. Therefore, an interface is literally equivalent to a Collection of Behavior Classes. This atomic treatment of behavior in Behavior Classes combined with the aggregating capability of Collections leverages the construction of optimal interfaces. This is because methods in MOP are recognized building blocks and can be referenced individually in order to construct a new interface. In Java or other languages there is no direct semantics support for method descriptions other than considering them as part of an interface; hence when a new interface is to be constructed it needs to be built entirely from scratch.[4]

Policy

Policies traditionally are used in the areas of Network Management and Distributed Systems [Marriott 1997]. Several policy languages have been developed to address

---

[3] This set comprises the domain of values and it is indicated by the *resultType* feature.

[4] In Java, an interface can extend another interface and inherit all the method descriptions of the latter. This facilitates the construction of new interfaces from other preexisting interfaces. Thus, if there were a requirement to create a new interface i1 with method descriptions that already exist as parts of interfaces i2, i3, and i4, i1 should simply extend i2, i3, and i4. However, this would entail i1 to inherit, along with the useful method signatures, others that are included in i2, i3, and i4, and are surplus/useless for i1. The only way to avoid this is to model numerous interfaces including only one method, and then let it extend merely the interfaces that refer to the methods it needs. This is exactly the approach MOP follows except that methods are directly described as Behavior Classes instead of being included in "thin" interfaces.

security issues [Sloman] such as access control, and network issues [IETF] such as allocation of network resources and configuration of devices to meet certain QoS criteria. In general, policies have been targeted for low-level (network level) and administrative control applications. What is missing is a dimension where policies can be used to specify high-level behavior and in particular, object behavior.

A Policy in MOP is tightly coupled with a Behavior Class. The latter intends to specify static characteristics of behavior, such as name of method and type of method arguments, and the former aims at describing the dynamic features of behavior; that is, the way this behavior is performed. Practically, a Policy is the service specification for a Behavior Class; that is, it implements the service the behavior class is meant to deliver.

Expressing Policies has emerged as a very challenging issue during this research. This is especially because of the main objective that policies aim to address, which is to describe object behavior. We have tried two ways of modeling. First, Policies are considered to be a set of Condition-Action rules. Based on the truth-value of a condition, the Policy continues either with executing a sequence of actions or with checking another condition. This representation has been applied in the first practical case study presented in the section "Case Studies." Second, a Policy is modeled as a set of linked nodes. Each node represents some primitive behavior (a Behavior Class). A node has as many outputs as values appear in the *resultValues* set of the respective Behavior Class. The Policy executes one node and then follows onto the next, according to the result. This is a more generic representation than the first and has been applied in the second practical case study. The convenience of both representations is that they can be modeled visually as graphs. This grants great flexibility in managing Policies and provides grounds for the implementation of user-friendly Policy management tools.

A dimension that is currently under consideration is to extend the Policy representation such that it captures events. State Transition Diagrams and events are broadly accepted in OO design paradigms, such as UML, as the means to model object behavior. Incorporation of events will also provide a strong modeling element for capturing the interaction between behavior components, which is admittedly a common and rather complex situation. This basically refers to a case where some behavior b1 starts, then suspends, waits for behavior b2 to perform, and then continues again in a direction that is dependent on b2's results; b2 starts upon the reception of an event sent by b1 and b1 receives b2's results through an event sent by the latter. Some relevant work is presented in "A Policy Description Language" [Lobo 1999], where an event-based Policy description language is proposed. Similarly interesting research is reported in "Integration of Behavior Models" [Frank 1997], "On the Representation of Objects with Polymorphic Shape and Behavior" [Papazoglou 1994], "Rule-based Behavior Modeling: Specification and Verification of Information Systems Dynamics" [Tsalgatidou 1991], and "An Integrated Method for Effective Behavior Analysis of Distributed Systems" [Cheung 1994].

A Behavior Class gets related to a MOP Policy with the keyword *implementedBy*. A Policy can be related to (implement) more than one Behavior Class and, conversely, a Behavior Class can be related to (be implemented by) many policies. This corresponds to a Java feature where classes can implement more than one interface and interfaces can be implemented by more than one class.

Policies do not get instantiated; only Behavior Classes do. This holds because the role of a Behavior Class is to represent a piece of behavior as a concrete entity. Therefore, it is sensible that *they* are instantiable. On the other hand, Policies simply describe a specification for the service that should be delivered by the associated method. A Policy is not a MOPClass, hence, it cannot have instances.

Collection Class

A *Collection Class* is a MOPClass with intent on materializing the concept of *aggregation*. It can be modeled as a structure that contains other MOPClasses (State, Behavior, Collection, and Relationship). Alternatively, we can view a Collection Class as an unordered set of classes and relationships that may contain a variant number of members each time a new Collection is defined. A Collection has the form *<id, name, description, type, MOPClass[] members>*. The first features are inherited from the root MOPClass. The *members* array keeps a list of the MOPClasses that are members of the Collection.

The keyword *memberOf* is used at the definition of a MOPClass to declare it as a member of a collection. However, it is preferable and more comprehensible to declare within a Collection the classes it includes. This is done with the keyword *members*, which is used in the definition of the Collection Class. The following example presents both alternatives of declaring members. It is assumed that the concepts belong to an XML schema that is mapped to MOP according to Table 7.1

```
CollectionClass Employee{            CollectionClass Employee{
type: XMLElementType                 type: XMLElementType
}                                    members: Name
StateClass Name{                     }
type: XMLElement                     StateClass Name{
memberOf: Employee                   type: XMLElement
contentType: String                  contentType: String
}                                    }
```

In instances of a Collection, each member may be instantiated more than once. This, in fact, shows that each member can have multiple values in one Collection instance.

There are two operators that can be used with a Collection Class. The first is *CollectionClass[] memberOf (MOPClass)*, which applies to any MOPClass and retrieves an array of Collections to which the MOPClass belongs. It is common to use this operator as a keyword in clauses of the form A *memberOf* B to state that A belongs to Collection B. The second operator has the reverse effect. It is *MOPClass[] members (CollectionClass)* and returns an array of MOPClasses that belong to a specific Collection.

A Collection can be defined without a name. This leverages the representation of a group of concepts when it is not necessary to reference this group explicitly by name. The definition of such a Collection leaves the *name* feature null.

Relationship

A *Relationship* in MOP becomes a first-class citizen since it is treated as a MOPClass. This fact contradicts the concept of a relationship, as it is perceived in ODMG. There,

"A relationship is not itself an object and does not have an object identifier. It is defined implicitly by declaration of traversal paths that enable applications to use the logical connections between the objects participating in the relationship." *[ODMG 1998]*

A MOP Relationship is captured as a binary association that links two MOPClasses. Therefore, it is a Collection Class in the sense that it *aggregates* two parties in the association. A MOP Relationship is unidirectional—there is an originator and a destination class. The start and end of the Relationship are respectively declared in the *from* and *to* section of the Relationship definition. A Relationship can be defined either as an independent class or within another class. In the latter case, the hosting class is assumed to be either the originator or the destination of the association, hence the *from* or *to* section is respectively omitted from the Relationship definition. Furthermore, a Relationship should, at definition, state its type/s. This implies that Relationships instantiate other more abstract ones. That is a benefit gained from considering a Relationship to be a MOPClass, therefore classification applies to it in the same way it applies to MOPClasses.

The basic features of a MOP Relationship are exhibited in the following example. We assume that the represented concepts are part of an ODMG schema whose semantic constructs are modeled in MOP according to the mappings shown in Table 7.2.

```
CollectionClass Employee{              CollectionClass Department{
type: ODMGClass                        type: ODMGClass
}                                      }
CollectionClass Department {           CollectionClass Employee{
type: ODMGClass                        type: ODMGClass
}                                      Relationship works for {
Relationship works for {               type: ODMGRelationship from
type: ODMGRelationship from            ODMGClass
ODMGClass                              to: Department
from: Employee                         }
to: Department                         }
}
```

There are two specific operators that apply to a MOP Relationship; *MOPClass from (Relationship)*, which identifies the originator class of the Relationship and *MOPClass to (Relationship)*, which returns the destination class. As shown in the example, *from* and *to* can additionally be used when referring to a Relationship in order to more clearly identify it by mentioning its source or destination.

The semantics of a Relationship is very generic because it can associate different types of MOPClasses, for instance, State, Behavior, Collection Classes, and even Relationships, since the latter are also MOPClasses in their own right. Additionally, a Relationship is allowed to have its own attributes. This is a feature encountered in many OO modeling languages, such as UML. In MOP this is achieved by aggregating the MOPClasses that represent the attributes within the collection of the Relationship. Then, the Relationship would appear to contain the attribute MOPClasses in addition to the originator and the destination classes.

In models, such as the Extended-Entity-Relationship (EER) model, relationships can be one of only three types determined by their cardinality ratios, namely, one-to-one, one-to-many, and many-to-many. A MOP Relationship is different in that it stands alone as a concept. However, a more specialized type of relationship can be defined, if necessary, by the augmentation of a MOP relationship with a constraint. This is feasible as MOP Relationships are Collection Classes and therefore constraints can apply to them. Specific examples of such cases are studied in the sections that follow.

Mapping Data Models to MOP

In "A Framework that uses Repositories for Information Systems and Knowledge Integration" [Georgalas 1999a] and "The Role of Repositories in Integrating Information Systems and Enterprise Knowledge" [Georgalas 1999b], the conceptual role of repository technology in the integration of information systems and knowledge was analyzed. There, a model was presented which, among other things, facilitates the integration of information sources that support different data models (e.g., XML, OO, and Relational). The intention of the model is to represent, in subsequent abstraction layers of the repository, knowledge pertinent to the information sources and their content. Hence, in MOP terms, we have user data on level M0, then we describe the information schema of the database on M1, on M2 the data model is represented, and finally on M3 we describe *"abstract representation types"* that are *"generic"* and *"independent of model-specific features"* [Georgalas 1999a]. In this section we study the *genericity* and *flexibility* of MOP to represent different data–models—XML, ODMG, and Relational in particular. By doing this we aim to show that MOP can be placed at the last abstraction layer of the model (M3), above the layer of data-model descriptions, and hence it can provide leverage for the generic representation of a variety of information models with data and behavior characteristics.

XML in MOP

XML is described in Figure 7.2 as a meta-model of its main constructs. This meta-model is based on the specification of XML given in "XML-Data" by the World Wide Web Consortium [W3C 1998]. The structure of the information contained in an XML document is declared by a *schema*. The schema includes several sorts of *element types*. *Single* or *atomic*

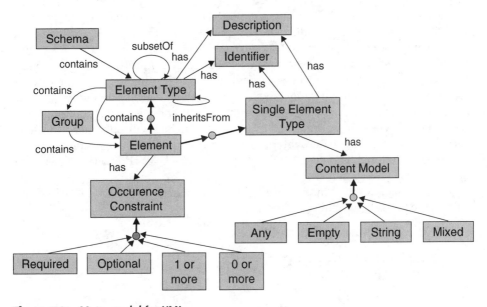

Figure 7.2 Meta model for XML.

Table 7.1   XML to MOP Mappings

XML CONSTRUCTS	MOP REPRESENTATION
Schema Element Type	Collection Class
Single Element Type *Identifier* *Description* *Content (Empty, Any, String, Mixed)*	State Class *Name* *Description* *ContentType*
Composite Element Type: *Single Element Type + (Required, Optional, OneOrMore, ZeroOrMore) Composite Element Type + (Required, Optional, OneOrMore, ZeroOrMore)*	Collection Class: *State Class +* *occurrenceConstraint Collection Class (of Composite Element Type template) + occurrenceConstraint*
Group	Collection Class with no name
Supertype	Relationship + subsetConstraint
Genus	Relationship + subsetConstraint + inheritanceConstraint

element types carry an *identifier* and optionally a description. However, more complex element types may exist, which consist of *properties/elements*. These types will be referred to as *composite element types*. Elements are element types that have been defined separately and can be, in turn, either *single* or *composite*. Each element within an element type specifies whether it is optional or required and if it occurs in the type 0,1, or many times. The structure of an element type is called *content model*. Specifically for single element types the content model determines whether the element type is Empty, a String, a mixture of characters and contents of element types declared in the same schema, or a mixture of element type contents without any free characters. A *group* indicates a set or sequence of elements within a composite element type and it is treated as a single element. Element types can be organized into class hierarchies with subtypes and supertypes. There, an instance of the subtype is also an instance of the supertype. When the supertype is declared as *genus* in the subtype, then the latter additionally inherits the supertype elements.

Table 7.1 illustrates the mapping of XML modeling constructs onto MOP. More analytically, the table shows that:

- A *schema* in XML maps to a Collection Class.

```
CollectionClass XMLSchema {
members: XMLElementType
}
```

This is because a schema contains element types in the same sense that a Collection Class includes MOPClasses.

■ An *element type* is modeled as State Class if it is single and as Collection Class if it is composite.

```
MOPClass XMLElementType{
type: CollectionClass, StateClass
}
```

■ An element type's identifier and description correspond to MOPClass name and description. For a single element type the content model corresponds to the contentType feature of the State Class. The *string* content model is equivalent to declaring a String contentType. *Any* is equivalent to a contentType that declares a Collection of State Classes. The Collection is constrained to contain State Classes of type XMLElementType, which belong to the same instance of XMLSchema as the single element type. A *mixed* content model similarly indicates a contentType of Collection Class. The Collection contains String or State Classes of type XMLElementType.

■ For composite element types the respective MOP Collection contains State Classes that represent single element type elements or other Collections that model composite element-type elements. In analogy to the *required* occurrence value, a MOP constraint is applied to the respective Collection member that forces it to be non-null for all instances of the Collection. Without this constraint, members can be null in some cases, which corresponds to the *optional* occurrence value. *OneOrMore* and *ZeroOrMore* values are covered by the property of the Collection members to acquire multiple values within a Collection instance.

■ A *group* is modeled as a Collection Class without a name.

■ *Subset* relationships and *inheritance*, declared respectively by the *superType* and *genus* XML attributes, are modeled as MOP Relationships with Subset and Inheritance constraints. The former constraint ensures that instances of XMLElement-Type type MOPClass, which is the start for a SubsetOf type Relationship, should also be instances of the MOPClass that ends the Relationship. The latter constraint forces members of a MOPClass, which is of type XMLElementType and ends a Relationship of type InheritsOf, to be members of the MOPClass that starts this Relationship.

```
Relationship SubsetOf{          Relationship InheritsFrom{
from: XMLElementType            from: XMLElementType
to: XMLElementType              to: XMLElementType
constrainedBy: Subset          constrainedBy: Subset, Inheritance
}                               }
```

Constraint Subset: ($\forall$i **instanceOf** this, k **instanceOf from**(i) $\Rightarrow$ k **instanceOf to**(i))

Constraint Inheritance: ($\forall$i instanceOf this, m memberOf **to**(i) $\Rightarrow$ m **memberOf from**(i))

A full example of an XML schema represented in MOP follows.

XML

```
<s:schema id='ExampleSchema'>
<elementType id="Name">
<description> The name of
some person </description>
<string/>
</elementType>
<elementType id="Person">
<any/>
</elementType>

<elementType id="Author">
<mixed> <element type="Name">
</mixed>
</elementType>

<elementType id="Title">
<string/>
</elementType>

<elementType
id="Introduction">
<string/>
</elementType>

<elementType id="Preface">
<string/>
</elementType>

<elementType id="Book">
<element type="#Title"
occurs=
  "REQUIRED"/>
<element type="#Author"
occurs=
  "ONEORMORE"/>
<group occurs="REQUIRED">
<element type="#Preface"/>
<element
type="#Introduction"/>
</group>
</elementType>

<elementType id="Price">
<string/>
</elementType>
```

MOP

```
CollectionClass
ExampleSchema {
type: XMLSchema
members: Name, Person, Author,
Title, Preface, Introduction, Book,
Price, ThingsRecentlyBought,
BooksRecentlyBought
}
StateClass Name {
type: XMLElementType
contentType: String
}
StateClass Person {
type: XMLElementType
contentType:
CollectionClass
constrainedBy  Any
}
StateClass Author {
type: XMLElementType
contentType:
collectionClass {
members: String, Name
}
}
StateClass Title{
type: XMLElementType
contentType: String
}
StateClass Introduction{
type: XMLElementType
contentType: String
}
StateClass Preface{
type: XMLElementType
contentType: String
}
CollectionClass Book {
type: XMLElementType
members: Title constrainedBy
Required, Author,
collectionClass {
members: Preface,
Introduction
} constrainedBy Required
}
```

```
<elementType
id="ThingsRecentlyBought">
<element type="#Price"/>
</elementType>

<elementType
id="BooksRecentlyBought">
<genus type="#Book">
<superType

type="#ThingsRecentlyBought"/>

<element type="#Price"/>
</elementType>

</s:schema>
```

```
StateClass Price {
type: XMLElementType
contentType: String
}
CollectionClass
ThingsRecentlyBought{
type: XMLElementType
members: Price
}
CollectionClass
BooksRecentlyBought{
type: XMLElementType
members: Price
Relationship inheritsBook {

type: InheritsFrom
to: Book
}
Relationship subsetsThings {
type: SubsetOf
to: ThingsRecentlyBought
}
}
```

```
Constraint Any: (∀i instanceOf this, m memberOf i ⇒ m memberOf
ExampleSchema)
Constraint Required: (∀i instanceOf this, ¬ (i = null) )
```

ODMG in MOP

ODMG is described in Figure 7.3 as a meta-model of its main modeling constructs. The meta-model is based on the ODMG specification [ODMG 1998]. The ODMG semantics is similar to any OO language, therefore we do not provide any detailed description; instead, we refer you to "The Object Database Standard: ODMG 2.0" [ODMG 1998].

Table 7.2 presents the mappings between ODMG and MOP. More analytically:

- A *database schema* is modeled as a Collection Class.

```
CollectionClass ODMGSchema{
members: ODMGClass
}
```

Every instance of ODMGSchema should include MOPClasses that represent ODMG classes of a database schema.

- A *class* in ODMG contains *attributes, relationships,* and *methods*; hence it is modeled as a Collection Class.

```
CollectionClass ODMGClass {
members: ODMGAttribute, ODMGMethod, ODMGRelationship
}
```

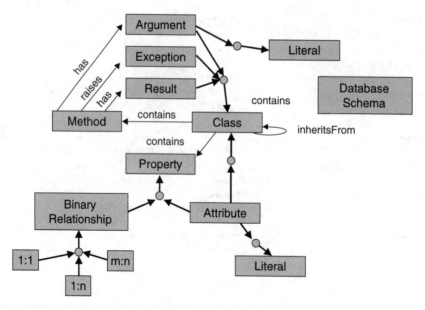

Figure 7.3 Meta-model for ODMG.

- An *attribute* can have as type either a literal, such as string or float, or another class that belongs to the same database schema. In the former case the attribute is modeled as State Class and in the latter as a Collection.

```
MOPClass ODMGAttribute{
type: CollectionClass, StateClass
}
```

Table 7.2 ODMG to MOP Mappings

ODMG CONSTRUCTS	MOP REPRESENTATION
Database Schema	Collection Class
Class *Attribute* *Relationship* *Method*	Collection Class *State or Collection Class* *Relationship* *Behavior Class*
Attribute	State or Collection Class
Relationship *(1:1, 1:n, m:n)*	Relationship + cardinalityConstraint
Method	Behavior Class
Exception	Behavior Class
Inheritance	Relationship + inheritanceConstraint

"The Object Database Standard: ODMG 2.0" [ODMG 1998] presents the ODMG-Java binding and it shows how ODMG literals map to Java classes that wrap up the Java literals. This mapping similarly applies to ODMG and MOP literals.

```
StateClass ODMGLiteral{
type: String, Character, Integer, Long, Float, Double, Boolean
}
```

- A *method* is represented as a Behavior Class. The types of its results and arguments are ODMGClass or ODMGLiteral. A method in ODMG raises an *exception* when an error occurs. An exception is modeled as a Behavior Class, which is related to ODMGMethod with the ODMGRaises Relationship.

```
BehaviorClass ODMGMethod {           BehaviorClass
argumentTypes: ODMGClass,            ODMGException{}
ODMGLiteral                          Relationship ODMGRaises {
returnType: ODMGClass,               from: ODMGMethod
ODMGLiteral                          to: ODMGException
}                                    }
```

- A *relationship* is mapped directly to a MOP Relationship. An issue is that a MOP Relationship is unidirectional, whereas an ODMG *relationship* is bidirectional. It is suggested that only one direction is kept and the designer chooses which one of the two related ODMGClass instances becomes the originator for the MOP Relationship. The cardinality ratios of 1:1, 1:n, and m:n are interpreted as cardinality constraints imposed on *ODMGRelationship*. Following, we express the *OneToOne* and *OneToMany* constraints assuming for the latter that the originator ODMGClass instance is the one sitting at the Many-end of the relationship. ODMGRelationship free of constraints represents the m:n case.

```
Relationship          Relationship          Relationship
ODMGRelationship{     ODMGRelationship{     ODMGRelationship{
from: ODMGClass       from: ODMGClass       From: ODMGClass
to: ODMGClass         to: ODMGClass         to: ODMGClass
}                     constrainedBy:        constrainedBy:
                      OneToMany             OneToOne
                      }                     }
```

$$\textbf{Constraint } OneToOne: (\forall i \textbf{ instanceOf this}, \forall k1, k2 \textbf{ instanceOf } i,$$
$$\neg(k1=k2) \Rightarrow \neg(\textbf{from}(k1)=\textbf{from}(k2)) \textbf{ AND } \neg(\textbf{to}(\ k1) = \textbf{to}(k2))$$
$$\textbf{Constraint } OneToMany: (\forall i \textbf{ instanceOf this}, \forall k1, k2 \textbf{ instanceOf } i, \neg(k1=k2) \Rightarrow$$
$$\neg(\textbf{to}(\ k1) = \textbf{to}(k2))$$

- *Inheritance* in ODMG is represented as a MOP Relationship augmented with the inheritance constraint. *InheritsFrom* is modeled exactly as in XML, as we examined in the previous section.

An example follows that illustrates the ODMG-to-MOP mappings in more detail.

ODMG

```
class Salary{              class Employee{           Class Professor
attribute float            attribute                 extends
base;                      string name;              Employee{
attribute float            attribute short           Attribute
overtime;                  id;                        string rank;
attribute float            attribute                 Relationship
bonus;                     Salary salary;            set<Section>
}                          void hire();              teaches inverse
class Section {            void fire()               Section::
attribute                  raises                    is_taught_by;
string number;             (no_such_employee);       }
relationship               }
Professor
is_taught_by
inverse
Professor::teaches;
}
```

MOP

```
StateClass Base{           BehaviorClass Hire {      Relationship teaches{
type:                      type:                     Type:
ODMGAttribute              ODMGMethod                ODMGRelationship
contentType:               }                         constrainedBy
Float                      BehaviorClass             OneToMany
}                          No_Such_Employee          From: Professor
StateClass                 {                         to: Section
Overtime{                  type:                     }
type:                      ODMGException             StateClass
ODMGAttribute              }                         Rank{
contentType:               BehaviorClass             type:
Float                      Fire{                     ODMGAttribute
}                          type:                     contentType:
StateClass                 ODMGMethod                String
Bonus{                     Relationship              }
type:                      raisesException           CollectionClass
ODMGAttribute              {                         Professor {
contentType:               type:                     type:
Float                      ODMGRaises                ODMGClass
}                          to:                       members: Rank
Collection                 No_Such_Employee          Relationship
Salary {                   }                         inheritsPerson{
type: ODMGClass            }                         type:
members: Base,             CollectionClass           inheritsFrom
Overtime, Bonus            Employee{                 to: Person
}                          type: ODMGClass           }
StateClass                 members: Name,            }
Name{                      Salary, Hire,
```

```
type:               Fire
ODMGAttribute       }
contentType:
String
}
```

Relational Model in MOP

The Relational data model, introduced by Codd in "A Relational Model of Data for Large Shared Data Banks" [Codd 1970], is described by the meta-model of Figure 7.4.

Table 7.3 presents the mappings between the Relational data model and MOP. More analytically:

- A *schema* is a Collection Class.

```
CollectionClass SQLSchema {
members: SQLRelation
}
```

An instance of SQLSchema aggregates MOPClasses that represent relations.

- A *relation* contains attributes, therefore it is modeled as a Collection Class.

```
CollectionClass SQLRelation{
members: SQLKey, SQLAttribute
}
```

- An *attribute* in the relational model can only be of literal type, such as integer or string, hence it is represented as a StateClass. Again, as in the case of the ODMG-MOP mappings, the relational literal types get mapped to the built-in MOP literals.

```
StateClass SQLAttribute {
}
```

- A *key* is a set of one or more attributes, and is mapped to a Collection Class. A key aims at uniquely identifying each tuple in a relation. In other words, a key instance

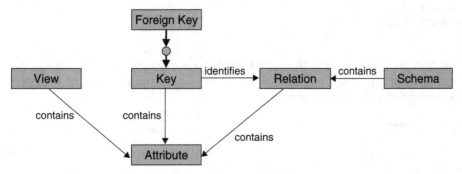

Figure 7.4   Meta-model for Relational data model.

Table 7.3 Relational to MOP Mappings

RELATIONAL CONSTRUCTS	MOP REPRESENTATION
Schema	Collection Class
Relation *Primary Key* *Attribute* *Foreign Key*	Collection Class *Collection* *State Class* *Collection*
Attribute	State Class
Primary Key	Collection Class
Foreign Key	Collection Class
View *Attribute*	Collection Class *State Class*

identifies one tuple and one tuple is identified by only one key instance. Therefore, we introduce the *Identifies* MOP Relationship that engages the *SQLPrimaryKey* and *SQLRelation* Collections into a 1:1 association. The 1:1 property of *Identifies* is represented by the OneToOne constraint, which was defined in the previous section.

```
CollectionClass              Relationship Identifies{
SQLPrimaryKey{               from: SQLPrimaryKey
members: SQLAttribute        to: SQLRelation
}                            constrainedBy: OneToOne
                             }
```

- A *foreign key* is a set of attributes that comprises the key of another relation. It is represented with the same Collection Class that models the respective key, and it is contained in the SQLRelation that models the relation of which the foreign key is part.

- A *view* is composed of attributes that stem from different relations. It is modeled as a Collection Class with *SQLAttribute* members.

```
CollectionClass SQLView {
members: SQLAttribute
}
```

An example is given next, in order to depict the representation of a relational schema in MOP. The underlined attributes correspond to the key and the italicized ones correspond to the foreign key.

RELATIONAL

```
Employee (EmpID, Name)
Department (SectionNo, DepartmentNo, EmpID)
```

MOP

```
StateClass EmpID{
type: SQLAttribute
contentType: Integer
}
StateClass Name{
type: SQLAttribute
contentType: String
}
CollectionClass
EmployeeKey{
type: SQLPrimaryKey
members: EmpID
}
CollectionClass Employee {
type: SQLRelation
members: Name,
EmployeeKey
Relationship
idenitifiesRelation {
type: Identifies from
SQLPrimaryKey
from: EmployeeKey
}
}
```

```
StateClass SectionNo {
type: SQLAttribute
contentType: Integer
}
StateClass DepartmentNo{
type: SQLAttribute
contentType: Integer
}
CollectionClass DeptKey{
type: SQLPrimaryKey
members: SectionNo,
DepartmentNo
}
CollectionClass
Department{
type: SQLRelation
members: DeptKey,
EmployeeKey
}
```

Case Studies

A MOP-based architecture is presented in "An Information Management Environment based the Model of Object Primitives" [Georgalas 2000]. The basic assumption therein is the existence of a set of heterogeneous data sources (e.g., XML, OO, or relational) and a network of software components that communicate in order to deliver a service to end users. Together they synthesize a *context*. Within the boundaries of this context, the architecture aims at offering the capability to conglomerate resources; that is, component *behavior* and *entities* stored in database schemata, under particular conditions in order to provide a user service of customized or more sophisticated behavior. In this setting, MOP becomes the means for representing and managing all context resources that are publishable and available to use. This holds mainly because of the powerful mechanisms MOP supports that facilitate primitive representation of resources, processing of primitives for the construction of complex aggregations, and specification of new behavior through policies. The architecture consists of a suite of tools that includes:

Extractors. They investigate the context to identify the published resources.

Wrappers. These are liable to convert existing resources into their MOP equivalents. The mappings between MOP and ODMG/XML/Relational described earlier play a primary role in implementing these wrappers, especially in the case of context resources originating from OO, XML, and relational databases.

Repository. It keeps descriptions of the MOP-represented resources.

Front-end graphical tools for service specification. Such tools facilitate the declarative definition of a service. *Service specification* is a description of the way a service should behave. The specification is delivered in the form of a MOP policy. These front-end tools are used to construct a policy. It is intended that the policy should either customize the behavior of an existent service or construct a new service by establishing rational[5] associations between context resources.

Service generator. Based on a service specification, the generator constructs a component that delivers the new service. If the specification aims at customizing the behavior of an existing service, this tool associates the new customizing policy with the component that delivers the service.

This architecture is a means to evaluate the MOP concepts in practice. It has been applied in two different functional scenarios that are briefly described next. Particular notice is given to MOPper, a prototype tool implemented in Java that is used mainly to construct graph-based MOP policies, or, service specifications. However, the functional description of the tool remains succinct as it is out of the scope of this chapter.

The first case, "Policy-driven Customization of Personalized Services" [Georgalas 1999c], assumes an environment (*context*) of services and assets (*context resources*) to which customers are subscribed, and where customers can obtain access by means of user-profiles. Examples of subscribed services may be directory or banking services and relevant assets can be agenda, accounts, and so on. The main objective here is to provide the capability at the customer's end to customize a service's behavior using parameters or functionality stemming from the same or other services to which he or she is subscribed. The MOP-based architecture complies satisfactorily with the requirements imposed by the problem. More specifically, the context resources are wrapped up and converted into MOP classes. Hence, parameters and service functionality become MOP state and behavior classes. They then populate a repository. The customer uses these resources to construct MOP policies, which, when associated with a service, will customize the service's behavior. MOPper has been constructed to serve this purpose.

A policy in MOPper is modeled visually as a Direct Acyclic Graph (DAG). The nodes of the graph represent conditions or actions. The edges specify the transition to subsequent conditions/actions. The repository content can be viewed through pop-up menus and is used to edit the node labels. The types of edges are TRUE, FALSE, or unlabelled. The first two define the transition in case of a true or false condition and the last shows transition from one action to another. After a MOP policy is graphically constructed it is then validated in terms of graph correctness and consistent use of the context resources; for example, if the argument values used in a MOP behavior class are of the correct type. Subsequently, it gets translated into a set of Java objects that logically represent the policy and its nodes. Finally, the service generator component associates the policy of the service to be customized and the policy gets saved for future use. Figure 7.5 illustrates MOPper and a policy that customizes the behavior of a cash transfer service. That is, a payer wishes to transfer cash to a payee but it is the payee's policy that determines to

---

[5] This term asserts that a policy, when viewed as a simple set of rules, utilizes operations and entities of the context to build rule conditions and sequences of action. Based on the truth-value of a condition, a particular flow of action is followed. Therefore, the rules can be considered as logical (rational) relationships established among the context resources.

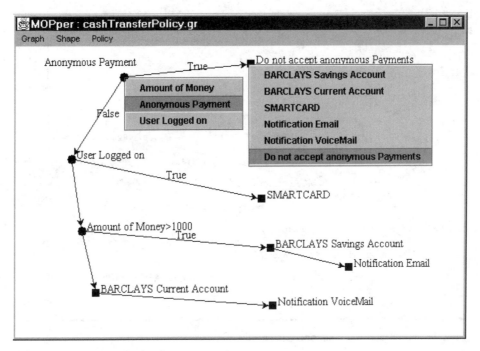

Figure 7.5 MOPper in the first case study.

what asset the money will be transferred—for example, deposit/current account or smart card. The repository content is shown in pop-up menus, to where the context resources appear to be referred, with the content of the MOPClass description feature. For purposes particular only to this case, the context resources appear separated in two pop-up menus, one specific to editing condition nodes and the other to editing action nodes. This has been achieved by grouping condition-specific and action-specific context resources into two separate Collection Classes.

The second case, "Policies for Context-Aware Session Control" [Rizzo 1999], assumes a telephony environment where callers and callees interact by means of agents. An agent follows a policy and negotiates with other agents in order to handle incoming phone calls. Again here, there are wrappers that convert the environment's operations in MOP behavior classes and a repository that keeps references to these. To demonstrate the aggregating capability of MOP, the wrapped up operations are managed in groups (in MOP Collection Classes). MOPper is used again to compose policies. This time policies are captured in a more generic form. The nodes in the policy graph represent behavior classes with several alternative outputs. Thus, instead of having conditional nodes with either TRUE or FALSE edges as outputs, there are operational nodes and outgoing edges with values stemming from the set of the permitted operation results.

The operations represented in the repository are viewed in pop-up menus, which hierarchize operations based on the Collections to which they belong. For each edge there is a pop-up menu dynamically created that visualizes the permitted outcome for the originator node. Figure 7.6 depicts MOPper and a call handling policy of an agent.

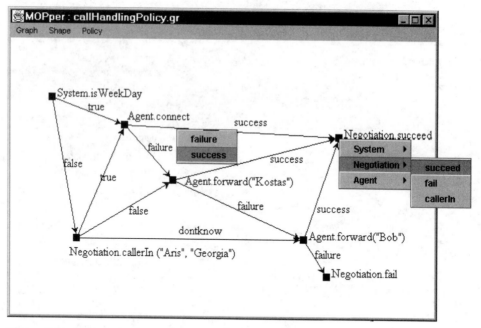

Figure 7.6   MOPper in the second case study.

After the graph is constructed, it gets validated and translated into a logical set of objects, as described in the previous case. Finally, the service generator creates a component that consists of the policy and an executing mechanism for it. This component constitutes a fundamental part of the agent that primarily determines the agent behavior over a negotiation.

Conclusion

In this chapter we described MOP, the Model of Object Primitives. It is a class-based model that analyzes and models objects using their primitive constituents: state and behavior. MOP contributes major advantages:

Minimal and rich. The semantics set includes only five basic representation mechanisms: state, behavior, collection, relationship, and constraint. These suffice for the construction of highly complex schemata. MOP additionally incorporates policies through which it can express dynamic behavior characteristics.

Cumulative and expandable concepts. The aggregation mechanism introduced by the Collection Class allows for the specification of classes that can expand incrementally. Since a class can participate in many collections, we can create Collections where one contains the other such that a complex structure is gradually produced including state as well as behavior constituents.

Reusable concepts. A MOPClass can be included into more than one Collection. Therefore, concepts modeled in MOP are reusable. As such, any behavior that is modeled as a combination of a Behavior Class and a MOP Policy can be reusable, which encourages the use of MOP in modeling software components. Reusability is a principal feature of components.

Extensible and customizable. MOP can be extended to support more semantics. Associating its main modeling constructs with constraints, more specialized representation mechanisms can be produced.

Use of graphs to represent MOP schemata and policies. MOP classes and relationships within a schema could potentially be visualized as nodes and edges of a graph. MOP policies are graph-based as well. This provides for the development of CASE tools, similar to MOPper, which alleviate the design of MOP-based models.

It is our belief that MOP can play a primary role in the integration of heterogeneous information systems both conceptually and practically. Conceptually, MOP performs as the connecting means for a variety of information models, and can facilitate transformations among them. It was not within the scope of this chapter to study a formal framework for model transformations. However, the XML, ODMG, and relational data model cases give good evidence that MOP can be used efficiently to represent semantics of diverse modeling languages. This is a necessary condition before moving onto studying model transformations.

Practically, MOP provides effective mechanisms to manage resources within a distributed software environment. Both practical case studies presented in this chapter show that MOP can assist in the construction of new components or in customizing the behavior of existing components. This is because MOP aids the representation and, therefore, the manipulation of context resources, state, or behavior, in a primitive form. Moreover, the adoption of policies as the means to describe the dynamic aspects of component behavior enhances MOP's role. Consequently, it is our overall conclusion that the Model of Object Primitives constitutes a useful paradigm capable of delivering efficient solutions in the worlds of data modeling and distributed information systems.

Four

Benchmarks and Performance

Database performance is an area where the relational vendors have often competed fiercely with each other on the well-known TPC benchmarks. Within the object database world, there has been no equivalent organization to TPC, but a few well-known benchmarks, such as OO1 and OO7 with their roots in the engineering world, continue to be used by many researchers. In commercial evaluations, such benchmarks tend to have little value, since they are not representative of many object database applications today. There are even fewer public benchmarks that attempt to compare both object and relational databases. Chapter 8, "A Performance Comparison of Object and Relational Databases for Complex Objects" by Bjørge is, therefore, particularly interesting. He uses part of a live system and describes his experiments in detail. The results show that an object database is not always faster than a relational database, which can, in fact, provide good performance in some cases. Bjørge concludes that it is important to undertake application-specific tests and pay attention to implementation details with any products under test, as such considerations may have noticeable performance implications.

Many database vendors from both the object and relational worlds have begun to offer strong Java support in their products. For object database vendors this would appear to be a natural extension to their previous offerings that supported C++ and Smalltalk. The Java language binding of the ODMG standard also appears to be the best supported by the pure object database vendors. However, we still do not understand many issues about the performance of such database systems using Java, and the language may bring with it its own special problems. Chapter 9, "Object Databases and Java Architectural Issues" by Danielsen, provides a good insight into some architectural issues, based on his evaluation of the Java language binding of a full-featured object database system. He discusses a number of general architectural issues as well as some more specific to Java, highlighting potential areas of concern and interest.

In any large-scale system development, questions of managing complexity and system scalability are perhaps uppermost in the minds of many developers, architects, and managers. Marquez and Blackburn describe one large-scale implementation that uses an object database in Chapter 10, "Addressing Complexity and Scale in a High-Performance Object Server." The chapter is also a very good example of academia and industry working together to develop answers to modern-day problems in using new technology. The discussion centers on how to tackle the issues of complexity and scale. One way to reduce complexity is to improve abstraction. Through the development of a prototype system, based upon Orthogonally Persistent Java (OPJ), the authors successfully show how complexity can be better managed. Furthermore, though scalability was not directly tested, their work looks very promising for the future.

A Performance Comparison of Object and Relational Databases for Complex Objects

This chapter was inspired by several different benchmark efforts; for example *The HyperModel Benchmark* [Anderson 1990], *The 007 Benchmark* [Carey 1993], *Fine-Grained Sharing in a Page Server OODBMS* by M.J. Carey, M.J. Franklin, and M. Zaharioudakis [Carey 1994], *A Performance Comparison of Object and Relational Databases Using the Sun Benchmark* by J. Duhl and C. Damon [Duhl 1988], and *A Test Evaluation Procedure for Object-Oriented and Relation Database Management Systems* by A.B. Larsen [Larsen 1992]. Some of the work described here has been reported previously in *Transition from Relational DBMS to Object DBMS: A Research of DBMS Performance, Advantages, and Transition Costs* by E. Bjørge [Bjørge 1999]. In that research, the goal was to study the transition from a relational DBMS (RDBMS) to an object DBMS (ODBMS)[1] for a real Knowledge-Based Decision Support System (KB-DSS) application. That application is object-oriented (OO), and an RDBMS is used today for storage management. In particular, one part of the OO model of the application was closely studied. The complex objects that were extracted from the OO model are the basis of the performance comparison and results presented in this chapter.

This chapter will demonstrate that even if an ODBMS is a "natural fit" for complex objects, it doesn't necessarily mean that it can outperform an RDBMS for all types of database operations. Benchmarking is not an easy task, and requires extensive knowledge about the products that will be used. Sometimes, a benchmarker may be unfamiliar with particular database technology—a situation faced by this author, who, although familiar with RDBMSs, had to start from scratch when it came to ODBMSs.

---

[1] In this chapter, ODBMS means "pure" ODBMS and not ORDBMS (Object Relational).

However, this proved to be an opportunity rather than a problem, and a great deal can be gained from simply undertaking a benchmarking exercise.

The performance tests discussed later in this chapter report results for one ODBMS and one RDBMS only. Some of the results (inserts) are similar to those reported in *Hitting the Relational Wall* by A.E. Wade [Wade 1998], whereas other results (deletes) were different.

The Application

The application used as a real-world test case from which to extract an OO model is a KB-DSS application called GeoX, and consists of a family of products delivered by the vendor GeoKnowledge [GeoKnowledge 2000]. The ultimate objective of KB-DSS is to improve the decisions for companies that attempt to locate more petroleum at less cost. One part of this GeoX family is the gFullCycle family member that supports rapid, early analysis of potential pre-tax and after-tax economic returns (NPV, IRR, and EMV) from an exploration project. The central part of the gFullCycle model is the Fiscal-Regime. Since the FiscalRegime was the most complex part and was fairly isolated from the remaining parts of the gFullCycle model, it was selected for the benchmark experiments. Presented next are the two different models (OO and relational) that were used to implement the database schemas for the benchmarks.

The OO Model

Figure 8.1 illustrates the OO model used in the ODBMS.

Each box represents a class. Those illustrated with a thick outline (TaxItem and Depreciation) are abstract classes in the database. Since there was a need for a top object in this model, the class FiscalSetting was chosen. The cardinality should read as follows: one FiscalSetting can have zero or more related FiscalRegimes. One Fiscal-Regime can be related to only one FiscalSetting. The cardinality [1] represents "or." This means that one specific ValueSerie is related to only one Depreciation or one Tax-Item, not both at the same time. The black arrows represent the "is-a-part-of" relationship. Those relationships that do not have any black arrows represent an "associated-with" relationship. Most of the relationships were implemented with the ODBMS vendors' 1:1 and 1:m bidirectional relationships (n:m is also present). Some safe pointers also were used where the relationship goes in only one direction. The white triangles represent inheritance in the model. The rest of the attributes in the classes are atomic types such as string, char, integer, and float. Each class has between 0–7 attributes, except for Distribution, which has 16 attributes (mostly floats). The classes of RevenueItem, ExpenseItem, ValueSerieType, ValueSerieItem, FunctionType, and DistributionType represent the type of a related class and contain only a few objects each that are collected in a class extent. Inheritance was not chosen here, due to the weakness of the object model when it concerns large heterogeneity in the data. For more about object data models weaknesses, refer to *Limitations of Object Data Models* by A. Girow [Girow 1997].

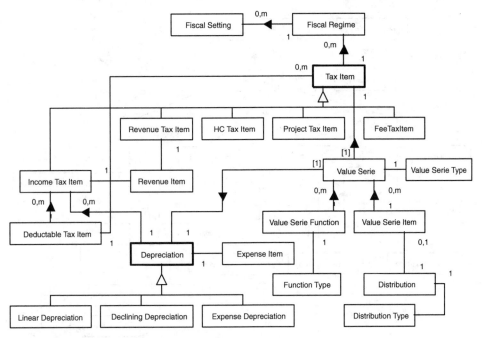

Figure 8.1   The OO model of FiscalRegime.

The EER Model

Figure 8.2 illustrates the related enhanced ER (EER) model for the RDBMS, based on the notation from *Fundamentals of Database Systems* by R. Elmasri and S.B. Navathe [Elmasri 1989].

This model represents the actual schema in the relational database, which means each box represents a physical table. The character *d* in the circle stands for disjoint, and this relationship is not mandatory. The largest difference between the OO and EER models is how the two abstract classes in the OO model have been implemented in the relational schema. This has resulted in two extra tables (DepreciationType and TaxBasisType) and the removal of six concrete inherited classes (now tables). The two extra tables contain only a few rows that represent the type of the object, similar to those already mentioned. Since the attributes have been removed from the models due to space limitations, the EER model has approximately 15 extra attributes compared to the OO model: Primary/Candidate/Foreign Keys that the RDBMS needs, and other requirements used to uniquely identify each row.

One Complex Object

In Table 8.1 the number of related objects/rows are listed, for one complex object. The benchmarks were based on fix-sized complex objects, using real values from the KB-DSS application.

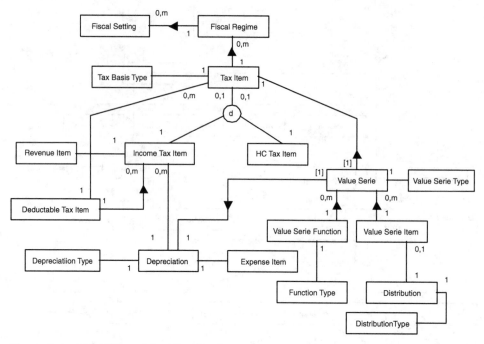

Figure 8.2   The EER model of FiscalRegime.

As illustrated in Table 8.1, an object consists of 20 more rows and is approximately 20–25 KB larger in the relational database than in the object database. The reasons for this are inheritance issues and extra attributes in the EER model. Due to the nature of RDBMS the relational schema has to contain many more indexes, too. Related to the RDBMS indexes are the ODBMS use of class extents. This issue will be discussed in the next section.

The objects/rows are related in the database as follows. First, the largest tree is six levels deep and there are two different kinds of trees. The first one goes from Fiscal-Setting to FiscalRegime, to TaxItem (IncomeTaxItem), to DeductableTaxItem, to Tax-Item (ProjectTaxItem or FeeTaxItem), to ValueSerie, and to ValueSerieFunction and ValueSerieItem. Distribution is not a part of this tree. The second tree goes directly down to Distribution (without passing DeductableTaxItem), passing Depreciation from the top FiscalSetting object. Table 8.1 shows that the last four classes/tables "contain" most of the data, because each IncomeTaxItem that exists in the database has about ten Depreciations of different types.

Database Operations

This section discusses the types of database operations found in the KB-DSS application. First, it does not have complex queries to handle the complex objects. The application brings all related rows (recall that it uses an RDBMS) raw from the database (few

Table 8.1   Comparison of a Complex Object in an ODBMS and a RDBMS

CLASSES/TABLES	OBJECT DATABASE	RELATIONAL DATABASE	EXPLANATION OF THE DIFFERENCE
FiscalSetting	1	1	
FiscalRegime	5	5	
TaxItem	-	30	An abstract class in the ODBMS
IncomeTaxItem	10	15	15 = incl 5 RevenueTaxItems
RevenueTaxItem	5	-	The rows are in the IncomeTaxItem table
HCTaxItem	5	5	
ProjectTaxItem	5	-	The rows are in the TaxItem table
FeeTaxItem	5	-	The rows are in the TaxItem table
DeductableTaxItem	20	20	
Depreciation	-	100	An abstract class in the ODBMS
LinearDepreciaton	40	-	The rows are in the Depreciation table
DecliningDepreciation	40	-	The rows are in the Depreciation table
ExpensedDepreciation	20	-	The rows are in the Depreciation table
ValueSerie	130	130	
ValueSerieFunction	420	420	
ValueSerieItem	420	420	
Distribution	200	200	
Total objects/rows:	1326	1346	Because of the abstract class: TaxItem
Total KB: [a]	Ca 56 KB	Ca 85–90 KB	Because of the extra need for keys and indexes

[a] Difficult to calculate exactly, since the RDBMS allocates a fixed size for tables and indexes.

joins, only on the m:n relationships that are on other parts of the application model) to transient memory. In transient memory all the raw tables are joined and the full tree is built. This shows us that it is not always necessary to use expensive joins in the database. Joining tables in transient memory should be faster than joining tables in the database. After the user has changed the status of the complex object, it is all saved back into the database. However, since it is fairly complex to determine which attributes have been updated, all the complex objects are first deleted and then just re-inserted. From these scenarios, the following database operations were developed for the benchmark.

Open and Close the Database

Since it is important to know how long such a process takes in general, this operation was also included. The following were tested:

1. Open a connection to the database.

2. Initialize libraries and event handling.

3. Send over/check user id/password (only for the RDBMS; ODBMS used operating system file-level security).

4. Open the database (for the ODBMS this meant also finding the database roots and database segments).

5. Start a write transaction.

6. Close the transaction with a commit.

7. Close the database/connection.

To gain a better understanding, separate results for some of these steps are presented next.

Pick Top Objects

When working with complex objects it is likely that there is a top object that represents the root. This is also true for this application, and it was interesting to observe the length of time it took to find this root. One of the intriguing questions was how the ODBMS would perform this task compared to the RDBMS. Many RDBMSs support stored procedures with the SQL query inside that will take as input the data being searched for. This should be faster than sending the complete SQL string to the server, so this was tested as well. The result of this small test gave the impression that it was possible to save about 5.5 milliseconds (ms) compared to sending over a SQL string of 60 characters that had to be parsed, validated, compiled, optimized, checked for permissions, and finally executed. The 5.5ms is actually a substantial length of time as we shall see later. In the ODBMS, since a Dictionary collection type (recommended by the vendor) was chosen as the class extent for the top objects, a query function could be used. The ODBMS vendor has developed a pick function for Dictionary collections. Both indexes in the RDBMS and ODBMS are of the type *Hash table* on a string attribute. The string that was searched for was approximately 17 characters long. Since rows in a table for an RDBMS are close together on the disk, a separate segment was created for the ODBMS for the top objects. This was because the tested ODBMS did not perform this by default, it was done to provide a more fair comparison. The advantages and disadvantages will be described later. This is the only operation where the transaction time (start and stop of a transaction) was not included.

Traverse Complex Objects

Since the KB-DSS application does not traverse the tree structure in the database itself, this operation has been implemented the same way for the RDBMS, as previously described. For the ODBMS, the data are traversed in the traditional way. To ensure that all attributes get accessed, every character and number is counted (rows and objects also). This ensures that the two different databases contain the same data. In other words, this operation does not compare the ODBMS traversal capability against the RDBMS traversal capability, but rather how fast can we place the related data (the complex object) into main memory before it is joined by the application (for the RDBMS case). The RDBMS at first glance should have an advantage here since all it does is transfer raw tables to the application. However, since it also has to create program variables to bind the rows that are returning, it is not that significant an advantage as maybe first assumed. To ensure that the rows become more effectively bound to the program variables, *array fetch* has been used in this process. A less effective way is to bind them one at a time. With the ODBMS, it is possible to access the instances directly during a tree traversal.

Copy Complex Objects

Since the traverse operation does not create a copy of a complex object in main memory, this operation was included. Due to lack of time, however, this operation was not implemented for the RDBMS, since it would not be an easy task to build a complex object in main memory. Additionally, such an operation is actually not necessary for an ODBMS, since it operates on the instances in the database directly. Another interesting problem arose when this operation was implemented, since the application did not use inheritance completely (recall it used a type table for some different object types in the database schema that could not be used in main memory). This was because there was a direct link to the type object in the "type table" (implemented as a class extent of type Dictionary). An extra transient attribute had to be implemented also because of this. This "transient" attribute would then receive a value instead of the pointer that was used in the database.

Inserts of Complex Objects

It was quickly apparent that this operation was arduous for the RDBMS compared to the ODBMS. This was one of the primary reasons why an ODBMS was interesting for the GeoX application in the first place. In the real application, each object is sent to the server as a string with the INSERT command. When many objects have to be inserted in this manner, there is a considerable client/server communications overhead. To see what could be done to optimize this procedure, sending more INSERT strings each time (several objects each time)[2] and using a stored procedure[3] were tested. For the string test, four ValueSerieFunctions were sent (in one long string) for each ValueSerie inserted, and each Distribution was inserted with a stored procedure.

The optimized insert procedure (both cases) was compared to a complete "one INSERT string at the time" operation. This can provide clues about how much such optimizing is worth. Since the ODBMS only uses six indexes and the RDBMS about 80 indexes, an interesting test would be to determine how much the indexing costs the RDBMS. Therefore, a special run was included where indexes for the RDBMS were removed with the optimized solution. The reason why there were so many indexes for the RDBMS is because of the nature of RDBMS. The Primary Key for the top object must be included in all subtables, each subtable needs extra attributes together with the Primary Key to uniquely identify each row, and then we have remaining Foreign Keys that are used. On top of this, some Candidate Keys also were implemented as indexes.

Deletes of Complex Objects

RDBMSs may support different ways to delete related rows. For example, the RDBMS product that the live gFullCycle system used at the time of these benchmarks supported DELETE CASCADE. The tested RDBMS, however, did not (only through triggers, but then all the implemented Foreign Keys would have to be removed instead), so the following ways were tested in advance, inside a stored procedure with an input parameter:

- Use of a cursor and a while loop
- Use of DELETE ...WHERE ... IN (SELECT ......) SQL expressions
- Use of a temp table and join

After several tests using different database sizes and 1–20 complex objects, method number 1 seemed to be the fastest. It was, for example, 1 second faster than method 2, when 20 complex objects were deleted at the same time. This could have changed if there were unique indexes on the main attribute in all tables (the attribute that represented one particular FiscalRegime, to which all subrows were related). An interesting result on these tests was that method number 3 was 30–50 ms faster than method 1 when the database contained only one complex object. This again can also be related to the missing unique indexes. The reason why extra indexes were not added was because of the insert results as we shall see later. The RDBMS had already too many in the first place, but the more important ones were used to uniquely identify each row in each table.

In the ODBMS there are at least two ways to delete all related objects: use each object destructor when traversing the tree structure or use the vendors CASCADE DELETE operation on their 1:1 and 1:m relationships. The latter was chosen since it appeared to be an effective way to delete complex objects. This assumption will be tested later, although one benefit was that some programming time was saved using this. An interesting remark from the vendor (that came later) was that they really did not recommend the use of these special relationships (which include the CASCADE DELETE functionality), since they felt that they were more of academic interest.

[2] This will be called tip #1.

[3] This will be called tip #2.

Updates of Complex Objects

Full results for this operation will not be presented here, because this operation produced similar results as the Delete first + then the Insert operation. However, the results are briefly mentioned since they confirm some of the assumptions regarding the delete operation.

Benchmark Considerations

In this section, we will discuss some general issues related to the database products used in the benchmark experiments, the configuration of the test environment, and so on.

The DBMSs Used

When undertaking performance benchmarks, the results will be dependent upon on which DBMSs have been used. Another important consideration is which kind of interface was used to interact with the DBMS. Because of vendor license agreements that prohibit publication of benchmarks results, the names of the DBMSs used in this chapter cannot be mentioned. The RDBMS used will be called RDBMS and the ODBMS used will be referred to as ODBMS. The versions that were tested are based on versions available in August 1998 and both are well-known commercial products.

The RDBMS was used with its own native C client/server interface, since the benchmark client was a C++ application. RDBMS has most of the relational database capabilities that we would expect from a commercial RDBMS. However, it did not have row-level locking at the time the benchmarks were run, and as mentioned earlier, it did not support CASCADE DELETE directly.

The ODBMS was used with its own C++ interface, which was not based on the ODMG standard [Catell 1997]. ODBMS is based on a page server architecture that locks at the page level. It is still possible to achieve object locking with the logical object clustering mechanism ODBMS offers.[4] It also transfers pages between the client and server, and the methods are run in the client memory space, not inside the server itself. Since it can be a disadvantage to run methods on the client for some operations (e.g., delete[5]), some of the tests ran the client program on the server to minimize client/server communication costs. Since RDBMS is server centric in nature, it was interesting to see how such tests influenced the results for ODBMS compared to RDBMS.

Test Environment

The test environment was based on a 10 Mbit Ethernet of UNIX servers and NT client PCs. This environment was not fully dedicated to the benchmark so to obtain equal load on the system for ODBMS and RDBMS, the tests were run when the load was low and stable. This was controlled with the UNIX system performance program Perfmeter v.3.6

---

[4] It had a maximum limit of 64 KB objects in the version tested.

[5] Then all the objects have to be transported over the network to the client before they can be deleted.

FCS. It should not be undervalued that the load on the system can influence the results, but since this KB-DSS application did not have many concurrent users the results should be fair. Another issue concerning this is that the tests were run in a single-user environment. The results that will be presented will, therefore, only give us an estimate of when there are several (but still few) concurrent users with a low load.

On the server side, both DBMSs were installed on a UNIX Sun Sparc 20 (clone) with four CPUs, 160MB RAM, 3 x 9GB disks, and with Sun Solaris 2.6. Both DBMS and databases were located on the same disk. ODBMS had a UNIX file-based[6] dynamic database size. It also had a dynamic log and write buffer.[7] ODBMS did not have a server cache like you normally would find in RDBMS. With RDBMS, the database and log have to be a fixed size, and this was set up with a 60MB database and 10MB log. The database for RDBMS was located on a UNIX raw device, which could give RDBMS a little advantage, but this was the setup at the institute where the benchmarks were being run. RDBMS was also set up with an 8MB server cache divided into 2KB buffer pools. Inside RDBMS it was possible to make different buffer pools sizes depending upon the kind of I/O. The default value is 2KB, but with more I/O, larger buffer pool sizes can be used (up to a maximum of 16KB). Even after several different query tests, larger buffer pools were not chosen by the DBMS so the 2KB buffer pools were kept.

On the client side, a Sun Sparc 10 (clone) was used with 1 CPU, 96MB RAM, and Sun Solaris 2.6. Only ODBMS had an 8MB client cache present because of the nature of ODBMS. To obtain access to this machine at off-peak periods (e.g., late at night or on weekends), a PPro 200 MHz with NT 4.0 was used with PC-Xware 5.0c. Using this, the client program could be run on the Sun Sparc 10 client in a UNIX window from this Windows machine. The introduction of this extra client should not have any real performance implications, since all it did was to send small strings back and forth to the UNIX client. Furthermore, the application itself was only a simple text-based one.

Warm and Cold Runs

When benchmarks involve caches, it is important to measure the differences when the caches are cold (are flushed completely) and warm (when the cache contain objects (pages)/rows that will be asked for). The comparison can make a significant difference in the reported results since it reduces I/O. So before each cold run all the caches were flushed by different techniques. Before each warm run the caches were filled several times with the objects/rows that were going to be involved in the runs. In the benchmarks, each cold/warm test was run five times, and each warm run for Open close operation, Pick top objects, and Traverse operation approximately 20–25[8] times. Five cold runs were chosen after it was evident that it produced no particular difference to run more tests, except for one run that is highlighted next. After the runs, the average with standard deviation was calculated.

---

[6] The vendor recommended a *raw device* that could provide a little performance advantage.

[7] To improve the write time on the server after a COMMIT.

[8] 5 * 5, and if some of them were influenced by the network, those were removed (down to 20 runs).

Database Considerations

In the KB-DSS application, the database would vary between 5MB up to 30MB. That is not very large when compared to many database systems today, but the complexity is still large. To see if there was any difference between the performance with different database sizes, 5MB was chosen as the small database (smaller than the caches) and 35MB (larger than the caches involved) as the large database.[9] To add even more complexity into to this procedure the tests were run with 1 and 20 complex objects, too: 1 and 20 top objects for the Pick top objects operation.

As pointed out by Hohenstein, Plesser, and Heller in *Evaluating the Performance of Object-Oriented Database Systems by Means of a Concrete Application* [Hohenstein 1997], object clustering can be an important performance factor for ODBMSs. The complex objects in ODBMS were not created in such object clusters because of the maximum 64KB limit it had. Since no changes were made to the complex objects after they were created, they were still clustered well on the disk before the operations were run. After a run of one specific operation, the database was deleted and created again.

Benchmarks Results

In this section, we will present and discuss the results obtained and draw some overall conclusions.

Database Sizes

The sizes of the databases are listed in Table 8.2. An empty database contains all its system components, the database schema, and space for data and indexes.

As stated, the database in ODBMS is smaller than in RDBMS for all three cases. This can be explained by the extra space RDBMS most likely creates in each table for later use and the extra rows/attributes the relational database contains.

Open and Close the Databases

The results for the open and close operation are listed in Table 8.3. The most important results from this table are presented in Figure 8.3. The results show that accessing the

Table 8.2   Database Sizes

	EMPTY DB	58CO[a] (SMALL DB)	423CO[a] (LARGE DB)
RDBMS	478KB	5MB	35MB
ODBMS	258KB	3.8MB	26MB

[a] Number of complex objects inserted with this database size.

[9] RDBMS sizes.

Table 8.3   Open and Close the Databases

IN [MS]		SMALL DATABASE				LARGE DATABASE			
		COLD RUN		WARM RUN		COLD RUN		WARM RUN	
		TIME	STD	TIME	STD	TIME	STD	STD	TIME
RDBMS	S	13.9	0.3	10.5	1.3	14.0	1.5	10.4	2.7
	C	604.7	7.9	246.6	7.7	618.5	38.1	244.3	6.3
	T	639.9	7.7	266.2	7.6	653.3	38.1	263.6	6.6
ODBMS	S	9.4	0.1	1.9	0.1	9.3	0.1	2.1	0.9
	1	476.3	15.3	96.2	2.0	488.1	9.3	106.2	3.3
	6	550.9	18.7	115.4	2.1	536.5	15.4	132.4	1.5
	C	926.8	4.1	145.4	8.2	984.3	11.3	208.3	3.9
	T	958.2	4.7	164.2	8.4	1018.2	12.7	230.4	4.4

StD   Standard deviation.

S   Only start and stop of the transaction.

1   Access of the main db root including the FiscalSetting segment.

6   Access of all the 6 db roots, including the main db root and segment.

C   Time before COMMIT will be taken.

T   Total time for the whole operation (= C + COMMIT time).

first db root is a demanding process for an open operation. It should be noted that it seems to be a progressive curve from the small to the large database, for ODBMS compared to RDBMS. Another interesting point seems to be that client cache for ODBMS

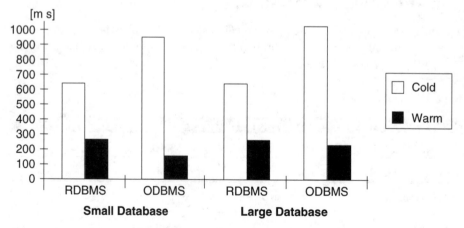

Figure 8.3   Open and close the databases.

has a better impact on the performance. That's not strange since the ODBMS can reduce the network activity this way.

Pick Top Objects

The results from the pick top operation are in Table 8.4, and the important results are presented in Figure 8.4. Again, from the figure can we see a more progressive curve for the ODBMS. When we know it is only 423 objects/rows in the top class extent collection (large database), something should be done to prevent this behavior. Still, we can see the advantage of having a client cache in the warm run, extra warm run, and the pick of 20 top objects. Of course it is bad practice to do 20 queries for 20 rows/objects, instead of one query for 20 rows/objects, but this example shows us the potential when several queries need to be run. Depending on what kind of ODBMS you are running, for some ODBMS it is possible to bring related objects together with the objects for which the query was meant. If the client needs those objects in the next query/traversal, those can then be retrieved quickly as shown here. All the top objects are located in the same segment, which is the reason for this fast performance. This could, however, lead to locking conflicts in a multi-user environment. Before the separate segment was created (could lead to no locking conflict), the time for picking 20 top objects in the small database was around 500 ms. This gives us a clue of the advantage and disadvantage in this picture. Let us now look at the more advanced database operations.

Traverse Complex Objects

In Table 8.5 and Figure 8.5 can we really measure the potential of ODBMS traversal and client cache capabilities. A positive sign for ODBMS is also its fairly stable performance from the small to the large database for both 1 and 20 complex object(s). Bearing in mind that it seems fairly expensive to access the main database root (more than 50 percent of the total traversal time) the results are impressive. As mentioned earlier, RDBMS does not have optimized indexes for this operation, which could

Table 8.4   Pick Top Objects

| IN [MS] | SMALL DATABASE | | | | LARGE DATABASE | | | | EXTRA | |
| | COLD RUN | | WARM RUN | | COLD RUN | | WARM RUN | | WARM RUN[x] | |
	TIME	STD	TIME	STD	TIME	STD	TIME	STD	TIME	STD
RDBMS 1to	40.6	3.1	8.1	0.4	41.4	5.4	8.4	0.5	8.8	0.2
ODBMS 1to	50.8	8.3	4.7	0.7	60.8	6.4	5.4	0.3	0.6	0.1
RDBMS 20to	200.4	7.5	161.3	5.6	194.7	28.5	159.4	4.2	158.9	5.7
ODBMS 20to	72.2	8.1	17.3	1.5	124.5	26.9	21.5	3.0	10.8	0.3

x   Runs the repetitions of the warm runs inside a transaction instead of outside.

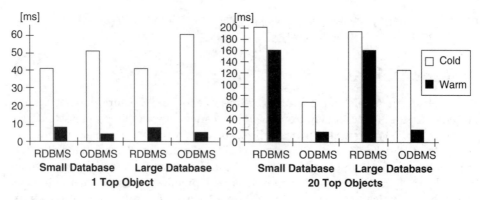

Figure 8.4 Pick top objects.

explain some of the results, but as we can see even a warm cache for RDBMS did not outperform ODBMS cold results.

Copy Complex Objects

Since this operation is implemented only for ODBMS it will be compared to the traversal operation for both DBMSs. Using this, we can measure how expensive it is to build the complex objects into main memory, too. A more fair comparison to RDBMS will then also be done since RDBMS actually creates memory variables for the returning rows in the traversal operation. In Table 8.6 we can find the results of this copy operation and the most important traversal operations times.

Table 8.5 Traverse Complex Objects

| IN [MS] | | SMALL DATABASE | | | | LARGE DATABASE | | | |
| | | COLD RUN | | WARM RUN | | COLD RUN | | WARM RUN | |
		TIME	STD	TIME	STD	TIME	STD	TIME	STD
RDBMS 1co	C	2551.3	69.3	1816.0	26.6	2639.0	47.1	1863.3	41.2
	T	2556.5	69.2	1821.1	26.7	2645.2	49.3	1868.6	41.4
ODBMS 1co	C	743.4	52.2	170.5	4.9	795.3	97.2	205.3	6.8
	T	755.9	51.6	177.6	4.6	810.4	98.1	214.6	6.9
RDBMS 20co	C	41297.9	230.7	36418.8	243.1	41533.6	316.1	37165.7	358.6
	T	41302.9	230.7	36423.8	243.1	41538.6	315.9	37170.9	538.6
ODBMS 20co	C	8217.2	215.0	2999.8	43.7	8530.0	337.2	3024.6	86.5
	T	8250.4	216.0	3024.2	44.1	8564.3	338.3	3052.8	87.5

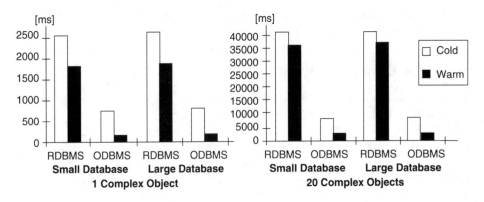

Figure 8.5 Traverse complex objects.

First of all, we can see that it's not particularly expensive to create complex objects into main memory as you traverse the structure in the database. For 1co, about 25 percent of the time is spent in creating the objects (small and large db) and about 35 percent of the time is spent in creating the objects for 20co (small and large db). When we compare the traversal results for RDBMS with ODBMS copy results, we still find that ODBMS is faster. Even if a little time is taken to build the complex objects from those raw tables that come from the server, ODBMS will still have an advantage in performance by a factor of

Table 8.6 Copy versus Traverse Complex Objects [x]

IN [MS]		SMALL DATABASE COLD RUN [z]		LARGE DATABASE COLD RUN [z]	
		TIME	**STD**	**TIME**	**STD**
RDBMS 1co [y]	T	2556.5	69.2	2645.2	49.3
ODBMS 1co [y]	T	755.9	51.6	810.4	98.1
ODBMS 1co	C	948.9	38.4	1096.4	130.0
	T	960.6	38.7	1112.3	133.1
RDBMS 20co [y]	T	41302.9	230.7	41538.6	315.9
ODBMS 20co [y]	T	8250.4	216.0	8564.3	338.3
ODBMS 20co	C	12892.3	333.7	12754.2	214.3
	T	12917.7	335.2	12782.1	215.7

x   A comparison between ODBMS copy operation and both DBMSs traversing operations.

y   The numbers come from Table 8.4 for both DBMSs.

z   Check Table 8.4 for the potential of a warm run.

at least three for the large database with 20co. Tests have shown that it took 20.7 ms to traverse those 1236 (1co) objects that this copy operation created.

Inserts of Complex Objects

The results from this insert operation can be found in Table 8.7. If we compare the values, RDBMS is challenged to insert all those rows. For the large database with 20co it is a 6.2 minutes difference, and that's about a 10-fold advantage for ODBMS. If we look at the 1co case, it is about a 7.6 times advantage, so we can assume we have a progressive curve here. However some of the difference can be explained by all the indexes within RDBMS. The TU times demonstrate this due to the difference of 9.4s (of 21.9s) between this special run with the normal run, in the large database for 1co. Another reason can be found indirectly on the COMMIT times. RDBMS has a very

Table 8.7   Inserts of Complex Objects

IN [MS]		SMALL DATABASE COLD RUN [z]		LARGE DATABASE COLD RUN [z]	
		TIME	STD	TIME	STD
RDBMS 1co[y]	TU	-	-	12501.3	207.4
	TT	-	-	19486.3	558.0
	T1	-	-	24158.3	364.3
	TS	-	-	25360.0	562.8
RDBMS 1co	C	21440.7	46.3	21871.1	322.5
	T	21456.8	46.4	21892.6	318.0
ODBMS 1co[y]	TT	-	-	2436.5	262.0
ODBMS 1co	C	2528.9	51.4	2361.5	115.7
	T	2799.6	50.3	2722.2	126.2
RDBMS 20co	C	412866.0	1943.3	410962.6	4880.5
	T	412888.2	1935.6	410979.8	4886.1
ODBMS 20co	C	34910.0	1587.4	35513.3	1427.3
	T	37185.9	1453.7	38073.2	1244.1

y   Runs that gives us a better picture of the situation.
z   Inserts should mostly be independent of a warm cache, but all caches have been flushed.
TU   Total time. Inserts without any indexes run on the client.
TT   Total time. Normal inserts, the client program run on the server.
T1   Total time. Inserts with tip #1 run on the client.
TS   Total time. Inserts of 1 and 1 row at a time in all tables on the client.

small COMMIT time because it has network overheads when the operation runs. This means when the COMMIT is sent from the client, the DBMS is well prepared.

For ODBMS the case is completely different since it has a client cache filled with objects before a COMMIT is sent. When a COMMIT is taken, the bundle of objects is sent over the network to the server. As we can see from the TT times, the network overhead for both DBMSs is around 10 percent of the total time,[10] with low network activity. Another reason why the RDBMS spends more time on this operation is the nature of ODBMS: It doesn't interpret the data types as RDBMS must do. From the optimized tips for RDBMS (see the section "Traverse Complex Objects") we can observe that we saved about 3.5s (T – TS). If we split those tips we save about 1.2s from tip #1 and 2.3s from tip #2. The technique that gave us the best results is hard to identify because of several factors, but if the whole operation was optimized like this we could save even more time.

When we compare the results (1326/46 objects/rows) with those found in A.E. Wade's *Hitting the Relational Wall* [Wade 1999], we actually find some similarities, even if they used two different kinds of DBMS systems, hardware, operation systems, and no network. On the run of 726 inserted parts (a tree of parts), the ODBMS used 1342 ms and the RDBMS used 15883 ms. On their run of 2184 inserted parts, the ODBMS used 2514 ms and the RDBMS used 46617. The similarities are apparent.

Deletes of Complex Objects

Until now the ODBMS has shown strengths, but if we evaluate the numbers in Table 8.8 and the values presented in Figure 8.6, we can see that this picture is different. Now suddenly RDBMS leads "surprisingly" by a factor of 2 for the large database for both 1 and 20co. This was interesting. Even with a warm cache and having the client program run on the server (TT) the performance of ODBMS didn't improve much—RDBMS was still faster. If we study the table more closely we find that the standard deviation for ODBMS is fair-sized in the large database for 1co. This also was noticed in the pretests that were run in advance. During an investigation of these runs it was clear that around each sixth run the transportation of pages from the server increases, both for warm and cold runs. After this was noticed, the number of runs for this special case was raised from 5 to 11. The last six runs were run in a new day with a new database and the same happened—one of the results was pretty slow compared to the other ones. They were approximately three times larger than the corrected values (TC times), where those two runs have been removed. Why this didn't happen to 20co in the large database is hard to determine, but it could have something to do with the large transportation of objects it had anyway. Recall that this ODBMS has to transport all its objects to the client before they can be deleted. As we can see, we don't save much time (compare TT and TC) if the client program is run on the server without any network traffic. Notice that we didn't receive any large standard deviation then. The main reason for the server suddenly to send many additional pages to the client was never found. One possible reason could have been that small portions of complex objects were spread together with other complex objects. When this happened, one or more

---

[10] Actually, RDBMS experienced a little network activity; the strings are sent from the server to the first switch box on the network and then returned to the server again. It was not possible to avoid this with the setup of RDBMS.

Table 8.8   Deletes of Complex Objects

IN [MS]			SMALL DATABASE				LARGE DATABASE			
			COLD RUN		WARM RUN		COLD RUN		WARM RUN	
			TIME	STD	TIME	STD	TIME	STD	TIME	STD
RDBMS 1co [x]	TT		-	-	-	-	1639.2	81.8	798.0	37.7
RDBMS 1co	C		1472.2	80.7	685.8	24.5	1441.0	215.4	703.3	10.0
	T		1616.9	86.7	742.7	24.4	1562.0	228.8	764.4	8.1
ODBMS 1co [x]	TT		-	-	-	-	2672.1	258.6	1973.8	100.9
	TC		-	-	-	-	2832.8	327.1	2340.9	376.9
ODBMS 1co	C		2042.7	47.0	1444.2	41.5	3384.4	1985.9	2747.7	1795.4
	T		2318.1	37.3	1718.6	43.9	3761.9	*1994.7*	3181.5	*1815.8*
RDBMS 20co	C		18183.9	857.8	12940.6	783.5	18074.9	1817.7	12558.8	210.7
	T		19882.4	670.7	14543.1	410.6	19843.6	1316.2	14998.1	437.8
ODBMS 20co	C		31216.5	440.7	26956.3	101.6	37725.3	402.1	32793.2	156.4
	T		33300.2	433.1	29025.0	142.6	40168.1	482.9	35117.6	173.0

x   Inserts should mostly be independent of a warm cache, but all caches has been flushed.

TT   Total time. Normal inserts, the client program run on the server.

TC   Corrected total time. Normal delete after removing two of the runs that have a large variance because of bad design.

extra complex object was also transported to the client. Additionally the cause may be from the segment that was created for those top FiscalSetting objects. If we compare the COMMIT times between the two DBMSs, it is interesting to notice that RDBMS has a faster commit than ODBMS in most cases. This is impressive since RDBMS also has to update many more indexes than does ODBMS.

There could be several reasons for the poor performance of ODBMS. First of all, RDBMS does have an advantage, since all the client program does is send one call[11] (the name of the top row) to the server and ask it to use its stored procedure and delete all the related rows. RDBMS has been developed for set operations, and when it can work with *set-at-a-time* it can be very effective. For deleting 1co the SQL command DELETE has

---

[11] 20 calls for 20co.

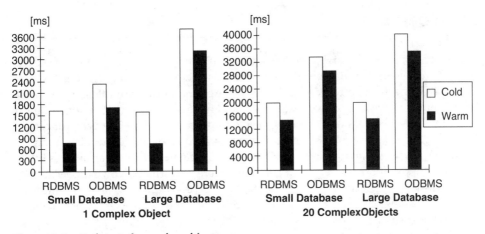

Figure 8.6 Deletes of complex objects.

been called only 47 times[12] for RDBMS. ODBMS has to traverse the structure and call the object's destructor 1326 times for one 1co. That doesn't seem effective compared to RDBMS. One reason why it is slow could have been the use of the vendor bidirectional relationships that were used. Recall that they included CASCADE DELETE functionality. It would have been interesting to create "traverse when you delete" methods instead and see if that could have improved the performance. The CASCADE DELETE performance of ODBMS was tested on main memory complex objects too (the ones the Copy operation created). For 1co it took about 360 ms and for 20co it took about 7200 ms. That is only about half of the time for the RDBMS, with a warm cache. So even in main memory this CASCADE DELETE (reference-integrity) functionality seems expensive.

For the insert operation we saw that our benchmark had similar results as reported in A.E. Wade, *Hitting the Relational Wall* [Wade 1998]. This is not the case for this delete operation. When they deleted 804 parts it took 6490 ms for the ODBMS and 18737 ms for the RDBMS. When they deleted 2412 parts it took 9964 ms for the ODBMS and 56000 ms for the RDBMS. In this benchmark, every third part in the tree that was a leaf object/row was deleted. Finding all those leaf nodes seems to be expensive, but why this steeper curve for the RDBMS? The answer may lie in the *set-at-a-time* data manipulation advantage a RDBMS has, which couldn't be used properly here.

Updates of Complex Objects

As mentioned earlier, this operation was not included since similar results could be obtained from the insert + delete operations, except for one case. In this exception, the problem with a large standard deviation for 20co in the large database was most apparent. This confirmed the assumption that the physical design of the database in ODBMS could have been improved. For 20co in the large database the standard deviation was around 10s of the 80s total for the complete operation.

[12] 5 loops (5 FiscalRegimes) for all nontype tables below FiscalRegime (5*9=45) + 2 for Fiscal-Regime and FiscalSetting.

Conclusion

Doing a benchmark for a given application is a difficult and time-consuming task. The reported results in this chapter are based on this author's first-time experiences with an ODBMS, and are, of course, related to how the operations were implemented. There are, of course, ways to improve them that could have led to different results. In most cases, the DBMS servers were used with standard set-up values. The value of tuning should not be underestimated. The benchmarks described here used fairly complex structures, and it was important that these were implemented as close as possible to the actual application before any adjustments were performed. However because of time pressures, little time was spent on exploring enhancements. Have in mind that n:m relationships have not been used in the tested complex objects, which actually could have given the ODBMS an extra advantage.

This chapter has shown that even if the ODBMS tested here were faster in some areas, the RDBMS also produced some good results. In particular, the RDBMSs delete capabilities were impressive, compared to the ODBMS. This was related to how complex objects were deleted. As long as the RDBMS can perform its work inside the DBMS server, and the ODBMS needs to transport all the related objects to the client and then delete them as they are traversed, it is not strange that the RDBMS can outperform the ODBMS. RDBMSs are optimized for set operations, and the delete comparison benchmark showed us exactly this. It is important to mention that it would have been interesting to test a manual method to CASCADE DELETE the related objects for the ODBMS, since the vendor did not recommend using their predefined bidirectional relationships. On the other hand we have seen the advantages that an ODBMS client cache can provide. A client cache is a powerful enhancement to reduce network activity and bring related objects closer to the client application.

The delete and update operations have also shown us how important physical design is for the ODBMS that was tested, even for relatively small databases. Some of the results have also shown a more increasing curve for the ODBMS when advancing from a small to large database. The RDBMS has been more stable in this situation. This is an important issue, particularly for developers with a strong programming background and without experience of physical database design.

CHAPTER 9

Object Databases and Java
Architectural Issues

Performance is an important success factor for most applications and databases. Using Java and an object database is no exception. In this chapter we will discuss a number of architectural issues that influence performance, both internally in an Object Database Management System (ODBMS) and its Java language binding. We will take a closer look at the importance of transfer units and caching strategies, locking and lock-models, flexibility of the ODBMS and its language binding, clustering, notification models, schema evolution, translation of pointers in the Java language binding, and a number of other interesting issues. The chapter is based on the authors' personal experience using one such commercial system. A developer should be aware of these issues, to prevent or minimize performance problems related to an ODBMS's architecture and its Java language binding.

ODBMS Architecture

The architectures of ODBMSs are fundamentally different from those of conventional relational and object-relational DBMSs. The ORDBMSs and RDBMSs send SQL queries to the server and receive a status and some records of data (optionally, if the query executed and returned data). All processing of queries is done by the server, as well as transaction processing, recovery, and so on. On the other hand, in many ODBMSs, the client plays a much greater role. Data are shipped between server and client, and the client performs much of the ODBMSs' processing (sometimes including query processing), as well as application processing. Other conceptual differences exist as well. For example, RDBMSs are based on the relational model first described by Codd [Codd 1970], whereas ODBMSs lack this commonly agreed model (recognized by many researchers, for example, [Atkinson 1989]; [TM-Lang uage 1996]; and [Cattell 1997]).

Object, Page, and File Servers

ODBMSs have originated from completely different camps through history, and the origination has affected the actual design of the database engines. Three major camps exist:

- Computer-Aided Design (CAD) and Computer-Aided Manufacturing (CAM)
- Programming language
- Database

None of the conceptual designs being presented should be considered superior: The most effective solution depends on the environment in which it runs, the application domain, and the applications used. Figure 9.1 shows conceptual designs of the ODBMS servers from the different camps. The gray regions mark elements of the ODBMS.

Object-servers have been developed from a database point of view, and accordingly the server parts of the ODBMSs are conceptually different than those originating from the other camps. The database camp wanted to create a professional object-oriented database system with object-oriented properties for handling complex objects and structures as found in Office Information Systems and other systems with similar requirements. Vendors having their origin in this camp include Versant, Itasca, and Poet, among others. In the object-server, the client application, and the server exchange objects, methods may be run at the client side or at the server side,[1] and concurrency control is done by the server on the server side.

Page servers originated from the programming language camp. This camp was in need of an object-oriented database to support them in the development of applications. Traditional DBMSs were not adequate for this purpose. ODBMSs originating from this camp include ObjectStore (Object Design), O_2 (Ardent), ONTOS, and GemStone. The page server exchanges pages of data (containing objects), methods are run on clients only,[2] queries are run on clients, and they support distributed concurrency control.

File servers originated from the CAD/CAM camp. A need to be able to handle complex data and structures was the driving force—no traditional databases were able to deliver with acceptable performance and concurrency control. In this camp, Objectivity has been the major contributor. The file server is actually a special kind of page server, with one major difference—in a file server you are not able to request a page and lock a page in the same message.

Performance Issues

Database systems should offer good performance to the application. To accomplish this, different kinds of optimizations and adaptations have to be performed. This section presents some of the most important issues related to performance of an ODBMS in this context.

[1] An object server may execute methods on the server side, but this is not a requirement.

[2] Some page servers can run methods on the server as well.

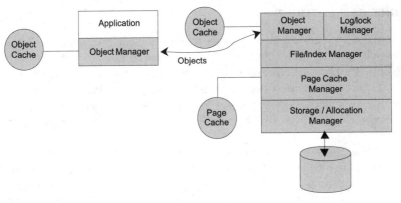

a) Object Server Architecture

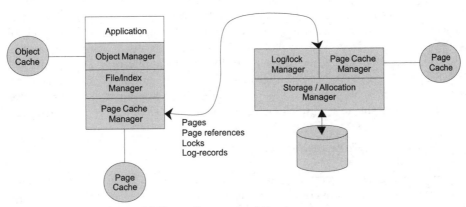

b) Page Server Architecture

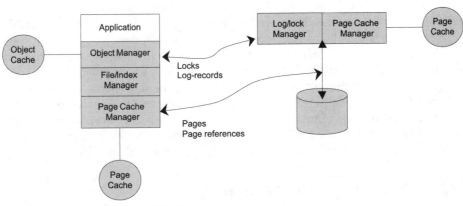

c) File Server Architecture

Figure 9.1 Examples of Object DBMS architecture.

Figures 9.1 a, b, and c appear in a slightly different version in DeWitt et al. [DeWitt 1990]. The copyrighted figures are used with permission of the VLDB Endowment. Other versions of these figures exists as well, e.g. in Manola [Manola 1994].

Transfer Units and Caching

The different kinds of servers exchange information with the client differently. Object servers exchange objects, and each object usually is transferred as a separate network package. If the objects exchanged are smaller than a page, an object server will use the communication channel heavier than a page or file server. On the other hand, if the objects span more than one page, the object server will transfer fewer packages than the page server, thus the page/file server will use the communication channel more heavily than the object server.

When an ODBMS accesses the disk, it will, as all other systems using disks, access one or more pages of the file system. The size of a page may vary, but is equal for all pages on a disk. When reading a page from disk, the page may contain several objects. An object-server would have both a page cache and an object cache on the server side, whereas a page or file server usually contains only a page cache (the object cache is bound to the client application). Figure 9.1 gives an overview of the different caches.

The difference in transfer units results in another difference between the ODBMSs. A client application connected to an object server is thinner than an identical client using a page or file server. The client of an object server contains an object cache and an object manager that manage the cache, in addition to the application. This is sufficient since the client and the server exchange objects. The page and file clients on the other hand, receive and send pages (and files). Accordingly, they need additional packages in the client to be able to separate the objects from the pages or files being exchanged.

Locking and Lock Models

The object server locks objects, the page server locks pages, and the file server usually locks containers (collections) of objects. Page and container locking may lock several objects, which may cause degradation of performance, forcing other transactions to wait for a lock to be released. On the other hand, if a reasonably good clustering or organization of objects is present and the applications take this into account, the probability of such situations can be reduced. At least one ODBMS has solved this problem by integrating a kind of hybrid functionality into the lock system. O_2 initially locks on page level, but if a page is locked by one client, and some other client requests an object (not locked by the first client) resident on the same page, the page lock is converted into object–locks, and the object is transferred to the requesting client.

Some ODBMSs support different kinds of locks and lock models. For example, Versant locks objects, but offers two different types of locks—hard and soft—in addition to custom lock models. Hard locks are held while some application accesses an object; soft locks enable other sessions to read and possibly alter the locked object [Anfindsen 1999].

Object Clustering (Physical Clustering)

Object clustering refers to the physical layout and organization in the database. Object clustering can be based on information provided by the application (to optimize transfer), by cluster settings (to optimize disk I/O), or by configuration parameters based on empirical information (may optimize both disk I/O and transfer). Chang [Chang 1989] found that performance could be increased by a factor of three for some CAD applications if an optimal clustering technique was applied. Object clustering is related to physical layout (it is by some vendors referred to as physical clustering as opposed to logical clustering). Object clustering can actually be performed in many different ways in an ODBMS [Chang 1989].

Generally, only one of the clustering types mentioned in Table 9.1 is applicable, but if the rules for clustering do not conflict, several clustering rules may be followed. The list in Table 9.1 uses the term *physically close* to indicate the organization of the storage. The organization usually takes one of two forms:

Pages. Objects are clustered according to the smallest physical unit read from disk. This is by far the most common technique.

Segments. Objects may be clustered in larger units; for example, when the user is able to specify a meaningful logical grouping or segmentation.

The largest performance gains are generally offered by page clustering, since pages are the unit of access from the disk. Another important observation is that if an object server is used (having an object as transfer unit) object clustering will primarily speed up performance on the server, not necessarily the client, since network transport is far slower than disk I/Os.

Object clustering usually focuses on optimizing a defined access pattern to data. This access pattern may of course change as the application and database undergo development. You should be aware that some ODBMSs are capable of changing the clustering strategy on the fly (with data in the database); still other ODBMSs require that the clustering strategy must be defined initially, before populating data into the database.

Logical Clustering

Logical clustering is related to where data are stored in a distributed environment (locality on servers). In such an environment, data are physically distributed between

Table 9.1 Clustering Schemes in ODBMSs

CLUSTERING STRATEGY	DESCRIPTION
Composite objects	If an object is part of another object (composite) it will be stored physically close to its owner.
References	Objects are stored physically close to each other based on relationships.
Object types	All objects of the same type are stored physically close to each other.
Indexes	Objects are stored physically close to each other based on a predefined index on an object's attributes.
Custom	Clustering is defined "on-the-fly"; for example, an existing object can be passed as a parameter to a new object, indicating that the new object should be stored physically close to the object passed as a parameter.

different servers, the network speed and bandwidth varies, and all users want optimal performance for their applications. Having data physically close to the consumer application is one way of providing better performance. This is, however, quite complicated to achieve, but some ODBMSs are capable of recognizing locality of objects. Versant is an example of such an ODBMS [Versant 1998]. Logical clustering is often combined with replication to ensure good performance and high availability.

Active and Passive Servers

Some ODBMSs can execute methods on both the client and the server side. These servers store the implementation of methods for a class in the database, and are labeled *active* servers, as opposed to *passive* servers, which are dependent on the application to support the methods for a class. An ODBMS that has an active server may reduce network traffic (e.g., when scanning through a collection of objects, the objects do not need to be transferred to the client to be processed). On the other hand, the processing of methods on the server side causes the server to work harder. The difference in performance of the two approaches becomes apparent when considering what happens when a large number of objects (e.g., 5–10,000) are traversed. The active server can process the objects on the server, not transferring the objects to the client, whereas the passive server has to get all the objects transferred to the client for processing.

Constraints

An object that is stored in the database may be subject to a number of constraints. It may be constraints regarding value of entered data (data integrity) or constraints regarding logical consistency (e.g., referential integrity) of an object and its collaborators, and so on. The constraints may be part of the data model in the object database, the client application, or invoked by the client application or the server automatically or manually. We generally separate these two types of constraints: data integrity and similar simple constraints that can be implemented in the data model directly (controlled by the ODBMS); and other constraints, usually related to logical consistency, based on a *notification model*. Simple constraints may also be included as a part of an application. The locality of these constraints may have some effects. It is usually more convenient to have the constraints as a part of the data model. This is due partly to simplicity (the constraints are defined in the database, and all changes to the objects from all applications are subject to identical constraints), and partly due to performance (optimized and centralized processing).

Notification Models

When an object changes its state in the database (either by locking or some other database event), there are two choices, shown in Table 9.2.

Both notification models will have an impact on performance. The utilization of the available notification model should be based on the need of notifications in the runtime environment of the application and on the logical constraints needed by the application and the data model (e.g., data integrity, referential integrity, business rules

Table 9.2   Active and Passive Notification Models

NOTIFICATION MODEL	DESCRIPTION
Passive	The ODBMS does not inform the application of the change. The application running has to query the database for information about the change.
Active	Application routines are invoked automatically as a result of some object being updated (change of state) or some other database event. An active notification model is similar to database triggers and constraint systems.

related to application domain, etc.). Active notification models may improve performance only in some cases.

For example, in a large print shop (printing books), they have a production system based on an ODBMS. A single book contains a cover, a number of pages of equal size and quality (predefined), and of course detailed printing information. However, this print shop is a little different than most print shops; they only print books on demand, and they are fully automated. Furthermore, all customers may request books online, and they receive information on the progress of the order frequently. A number of different situations may occur in a production system, and if a passive notification model were used in the ODBMS, all the programs controlling the production line would have to report the print progress to the customers. On the other hand, if the ODBMS supported active notification, the programs controlling the production line only report status to the ODBMS, and the ODBMS reports the print progress to the customers. In such an environment, the programs controlling the production line need to have reasonably good performance to be able to control the production line. By using an active notification model, one possible bottleneck is removed from the application context to the ODBMS. This, of course, has an impact on the performance of the ODBMS as well.

Schema Evolution

Applications that use ODBMSs change just as often as other applications, but due to the close relationship between the object model of the application and of the database, these changes have to be controlled differently than in a RDBMS or ORDBMS. For example, attributes may be added or removed from a class, methods may be removed or added to a class, the signature of a method may be changed, implementation of a method may change, and so on. All of these changes have to be reflected in the application and the database. Table 9.3 gives an overview of the most common conversion[3] strategies.

In an ODBMS these changes have an impact on the database schema as well as the objects in the database. None of the changes should make the database unavailable. The different ODBMSs handle these situations differently, and all of the solutions either have an impact on performance or on availability.

Emulation will degrade performance since all interaction with old instances is performed via a set of filters, supporting the new-style operations on the old-style data

---

[3] Some vendors use the term "transformation" instead of "conversion."

Table 9.3   Schema Evolution Conversion Strategies

CONVERSION STRATEGY	DESCRIPTION
Emulation	All interaction with old instances is performed via a set of filters, which supports the new-style operations on the old-style data format. Under this scheme all data associated with the old type is retained, and the filter functions are masking their presence to the programmer. This makes it possible to run old versions of the applications towards old instances of the data [Skarra 1987].
Eager conversion	Write and execute a one-time program that iterates over all instances of the old types in the system, converting them into instances of the new types using some user-specified constructor.
Lazy conversion	Whenever an old instance is found, automatically convert it to a new instance. If this is done when an old object is read it would make read operations much more expensive. It also requires that all changes to the data model include default values for old instances of a previous schema.

format. Eager conversion will not degrade performance, but some objects may be unavailable due to differences in versions between the class defined for the objects and the objects themselves during the conversion. Another, and possibly more convenient, approach in this context is to unload the database or class, change the definitions, and reload the data again. Finally, using lazy conversion will also degrade performance because whenever an old instance is found, it will automatically be converted to a new instance, and stored. Ferrandina et al. [Ferrandina 1995] gives an overview on how schema evolution is handled in the O_2 object database, supporting both lazy and eager conversion.

Indexing

As in relational and object-relational databases, object-oriented databases can create indexes on a collection of data. Indexes in object databases have other properties than their counterparts in RDBMSs and ORDBMSs though; they usually refer to all instances of classes inheriting from a class that is indexed. Indexes are used during lookup in collections or to optimize some kind of query in the database. The maintenance of indexes involves some overhead to the insert, update, and delete operations. Some ODBMSs do not support unique indexing; others support only indexing on single attributes [Anfindsen 1999]. Other indexing schemes may be supported as well. For example, ObjectStore and Jasmine support path indexing (an indexing scheme that may optimize access to certain predefined relations between objects).

Tuning Opportunities

ODBMSs and ODBMS applications can be tuned. The tuning parameters focus on different aspects of the different tuning targets. The tuning parameters may address sizes related to buffers in the client, the server, and how the client and the server interact with each other. For example, in the server it is usually possible to configure an initial heap size, how the heap should increase its size, the size of the page or object cache (if an object server), the number of cached user-defined classes, lock timeouts, the maximum number of concurrent transactions, users, and so on. Often the size of one parameter is dependent on another. Tuning the various components, and how they interact, is often both complex and time consuming. Fortunately, most ODBMSs offer a number of utilities that help the Database Administrator (DBA) with these tasks. These utilities usually include tools for collection of information on how objects are accessed, hit rates, and so on, which may help the DBA create the best possible indexing or cluster settings. Other utilities may collect information (snapshots and/or statistics) related to other parts of the ODBMS (e.g., logging, locking, cache coherence, etc.). Some ODBMSs even include tools for analyzing the information generated by such utilities.

Tuning an ODBMS requires knowledge about the run-time environment (both client and server, and distribution if present), the data models, the application, the ODBMS and its tuning options, and to some extent, the application domain (e.g., access patterns). Another important aspect is to have real amounts of data. Only then can we expect to successfully tune the ODBMS and its database, optimizing performance.

Transaction Models

Some ODBMSs support several kinds of transaction models. For example, Versant supports short transactions with the traditional ACID properties [Härder 1983], long transactions, and closed nested transactions. It is also possible to create your own lock models (optionally relaxing the ACID properties), or to use an optimistic locking scheme (timestamp ordering) instead of the traditional two-phase locking [Danielsen 1999].

Nested transactions may be implemented using several threads, which again may improve the performance of the transaction. On the other hand, programming nested transactions are more complex than the traditional short and flat transactions. Using an optimistic locking scheme postpones the concurrency problems until commit-time, which in some cases may improve performance.

Some applications and domains may enjoy the benefits of different transaction models, both related to functionality and to performance. We should carefully consider whether the targeted application (and domain) requires such transactional properties.

Multithreaded Database Clients

Support for multithreaded database clients is important in multitier systems. In such systems a server (e.g., CORBA server) in the middle tier handles a number of different clients (CORBA clients). The CORBA server acts as a single database client to the database. To avoid blocking of the different CORBA clients due to concurrent requests issued by different CORBA clients, the ODBMS should support multithreaded clients.

However, currently not all ODBMSs support multithreaded databases clients. Examples of ODBMSs that support multithreaded clients are Versant, Jasmine, and Objectivity.

Storage Reclamation

Data are inserted, changed, and deleted in a database as time goes by, resulting in unused or unreferenced pages. These kinds of pages may be reclaimed by the database system using some kind of reclaiming strategy. The strategy chosen by different ODBMSs differ, but generally two approaches are used:

Explicit reclamation. The DBA of the ODBMS will make the system unavailable, and explicitly perform some kind of reclamation procedure restructuring the database; that is, a kind of offline garbage collection in the store or database.

Implicit reclamation. The reclamation process is performed by the ODBMS at run time, preferably when the ODBMS is not used, and as a background activity. This kind of reclamation strategy may in some cases result in performance hiccups (temporary degradation of performance). This represents a kind of online garbage collection in the store or database.

Inaccessible pages may degrade performance by forcing the ODBMS to perform disk I/Os that do not return data, and if the database does not reclaim these pages, the database files will continuously increase in size and performance will be degraded.

Java Language Binding

Offering persistence to objects in Java may be done in a number of ways. For example, a class may inherit persistence capabilities from a predefined persistent class. The object instantiated from this class may either be persistent or transient, but the operation of moving the data between transient and persistent areas must be performed explicitly [Lausen 1997]. This principle is generally known as *persistence-by-inheritance*. Another way of offering persistence to an object is to let the object obtain its persistent capabilities when instantiated. This principle is generally known as *persistence-by-instantiation*. A third way, and the most intriguing solution as well for Java, is to make an object persistent if the object is reachable (using object references) from another persistent object. This is generally referred to as *persistence-by-reachability*.

In this section, we will focus on the Java language binding defined by the Object Data Management Group (ODMG) in *The Object Database Standard: ODMG 2.0* [Cattell 1997], and how it may be implemented. ODMG defines the design principle of the binding as follows:

"The ODMG Java binding is based on one fundamental principle: the programmer should perceive the binding as a single language for expressing both database and programming operations, not two separate languages with arbitrary boundaries between them." *[Cattell 1997]*

Thus, all ODBMSs claiming ODMG-compliance of their Java language binding supports this binding based on the persistence-by-reachability paradigm outlined earlier.

Implementing Persistence

Implementing the persistence-by-reachability paradigm into the Java language binding of an ODBMS requires that the extra code needed to make objects persistent has to be inserted into the source or byte code of the program. The process of inserting the extra code may be done before compilation of the Java source using some kind of preprocessing, or after the Java-source has been compiled, by analyzing the byte code generated by the compiler and inserting other byte code sequences to perform transactional controls and database operations. The result of either strategy (pre- or postprocessing) is byte code that would make the program run only on those platforms that support the defined transactional and database framework. Another possibility would be to modify an existing Java Virtual Machine (JVM). This latter approach is taken mostly by research projects, for example, PJama—a type-safe, object-oriented, orthogonally persistent programming language based on Java [Atkinson 1996].

Some ODBMSs do not support Java's object model directly in the database. Instead, the database includes an internal object model. One of the major causes for this situation is related to the difference in the internal representation of an object and the difference in the type and run-time systems of the different programming languages supported by an ODBMS. For example, both Java and C++ have their own Date class, but they do not have identical properties. For a Date object created in Java to be interpreted correctly by a C++ application, the ODBMS has to ensure that the state of the object is preserved in such a manner that both languages may access the object and interpret its contents correctly. The easiest solution to this problem is for the ODBMS to store the object using its own data model and to translate the object to the correct representation when retrieved from a C++ or Java application. Another option would be, of course, to ensure that all objects that are accessed from different programming languages used the ODBMSs data model instead. The latter approach would still comply with the ODMG's statement earlier, and might improve performance of the application in question.

Translation of Pointers

Every persistent object in an ODBMS has a unique identifier. The identifier is usually some kind logical reference (logical object ID) to the physical location of the object. When a client application accesses such an object, this logical reference is used to read in the object from the database into the client. The identifier then usually is converted from its external form (logical object ID) to an internal form of the actual programming language (direct memory pointer). This operation is known as *pointer swizzling* [Moss 1992], or just *swizzling*. The basic trade-off in swizzling is obvious: the conversion costs something up front (and at the end of the program, to convert direct memory pointers back to logical object IDs), but saves a little each time a reference is followed. The trade-offs in swizzling give rise to two different schemes:

   Eager swizzling. Whenever a pointer to a persistent object is swizzled, all pointers to objects referenced from this object are (optionally read from the database, dependent on implementation) swizzled as well (if not already read and swizzled).

Lazy swizzling. Objects are swizzled only when their reference is accessed (if not already swizzled).

Consequently, if eager swizzling is used, whenever a persistent object is referenced, all objects contained (e.g., in an array) within the object referenced will be read in and swizzled. This kind of swizzling takes time, but if most of the contained objects are accessed, this may be a good approach. On the other hand, if only a few of the contained objects are accessed, lazy swizzling may be a far better approach.

Another aspect of swizzling is whether or not a swizzled pointer can refer to an object that is not main memory resident. This gives rise to two other swizzling related schemes; indirect and direct swizzling [Kemper 1993]:

Direct swizzling. Direct swizzling places the in-memory address of the referenced persistent object directly in the swizzled pointer itself. As a consequence, direct swizzling is concerned only with objects being main memory resident.

Indirect swizzling. When indirect swizzling is used, the reference to the persistent object is replaced by a pointer to some intermediate data object (usually called fault block) that points to the targeted object when it is in memory.

Consequently, the direct swizzling scheme is faster than the indirect swizzling scheme because no extra overhead is added concerning maintenance of fault blocks and the extra level of indirection. On the other hand, indirect swizzling is more flexible, which may improve performance. For example, the indirect approach makes it easier to support incremental uncaching of objects (instead of unswizzling all pointers that reference an object, only the fault block is set to null). This is exemplified by Figure 9.2(a) and (b), where solid lines indicate references based on direct memory pointers and dashed lines indicate inter-object references (the figure does not show cells related to chaining of the hash table). In Figure 9.2(a), *object 4* may be removed from main memory without updating the references to it in the other objects (an update of *object 4's* descriptor is sufficient). In Figure 9.2(b), the *Reverse Reference List* (RRL in the figure) has to be traversed to update the references to *object 4* in other objects (indicated in Figure 9.2(b) as dotted lines).

Eager/lazy swizzling may be combined with the indirect/direct swizzling, which together constitute the four main schemes of swizzling (eager direct swizzling, eager indirect swizzling, lazy direct swizzling, and lazy indirect swizzling). Not surprisingly, a number of other swizzling techniques exist; for example, Texas uses swizzling at page-fault time [Singhal 1992]. White gives an overview of the different dimensions and techniques of pointer swizzling as well as a performance study of some of the techniques [White 1994].

Suppose that a language binding does not use swizzling to translate object identifiers between their external form (logical object identity—LOID) and the internal form used in a programming language (OID). Instead it uses a hashed table (Figure 9.2(c)) that keeps an entry for each LOID being used. The hashed table is part of the client cache. Each entry in the table keeps information about the object; for example, the memory address of the object, if the object is dirty, and so on. A pointer to an object in the client cache would be nothing else but a pointer into the hashed table, and consequently no hashing is required when referencing an object, but one additional dereference is necessary to get to the physical address of the object.

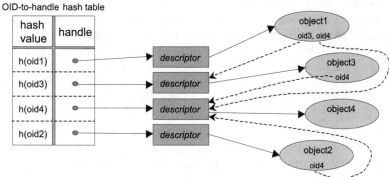

a) References between objects using indirect swizzling

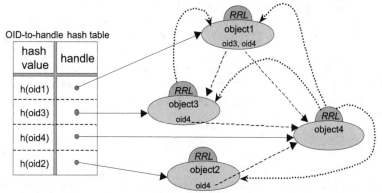

b) References between objects using direct swizzling (requiring all objects in memory)

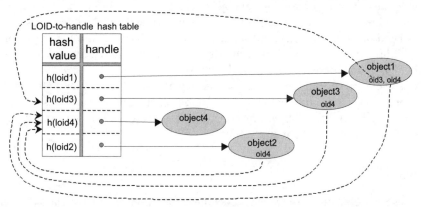

c) References between objects using a hash table for lookup (no swizzling)

Figure 9.2 Techniques for referencing persistent objects: indirect swizzling, direct swizzling, and no swizzling, using a hash table.

Solid lines symbolize references based on direct memory pointers, dashed lines shows inter-object references, and dotted lines show inter-object references maintained by the reverse reference list (RRL).

When developing applications for use against an ODBMS, the developers should know which mechanisms the language binding makes use of for translation between the logical object IDs (persistent identifiers) and object references in the programming language. This is important since the language binding of the ODBMS in question predefines the scheme used for translation. For example, Versant uses a technique similar to the hash-table lookup in Figure 9.2(c) [Apostrophe 1996], as does Objectivity [Objectivity 1998]. Texas, on the other hand, uses a swizzling technique closely related to lazy indirect swizzling (but based on page faults instead of object faults).

Choosing the wrong application design may influence performance. For example, if the language binding uses an eager swizzling scheme, and the application being developed uses a number of arrays, the application may experience performance problems, especially if only a few of the objects are used in the array each time the array is accessed by the application. This is due to the incompatibility between the principles of eager swizzling (for an array; swizzle in all objects referenced by the array) and the application design (accesses only a few of the objects in the array). Consequently a number of objects not used by the client application are transferred and swizzled in the client, but never used.

Programmers should be aware of the swizzling scheme, or lack of such, used in an ODBMS to avoid possible performance penalties due to the technique applied for translation between logical object ids in the database and object references in Java.

Client Overhead

An object in Java has no persistence capabilities on its own (other than serialization). However in an ODBMS application, persistence capabilities are added to the object either by post- or preprocessing the source or byte code. The objects that are read from or written to the database contain logical object–references; the objects in a Java application contain in-memory pointers as references. Consequently, these references have to be translated between the two representations (e.g., swizzled). Another important aspect of reading and writing objects to the store is the transactional framework used during the operation. These issues may influence performance.

ODBMSs use different implementations, but they all base their implementation on the use of proxy objects or other helper objects (or both), or similar techniques. This, of course, has an impact on the memory consumption of an application, and consequently performance of the client application.

Libraries

ODMG does not define how a Java class becomes a persistence-capable class [Cattell 1997]. Additionally, ODMG has its own object model, different to both Java and the ODBMSs. To support the ODMG data–model, a number of design choices have been made by the ODBMS vendors.

It is quite obvious that an ODBMS has to offer some kind of low-level interface to support a Java binding. This low-level package must include a number of ODBMS-interfacing classes, such as conversion classes (between the representation offered by the ODBMS and the representation used by Java) for arrays, strings, and so on. Additionally, this low-level package would need to support the basic operations of the transactional and database framework offered by the ODBMS. Such a package would not support the persistence-by-reachability paradigm outlined earlier, but rather would offer a fast and reliable interface for transferring data between the application and the DBMS. Programs being developed that use only this package would be able to exploit every low-level capability of the ODBMS in question, offering a maximum of performance. However, this approach may be expensive; the time used during development and testing will increase, and the application will become very dependent on a nonchanging functionality of the low-level classes used.

Developing larger applications or larger parts of applications based on the low-level library in most cases is not a good solution. ODBMS vendors offer instead a set of classes founded on these low-level classes, but still proprietary to the ODBMS in question. The actual organization of these more abstracted classes and packages may vary depending on which database camps the vendors belong to, and the capabilities of the ODBMS and its Java binding. From a more abstracted viewpoint, these classes often give simpler and more secure access to the database while supporting the transactional and database framework offered by the ODBMS. Using these two sets of classes (low-level and abstracted classes), the Java language binding defined by ODMG is implemented, thus supporting the object model defined by ODMG. ODBMSs are also capable of supporting other object models, such as component models for the World Wide Web, based on the two sets of classes on which the ODMG Java binding is based.

Availability, Flexibility, and Performance

Java is still a fairly new programming language, compared to C++, C, and Smalltalk, and the ODBMS vendors have developed a number of libraries for C and C++ to make these languages capable of exploiting most of the capabilities provided by their ODBMS. The Java language binding is fairly new compared to the C++ binding, and usually some of the special features available to the C++ binding are unavailable for the Java binding. For example, an ODBMS may support long transactions in its C++ binding, but in the Java binding long transactions cannot be used. This aspect is not directly related to performance, but is of such importance that it should be mentioned.

An important factor to performance is the flexibility offered by the ODBMS in regard to multiple paths to resolving a single problem. For example, when deleting or dereferencing an object in Java it is sufficient to set the object to null, and setting a persistent object to null should be no different. If some other object is referenced from the object being deleted, this object is dereferenced/deleted as well if no other objects reference it. Most ODBMSs support this kind of functionality, but some offer a number of additional options. Versant, for example, offers in addition to single delete (only the object being set to null is deleted, nothing else), group delete (a group of objects may be deleted, contained in a vector), class delete (deleting all instances of a class), or predicate-based delete using a query language (VQL). These different delete options have different consequences related to the number of network calls, locality in cache, and consequently performance. Similar options may exist for basic and more complex operations. Such options should be investigated to determine how they influence performance in each case.

Caching and Tuning

When a transaction commits, the changes made to objects in the client are sent to the database (how and when the data are sent may vary). One of the important questions in this context is whether or not the cache (object and/or page cache) should be cleared. Preserving the cache may degrade performance if the objects in the cache are not reused. However, if the objects are used again, preserving them in the cache may increase performance. Another related issue is whether or not the locks set by the previous transaction should be released. If the objects are cleared from the cache, preserving the locks may seem like a waste of resources, but if the cache is preserved and the objects are referenced again, this will increase performance since no extra locks have to be acquired and those objects resident in cache do not need to be sent from the server again. Hohenstein et al. illustrates the effect of such tuning opportunities [Hohenstein 1997].

It is often possible to tune distinct parts of the client application related to the ODBMS architecture; for example, the initial and maximum size of the object cache may be set, how and when swapping of objects should occur, and so on. The number of tuning possibilities is limited, but in an environment where performance is of great importance these parameters should be investigated as well.

Navigational Access versus Queries

Most Java applications use navigational access; that is, the application uses object references to navigate between the objects in the application and database. Using object references makes the performance of the application very dependent on how the database translates logical object IDs to in-memory references (e.g., swizzling or hash-table lookup), how the client and the server exchange data (e.g., objects or pages), whether the ODBMS is an active or a passive ODBMS, and the length of the path (the number of object references that need to be followed to reach the target object).

Fortunately ODBMSs offer an alternative path using a query language. Danielsen investigated the difference in performance using navigational access and queries to retrieve unique objects [Danielsen 1999]. The test used a binary search tree with 450,000 occurrences (a balanced version of such a tree contains 19 levels, but the tree used in the test had more). Danielsen came to the conclusion that the average time used to retrieve unique objects was close to zero when a unique index was used, compared to the time used to navigate through the binary search tree to get to the unique object. The evaluation presented in Danielsen was based on PJama [Atkinson 1996] and Versant. The results of the test would have been different if the ODBMS had to transfer the data to the client to execute the query.

JIT Compilers

A Just-In-Time (JIT) compiler is a program that turns Java byte code into instructions that can be sent directly to the processor. It compiles the byte code into platform-specific executable code that is executed immediately. The client will usually get improved performance, especially if the method executable is used repeatedly. The effect, however, may be limited if the application is waiting for the database most of the time.

Evaluating Performance and Benchmarking

Developing applications that work well using a particular ODBMS requires knowledge on how the ODBMS should be exploited. However, most developers initially do not know enough about the ODBMS and its language binding to be able to fully exploit the ODBMS, getting optimal or close to optimal performance. To be able to exploit the performance capabilities of an ODBMS fully, the different aspects of the ODBMS and its language binding have to be investigated.

A number of different techniques may be explored for this purpose. One possible solution is to port some of the critical parts of an existing application to one or several ODBMSs and evaluate. Hohenstein et al. report on such an activity evaluating three ODBMSs and one RDBMS [Hohenstein 1997]. Another possibility is to use one or several benchmarks, for example, the OO7 benchmark [Carey 1993] and JUSTITIA [Schreiber 1994], and base a performance evaluation on them. A third possibility is to write your own benchmarks focusing on the issue you want to explore. Danielsen demonstrates such an attempt [Danielsen 1999]. Chaudhri gives an overview of a number of different benchmarks related to ODBMSs [Chaudhri 1995].

Conclusion

Developing applications in Java and exploiting the capabilities of an ODBMS requires knowledge about the architecture of the ODBMS and its Java binding, as well as knowledge on application development and the problem domain. We have not discussed application development and problem domains, but we have looked at a number of architectural issues that influence performance. Some of these issues are related only to special properties that may or may not be present in the ODBMS or language binding (e.g., swizzling). Other issues are conceptual; for example, object versus page servers, active versus passive server, and notification models.

To undertake a complete and exhaustive list of all architectural issues that influence performance in an ODBMS, its Java binding, and applications would require a book or three, or even more, not a single chapter!

To be able to exploit the ODBMS and its language binding fully, we need to know the importance of these issues and how the ODBMS works in this context. However, the most important success factor in this context is the application itself, and its design. If you miss there, you have missed the train.

Addressing Complexity and Scale in a High-Performance Object Server

The so-called "information explosion" has led to an enormous demand for networked information, which in turn has placed enormous pressure on information servers. The design of high-performance server technology has thus become a hot topic in computer science. In this chapter we describe how our exposure to a large real-world application has shaped our response to two key issues for high-performance object-server technologies—the management of complexity and the management of scale. The Australian Bureau of Statistics' Business Register (ABS-BR) is an object-oriented database (OODB) application that forms a register of all businesses in Australia. The register is fundamental to much of the Australian Bureau of Statistics' (ABS) economic survey activity and is used by many branches of the large organization. The basis of the register is an object model that reflects the business structure of all Australian businesses, from large multinationals to corner stores. There are over 100,000,000 objects in the register and it is constantly updated, both through operator-driven data entry and the batch processing of data from other government agencies. Specific requirements are acceptable response time for interactive access for more that 100 users, long and short transaction support, efficient storage and online access to historic information, flexible object version views, and schema evolution support. The challenges raised by the Business Register (BR) are dominated by the problems of complexity and scale. Our response to these challenges has been guided by our view that *abstraction* has a basic role in addressing complexity and scale, and by our use of *Java* as an implementation context.

In this chapter we report not only on our approach, but also on novel technological outcomes that stem from our exposure to the challenges highlighted by the ABS-BR.

These outcomes include portable orthogonally persistent Java, a system for object versioning, a proposal for schema versioning, and a system architecture for scalable object servers based on a separation of programming language and storage system concerns. The outcomes are examined in the context of an ABS-BR technology demonstrator—a small-scale version of the ABS-BR built to test and showcase new technologies for high-performance object servers. This work brings to light a number of key lessons for the OODB application developer. First, appropriate use of abstraction is crucial to managing complexity. We explore this theme with respect to a number of concerns, including persistence, storage reclamation, versions, and schema evolution, each of which are major sources of application code complexity. The second key lesson is that a modern object-oriented language such as Java can provide an excellent implementation context for a large-scale OODB application. This theme is explored with attention to features of Java such as type safety, automatic garbage collection, and dynamic binding. We also discuss how we were able to use Java to achieve an extremely high level of abstraction over major sources of complexity without major sacrifices with respect to expressiveness or performance. We also make some observations about the ODMG-3 standard and the extent to which it has been able to address adequately such abstraction issues in the context of Java.

The communications revolution has made possible the explosive growth in the Internet currently being witnessed. This growth has lead to a corresponding explosion in demand for networked information and has thrown server technology under the spotlight—its capacity for scalability and robustness now the subject of great scrutiny. Although relational technology has an important role to play in some application domains, there are others where object technology is better suited. So it is that high-performance object-server technology has become extremely important, any advance in the utility and scalability of such systems being of direct relevance to a large and rapidly growing market.

It was in this setting that we began a project with the ABS to examine their BR application with a view to exposing us to a large real-world problem, and allowing the ABS to see something of what the research community was doing to address the sort of problems they were facing. Through discussions with programmers and managers from this large project we were able to get a first-hand view of some of the major problems faced today by implementers of large-scale object server applications. We were thus provided at once with both a source of motivating problems and a testing ground for our ideas.

Our exposure to the ABS-BR led to the identification of two major barriers: *complexity* and *scalability*. We approached the problems raised by these barriers through a two-level strategy that involved the use of *abstraction* at a high level and the use of Java at an implementation level. Abstraction serves to separate concerns and reduce complexity, both of which aid scalability. Our choice of Java as an implementation environment was based on many of its popular features, but above all, on its capacity to be semantically extended—a feature that allowed us to efficiently and portably realize our strategy of complexity reduction through abstraction.

Part of our goal in working with the ABS was to provide us with a context for testing and analyzing our ideas. It was in this light that we built the ABS-BR demonstrator. The demonstrator implements a cut-down version of the ABS-BR over synthetic data,[1] using Orthogonally Persistent Java (OPJ) with orthogonal versioning. These extensions to Java were developed by our research group and utilized underlying stores built to the PSI [Blackburn 1998] storage interface by the group. The outcomes of this major implementation experiment are reported in some detail later in this chapter. Suffice it to say here that through the abstractions provided by orthogonal persistence and orthogonal versioning, our implementation was enormously simplified. As to whether our objectives with respect to scalability were met, it is harder to say, as we were not able to replicate the full ABS-BR for a variety of reasons.

Our experience with the ABS-BR offers two major lessons for OODB application developers: Appropriate abstractions can *greatly* simplify your implementation; and Java is a language with sufficient strength to be used in major implementations and with sufficient flexibility to realize readily such abstractions. These lessons are significant because complexity is the major source of implementation and maintenance cost overrun, and the identification of an appropriate implementation language for a large OODB application is critical.

The remainder of this chapter is structured as follows. In the first section, the ABS-BR application is described and key challenges that it raises are discussed. The next section outlines our approach to the challenges of complexity and scale in terms of a high level strategy based on the use of abstraction and an implementation strategy based on the use of Java. This is followed with a discussion of four key technologies used to address the ABS-BR challenges: orthogonally persistent Java, orthogonal versioning, the semantic extension framework for Java, and PSI, a persistent storage interface. We then describe our ABS-BR demonstrator, which demonstrates the use of the aforementioned technologies in a scaled-down implementation of the ABS-BR. In the last section, we analyze the performance of the ABS-BR demonstrator and discuss the implications of the lessons of the ABS-BR, particularly in the context of the ODMG standard [Barry 1998]; [Cattell 1999].

The ABS Business Register

The ABS Business Register (BR) is a register of all businesses in Australia, from transnationals to corner stores[2]. The Register contains details of 900,000 businesses, employing more than seven million people and operating from about 1,000,000 locations. The Register is the source of all sorts of statistical information about Australian businesses. It can provide information on businesses in particular regions, or about the main regions of activity for a particular industry. Customized reports can provide information such as numbers of businesses classified by industry, employment size range, and region. This information can be combined with other ABS economic information (Census of Population and Housing, specialized industry and labor statistics, etc.) to examine profit margins for particular industries, and to benchmark a business against other businesses of similar industry and size. However, information in the Register that could identify individual businesses remains confidential. The ABS makes available aggregated BR data,

---

[1] Strict privacy legislation prevents us using live ABS data. We were therefore restricted to the use of a synthetic facsimile of the Business Register data.

[2] For more information about the ABS Business Register, please refer to [Australian Bureau of Statistics].

which is used by companies all over Australia to analyze business markets, establish business profiles of a particular area, and as a tool for other market research problems.

Many different sources are used to update information on the ABS Business Register, and updating is done on a continuous basis. Most new employing businesses are identified and included on the Register within one to six months of commencing employment of staff.

The BR is currently implemented using OODBMS technology, each business modeled according to a complex schema that reflects real-world business structure, including concepts such as legal entities, enterprise groups, and locations. Key issues for the BR include *scalability*, *complexity*, *reliability*, *change management*, and *heterogeneity* of computational environment.

Scalability concerns include:

Storage. The database currently has over 100,000,000 objects using more than 10GB of storage space.

Processing capacity. The system must be able to respond to queries in a timely manner and be able to batch-process large quantities of data from external sources.

External IO. A large number of external clients must be supported simultaneously.

The complexity of the database is evidenced by a large schema and the need to preserve information about complex statistical data dependencies. This complexity is exacerbated by the difficulty of maintaining persistent-to-transient data mappings, and the demands of explicit storage management (alloc/free). As a central resource for the ABS's economic statistics, the reliability of the system is of paramount importance from the perspective of both data integrity and availability.

Change management places considerable demands on the system at a number of levels:

- The capacity to deal with long transactions (update transactions on large companies can take many days by virtue of the complexity of the data entry task)

- The need for object instance versioning to allow for retrospective queries and changes

- The need for schema versioning in order to support schema change and retrospective use of the data and associated schema

The BR must do all of this in support of a wide range of users, including system operators, data entry personnel, and statisticians who exist within a diverse heterogeneous computing environment.

Key Issues Raised by the ABS-BR

The challenges of the ABS-BR and the difficulties faced by the ABS in realizing and maintaining a solution indicate a number of issues that we see as being of broad relevance to high-performance object-server technology. It is these issues that have been the focus of our research effort centered on the ABS-BR. Of these, the first four relate to system requirements that led to significant complexity for the ABS-BR application programmers, and the last relates to scalability. The challenges of the ABS-BR can be broadly classified as those of *complexity* and *scalability*.

Figure 10.1 illustrates some of the important concepts in the ABS-BR. *Historic snapshots* are globally consistent snapshots of the BR that define the resolution at which historical queries are made. The *common frame* is the current stable view of the BR (typically corresponding to the last historic snapshot). The *current view* is the view of the database that includes all updates since the last historic snapshot. *Dependent source feedback* refers to updates that in some way are a function of the database itself (e.g., where change in the database triggers the collection of new data items for the database). Such data items constitute a feedback loop and must therefore be excluded from certain statistical analyses. Long and short transactions are depicted with respect to different views of the BR.

Need to Reduce Impedance Mismatch

Many OODBMS systems expose application programmers to the existence of transient (in-memory) and persistent (database) copies of the same data. In some cases the OODBMS maintains only the persistent copy, leaving the programmer with the task of managing mappings between, and coherency of, persistent and transient copies. The transient copy is used for implementing and realizing the application *logic*, and the persistent copy must be maintained in order to ensure that changes are made stable, that transactional semantics are observed, and to facilitate intertransactional data sharing. This adds substantial complexity to the programmer's task, sometimes doubling the size of the schema (with transient and persistent analogues of each class). In the case of the ABS-BR, this issue was a *major* cause of implementation complexity. An environment that allowed the programmer to abstract over the issue of persistent storage management would greatly simplify the task of the application programmer.

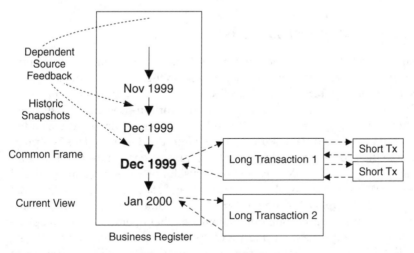

Figure 10.1 The ABS-BR showing historic snapshots, a common frame, long and short transactions, and an example of dependent source feedback.

Need for Automatic Storage Management

Discussions with ABS-BR's application programmers revealed that storage management (alloc/free), particularly with respect to persistent data, was a major cause of complexity. Indeed, the complexity was so great that the problem of storage reclamation was deferred, with the consequence that the database grew monotonically at a rate in the order of 1GB/month. The additional cost of disk storage was deemed insignificant when compared with the programming effort needed to address (safely) the intricate and complex problem. Not surprisingly, the possibility of support for automatic storage management (through the use of garbage collection) was greeted with enthusiasm by the ABS-BR application programmers to whom we spoke.

Need to Support Historical Versioning

An important requirement of the ABS-BR is that it supports historical queries. Furthermore, additional statistical requirements such as the need to avoid dependent source feedback add to the complexity of historical queries. In the context of these requirements, OODBMS support for versioning was deemed inadequate, and versioning support was built in explicitly at the application level, substantially adding to the complexity of the application. Not only must the application manage persistent and transient copies of objects (as mentioned earlier), but also multiple versions of the object, each with its own persistent and transient copies. All of these many instances, when viewed at an appropriate level of abstraction, amount to a single object seen in differing contexts. Unfortunately, application programmers are not afforded this simple abstract view. Instead they must deal explicitly with the many different faces of the same logical object. A programming environment that could provide programmers with a level of abstraction where such details were only exposed when necessary would again substantially reduce the complexity of the application.

Need to Support Long Transactions

Updating the records for a large company in the ABS-BR can take days of data-entry time, and yet such updates must occur transactionally, so there is a clear need for long transactions to be well supported. In the ABS-BR, application programmers copy data out of the database into a temporary space (called the work-in-progress or WIP store) for the duration of the long transaction to avoid lock conflict problems. At the end of the long transaction, updated data is brought back into the database. This is a pragmatic solution to the problem of dealing with long transactions without built-in support from the underlying OODBMS. However, this solution does not scale well and bypasses the OODMBS' transactional isolation by taking data outside of the OODBMS' scope. Ideally the OODBMS would provide an abstract solution whereby the distinction between operations within a long transaction and other operations would be evident only from the context—the same query and update code executed in the different contexts would have the appropriate semantics. The programmer should not have to be exposed to long transactions when writing application logic.

Need for Scalability

A system like the ABS-BR places enormous demands on scalability. In large part, the performance demands of the ABS-BR can be characterized in terms of throughput. In principle, this should allow the application programmer to be heavily insulated from the scalability issue, the onus falling on an underlying OODBMS capable of executing user queries at the requisite rate. In fact, the ABS-BR programmers were heavily exposed to the question of scalability as issues like locking strategies and their impact on performance came to the surface. The challenge therefore exists to build OODBMSs capable of scaling while insulating users from the mechanisms critical to that performance.

Approaching a Solution

Having discussed major challenges raised by the ABS-BR project, we now go on to describe our approach to addressing them. The approach is two-pronged: At the conceptual level, our approach rests on the power of abstraction as a tool for conquering complexity, and at a more practical level, we depend on the use of *Java* as a powerful environment for constructing a solution.

Abstraction as a Tool

The enormous complexity of a large object database application like the ABS-BR is a product of the intersection of multiple domains of complexity. Although the complexity of the essential system that the ABS-BR seeks to model is moderate, secondary issues that the application programmer must deal with such as *persistence*, *historical versioning*, and *scalability concerns* appear to impact on the system complexity in a multiplicative rather than additive manner. By separating concerns and providing abstractions, the application programmer is able to focus on the primary objective—the core application logic. It is for this reason that we see abstraction as the key to conquering the complexity of such applications. Furthermore, abstraction can be a key to addressing scalability through the clean separation of application and store-level scalability issues. The following sections detail three important applications of this approach.

Orthogonal Persistence

As noted earlier, the complexity of the ABS-BR implementation is in large part a consequence of the *impedance mismatch* between the programming environment and the underlying storage technology. This impedance mismatch is manifest in complex mappings between persistent and nonpersistent classes and instances. We see this as a prime example of the need for abstraction—abstraction over persistence—and we see orthogonal persistence as a solution to that problem. Orthogonally persistent systems are distinguished from other persistent systems such as object databases by orthogonality between data use and data persistence. This orthogonality comes as the product of the application of the following principles of persistence [Atkinson 1995]:

Persistence Independence. The form of a program is independent of the longevity of the data that it manipulates.

Data Type Orthogonality. All data types should be allowed the full range of persistence, irrespective of their type.

Persistence Identification. The choice of how to identify and provide persistent objects is orthogonal to the universe of discourse of the system.

These principles impart a transparency of persistence from the perspective of the programming language that obviates the need for programmers to maintain mappings between persistent and transient data. The same code will thus operate over persistent and transient data without distinction. The third principle states that all data required by computation within some system will implicitly persist. This infers a form of transitive persistence and an implicit rather than explicit mode of identifying persistent data. A consequence of this is that orthogonally persistent systems provide automatic storage management through the use of garbage collection with respect to the implicit persistent roots of the system—thus addressing the second key issue raised by the ABS-BR.

The abstraction over storage provided by an orthogonally persistent implementation environment would thus facilitate substantially simplified construction for the ABS-BR through the removal of the language/database impedance mismatch and the introduction of automatic storage management. By greatly reducing implementation complexity, the use of orthogonal persistence would also have the significant side effect of reducing maintenance costs.

Although orthogonal persistence provides a nice solution to the problem at hand, in fact, few implemented orthogonally persistent systems exist, and, until now, none exist that are capable of adequately supporting many of the other demands of the ABS-BR such as transaction and version support. The filling of this gap with a portable orthogonally persistent Java (OPJ) [Marquez 2000] has been a major focus of our research group, and is the subject of further discussion.

Orthogonal Versioning

The concept of orthogonal persistence, which has been under development since the early 1980s, has a natural analogue in orthogonal versioning. Whereas orthogonal persistence allows the programmer to abstract over the concern of persistence, orthogonal versioning abstracts over versioning. This allows the programmer to write code without regard to the issue of versioning except insofar as that the programmer finds it desirable to explicitly do so.

In concrete terms, a programmer designing and building a class for the Business Register is able to focus on the business logic, ignoring the issue of versions. At some high level in the BR implementation, means would be provided for allowing the BR user to define a version context (*now, last quarter, Q2 2000*, etc.). Operations over the BR would then be executed using the *same code*, from the *same classes*, in the *new context* specified by the user. The implementation code thus remains abstract with respect to versions, except at the few points where it is desirable for the version context to be explicitly set, yet the entire BR operates with respect to fully versioned persistent data.

The first two principles of orthogonal persistence have obvious analogies in orthogonal versioning:

Version Independence. The form of a program is independent of the version of the data that it manipulates.

Data Type Orthogonality. All mutable data types should be allowed to be versioned, irrespective of their type.[3]

A meaningful implementation of the concept of version independence must provide transparent support for *configuration management*[4] in order to facilitate transparent access to and manipulation of a consistent collection of component versions of a complex object. The importance of configuration management has been widely recognized in areas such as CAD, CASE, and Web document management systems. One of the consequences of configuration management support is the need to be able to generate new versions of an object transparently. For example, a new version of an object must be created the first time the value of the object is updated within the scope of a new configuration. That is to say, versions are not generated for each update to an object, but rather new versions are generated at the granularity of the instantiation of new configurations.

To our best knowledge, the concept of orthogonal versioning is new and previously unimplemented. Our implementation of orthogonal versioning in the context of Java and its application to the BR demonstrator are the subjects of later sections.

Abstracting over Distribution and Storage Technology

Ideally, an application developer should not have to be exposed to the particulars of system architecture and storage technology. Whether the technology used to deliver requisite performance is uniprocessor, SMP, cluster, or some other technology, it should be transparent to the programmer implementing the business logic of the application. The application programmer should not need to be concerned with the choice of vendor for the underlying transactional store. Of course an orthogonally persistent development environment will abstract over the storage technology. However, the *implementer of the orthogonally persistent environment* will have to face this issue, and his or her approach will impact on the flexibility of the end product. While developing the orthogonally persistent environment reported in this chapter, we were faced with these issues of abstraction, and our response to them centered on the use of PSI [Blackburn 1998].

PSI was borne out of an appraisal of the problems inhibiting the development of high-performance orthogonally persistent systems, and the view that a separation of storage and language concerns was an essential step to alleviating those problems. PSI thus represents an abstraction over storage at a low level in the implementation hierarchy. Crucial

[3] The principle of Data Type Orthogonality applies only to *mutable* types, as the concept of versioning makes no sense except where the object may be mutated. Another way of looking at this is that immutable types are trivially versioned, but because the objects are immutable and therefore never updated, all versions of the object present the same value.

[4] The term configuration is used to denote a consistent view of a set of versioned objects. This is analogous to the concept of a release in the context of a software management system—a software release corresponds to a consistent set of files, each at a particular (but typically different) point in their own version history.

to the abstraction over storage is the separation of *scalability* issues associated with the store from those associated with the application. This abstraction thus plays a central role in our goal of scalable object-server technologies.

A key feature of the PSI architecture is the concept of a single image store. The single image store abstraction allows a storage system to be seen as uniform and single level, when in fact, it may be implemented at different levels, and in a distributed fashion. In the PSI architecture, objects are accessed directly through a cache that is shared between storage and language layers. The PSI interface mediates access to objects in the cache to ensure coherency of data. This mediation is done through a transactional mode of operation, with all data access occurring in the context of some transaction and so being subject to transactional semantics.

The simplicity of the PSI interface makes it possible to add PSI compliance efficiently to transactional object storage systems by adding a thin interfacing layer. A language system that works to the interface can utilize any store that implements the PSI interface, and so has a great deal of portability with respect to storage technology.

Java as a Development Platform

Java is becoming an increasingly popular choice of programming environment. There are many reasons for this, some of which where behind our decision to choose Java as the basis of our ABS-BR demonstrator implementation project. We view this choice as a significant facet of our approach, and so place it at the same level as our discussion on the role of abstraction in our approach.

Leveraging Java's Attributes

Of Java's many attributes, three stand out as being particularly important in the context of the ABS-BR.

Usability

As a modern object-oriented programming language, Java provides its users with numerous features that enhance its usability, including type-safety, encapsulation, and automatic memory management. Furthermore, rapid advances in Java Virtual Machine (JVM) technology allow these features to be delivered to the user with rapidly diminishing performance overheads [Alpern 1999]. In the context of the ABS-BR these usability concerns are significant with respect to the development and maintenance of the ABS-BR application. At present, *enormous* resources are devoted to development and maintenance, and issues such as the lack of automatic memory management in C++ are among the greatest concerns.

Portability

Another of Java's most outstanding features is portability. Not only may compiled Java code be executed on any platform for which a JVM implementation exists, but micro-applications (applets) may be transmitted from client to server across the Internet, executing on any client platform that has a JVM. This feature is particularly significant in the ABS-BR context, where the execution environment is strongly heterogeneous, ranging from large UNIX servers to desktop PCs, and is distributed (through the ABS WAN) across Australia. In such an environment, a server-oriented JVM could be run at the server [Alpern 1999], while clients could simply utilize Java implementations within their browsers. The ABS-BR implementation could be built purely in Java, from the business logic all the way through to the GUI presented to desktop users. This would short-circuit the impedance that currently exists between the UNIX-based C++/OODBMS server application and the Windows-based client-side GUI application.

Concurrency

Java's support for concurrency is another key feature in the context of the ABS-BR. Concurrency is essential to delivering server-side performance, both in terms of throughput and responsiveness. In this setting, a language such as Java, which has strong support for concurrency, is a major advantage. The demand for highly scalable JVMs for just such applications has led to major research efforts within industry to develop high-performance server JVMs capable of exploiting hardware and operating system support for concurrency through threads [Alpern 1999], a move which seems destined to deliver such JVMs commercially in the very near future.

Java's Capacity for Extended Semantics

Earlier, we discussed the importance of *abstraction* as a tool for resolving complexity, and introduced the concepts of orthogonal persistence and orthogonal versioning as powerful applications of this principle. Both of these comprise *orthogonal semantic extensions* to the programming language. In other words, the semantics of the programming language must be extended to orthogonally (transparently) support additional semantics (in our case persistence and versioning). The orthogonal persistence literature [Atkinson 1995] includes numerous papers addressing the question of how the semantics of persistence can be orthogonally integrated into a programming language.

One of the key breakthroughs in our quest to build an orthogonally persistent Java was the realization that Java has an extremely powerful capacity for semantic extension in its provision for *user-definable class-loaders*. This mechanism allows a custom class loader to be written (in Java), that intercepts (and possibly modifies) classes as they are loaded. This allows the language to be extended semantically through the use of custom class loaders. Significantly, this approach is portable, as it does not depend on modifying the compiler or the virtual machine.

Engineering a Solution

Having outlined our approach, we can now discuss the technology we developed and applied to our implementation of a BR demonstrator. We begin by discussing our implementations of Orthogonal Persistence for Java (OPJ) and Orthogonal Versioning for Java (OVJ). Central to the development of each of these was the Semantic Extension Framework (SEF) for Java, the subject of the next section. Finally we discuss our use of PSI to abstract over storage concerns that allowed us to implement OPJ in a storage platform neutral manner.

Orthogonal Persistence and Versioning through Semantic Extensions to Java

Earlier, we argued for orthogonal persistence and orthogonal versioning as powerful examples of simplification through abstraction. The realization of each of these in the context of Java depends on *orthogonally* extending *the semantics of Java*. That is, the normal semantics of Java must be preserved but transparently extended to support new semantics (in our case persistence and versioning). In the following sections we describe the nature of the semantic extensions we have made to Java in order to realize Orthogonally Persistent Java (OPJ) and Orthogonal Versioning for Java (OVJ). We also discuss the technology used to extend Java semantically in an efficient and portable way.

Orthogonally Persistent Java

The primary function of orthogonal persistence is to *abstract over storage*, allowing the semantics of object persistence to become orthogonal to all other object semantics. This leads to the first-order goal for OPJ of making transparent the movement of data between primary and secondary storage, providing the user with the illusion of a single coherent level of storage. Of course there are many second-order goals and requirements for an orthogonally persistent system, but a detailed discussion of these is beyond the scope of this chapter. If you are interested, see Atkinson and Morrison's review of orthogonal persistence [Atkinson 1995], and a detailed account of our OPJ implementation [Marquez 2000].

Although our OPJ implementation (ANU-OPJ) is not the first implementation of OPJ [Atkinson 1997]; [Gemstone Systems 1999], a number of important features make it unique:

- Our implementation strategy based on the semantic extension framework gives our implementation portability and access to the fastest JVM technology.
- ANU-OPJ is fully transactional.
- ANU-OPJ has a natural and clean approach to identifying persistent objects.

These differentiating characteristics come with strong performance results (presented later). In the remainder of this section we briefly discuss four aspects of the ANU-OPJ implementation before addressing its limitations.

Read and Write Barriers

At the core of any orthogonal persistence implementation must lie mechanisms that transparently fetch data from storage on demand and transparently write updates back to storage when necessary. Such mechanisms depend on read and write barriers—traps that transparently catch user attempts to read or update data. Efficient and transparent implementation of read and write barriers are thus essential to any OPJ implementation. The approach taken by ANU-OPJ is in keeping with our theme of transparent semantic extension. Java semantics are transparently extended by the insertion of byte codes that implement the barriers each time an attempt is made to read an object (e.g., through the `getfield` byte code) or update an object (`putfield`). These additional byte codes are added in a stack-neutral manner at class-load time, a modified class loader transforming every `getfield` and `putfield` byte code accordingly. The efficiency of this approach is largely a function of the Virtual Machine (VM) technology on top of which it is used— a compiling VM will fold these checks into a small number of machine codes, and an interpretive VM will be somewhat inefficient. The basic read barrier implementation is composed of a check to see whether the object had already been read. If the object had already been read then nothing was done; otherwise, a call was made to the storage layer to read the object in from storage. The basic write barrier consists of the setting of a dirty flag that was checked at transaction commit time. Any dirty objects are written back to the store as part of transaction commit. Implementing read and write barriers for all classes including system classes, was not trivial, nor was it trivial to implement the barriers efficiently. Details of the various approaches used and their performance are included in our detailed account of the OPJ implementation [Marquez 2000].

Persistence Identification

The means of identification of persistent objects is another important facet of an orthogonally persistent system. In most systems, known roots are used as the basis of persistence by reachability—any objects transitively reachable from the roots are implicitly persistent. Whereas other OPJ implementations accomplish this by introducing *explicit* user-definable and retrievable named roots [Atkinson 1997], [Gemstone Systems 1999], ANU-OPJ takes an alternative path, making nontransient class static members implicit roots. Any object transitively reachable from the static class member of a class is implicitly made persistent. This approach seems to be truer to the *principle of persistence independence* because it allows any Java code to become transparently, implicitly persistent without any modification whatsoever. The value of this feature is borne out in our experience with the ABS-BR demonstrator (discussed later), which was built from scratch without explicit concern for persistence in a conventional Java development environment, and yet ran persistently, as intended, without modification once the nonpersistent Java was replaced by ANU-OPJ.

Concurrency and Transactions

Concurrency is of utmost importance to our motivating example, the ABS-BR, and yet the intermix of concurrency and persistence has been a major stumbling block for orthogonal persistence [Blackburn 1998a]. The root of the problem lies in the conflicting approaches to concurrency traditionally taken in the programming language and database fields. On one hand, programming languages typically adopt, for reasons of flexibility and expressibility, a *cooperative* concurrency model centered on the use of shared variables. On the other hand, for reasons associated with the need for coherent stability, database systems typically adopt a concurrency model centered on the use of *isolation* through transactions. The chain and spawn transaction model presented in Blackburn and Zigman's work, "Concurrency: The Fly in the Ointment?" [Blackburn 1998a] provides a way out of a difficult problem[5] that arises when trying to make an orthogonally persistent environment fully transactional and capable of inter- (and intra-) transactional concurrency. This model

---

[5] The problem arises because when all computation is transactional and intertransactional concurrency is desired, some form of nesting is required. Yet, the basic building block of transactions—the ACID transaction [Härder 1983]—cannot be nested because of a contradiction between the atomicity of the parent and the irrevocability of the child. For further information, see [Blackburn 1998a].

is provided by ANU-OPJ, allowing users to work in a concurrent and yet fully transactional environment. Transactional isolation is ensured cheaply by ANU-OPJ by leveraging Java's existing class-loader isolation. ANU-OPJ ensures that each new transaction is run in the context of a different class loader and Java ensures that Java objects remain isolated on a transactional basis. Transactional guarantees provided by the underlying store are also leveraged by ANU-OPJ to ensure that correct transactional semantics are observed.

Implementation Strategy

The key to the ANU-OPJ implementation strategy lies in its use of the Semantic Extension Framework, (SEF). The semantic extensions embodied by ANU-OPJ are injected into classes at class loading time, thus giving normal Java programs orthogonal persistence semantics. This contrasts strongly with the dominant approach of modifying the Java virtual machine, which is motivated by the performance gains to be made by building the semantic extensions into the virtual machine at the lowest level. Interestingly, ANU-OPJ is able to outperform an OPJ built using this approach (discussed later). This appears to be the product of two factors. First, in a compiling JVM, such as one with a Just in Time (JIT) compiler, the byte codes added by the SEF are compiled and optimized just as they are in the built-in approach. Second, for the built-in approach to maintain its advantage, the semantic extensions must be built into each new release of the parent JVM—a demanding task given that the semantic extensions must be added to the component of the virtual machine most targeted for improvement (the interpreter and/or compiler).

Limitations

ANU-OPJ is relatively young, and so holds plenty of room for improvement. Aside from performance improvements, ANU-OPJ in its current form also embodies a number of limitations. Although most of these are minor, its current incapacity to make threads persistent is at odds with its claim to orthogonal persistence.[6] However, we believe that this problem can be overcome relatively easily by borrowing an approach used in the context of thread migration [Hohlfeld 1998].

Orthogonal Versioning in Java

Object versioning is a natural concept in many object-oriented applications. Versioning becomes important in applications where an exploratory or iterative approach over the object store state is needed. In the ABS-BR demonstrator, we utilize object versioning both as a means of facilitating queries and updates against historical data, and as a practical means of efficiently implementing long transactions. This is all done through our implementation of Orthogonal Versioning for Java (OVJ), the subject of the remainder of this section.

As with OPJ, OVJ consists of semantic extensions to Java, and like OPJ, OVJ utilizes the Semantic Extension Framework (SEF) to realize these semantic extensions. Here we describe OVJ as implemented on top of ANU-OPJ, although OVJ can be integrated into other modes of persistence support for Java such as an ODMG-3 transparent persis-

---

[6] This limitation is common to the two other major OPJ efforts [Atkinson 1996], [Gemstone Systems 1999].

tence implementation. Our OVJ does not depend on explicit support for versioning within the underlying object store. In fact, our first implementation of OVJ was built on top of the SHORE OODBMS [Carey 1994a], which has no support for versions.

Figure 10.2 illustrates the abstraction provided by OVJ, and depicts the relationship between versions and configurations. In this example, the global environment includes many different configurations; the depicted object only has versions in four of these. The power of the abstraction over versions provided by OVJ is seen in the left side of the diagram, which presents a simple view of the object in a particular configuration context; the underlying situation (which OVJ abstracts over) is the complex version tree depicted at the right. The importance of a configuration context is that it allows the denotation of versions to be implicit rather than explicit, which is essential to our goal of transparency. Having established a configuration context (perhaps implicitly), user computation proceeds, oblivious to the issue of versions, over a normal object graph, which, in fact, corresponds to some projection of a versioned object graph into the Java heap space. In the remainder of this section we discuss four major aspects of our OVJ implementation.

Run-time Overhead

An important goal in designing OVJ was minimizing the performance impact on objects that are naturally transient and so are unaffected by versioning. This is achieved by applying versioning to objects only at the time that they first become persistent. Any object that never becomes persistent because of its transience avoids most of the overhead associated with versioning. However, some overhead is unavoidable, even for transient objects. Under OVJ all instances[7] include an additional field that is used for storing a reference to version information for that object, regardless of whether the particular instance is sufficiently long-lived to be subject to versioning. Additionally, the read and write barriers of OPJ are extended slightly (all objects are

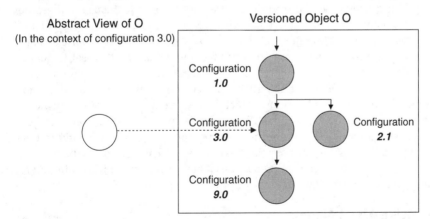

Figure 10.2   A versioned object in OVJ. The user's perspective (left) abstracts over the complex version hierarchy (right). The particular version of the object seen by the user is an implicit function of context (in this case, configuration 3.0).

[7]Although under OVJ *all* classes are subject to versioning in order to maintain orthogonality, the underlying versioning framework, which we describe here, allows versioning to be scoped with respect to some part or parts of the Java class hierarchy.

subject to the barrier overhead). In addition to these overheads that are imposed on all instances, those instances that are sufficiently long-lived to be versioned are subject to a small space overhead that is used to link instances that correspond to different versions of the same object. A run-time overhead must also be paid on the first access to an instance that corresponds to a specific version of an object.

Orthogonality with Respect to Versioning and Persistence

To ensure the persistence of all versioned objects, in the context of OVJ, OPJ's approach to defining persistent roots is extended by making all *versions* of nontransient static class members roots (in OPJ persistence is defined in terms of reachability from the static class members). In order to meaningfully fulfill the principle of version independence, OVJ must provide transparent support for configuration management. In other words, there must be means for transparently accessing and manipulating a consistent collection of component versions of a complex object. This approach provides a transparent and simple abstraction over versioning by allowing the basic versioning classes to be extended and customized. The versioning framework on which OVJ is constructed also provides a very general and powerful approach to versioning that has application to many different contexts, and that need not be as transparent.

The Configuration Hierarchy

A configuration represents a set of versioned object versions, each configuration containing no more than one version of a given object. Each configuration except the first has a parent, and each may have any number of children. Thus, a linked set of configurations corresponds to an n-ary tree, and a linear sequence of configurations corresponds to a branch. In Figure 10.2, a subset of the nodes comprising a configuration tree can be seen in the version tree of object O. Although the very purpose of OVJ is to provide a means of abstracting over versions, it is necessary to provide the user with some way to control the configuration hierarchy explicitly. Minimally, such control might just involve a means for instantiating new configurations (akin to ABS-BR historical snapshots). OVJ also provides a much more powerful facility that allows the user to generate and manipulate a configuration hierarchy in quite general ways, including branch generation and configuration tree navigation. The current implementation does not support automatic configuration merging (which derives a new configuration by merging two or more existing configurations). However, a special class of configuration exists, whose instances may have more than one parent configuration (configuration merges create cross-links in the configuration n-ary tree). OVJ also supports the concept of configuration freezing. A configuration may be labeled as frozen, with any attempt to write to a member of that configuration triggering an exception.

OVJ's Underlying Object Model

In this section we describe something of the model underlying OVJ's implementation. Although this detail is not exposed to the user of OVJ, it may give you a better understanding of some of the issues faced in implementing OVJ. The basis for OVJ is a versioning framework that is implemented by semantically extending Java classes at class loading time through use of the semantic extension framework. For a class to be versioned, it must be (transparently, by the SEF) either made to inherit (directly or indirectly) from the class VersionView, or made to implement the interface ObjectVersioning. Each instance of VersionView includes a reference to a configuration instance and to the specific version instance associated with the given configuration.[8] (Such an instance corresponds to the object on the left in Figure 10.2, which in practice would also refer to the configuration instance corresponding to 3.0.) Each of the specific version instances are instances of an automatically generated class that corresponds to the base class of the object, but contains only those fields that must be made persistent and with the addition of fields that link the various versions of the instance (these instances correspond to the gray objects on the right in Figure 10.2). This approach of dynamically creating new classes in a manner that is transparent to the user is common to OPJ, and although beyond the scope of this chapter, is described in some detail in the work by Marquez, Zigman, and Blackburn [Marquez 2000].

Versioning API

OVJ provides a versioning API for all objects, which includes the following methods:

```
public ObjectVersioning getClosestVersion(String name);
public ObjectVersioning getCreateVersion(String name);
public void deleteCurrentVersion();
public ConfigurationInterface getConfiguration();
```

The first two, getClosestVersion() and getCreateVersion(), both return an instance of the object corresponding to the given configuration. (If the configuration does not exist an exception is thrown.) If such an instance version does not exist, the first method will return the closest ancestor and the second will create a new version. The third method separates the associated specific version from the other versions of the object. The last returns the configuration associated with the instance it is called over.

SEF: The Semantic Extension Framework

Fundamentally, both OPJ and OVJ constitute *semantic extensions* to Java, in one case to support persistence, in the other to support versioning. We implement these extensions through use of the Semantic Extension Framework (SEF). The SEF is a *general* framework that was developed after our experience with ad-hoc approaches that we used in our initial implementations of OPJ and OVJ. Aside from its generality, the SEF is distinguished by its use of Java's class loading mechanism, which allows the extensions to be applied dynamically and gives the process portability. Despite its generality, simplicity, and portability, we show later that it can outperform a solution based on direct modification of the Java virtual machine.

---

[8] An instance of VersionView may also reference a *virtual configuration*. A virtual configuration represents the set of versioned object versions that satisfy a given condition. Virtual configurations typically span a configuration subbranch.

Semantic Extension: Goals and Implementation Constraints

The "write once, run anywhere" philosophy has been central to the success of Java. The approach we have taken to semantic extensions is in keeping with this philosophy of portability. Though this could be viewed as a limitation (restricting the programmer to the mechanisms offered by standard Java rather than extending Java), it enables implementations to exploit the best Java technology available (since it can run on any virtual machine and use any compiler).

A system that extends the semantics of Java should maintain fundamental properties of the language and run-time system including *separate compilation, dynamic class linking, modularity,* and *portability*. Original language semantics must be maintained in order to preserve the properties of separate compilation and dynamic class linking. New properties, such as fields and methods, may be added to a class only if the existing API contracts are respected. Furthermore, any semantic extensions should compliment existing semantic change mechanisms such as inheritance and overloading.

An important objective is that the semantic extensions can be composed *dynamically*. Many semantic extensions such as program instrumentation and profiling are volatile by nature. These semantic extensions should be applicable to other more permanent semantic extensions, such as orthogonal persistence or object instance versioning. Consequently, the specific set of semantic extensions to be applied may be known only at run time, emphasizing the need for dynamic composition of semantic extensions. In fact, it could even be of interest to extend dynamically the semantics of classes already loaded (e.g., the dynamic instrumentation of a program already running). However, the JVM specification forbids modifications of classes after they have been loaded, so the only possible solution in this case is the use of a modified JVM with advanced support for introspection.

Semantic Extension through Byte-Code Modification at Class-Load Time

Until now, efforts to extend Java's semantics to support persistence could be classified in terms of two approaches: those that modify the Java virtual machine [Atkinson 1997]; [GemStone Systems 1999]; [Kutlu 1998], and those that use a modified compiler or postprocessing to produce modified byte codes [Hosking 1998] (in some cases both approaches have been employed). The first approach clearly violates the goal of portability—the semantics will be available only on modified virtual machines. The second approach produces portable byte codes, but requires each producer of semantically extended code to have access to a modified compiler or preprocessor. Moreover, the compilation approach precludes the dynamic composition of semantic extensions. Byte codes produced under the second approach indelibly embed the semantic extension, and so are no longer able to exhibit their original semantics.

The approach we have taken is to transform byte codes at class load time, a technique that has been used in other contexts [Bokowski 1998]; [Agesen 1997], but until now has not been applied in the context of persistence. The approach has numerous advantages including portability with respect to the target machine and portability of the users' byte-codes. (Unlike the second approach mentioned earlier, the byte-code modifications happen inside the JVM and so are not visible to the user and do not affect the source byte–codes.) The basis for the technique is Java's support for user-defined class loaders that may modify the content of a class file before loading the class into the JVM. The virtual machine will apply all of the usual checks to the modified class. By using a user-defined class loader to introduce semantic change, standard compilers and virtual machines may still be used.

A Declarative Semantic Extension Language

As we have said already, our initial implementations of OPJ and OVJ were made by constructing custom class loaders that made *ad-hoc* byte-code transformations. This experience with an ad-hoc approach directly motivated the development of the SEF, which has been used as the basis for our subsequent OPJ and OVJ implementations. Our distaste for the ad-hoc approach was driven by many factors, but the fundamental one was that byte-code transformations are difficult and error prone. A simple mistake during the transformation process can destroy type safety or the semantics of the program, and may lead to the byte-code modified class being rejected at class loading time. So just as a compiler raises the level at which the programmer is able to specify a program's semantics (through the use of a high-level language), the SEF raises the level at which semantic extensions may be specified. In each case the programmer is able to avoid the complexity and hazards of working at too low a level.

The declarative language of the SEF is characterized by a class-based naming protocol for defining the *scope* of semantic extensions and the use of Java to specify the *semantics* of the extensions. Thus users encode semantic extensions in Java classes, and the naming of the classes reflects the scope of the extension. For example, the semantic extensions specified in a class named `javalangObject` will be applied to all classes that inherit from the Java class `java.lang.Object`.

Semantic extensions can include the addition of new fields and/or new methods to the modified class(es). The SEF has a convention for adding specially named methods that function as triggers. Trigger methods are invoked automatically on the occurrence of certain events such as field accesses, array accesses, method invocations, and parameter loading. Both pre- and posttriggers are supported, allowing the trigger method to be executed either immediately before or immediately after execution of the triggering event. Trigger methods are defined through the use of a simple naming convention—`pregetfield()` identifies a method that will be invoked prior to any execution of a `getfield` byte code in classes falling within the scope of the extension definition (similarly `postputfield()` will be invoked after any execution of a `putfield`).

These concepts are illustrated in Listing 10.1. The name of the class (`java$lang$Object$`) indicates that the *scope* of the semantic extension is the class `java.lang.Object` and all of its subclasses. The *semantics* of the extension are limited to a single method `pregetfield`, which, as a special trigger method, will be invoked immediately prior to the occurrence of any `getfield` byte code in any class within the scope of the extension. In this example, the trigger instruments a trace message, with the `showAccess` method of the class `Tracer` dynamically determining whether or not the message will appear.

```
public class java$lang$Object$ {
    protected final java.lang.Object pre$getfield$() {
      if(Tracer.showAccess(this))
        System.out.println("Going to access object "+this);
      return this;
    }
}
```

Listing 10.1 A declaration of a parametric semantic extension to achieve trivial instrumentation.

The semantic extension framework is invoked each time a user class is loaded. This action triggers a special semantic extension class loader to search for and load any semantic extension classes that are applicable to the user class being loaded (according to the scoping rules already described). The semantic extension class loader relies on the same visibility rules as all other Java class loaders. This means that a whole suite of semantic extensions may be turned on or turned off by simply including or excluding the path containing extension classes from the class paths visible to the JVM (which can be done trivially either by changing the CLASSPATH environment variable or by setting the -classpath option on the JVM command line).

Further Implementation Issues

A detailed account of the SEF and its implementation is beyond the scope of this chapter—refer to the work of Marquez, Zigman, and Blackburn [Marquez 2000] for details. However, we will briefly mention two implementation issues. The first of these is the way that the SEF deals with system classes. Because Java system classes are not directly modifiable, the SEF uses a proxying approach whereby references to the target system class are redirected transparently to a proxy for the system class. Although the SEF cannot *modify* any of the system class methods, the proxy mechanism can be used to *redefine* any of the methods, calling back to the unmodified system class if desired. Extensions defined with respect to a system class are, of course, applied to any class that inherits from the system class. The second important issue is the impact of the SEF on Java's introspection mechanisms. Because the SEF rewrites classes and in many cases generates new classes, methods such as getClass() may return unexpected results. Fortunately the SEF can rectify such confusing side effects automatically by semantically extending Java's introspection mechanisms to reflect the desired behavior.

PSI: Abstracting over Storage

By abstracting over storage, the application developer is freed from explicit concern for the characteristics of the underlying storage architecture—whether the system is scalable, distributed, or what the interface of the particular system is. Furthermore, as the demands of the application change, the choice of most suitable storage platform may also change. If the application, through a layer of abstraction, has become independent of the particular storage platform, the storage system may be changed without perturbing application code. In this section we identify PSI, which is an instantiation of the *transactional object cache* architecture.

Central to the architecture is the *cache*, to which the underlying store, the language run–time, and the application may have direct access. A *transactional interface* mediates the movement of data in and out of the cache, giving the language run time (and through it the application) transactional guarantees of atomicity, isolation, coherency, and durability with respect to its accesses to the cache. A layering of storage and programming language concerns is explicit in the architecture.

The explicit acknowledgement of the centrality of the cache and the provision for mediated direct access to it contrast with other architectures for persistent systems [Matthes 1996]; [Munro 1994] that provide the abstraction of a persistent heap, implemented with a relatively expensive procedure call interface for data access. This aspect of the transactional object cache architecture makes it far more conducive to high performance implementations than such alternatives.

By providing an abstraction over the object store through layering, the architecture is transparent to the distribution of the underlying store, and coupled with the concurrency control delivered by the transactional interface, facilitates the implementation of multi-user, client/server, or highly scalable multiprocessor implementations independently of the language run time/application [Blackburn 1998]. We characterize this property of distribution transparency from the perspective of the run time and application with the term *single image store*. See also Figure 10.3.

PSI: A Transactional Object Cache Interface

At the heart of the transactional object cache architecture is an interface between the language and store layers of a persistent system. A realization of the architecture is

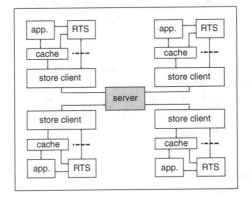 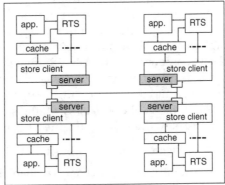

Figure 10.3   Client server (left) and client peer (right) realizations of the underlying object store. The abstraction over store architecture provided by the transactional object cache architecture gives distribution transparency to the client application and run-time system. PSI is an instantiation of the RTS/store interface visible at each node.

dependent on the identification of a suitable interface. To this end we have developed PSI, a software interface definition [Blackburn 1998].

In designing PSI, we sought to balance a number of objectives:

- To flexibly support the needs of persistent programming languages (PPLs)
- To strongly separate storage and programming language concerns
- To admit small and fast PPL implementations

This combination of objectives presented a constrained trade-off space for the interface design, within which PSI represents just one point.

The underpinning for the PSI definition is an abstraction of the transactional object cache architecture [Blackburn 1998]. The abstraction is based on three distinct facets of the behavior of the transactional object cache: stability, visibility, and availability. A number of abstract operations over the store such as ReadIntention, WriteIntention, and Commit are identified, and their semantics defined in terms of the three previously mentioned domains of behavior. The well-defined semantics of these primitives were then used as the basis of a definition of the semantics for each of the PSI calls.

Having defined the PSI interfaces, we have constructed bindings to the SHORE OODBMS [Carey 1994a] and to Oracle's object cache and relational interfaces. In addition, a high-performance object store under development within our lab also has a PSI interface. Thus the scalability of the ABS-BR demonstrator is in large part a function of the choice of underlying storage system.

Implementing the ABS-BR Demonstrator

Recall that our goal in the ABS-BR project was to expose ourselves to a large real-world problem and then to develop and test new technologies in the context of that problem. The ABS-BR and the challenges that it gives rise to were the subject of the section "The ABS Business Register," and in the section "Approaching a Solution," we discussed an approach based on the use of abstraction as a methodology and Java as an implementation context. In the preceding portion of this section we have outlined the development of technologies that put our approach into practice. We can now discuss the implementation of a first prototype of the ABS-BR demonstrator, which is a realization of key components of the ABS-BR using the previously mentioned technologies.

The demonstrator is built in Java and uses OPJ and OVJ for transparent support for versioning and persistence and, through OPJ, uses PSI to gain portability with respect to, and leverage the scalability of, the storage back-end. The application has a user interface built using Swing (Figure 10.4), and allows the user to

- Navigate the BR's core business unit hierarchy
- Create, query, and update company information
- Use both long and short transactions
- Access historical snapshots of the database

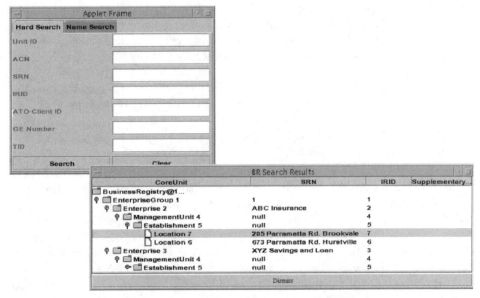

Figure 10.4 User interface of the OPJ/OVJ-based ABS-BR demonstrator. Shown are the startup window and a query window displaying a set of company hierarchies that satisfy a user query.

A single programmer constructed the demonstrator over a period of four months. The system is written entirely in Java and was developed using a popular integrated development environment. Because of the orthogonality of OPJ and OVJ, the code is pure Java and is devoid of the explicit persistence and version management code that are dominant contributors to the complexity of the original ABS-BR. In the remainder of this section we discuss three significant aspects of the demonstrator implementation.

Implementation of Long Transactions

Long transactions are very important to the ABS-BR because updates to large companies can take days of data-entry time. As discussed earlier, in the absence of support from the underlying OODBMS, this need is addressed in the ABS-BR by copying data out of the database into an external space called the work-in-progress (WIP) store for the duration of the updates. This pragmatic approach is far from ideal because it does not scale well (all data used must be copied), and it bypasses the database's transactional mechanisms.

Our solution is to view long transactions as an application of object versioning. Looked at this way, a long transaction corresponds to a branch in a configuration hierarchy and the commit of a long transaction corresponds to a configuration merge (bringing the branch back into the main line). Because a branch in a configuration hierarchy is a *logical* duplication of the database, (short) transactions operating over the mainline and branch will not conflict and so can operate concurrently. Yet because the duplication is *logical* rather than *physical* no unnecessary copying occurs. Operations within the long transaction are composed of normal transactions with respect to the appropriate configuration branch of the object database. Using this approach, a user query can occur concurrently with a long-running update to one of the companies queried without conflict. In general, branch merges can generate conflicts that must be manually resolved, and conflict resolution is avoided in the ABS-BR prototype by using a simple system of high-level locks to ensure that (rare) conflict-generating transactions do not execute concurrently.

Because this solution is based on the use of versioning through OVJ, aside from calls to start and end a long transaction, it is completely orthogonal to user code.

Implementation of Historic Versioning and Dependent Source Feedback

The need for historical versioning is a key requirement of the ABS-BR (Figure 10.1). In particular, the ABS-BR has the concept of *historic snapshots*, globally consistent historical views of the database, and *common frames*, means for retrospectively updating historical data. Both historical snapshots and common frames were trivially implemented through the application of OVJ's configuration management features. Branched configurations are a natural solution for the implementation of historic snapshots. Any configuration in the initial branch (main line) is a historic snapshot, except for the last one. A configuration status is frozen once a descendent configuration in the same branch is created. A common frame corresponds to a new branch created to allow changes to an historic snapshot.

OVJ's configuration management also provides a solution to the problem of dependent source feedback. Virtual configurations allow configurations to be defined conditionally, and so in the case of dependent source feedback (DSF), virtual configurations can be used to exclude or include object versions that are affected by DSF from any query.[9]

Analysis

The goal of the ABS-BR demonstrator was to provide a context for evaluating the technologies we have developed and the approaches that they embody. This section focuses on that evaluation and concludes with a brief discussion of alternative approaches and directions for future work.

Evaluation of the ABS-BR Demonstrator, OPJ, and OVJ

An evaluation of the ABS-BR demonstrator must include both qualitative and quantitative aspects of both the demonstrator development and the underlying technologies.

Productivity

In large part, ABS-BR productivity concerns stemmed from a high degree of code complexity induced by persistence, versioning, and explicit memory management. We

---

[9] At the time of writing, support for DSF-free queries through virtual configurations is still under development.

briefly analyze the ABS-BR and the demonstrator with respect to two aspects of overall productivity—development and maintenance costs.

Development

The ABS-BR was developed using state of the art commercial OODBMS technology. The development, including a detailed analysis phase, took a team of around fifteen programmers three years (45 person years). The business logic of the application comes to more than 90,000 lines of C++ (not including the graphical user interface). Much of this is accounted for by the use of templates for the generation of an object versioning mechanism, maintenance of explicit persistent to transient mappings, and explicit memory management through `alloc` / `free`.

By contrast, the development of the ABS-BR demonstrator prototype took one programmer four months. The demonstrator implements the core ABS-BR schema and about 25 percent of the total functionality in just 3400 lines of Java. An additional 3050 lines of Java implement an advanced graphical user interface using Swing (the GUI includes support for drag and drop, hierarchical displays, etc.). The ease of development was highlighted by the fact that the first version of the demonstrator was developed as a nonpersistent Java application entirely independently of OPJ and yet ran persistently *without modification* once OPJ became available.[10] Although the demonstrator does not implement user help, data migration, and other such peripheral functionality, the simplicity of the demonstrator implementation indicates that the use of Java, OPJ, and OVJ facilitates a *substantially* simpler (and thus cheaper) development process.

Maintenance

Though it is not possible to make meaningful comparisons about the *actual* maintenance costs of the respective systems, two characteristics stand out as indicators that maintenance costs for the demonstrator would likely be substantially lower than for the ABS-BR. First, the complexity of the code is dramatically reduced, yielding substantially shorter and simpler code. For example, the class `coreu`, which implements the important CoreUnit in the BR application, is 3113 lines of C++ code in the ABS-BR and 1213 lines of Java in the demonstrator. Since code size and code complexity are key factors in software maintenance costs, it seems likely that the demonstrator code would have appreciably lower maintenance costs. Second, the implementation of versioning at the level of application code through templates adds a great deal to the complexity of the ABS-BR code and, again, is likely to be a significant ABS-BR maintenance cost that will not be incurred by the demonstrator.

Performance

Ideally we would present results directly comparing the performance of the ABS-BR with that of a complete ABS-BR demonstrator implementation. However, although the demonstrator currently implements the most important functionality for such a comparison, it is not possible to access ABS-BR source data, and for a variety of reasons it would not be practical to benchmark the ABS-BR against some other data source.

---

[10] OPJ was being developed concurrently and so was not available until after the first demonstrator prototype was ready.

All the benchmarks presented in this chapter were executed on a single Sun Ultra-170 with 128MB of RAM and separate hard disks for the persistent store and log.

In a first empirical performance analysis, we have compared the user interface over a database of half a million objects using a transient version (that loaded serialized data at initialization time), an orthogonally persistent version, and an orthogonally versioned version. The response time of the navigation and update of the company graph was quite similar in all three versions. We attribute this favorable result to the high overhead of the Swing interface that helped to overshadow the read and write barrier overhead of the persistent versions.

We have also evaluated the performance of the key underlying system—OPJ. The primary role of OPJ is as a persistent object system, so we compare it here against a number of alternative systems using a standard OODBMS benchmark, OO7 [Carey 1993].

In the results that follow, we include performance figures for our first two implementations of OPJ (ANU-OPJ-shell and ANU-OPJ-façade), each of which used different swizzling policies [Marquez 2000]. The results show performance problems for both systems when executing cold.[11] In the case of ANU-OPJ-shell, we attribute this largely to eager memory consumption for the allocation of shell objects in the swizzling process. Whereas for ANU-OPJ-façade, we believe that the poor results are due largely to extensive use of the Java Native Interface (JNI) and the substantial cost incurred on each transition of the Java/C++ interface. Additionally, some of the transformations used in the façade approach may reduce the opportunities for code inlining and optimization by the Just in Time (JIT) compiler [Marquez 2000].

In both of these implementations, native methods were used for the time-consuming tasks associated with read barriers, such as object faulting and reification. However, instrumentation of the system demonstrated that the barriers performed substantially better when the kernel of the barrier was implemented in Java rather than as native methods. This is attributed to the substantial overhead of native method invocation and the capacity for the JIT to optimize frequently executed code. In future implementations we hope to reduce our use of JNI and C++ substantially.

Benchmarking Environment

We have used the OO7 benchmark [Carey 1993] to evaluate the systems. The results presented here compare the performance of ANU-OPJ (ANU-OPJ-shell and ANU-OPJ-façade), PJama [Atkinson 1997] (versions 0.5.7.10 and 1.2), PSI-SSM (a SHORE-based implementation using C++), and Java running without persistence. The PJama implementations are unable to take advantage of JIT technology, whereas ANU-OPJ can leverage this technology to produce competitive performance and portability. The small OO7 benchmarks are used since we were not able to run the medium database over any version of PJama or PSI-SSM.

It is possible that the hot[12] times could degrade as the database size is increased. In this case, techniques such as object cache eviction and promotion will become a necessity. None of our implementations support these techniques, but this support could easily be built on top of the normal Java garbage collection (using finalizer methods

---

[11] Cold execution times are for the initial run where the data have not been faulted into memory and must be retrieved from the underlying store.

[12] Hot execution times are for runs where the data have already been faulted into memory.

and weak references), with the support of an object cache that can flush objects and still maintain their locks.

The same Java code was used for the ANU-OPJ, PJama, and JDK systems with only minor modifications required for each. For the base code to run on either ANU-OPJ-shell or ANU-OPJ-façade it was only necessary to insert a call to Chain() at the point where the benchmark required a commit. The nonpersistent version (JDK 1.2.2) needed minor changes to allow the generation and benchmark phases of OO7 to occur in a single execution. For PJama it was necessary to add code that opened the store, retrieved the persistent roots, and called stabilizeAll() at the point where the benchmark required a commit.

For PSI-SSM, the OO7 benchmark was implemented in C++. The implementation does not use swizzling, but instead explicitly translates persistent references to pointers at each traversal, and makes explicit update notifications. Smart pointers [Lippman 1991] were used to perform the reference translations, affording a degree of syntactic transparency.

Both version 0.5.7.10 (which required JDK 1.1.7) and version 1.2 of PJama were used. JDK 1.2.2 (with the Hot Spot JIT) was used to execute the ANU-OPJ-shell, ANU-OPJ-façade, and nonpersistent (JDK) versions of the OO7 benchmarks. ANU-OPJ-shell, ANU-OPJ-façade, and PSI-SSM used the Shore storage manager.

Performance Results

Each impulse reported corresponds to the normalized average execution time for ten executions of a particular benchmark. The benchmarks reported here are traversals t1, t2c, t3b, t4, t5do, t5undo, t6 to t10, and wu, and queries q1 to q8, in this order.[13] The results are presented separately for the traversals and queries because of markedly different characteristics of the two benchmark groups.

The cold execution results in Figure 10.5 indicate that ANU-OPJ implementations perform worse than PJama1.2 when cold (2.2 times slower than PJama version 1.2 on average). We attribute these results to the excessive context switching between Java and C++ using JNI.

The hot execution results in Figure 10.6 indicate that ANU-OPJ-shell implementation performs well when hot (five times better than PJama version 1.2 and three times better than the ANU-OPJ-façade implementation on average), outperforming both PJama implementations in almost all the operations. The ANU-OPJ-shell performs better than any other implementation in read-only operations (almost eight times better than PJama 1.2 on average), even outperforming a C++ based implementation over the same store. We attribute the strength of these results to the JDK1.2.2 JIT compiler and to the cost of explicit reference translation in the C++ implementation.

Read and Write Barrier Overhead

Figure 10.7 compares the ANU-OPJ shell and façade implementations with a nonpersistent implementation of the OO7 benchmark operations. This graphic demonstrates a moderate overhead for all query operations (150 percent on average). However, traversal operations were much more expensive (370 percent on average), largely as a consequence of greater transaction commit costs for that group of benchmarks. We

---

[13] It was not possible to present results for the complete suite of OO7 benchmarks. Benchmarks t2a, t2b, and t3a did not run in either ANU-OPJ implementation or PJama. Benchmarks "i" and "d" did not run due to an unidentified failure in the Shore storage manager.

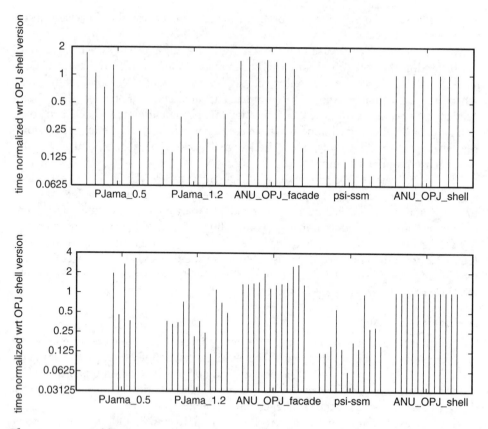

Figure 10.5   Cold query (top) and traversal (bottom) times relative to corresponding ANU-OPJ-shell time.

believe that the query results are significant, because they suggest that the run-time efficiency of the Java language environment is unlikely to be a stumbling block to the use of Java in the context of persistent data management.

Scalability

We have not been able to make a detailed scalability analysis of the ABS-BR, OPJ, or OVJ, although we have shown that the demonstrator will scale to at least half a million objects.

However, the key scalability properties of the ABS-BR lie in its *architecture*, and in large part are independent of OPJ or OVJ but depend instead on the scalability of the underlying object database. The use of the PSI interface allows OPJ to utilize any underlying store that supports the interface—we have trivially constructed bindings for a number of databases, including Oracle. The fact that user code is unaffected by the choice of OODBMS liberates the developer, enabling users to choose the OODBMS that best suits their demands at any time without impacting *any* of their application code (of course a once-off data migration will probably be necessary).

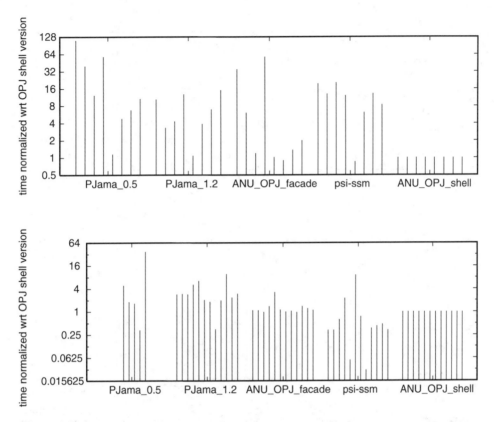

Figure 10.6   Hot query (top) and traversal (bottom) times relative to corresponding ANU-OPJ-shell times.

Commercial Alternatives and Related Work

The focus of this chapter has been the challenges of high performance object database applications and the development of technologies that address them. We have presented some quite specific solutions to these problems and demonstrated their utility. Although our solutions have direct commercial application, at this stage they lie in the realm of academic research. However, there are alternative approaches available, including commercial ones, some of which were developed independently during the course of our work. In this section we briefly look at some of these.

OPJ Alternatives

To this point there have been no commercially available persistent object systems that fully implement orthogonal persistence for Java. Some would argue that this reflects a long-held commercial perspective that orthogonal persistence is an impractical technology [Carey 1996], and it certainly seems true that orthogonal persistence

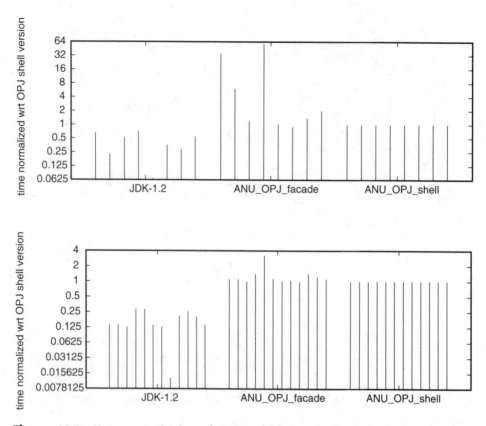

Figure 10.7 Hot query (top) and traversal (bottom) times for a nonpersistent implementation (JDK) and ANU-OPJ-façade relative to corresponding ANU-OPJ-shell times.

researchers have not been sufficiently pragmatic in their efforts to have the technology commercialized. Nonetheless, recent developments indicate that technological advances (particularly with respect to Java) and growing demand for object technology are bringing vendors ever closer to the orthogonal persistence ideal. This shift is most notable in a progression of ODMG standards, the most recent of which, ODMG 3.0, has led to the proposal of a new standard for persistence of objects in Java—the Java Data Objects standard [Sun Microsystems 1999].[14] This specification is expected to play a fundamental role in the portable implementation of container-managed persistence in Enterprise JavaBeans (EJB) [Sun Microsystems 1997] servers. Thus Java Data Objects implementations probably correspond to the closest commercial offering to OPJ, and could serve as a close substitute to OPJ in developing a solution such as the one presented here. Indeed, we have used the SEF to develop our own JDO implementation and have built a version of the ABS-BR using JDO rather than OPJ.

---

[14] At the time of writing, the JDO proposal had just been "approved for development" under the Java Community Process (JSR-12). See http://java.sun.com/aboutJava/community-process/jsr

Unfortunately JDO has a number of serious deficiencies. Notably, although JDO implements persistence by reachability, persistence is *not* type-orthogonal. Thus an object may be reachable from a persistent root but of a nonpersistent type, leading to dangling pointers in the persistent object graph. Furthermore, JDO does not have the pure transactional model of our OPJ implementation, but rather intermixes transactional and nontransactional computation. This has two significant consequences: transactional isolation is not enforced within the JVM, and in order to implement abort semantics in a manner that is visible to nontransactional computation, JDO implementations must explicitly restore cached objects that were updated in any aborted transaction.

OVJ Alternatives

Some commercial OODBMSs, such as O2 [Lee 1999], Ode [Lieuwen 1999], and ONTOS [ONTOS 1996], provide object versioning support as part of their programming language environment. Most of these products do this through hard-coded version semantics and lack support for configuration management. Thus programmers must manage configurations through the use of basic versioning functionality and dynamic binding. An exception is ONTOS, which provides the concept of configuration streams that correspond to configuration graphs [ONTOS 1996], but it still has quite rigid versioning semantics. None of these offers the transparency provided by OVJ, so none are able to fill the same role of hiding object versioning management complexity from the application programmer.

The concept of database versions in multiversion databases [Gancarski 1995] is perhaps the closest in the literature to our notion of transparency. A multiversion database may be seen as a generalization of a conventional (monoversion) database, each database version being equivalent to a conventional database. The language DML [Gancarski 1995] includes the concept of a default database version (configuration) that is similar to our concept of an implicit configuration context in OVJ, but DML is limited to a query language.

Directions for Future Work

The work presented here directly addresses some of the major issues facing implementers of high performance object server technology. Nonetheless many challenges remain. Perhaps the most pressing of these is schema evolution and schema versioning. Although we have discussed at some length the motivation for and implementation of transparent *data* (object instance) versioning (realized as OVJ), schema versioning concerns *meta-data* (class) versioning. This is very important because just as data changes over time, so too does meta-data—both because systems modeled by the meta-data change and also because the way systems are modeled changes (improvements in algorithms, bug fixes, etc.). Thus different historical instances of a single object may have been created by different classes, according to when they were created.

Although we have not reported our work on schema versioning, we have been researching this area actively and are in the process of implementing transparent support for schema versioning that we will employ in the ABS-BR demonstrator. We are also working on a number of other topics related to the ABS-BR, including extending OPJ to applets.

Conclusion

Object server technologies are becoming increasingly important; however, large applications—such as our case study, the ABS-BR—are facing major challenges in the form of complexity and scale. The task of implementing the application's business logic is clouded by the need to manage concerns such as persistence, transactions, versions, heterogeneity, and distribution. The consequence of this is complex code, large applications, long development times, and high maintenance costs.

We have used the ABS-BR case study as a forum for examining these problems and as a platform for evaluating new solutions. The approach we have presented here is deeply rooted in the principle that *abstraction* is the key in the fight against software complexity, and has been shaped by our use of Java as a development context. In our implementations of Orthogonally Persistent Java (OPJ) and Orthogonal Versioning for Java (OVJ) we have shown how effectively this principle of abstraction can be applied to the problem at hand, and demonstrated the utility of Java as a context for implementing such solutions.

Although the commercial viability of such a pervasive application of the principle of abstraction has at times been questioned [Carey 1996], we view the emergence of Java as a turning point in that quest. To us, the cleanness, efficiency, generality, and portability of the solutions we have developed are indicators that the approach is on the cusp of being commercially viable. The progress of the new Java Data Objects (JDO) standard suggests to us that industry is beginning to think so too.

The message to OODB application developers thus is clear: modern programming language technology is opening up powerful new languages as realistic implementation choices, and such languages provide a realistic means for powerfully and radically applying abstraction as the key to the fight against application complexity. This realization will open the door to new, cleaner, development approaches, and should lead to simpler, cheaper OODB applications.

PART

Five

Database Development

Chapter 11, "The Unified Modeling Process in Web-Deployed, Object-Oriented Database Systems" by Janssen, Rine, and Damiani begins with an overview of the issues in designing object oriented applications, including a methodology that they have been developing for several years to improve team productivity and quality. They provide particular attention to the design and development of those aspects that include a persistent common object model. Second, they describe their experiences with development using the Unified Modeling Language (UML) in Rational Rose and an Object-Oriented Database for an application called B2C_Sys. Finally, they discuss some future directions.

Many universities and colleges have been teaching courses in object databases for a number of years, but we are not aware of any published papers that describe experiences that lecturers have had with this technology or the successes/problems their students have encountered using object databases for practical assignment work. Chapter 12, "Teaching Object-Oriented Database Concepts" by Tari, Craske, and Bukhres, is, therefore, a very useful contribution. The chapter provides a discussion of the teaching methods used, some of the practical assignments that were set, and some of the issues and problems that students encountered. This chapter also provides some details about the teaching material used and should serve as a good reference to many lecturers and students.

Sometimes when dealing with a new technology, it can be useful to have a "quick start" guide that provides some useful information for developers to get them up to speed quickly. Furthermore, any pitfalls to avoid or "gotchas" to use can also be very valuable. Chapter 13, "Building a Jasmine Database" by Fallon, falls into this category. Based upon his experiences using Jasmine over a period of time, he uses his knowledge to good effect by describing some examples using particular product features. Although the chapter is obviously focused on one particular object database, you should become more alert to product-specific issues when evaluating different object databases. Furthermore, the number of Jasmine developers is growing and many of them are still using the current GA version of Jasmine and may find the ideas presented in this chapter to be helpful.

One of the major benefits that object databases claim over relational databases is that they use existing programming languages and manage both transient and persistent (database) objects in a similar way, overcoming the often-quoted "impedance mismatch" problem. This should make the task of the developer easier, since the language used for application development is the same language that the database understands. In reality, some extensions to existing languages typically are needed to manage database operations, such as opening/closing a database, transactions, and so on. Chapter 14, "Seamlessness and Transparency in Object-Oriented Databases" by Kaplan and Wileden, shows that for products that follow the ODMG standard, seamless persistence is not possible since transient and persistent objects are treated differently, with the result that transparency is lost. Furthermore, the problem is greater for multiple language bindings. Through their research work, the authors also report upon their experiences with multiple language bindings.

CHAPTER 11

The Unified Modeling Process in Web-Deployed, Object-Oriented Database Systems

It is generally accepted that, when an object model specifies object persistence, an object-oriented database is the most natural means for implementing that persistence. However, there is an ongoing debate among database developers concerning object modeling as an effective way to develop object-oriented database applications, especially those involving distributed object databases. The reasons for this may include a database programmer's need to do the additional modeling step prior to actual coding of an application, or management's belief that the modeling adds cost to development, or a belief that present relational database technology is higher performing. However, some believe that object modeling can reduce costs substantially and improve the odds of developing an application that actually meets end-users' requirements. Especially in designing large, complex systems it is becoming common for systems analysts and designers to use The Unified Modeling Language (UML), and for programmers to follow UML design during implementation. This approach has become the culture in some software development houses, and it is likely that other companies will need to follow suit in the use of object design tools to remain competitive. This is critical in the rapidly changing global economy, where those who *do it best* grow, and the others fade away. Therefore the question for those developing software is most likely to be how, rather than if, they will use design and development object tools to increase software quality and object-oriented toolkits such as Objectivity when developing object-oriented (OO) database applications.

Several approaches have been suggested for OO design, including OMT [Rumbaugh 1991], OOA/OOD [Coad 1990, 1991], OOD [Booch 1991], and UML [Burkhardt 1995]. Of these, UML and the encompassing Unified Modeling Process (UMP) methodology are considered in this chapter, since their capabilities cover the other alternatives. A comparison of various UML tools can be found in Wasserman's *Proceedings of the Technology of Object-Oriented Languages and Systems* [Wasserman 1998]. In recent years UMP has become a *de facto* standard among software engineers. A primary reason for its widespread acceptance is that UMP/UML is capable of full system specification. However, even though a good idea, UMP/UML for OO database application development still has not become widespread because of continued use of legacy relational database systems commitments.

In this chapter we first describe two primary aspects of UMP: unified modeling (UM) and the Unified Modeling Language (UML). Then we explore the use of UMP/UML for OO database application development in particular. We provide a simple example with a popular UMP modeling tool, Rational Rose. Using a new Rose plug-in called Rose Link, we design and automatically generate C++ code for an object-oriented database management system, Objectivity/DB (www.objectivity.com). Objectivity/DB complies with the ODMG standard [Cattell 2000]. Rose Link adds the capability to Rational Rose to generate the Objectivity/DB schema automatically, in addition to the application code that Rational Rose generates from UML.

Finally, in the last sections of this chapter, we explore the issues associated with UMP/UML for the specialized case of deployment of distributed OO databases over the Web and Internet. We illustrate this approach for the development of a simple Web-deployed application using optional implementations of TCP/IP sockets, servlets/RMI, XML, and CORBA, and discuss some issues, limitations, and tradeoffs associated with each. Potential problems with Internet deployment are described and solutions are provided.

Objectivity/DB Architecture

Throughout the chapter we shall extensively refer to the Objectivity Object-Oriented Database Management System (OODBMS). Objectivity employs a homogeneous, federated database system perspective. This means that a single OODBMS logically may contain one or more databases, each provided with its data type information (e.g., its schema) and its boot file information (e.g., its lock server host). From the application point of view, logical databases are used to store objects, but Objectivity supports a simple though flexible hierarchical internal structure that we shall now briefly review.

Though an Objectivity federated OO database may well be stored physically in a single file, each database logically consists of a system-created default *container* and a user-defined *container*. The federated OO database will be composed of multiple containers, each belonging to a single logical database.

The default container holds basic objects that were not specifically placed in user-defined containers. In turn, containers logically hold basic objects, which are physically clustered together in memory pages and on disk.

The internal organization of an Objectivity container can be sketched roughly as follows: Pages are the unit of retrieval and caching, and generally are not exposed to the language interfaces. Each page contains a number of slots (again, not exposed to the language interfaces), which in turn contain database objects; a basic object cannot belong to more than one container. Large objects occupy one slot, but may span multiple pages. The basic object is the fundamental storage entity of Objectivity/DB, and is the natural conceptual modeling unit, directly accessible to application layers.

In this chapter we refer to Rational Rose 2000, the Objectivity Rose Link add-in Beta 4 version, Objectivity/DB Version 5.2.1, and Microsoft Visual C++ Version 6.0 development software.

The Unified Modeling Process (UMP)

As mentioned earlier, unified modeling (UM) is an international *de facto* standardizing movement among systems, information, and software engineers to bring about a uniform way for sharing common modeling and design work. Older engineering disciplines (e.g., digital systems engineering, electrical engineering, civil engineering, chemical engineering) are able to both transmit and share standardized models and designs between, for example, designers and manufacturers. Older engineering disciplines are also able to promote industries based upon common parts and common interfaces. To an extent, these abilities that older engineering disciplines have are lacking in the newer systems, information, and software engineering disciplines. The lack of these abilities inhibits both technology transfer and development.

UM has been promoted in part by the Object Management Group (OMG) whose activities and progress can be explored through their Web site at www.omg.org. Through recent work of the OMG, software tools developers, universities/colleges, and publishers, a common discipline is emerging that should benefit systems, information, computer, communications, and software engineers. These benefits include a common modeling and design language, a common development process architecture, and common interfaces. Benefits such as these may encourage the interchange of components in the form of requirements components, model components, design components, and binary components.

Unified Modeling Language (UML)

The Unified Modeling Language (UML) is meant to be a commonly accepted modeling and design engineering notation that can be used effectively by systems, information, software, computer, and communications engineers. The UML is meant to be an improvement over past generations of such languages (e.g., entity-relationship languages (ER), data flow languages (DF), state transition languages (StateCharts), formal languages (Z, Object-Z, B), OMT, and requirements defining languages). UML covers the capabilities of these earlier notations. Moreover, since UML is meant to be promoted as a *de facto* standard it can, therefore, improve the prior status of CASE tools by requiring that all future tools support work using only the standard UML. Hence, to an extent, UML becomes a standard interface to which all tools must adhere.

The UML is an end-to-end software programming, systems modeling and designing, and information modeling and designing language. The language is similar to other programming languages in that it has a context-free grammar, a structure editor, a debugger, and an interpreter-compiler. The language has a standard definition, and it is compiled into another form that can be read easily and used by other tools. UML is similar to other information defining and manipulating languages in that information beginning at the data requirements level can be defined and later manipulated. The language is successfully being used as a total systems engineering language.

UML Programming Environment

The UML programming environment is meant to support directly work inside the Unified Modeling Process (UMP). The UMP is at the abstract level defined by a four-level horizontal or a five-level vertical architecture where programming is a well-defined set of work tasks for the development of a total system from requirements through to deployment and maintenance. The paradigm for the well-defined set of managed work steps is consistent with the modern *spiral development model* [Sommerville 1997]. Most managed development paradigms such as the spiral model include an ongoing evolutionary, iterative, risk managed set of work categories composed of enterprise modeling work, requirements specifying work, design work, validation and verification work, leveraging of reusable assets work, deployment work, and maintenance work. These sets of work are all identified within the UMP. In this sense most systems engineering combinations of software, information, and communication can be programmed. Moreover, deployment of the programmed end-products is a systems engineering combination of tasks executed through software, computers, communications, people, and other equipment.

The UMP architecture can be described from several perspectives. From the four-level, horizontal-layered perspective the UMP architecture can be viewed as follows:

Use cases view. Enterprise modeling and requirements

Logical view. Detailed specification of logic design

Components view. Software architecture and components

Deployment view. Installation to computer-communication systems

Work at the Use cases view is concerned with the development of the enterprise model, encapsulating required system services. Even in a general sense, software or information systems are never developed in isolation without any context. Usually, software or information systems are developed for either a particular enterprise or a marketplace of common enterprises. If, for example, engineers are developing an electronic-commerce–oriented information system, then it might be for a specific company or for a market place of similar companies. In either case the UML programming environment requires that we begin with a specification of a program.

In our example the program specification would be for B2C_Sys, a distributed system for business-to-consumer (B2C) e-commerce, run by a multinational company having branches and warehouses in several different countries. This example is a simplified version of a real system recently designed and implemented for a European company. To keep the example size manageable, here we shall assume that a single Web site (possibly replicated for performance) is the customers' entry point to the system. Data about customers, articles, and article availability are stored in a homogeneous federated Objectivity OO database, as well as in a variety of heterogeneous data sources. For the sake of simplicity, we shall assume the object schema to be the same everywhere, and each copy of the Objectivity database will contain local data about

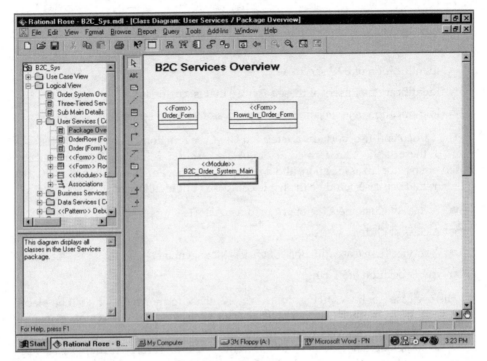

Figure 11.1 Specifying the B2C e-commerce system in a UML environment.

customers residing in the country and articles available at the local warehouse. The Web server receives an order and subdivides servicing it among branches and warehouses according to distance, cost, and availability, while trying to assign it to a single branch whenever possible. In principle, this is a rather difficult linear programming application, but we shall not deal with this aspect of the problem in this chapter.

It is however worth noting that the choice of OO storage for this application is due to the peculiar nature of the articles, which are complex hardware systems for shop-floor automation that the user can customize while visiting the Web site, by choosing the hardware cards and adapters they will include. OO storage particularly is suited to modeling and querying data characterized by such a high level of composition.

Figure 11.1 models the B2C_Sys program as a clean separation between the Web-based interface and the order system module that constitutes the back-end of our system. Each Order_Form accessible via the Web is composed of a set of Rows_in_Order_Form, which is the input to the Order_System module. Once the model has been programmed in the UML programming environment, the units (e.g., administrative units, cost unities)—represented by the package construct in the UML—that are stakeholders of the B2C_Sys UML program are identified. It may well be that although the enterprise model has been identified as having 30 units, only 12 of these units are directly stakeholders in the B2C_Sys, in the sense that only these 12 units will use the services of the system once it is deployed. In our case, each branch's Order_Administrator and Store_Administrator units are natural stakeholders to the system.

The next phase of work is the beginning of the use cases analysis of each active unit. Three kinds of use cases information need to be identified during use cases analysis of the B2C_Sys unit:

- Identification of B2C services
- Identification of users of these services, that is, customers
- Identification of associations between customers and services

The valued end-user services are termed Use Case functions. The external classes of users of these services are termed actors. A use case is a defined ordered triple composed of an actor, an association, and a use case function. For example, in the B2C_Sys an identified use case could be the triple composed of the following:

- A class of Customers (actor is Customer Actor)
- A class of Orders
- A service (Use Case function) of Order_Management
- An association of Placing

So, the use case can be written as follows, in sentence form: An Order shall be placed by a Customer. Another Use Case will involve the Order_Administrator, managing Orders, and the distributed Customer Register.

Upon completion of use cases analysis in the B2C unit, Figure 11.2 depicts a simplified portion of the active unit in the UML program B2C_Sys.

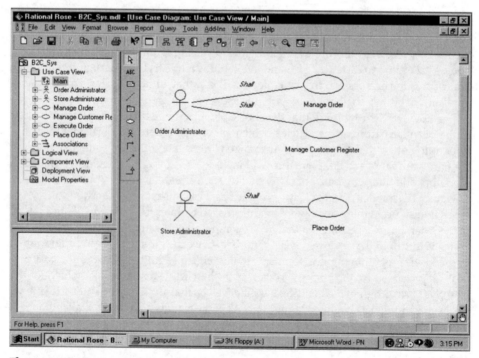

Figure 11.2   Some use cases of the B2C_Sys.

It is easy to see that in our Web-based B2C_Sys UML program each Order is a User Services complex object, composed of interface objects Order_Rows (i.e., the rows in the Web form filled in by the customer on the act of purchasing). In turn, each Order Row has to be associated to a Business Object belonging to Business Services, namely an Article (composed of Parts). Finally, Articles (as well as Customers) objects must be made persistent by a Data Service.

Being the Database Management System OO, persistency can be acquired straightforwardly by providing application space objects with permanent database OIDs, as shown in Figure 11.3.

In Objectivity, each persistent object is uniquely identified by a 64-bit OID, broken up into four 16-bit fields. The resulting three-tiered system is depicted in Figure 11.4.

In the next sections we shall first deal with implementing the Data services layer of our B2C_Sys, via an Objectivity federated database. Then, we shall examine specific problems posed by the necessity of Web-based deployment.

Using UML for Data Service Design

As Objectivity/DB complies with ODMG-98, it is possible to implement the standard's powerful semantics, from UML object model, to Objectivity/DB schema. Although substantial progress has been made, complete automation from object model to object schema is generally not possible without manual intervention and coding as we illustrate in the next section. This is because there are usually several problems that must be

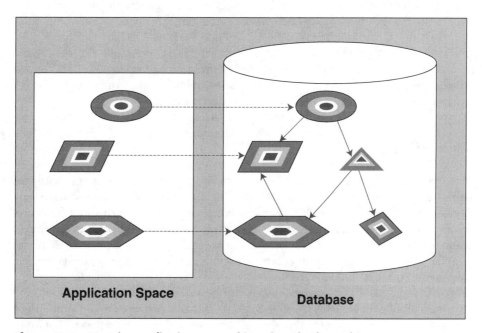

Figure 11.3 Mapping application space objects into database objects.

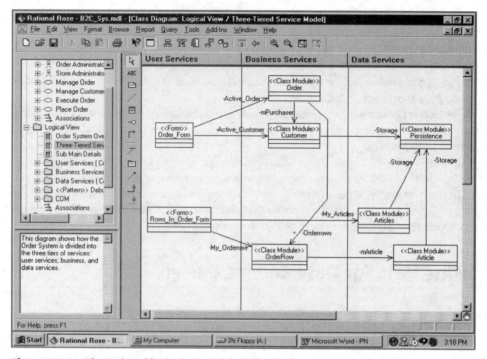

Figure 11.4   Three-tiered logical view of the B2C system.

overcome before complete automation can be achieved. In general, automation is possible when an object model is defined with all semantic information; as we will illustrate later in this chapter, complete automation is prevented by software- and hardware-specific implementation constraints. Therefore, in practice it is generally not the goal to attain specification of every detail of program operation with UML, but to facilitate the development via a combination of automated and manual steps.

One issue of debate is whether it is cost effective to model with UML prior to development. Some believe it is best to minimize modeling costs, by limiting the modeling effort to only the details required to generate language-specific function shells such as C++, and to code the functions manually. This would be especially true when the effort to model deeper, more complete specifications produces only marginal Objectivity gains. Furthermore, many functions are provided by libraries of reusable software components, such as Java Beans or C++ libraries. In these cases it is usually not cost effective to redesign and develop functions again, especially when those functions already have proven reliability and cost effectiveness. Consider for example communications software libraries that include e-mail functions. Although possible to model an e-mail system in detail within an application, it would not be cost justifiable, and added value would be unlikely. For these reasons it is important to consider the utility and cost benefit before deciding upon the depth and detail of a modeling effort. There are no set rules because each system is different. But one simple rule-of-thumb might be, if in doubt, to limit the amount of time effort expended in UML to the level of functional shells. Exceptions to this rule would be especially complex functions, and other cases where the utility and cost benefit of modeling the details with UML is indicated.

One means of reducing development cost and improving quality is through automated code generation from UML. For example, Objectivity/DB offers a high degree of integration with Rational Rose, a popular object-modeling tool from Rational Software. Integration may be accomplished by a plug-in to Rational Rose that provides the capability to generate Objectivity/DB Data Definition Language (DDL) schema statements, and other C++ classes. Furthermore, users can reverse-engineer Objectivity/DB schema back to Rational Rose, allowing software engineers to generate models that can easily be understood and modified in Rational Rose. This functionality gives Objectivity/DB "round-trip" engineering integration with Rational Rose, something that, to our knowledge, few other OO databases offer.

As part of its integration with Rational Rose, Objectivity/DB does the following:

Creates Objectivity DDL files and schemas database from a Rose model. Objectivity/DB makes a class persistent by clicking on the Persistent Radio Button, or by deriving a class explicitly from a persistent base class such as ooObj, the abstract base class used by Objectivity for the persistence hierarchy. Also, any class that is derived from a persistent class is implicitly considered as persistent, regardless of whether or not the derived class is tagged as persistent. Associations and propagation properties can be defined in Rose. For example one dialog box would be the default dialog of Rational Rose C++ add-in. Because it is a language-independent case tool, the Detail Tab has a Persistence Radio Button, although standard C++ does not support persistence. For Rose C++ code generator, this does not have any meaning and has no effect to the output code. With Rose Objectivity Link, Article, the class marked as persistent becomes a subclass of ooObj and is generated into a DDL file. To some model elements, "Objectivity"-specific properties are added. For example, association has some properties to define Objectivity-specific behavior, such as propagation.

Reverse engineering from Objectivity schema. Objectivity/DB in principle can reverse-engineer an existing schema into a Rational Rose model. It will create a Rational Rose model with all user-defined classes, associations, inheritance, hierarchy, and so on, including appropriate properties on each of the model elements such as propagation. By using both reverse and forward functionality, the user can generate DDL files from an existing schema database. This might be useful for users who use active or dynamic schema. For example, it can generate C++ DDL from existing schema defined in Java. Or it can generate C++ DDL after the existing schema is modified by using Active Schema functionality. The schema classes reversed from the Objectivity schema database belong to one component—Single DDL file. Because the Objectivity schema database does not have any information about the schema file in which the class is defined, the user has to assign the classes to a specific component.

Schema Evolution. A user in principle can modify existing class definitions in Rational Rose. In some cases, the modifications are automatically affected to the schema via generated DDL. Users may have to add some pragmatic statements manually for some schema evolution case.

OO Database Development with UML Example

Now we are ready to describe the process of translating the UML example to machine-readable object database schema and C++ code. In particular, the Objectivity/DB schema is generated using a new plug-in to Rational Rose developed by Objectivity, Inc.

The process of generating the schema for the Rational Rose UML example described in the beginning of this chapter requires four primary steps:

1. The UML model in Rational Rose is updated with the Objectivity properties that describe where the Objectivity/DB resides (termed "Boot File Directory"), and the location of the C++ Project file. This can be obtained by creating the UML model in the Objectivity framework directly, by importing an existing model into such a framework, or by using the Rational Rose integrator tool.

2. The classes of objects that require persistent storage are made "persistence-capable." In Objectivity these classes are derived from the class of basic objects (ooObj) or the class of "container" objects (ooContObj). Figure 11.5 shows the UML class that is used in our model to provide persistence to the Article class.

3. All associations must be defined. Rose Link provides options for:

    (a) inline association types (long or short)

    (b) propagation of delete to the associated object

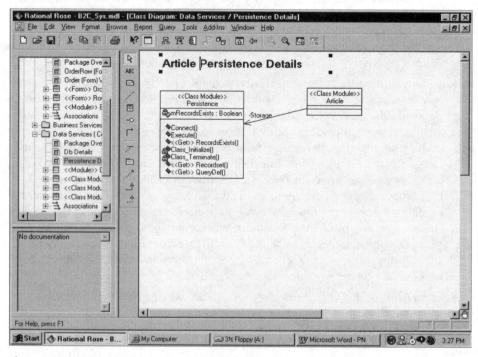

Figure 11.5 Giving persistence to the Article class.

(c) copying the behavior to the associated object

(d) propagation of locks to the associated object

(e) version control

4. Finally, a schema for Objectivity/DB is generated using the Rose Link plug-in in Rational Rose.

Before we begin, it is important to note that UML does not model some of the constructs that generally are needed in Objectivity/DBs, such as indices, and other features that cannot be modeled with UML in its current form. Rose Link provides for incorporation of all these features of Objectivity/DB by allowing the embedding of code references before the DDL generation in the Microsoft Visual Studio environment. This means component code files written in C++ and stored in the Visual Studio can be included in the DDL generation, providing a means of maintaining and reusing code independently of the UML. Once this manual step is completed, Rose Link is used to generate the new Objectivity/DB schema definition.

So we see that Rose Link does not yet provide completely automated application code generation and schema definition from UML. However, it does a significant part, and the UML to code techniques will continue to improve.

Once a model has been created or imported in the Objectivity framework, one starts by making selected classes persistence-capable. The procedure to do so is shown in Figure 11.6.

Then, association properties must be defined in the proper way; for instance by setting whether object associations are to be in long or short format (Figure 11.7).

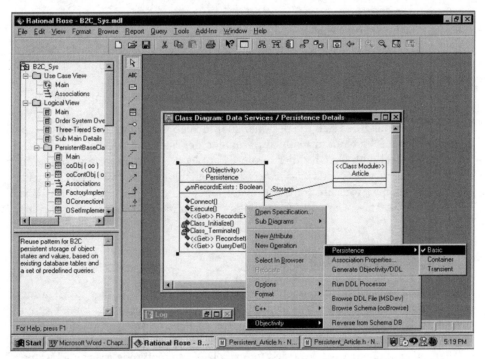

Figure 11.6 Adding persistence in Objectivity.

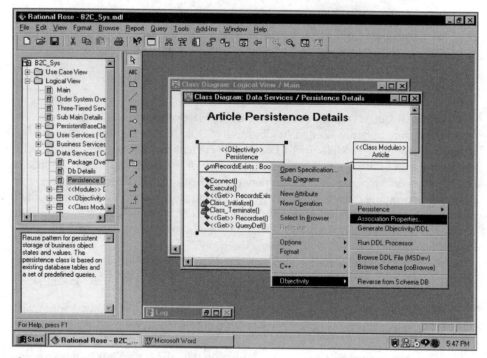

Figure 11.7 Setting association properties.

The rationale for this operation is that UML provides a wide spectrum of association definitions that must be mapped to the more restricted set of Objectivity DDL relationships. The Objectivity framework sets default properties for this mapping that can be adjusted manually by the software designer.

Then, class attributes must be dealt with (Figure 11.8) to ensure proper mapping to Objectivity type space.

While performing this step the designer should keep in mind that some C++ types (e.g., pointer types) are not formally applicable to persistence-related classes. Though we shall not deal with technicalities in our example, it is also important to note that some subtle language dependencies may be hidden in this step: for instance, persistence-capable classes may well use transient ones as members in C++, whereas this is not allowed in Java. Then, Get and Set methods are required to be set for the attributes (Figure 11.9).

Generating DDL Classes

To generate DDL files, a component must be defined for each DDL class definition; moreover an additional standard component (included by default in the Objectivity framework) is needed for the federation. The latter is automatically added by the Objectivity framework. See Figure 11.10.

Then, a Component must be added for each DDL, stereotyping it as an Objectivity DDL (see Figure 11.11). Classes then must be assigned to the new component, as shown

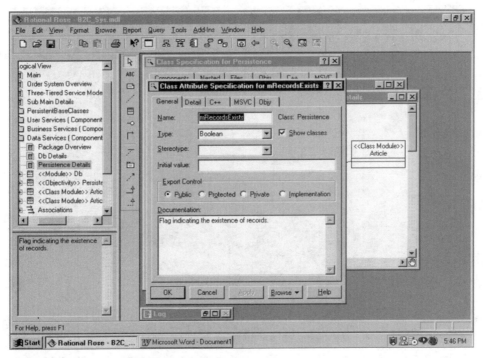

Figure 11.8 Dealing with attribute types.

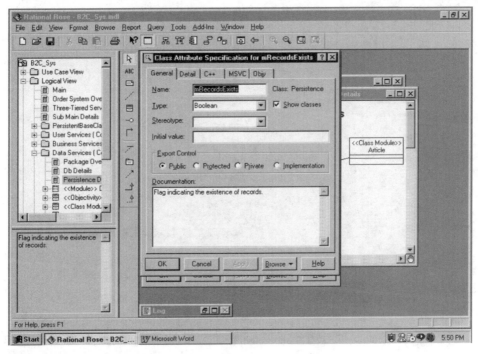

Figure 11.9 Generating Get and Set methods for an attribute.

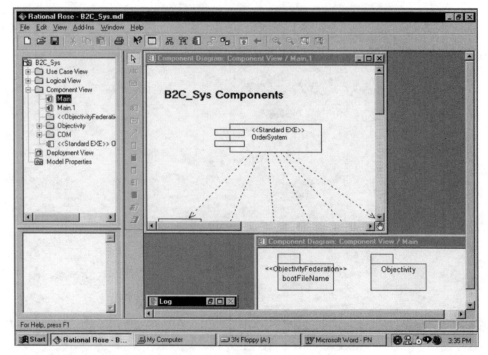

Figure 11.10 Component view of the B2C system after importing it in the Objectivity framework.

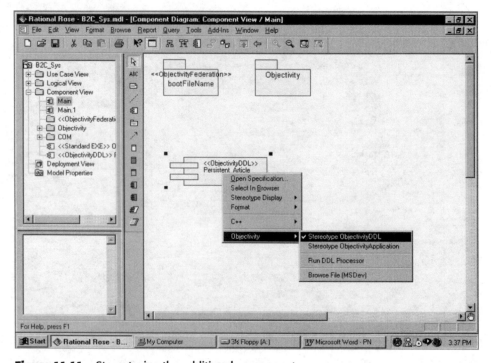

Figure 11.11 Stereotyping the additional component.

in Figure 11.12. After assigning persistent classes to the additional component, DDL file generation can be performed from the Federation Component (Figure 11.13).

Note that Rational Rose does not support ordering of the DDL at this stage, and a text-based utility called DDL processor must be run if the DDL code must be generated or processed in a specific order.

At this point the schema is generated by Rose Link as illustrated in Figure 11.14, showing the C++ header for the Article Class in the upper window and the *Get* and *Set* operations in the lower window.

Additional modification of the generated code may be necessary to gain performance or other kinds of improvements. For example, an index can improve performance in Objectivity/DB for functions such as search or lookup. In our example customers can be accessed by name, last name, and first name, using a hash table index. Another common retrieval is by Article number, so we manually added an index also. Since UML cannot represent the index, care needs to be taken when reverse-engineering to avoid loss of information. These same lines of code will need to be entered manually each time a new schema is generated from the Objectivity/DB.

This concludes the example and demonstrates some advantage of using UML in OODB design. There are potential disadvantages that we will not cover here, such as vendor dependence. It is possible to get locked into a vendor-specific product when developing a large application with a tool like Rational Rose, since there is no easy way to migrate to another vendor. In the future this may not be a problem because the Object Management Group (OMG) is working toward the development of a vendor-independent standard, XMI, that would make interchanging UML possible between software modeling tools

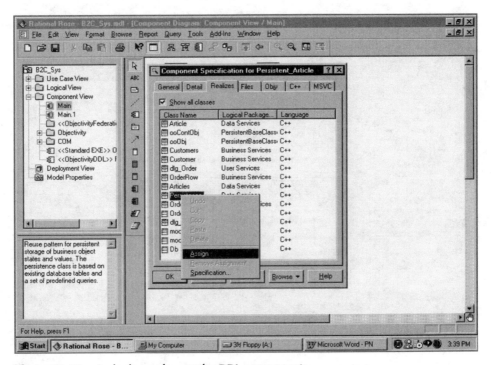

Figure 11.12   Assigning a class to the DDL component.

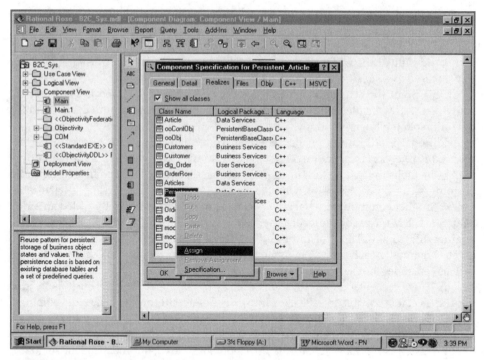

Figure 11.13 Generating DDL files from the Federation Component.

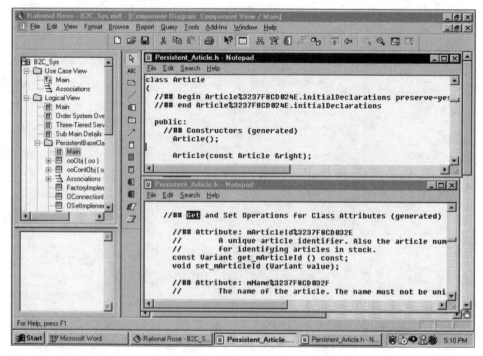

Figure 11.14 Code generated by Rose Link.

[Brodsky 2000]. Another problem, potentially more serious, is the complexity that Web- and Internet-distributed applications add to OO database modeling and the corresponding deployment. In the final section we focus on this aspect in particular.

The Web Deployment Challenge

As we have seen in previous sections, the object-oriented (OO) paradigm and conceptual modeling tools are being transported from application design to database modeling. As early research had indicated [Parent 1992]; [Sjolin 1994], this paradigm shift is proving particularly useful in application domains characterized by high composition of basic entities and multiple abstraction levels.

The use of UMP in designing applications involving OO databases allows designers to retain a more realistic mental model of complex application domains, and can help prevent several well-known design traps, for most being the famed *impedance mismatch problem* of traditional database technologies [Woodfield 1997].

Indeed, current UML-based CASE tools in general are able to deal with database application requirements at a higher level of abstraction. They can produce executable application code, *tightly coupled* with the OO database, provided that the domain representation defined at the specification/design level is firmly grounded on a sound paradigm such as UMP.

Sometimes the CASE tools' performance may not be entirely satisfactory. For instance, the compilation of automatically generated classes or methods can be slow if compared with standard IV generation imperative languages. However, several research results and case studies have documented the advantages of uniform conceptual modeling for database applications. A detailed European case study can be found in "Lessons Learned" [DOOR Esprit Project 1997]. This widely held opinion, notwithstanding early expectations of seamless design and implementation using CASE tools, is still at least partially unfulfilled. Indeed, to deliver on its promises, UMP design must be able to produce OO database applications that are both reliable (i.e., correct and robust) and performing. Under these conditions the other quality factors advertised for the method, in particular the increase in reusability and extendibility, will yield the expected benefits for software practitioners. However, recent experience has shown that this is not always the case, as database software architectures require different deployment techniques, in turn requiring ad-hoc (and sometimes awkward) solutions at the design and implementation levels. In this section we shall try to identify the deployment-related factors still hindering the full exploitation of UMP for OO database applications development, outlining how they could be overcome by future research.

Process-Driven versus Project-Driven Deployment

Unlike relational databases, OO databases still lack consolidated practices, let alone standards, for Web-based deployment. The main reason for this problem is that their deployment is seldom entirely *process-driven* using a standard methodology; much more often, the last stages of the lifecycle are *project-driven* and characterized by customer-specific needs and execution environments. Today, customer-specific deployment toolsets are adopted for each single project. This is due mainly to the rapid evolution of Web-aware software architectures. Databases' complex deployment techniques are difficult to specify entirely at the level of *UML deployment diagrams*. Each UML model contains a single deployment diagram, which shows the connections between its processors and devices, and the allocation of its processes to processors.

Figure 11.15 shows a deployment diagram illustrating a possible client/server deployment of the B2C_Sys.

Information about the mapping of components to processors, though useful, does not usually identify the auxiliary classes and concepts that have been introduced into the design for deployment purposes. For instance, the diagram in Figure 11.15 could describe socket-style connection (via the `java.net` class) as well as remote method invocation (through the Java *RMI* interface). Identifying and describing deployment-related classes, as we shall see, is the key to effective deployment automation.

Existing software architectures for OO database deployment [De Ferreira Rezende 1998] rely on developers and system administrators to port and install application-specific functionality to all sites in the systems. The rapid pace of change in Internet-related technologies, and particularly in Web deployment techniques, is the main reason for the variety of ad-hoc approaches used for application deployment.

So, much work needs to be done on how to automate the software deployment process during the whole software lifecycle by a single methodology, and to provide standard tools to automate deployment.

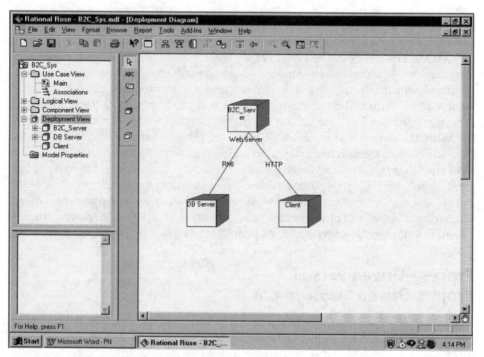

Figure 11.15 UML deployment diagram.

Some preliminary work on identification of possible risks connected to the deployment challenge and the corresponding contingency can be found in [Rodriguez-Martinez 2000]. Specifically the following risks have been described:

- High cost of development in terms of personnel training due to the use of a new advanced technology

- Higher costs than expected in terms of integration of an object-oriented database within a context of existing software

- Other costs associated with the uncertainties related to the use of advanced design tools that could be poorly supported by the suppliers and not extensively tested, with possible delays in the application development

An additional challenge is posed by the trend toward large, distributed organizations, and information systems are growing in heterogeneity as well as in size. OO technology, successful as it is, needs to coexist both with legacy systems (such as conventional relational databases or object-relational ones) and with an increasing number of heterogeneous data sources adopting different data models. Moreover, an increasing amount of information, both at the corporate and department level, is being made available through unstructured and semistructured data sources such as collections of text documents (e.g., e-mail messages) and static Web sites. Although all these data sources currently are managed and accessed by applications independently from one another, it is widely recognized that, in the fullness of time, they will have to be accessible in an integrated and uniform way to both end users and software application layers by imposing a global schema on top of the individual schemata used by each data source.

Web technology is unanimously considered to be the "right" glue to put different data sources together. After more than five years from the first approaches, though, Web-based deployment of applications involving "pure " OO databases such as Objectivity is still more an art than a science.

Deployment Quality and Effort

From the UMP designer point of view, Web deployment of OO databases should indeed be easy, as these data sources provide both the logical structure description (their OO schema), and the knowledge of instance information. Both information and *metainformation* can be used to format and present the content of an OO database via XML documents or even HTML pages.

However, when data are integrated in a naive fashion, semantic discrepancies among the various data representations may well occur; for instance, some information may be missing in some sources, an attribute may be single-valued in one source and multivalued in another, or the same entity may be represented by different classes in different sources.

Considerable development effort is required to ensure via the application layer that the integrated OO data are well structured and conform to a single, consistent abstract schema. Substantial programming effort is also required if one or more of the information sources change, or when new sources are added.

Deployment techniques greatly influence the amount of this effort and overall system performance.

Control of Application-Data Source Coupling

A fully fledged integration architecture, while allowing for sophisticated interaction styles between applications and data sources, should not hinder the possibility of close coupling (e.g., by shared storage, memory, or locality) of application and specific data sources in order to achieve the desired performance level. Experience with Objectivity, as well as with other OO databases has shown that tight coupling between applications and data is one of the strongest points of OO database technology. Web-based deployment and integration may well endanger such coupling, as using XML as an interchange format and/or HTML for presentation makes updates more awkward.

Stateful Transactions

Another important feature is keeping a stateful connection with the OO database for performance. But since the HTTP protocol is stateless—that is, HTTP servers do not retain open session information from one connection to the other—there is an increasing need for intermediate modules that answer database requests in a stateless fashion, yet guaranteeing that the database stays open for future requests.

Security Awareness

Applications that need to work across the Internet typically are deployed across great conceptual, spatial, temporal, and physical distances, often through several firewalls, as most corporations have elaborate firewall systems in place to prevent unauthorized access. Internet or Extranet deployment of database applications requires specific access control measures to ensure accuracy and confidentiality of data interchange. These measures may include:

- Two-step verification of the user's identity, based on both a password and a physical token such as a smart card (often called *two-factor authentication*)

- Three-factor authentication, which includes a physiological factor too, such as eye retina or fingerprints

- Support for a public-key security infrastructure, such as SSL

- Digital notarization of important transactions via a third party to ensure accuracy and timeliness

- Integration of the Internet-specific security with the existing enterprise security infrastructure to ensure seamless, end-to-end security

It is easy to see how a high level of security awareness may greatly influence deployment decisions.

Indeed, both corporate-wide networks and the global Net can be envisioned as composed of tight *security cells*, whose boundaries are delimited by firewalls. Many administrators would like to avoid opening special "holes" in their firewalls for business applications. A successful Internet-based deployment should guarantee the application to be able to navigate its own firm's firewall to call out to external business objects, as well as other firms' firewalls in order to invoke their internal business objects.

As we shall see, some deployment techniques involving remote access may require an additional installation burden in terms of configuring firewall traversal, or may be simply unfeasible for security reasons.

Web-Based Deployment of OO Databases

Although interaction between relational databases and Web components has been defined by the ubiquitous ODBC/JDBC family of standards, a standard interaction protocol between Web-based components and OO data sources must still be specified.

Currently, Web-based database access is obtained via three distinct deployment techniques:

- Java servlet/Remote Method Invocation (RMI)
- XML Mediators
- CORBA Shells

In the sequel, we shall briefly discuss these techniques.

Servlet-Based Deployment

Servlets are Java objects that conform to a specific interface (defined in the standard package `java.servlet`), run on the server side, and can be integrated seamlessly with most Web servers via a servlet engine (Figure 11.16).

Physically, the servlet engine usually is implemented as a `.dll` file that routes servlet requests to the Java Virtual Machine using threads of hosting server, by means of a URL to path/name mapping.

Two standard servlet classes have been predefined by JavaSoft: the GenericServlet and the HttpServlet. Both of these classes implement a standard servlet interface consisting of three methods.

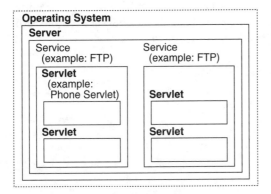

Figure 11.16 The servlet engine.

init() method. Offers one time initialization for opening files, starting helper threads, etc.

service() method. Offers stdin/stdout functionality, taking two parameters: a ServletRequest Object and a ServletResponse Object.

destroy() method. Offers garbage collection if necessary.

Servlet-based deployment, often coupled with Java's *RMI* capability, is currently among the most widespread Java-based database deployment technique. In its simplest form, servlet-based deployment involves turning the Web server into a fully-fledged database client. Such a client can have local access to the database, or can access it remotely. The latter technique involves two options: connecting to the Objectivity server using the low-level *socket* interface, or via an RMI interface.

Both options will allow the servlet code activated by the Web server to perform the basic Objectivity client–server handshake, including caching and the Objectivity primitives for Initialize, Begin Transaction, and Commit.

It should be noted however that transactions are thus originated on the Web server and not on the clients, as direct socket connections using Objectivity clients would ensure.

Writing servlets to access OO databases can sometimes be awkward, especially for language-dependency problems (servlets are mandatorily Java); in the case of Objectivity, due to Objectivity C++ and Java interoperability, the language used to generate the objects is irrelevant. Moreover, writing the code allowing servlets to access a local database is straightforward, as the Java classes representing database objects can be instantiated directly inside the servlet code, leaving it to the programmer to call their methods.

Namely, with reference to the Article class defined in previous sections, code like the following will be sufficient:

```
import com.objy.db.app.*;

public class Article extends Object {
    public String ODLName() {
            return "::DatabaseDerby::Article";
            }}
```

As anticipated, servlets can address the database classes either *locally*, as in the preceding example, or *remotely*, by retrieving such classes from an RMI server extending the Java/RMI interface. In the following example an RMI client requests a remote RMI server to store and retrieve objects using Objectivity For Java.

```
import java.rmi.* ;

public class ArticleClient
{
    //
    // Constructor.
    //
    ArticleClient( )
    {
        // Set the client security manager.
```

```
..-..
        // Get a remote server object from RMI Registry.
        StudentInterface server = null ;
        try
        {
        server = (ArticleInterface) Naming.lookup( "ARTICLE-SERVER" ) ;
        }
        catch ( Exception exception )
        {
    System.err.println ( "Error in registry lookup( ). " + exception ) ;
        }

        // Tell server to store an article.
        try
        {
            System.out.println( "Storing Article no. 1201" ) ;
            server.storeArticle( "1201" ) ;
            System.out.println( "   Article is stored." ) ;
        }
        catch ( RemoteException exception )
        {
        System.out.println( "Error in store invocation. " + exception ) ;
        }

        // Tell server to lookup that article.
        try
        {
            System.out.println( "Retrieving article no. 1201." ) ;
            Student student = server.lookupArticle( "1201" ) ;
// Object article is now available at the client side.

        }
        catch ( RemoteException exc )
        {
    System.out.println( "Error in lookup invocation. " + exception ) ;
        }
    }
    //
    // Main.
    //
    public static void main( String args[ ] )
    {
        // Create the client instance.
        ArticleClient client = new ArticleClient( ) ;
    }
}
```

If the database server lies behind a firewall with respect to the Web server, some additional manual configuration work may become necessary. Socket-based connections are least likely to cause problems, as TCP connections can be duplicated transparently by proxy-based firewalls.

As far as the problem of multiple data sources integration is concerned, servlets allow users to collect HTML information from multiple databases, providing an entry point into Objectivity's Single Logical View.

Indeed, servlets are easier to maintain and administrate than PERL script or C/C++ programs because they are dynamically loadable and provide easier scalability than other deployment techniques.

The availability of standard Java interfaces for servlet and RMI servers suggests the explicit integration of the corresponding classes in the UML design as the first step towards automatic servlet-based deployment. The servlet is a generic, dynamic container for application-specific classes, which can be obtained locally or via remote access. This could be instrumental in fully automating servlet-based deployment; however, to this date servlet-based deployment of Objectivity must be performed manually, as its steps are process- and even server-dependent.

XML-Based Deployment

XML-based deployment techniques rely on the use of *wrappers*, encapsulating databases and providing XML output, and *mediators*, providing to application layers some local caching and easy access to XML data (Figure 11.17).

Several mediator-based architectures have been proposed so far, some of them as research prototypes [Papakonstantinou 1995], others as commercial products. To deal with the problems posed by the integration of heterogeneous data sources, current

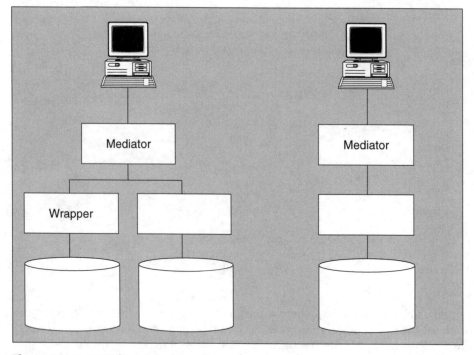

Figure 11.17 XML-based deployment.

mediator-based architectures rely on each wrapper to *publish* the information contained in the associated data source as XML data. The Objectivity Article suite will include a tool, *Xhive* (www.xhive.com), which integrates the OO database and has the capability to store, retrieve, and query XML documents, or XML document fragments conforming to the main W3C XML-related standards such as DOM, XPath, XLink, and Xpointer.

In principle, the XML-based deployment scenario lends itself to deployment automation particularly well. The MOCHA system [Rodriguez-Martinez 2000] provides a framework suitable for automating deployment of application-specific functionalities, delegating deployment to a software layer that *ships* to interested clients the Java classes through which they may access the required XML information.

CORBA-Based Deployment

OO databases increasingly rely on software architectures exploiting the CORBA 3.0 standard. As we shall see, CORBA-based deployment allows for obtaining Java objects representing database content from a remote server in a language-independent way. From the architectural point of view, CORBA-based access can be made either at the server side, not unlike what happens in the servlet-RMI technique discussed before, or at the client side. In the sequel, we shall briefly discuss server-side deployment.

CORBA environments and OO databases are indeed complementary and can be used jointly to provide a fully distributed, language-independent execution environment for persistent object application. CORBA environments include a rich set of distributed services that enlarge Java possibilities, such as transaction services, security services, naming services, or trading services. On the other hand, Java simplifies the code distribution in CORBA execution environments because its code can be managed easily from one server, and most of all, it provides a portable OO infrastructure.

UMP-based design of integration architectures for OO databases needs innovative, CORBA-compliant design patterns [Mowbray 1997], describing a standard interface all components should provide, and the communication protocols within the architecture. The same, however, can be said for deployment techniques. CORBA-based deployment techniques of OO databases are promising inasmuch as they could allow bringing back the deployment stage under the umbrella of design methodologies. Namely, they are aimed at satisfying the following requirements:

OMG-compliant interface. CORBA compliant wrappers for OO databases offer a standard OMG-compliant interface, with persistence, transaction, and query services.

UMP-based integration. Unlike other database connectivity solutions, *CORBA* wrappers allow UML classes defined at the design level to be used in implementation code.

Web awareness. Since most OO databases provide Java and C++/ODMG-compliant interfaces, it is not only feasible but also very simple to integrate them in a Web server framework based on the CORBA environment.

Heterogeneous platforms. CORBA and OO databases jointly provide a fully heterogeneous platform. For instance, a client from an INTEL PC will be able to access an Objectivity database managed on SPARC or RS-6000 platforms.

Multiple servers. An OO database system may manage a distributed database, that is, a set of ODL schemas and the corresponding OO databases, distributed on a set of disks inside a network.

From the security point of view, several CORBA systems support both SSL and two-factor (but not three-factor) authentication in their implementation, although these features are still immature. Although these features are currently proprietary, recently they have been standardized for Version 3.0 of the CORBA specification.

A word of caution is necessary however: Full usage of CORBA in implementing the colloquium between Web components and OO data sources is still in evolution, and unexpected problems may arise. Again, experience [DOOR Esprit project 1997] has shown that establishing a connection of a user interface to OO databases via some CORBA implementations may be awkward, and even not possible. Database vendors are solving these problems, but they still affect deployment in many ways.

When accessing an OO database "from outside," CORBA's Interface Definition Language (IDL) allows us to define a *CORBA wrapper*, that is, an external syntactical interface to the database. Using IDL, the designer defines the syntactical interface selecting the methods needed for the particular purpose of the view. This view can then be used by a client outside the database (i.e., a client that runs in a process but is not a native client). The designer of the syntactical interface has then to implement the wrapper on top of the OO database, inside another process that is a native client. It should be noted that the definition of a syntactical interface does not guarantee any quality of service.

CORBA architecture acts as a software bus between the application layer and the database. This deployment technique involves *flattening* the dynamic relationships among objects defined during the OMP process, translating them into interactions on the CORBA software bus.

CORBA-Based Deployment Example

We shall now use a very simple example to outline a standard CORBA-based deployment technique aimed at providing a standard link between design-level classes and the implementation-level OO database interface. Of course, this example intends only to show how, in principle, CORBA can make deployment independent from technology and project-related choices (providing a monolithic or Web-based client, using a Java *servlet* or an *applet* as a query interface, etc.), bringing it back under the methodology's umbrella. The basic idea can be outlined as follows.

A CORBA Server is deployed as a generic OQL server. In our example, the server is a *Factory* object, used to create Servants that deal with clients' requests, according to the well-known Factory design pattern [Mowbray 1997].

Web-based Clients (e.g., Web-deployed Java servlets or applications) ask the Factory object for an *O-Connection* to be created and opened. The O-Connection syntactical interface should be designed to provide roughly the same functionality as the JDBC Statement for relational databases. Often, however, a subset of those functionalities may turn out to be sufficient. Each O-connection is the Web-based equivalent of a database session, during which clients may freely execute OQL commands.

Before providing a description of this deployment technique, we need a few notions about CORBA-compliant invocations of distributed services. CORBA objects must provide a syntactical interface written in an Interface Definition Language (IDL); objects themselves are to be implemented via inheritance or delegation as Servants— in other words, network objects whose methods can be invoked remotely by other objects that possess a valid reference to them.

On the other hand, a CORBA server object will instantiate the Object Request Broker (ORB), the standard software bus connecting clients and servants; then it will forward clients' requests to servants, hiding their physical location. Normally, the server starts by instantiating a servant and connecting it to the ORB, so that clients can obtain a remote reference to it. Such creation is realized by an Object Adapter (the simplest implementation of which is the Basic Object Adapter or BOA of the version 2.0 of the standard). However, servants can also be created by other servants connected to the ORB (again, according to the Factory design pattern). In our example, we shall utilize this latter method for deploying servants allowing remote access to OO databases.

To invoke a servant, clients instantiate a local object (proxy or stub) representing a remote service to it. When the client invokes a method of the local proxy, the proxy marshals the input parameters and communicates them to the server via the ORB. The ORB forwards them to the BOA, which decodes the parameter according to the local type system and passes them to the skeleton, which is the entry point to the servant's implementation. If any return parameters are specified for the call, the procedure is repeated. By allowing both communicating objects to provide local proxies CORBA can be used to support a symmetric programming model.

Implementation Guidelines

We are now ready to provide some implementation guidelines. First of all, we observe that implementations of servants Factory, O-Connection (together with the ObjectSet object that will hold query results) can be done either via inheritance or delegation; for the sake of simplicity, here we shall briefly discuss the inheritance-based one. Using this technique, the interface implementation can be obtained simply by defining Java classes inheriting from the skeletons, as depicted in Figure 11.18.

Then, the server object (Server.java) must be implemented, which instantiates the ORB, BOA, and Factory. Its sample code is:

```
//ORB init
  org.omg.CORBA.ORB orb = org.omg.CORBA.ORB.init(args, props);
    //BOA init
    org.omg.CORBA.BOA boa = orb.BOA_init (args, props);
    //Factory init
    Factory_impl f = new Factory_impl(orb);
       //connect Factory to the ORB
    orb.connect (f,"FactoryServant");
```

In the preceding example, for the sake of simplicity we used the well-known Named Servant technique to associate a string name with a servant, while connecting it to the ORB via the `connect` method. Note that, when instantiating the Factory servant, the ORB is passed to the constructor. This way, the `CreateConnection` method instantiates an O-Connection object, connecting it to the ORB, according to the Factory design pattern.

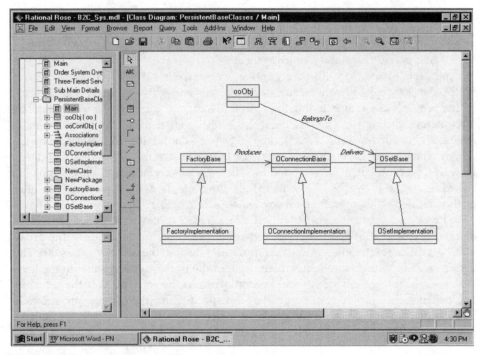

Figure 11.18 Deployment-related classes.

Clients obtain references to the servant Factory from CORBA's Naming Service, using the Factory servant's name. This can be done by invoking the get_inet_object method as shown in Listing 11.1.

The get_inet_object method will need the following parameters: the host where the Server is running, the port it is listening on, and the name of the object a reference to which must be obtained. Then, specific objects can be retrieved from the remote server much in the same way as illustrated earlier for RMI.

Of course, several other architectural issues need to be solved in order to evolve the previous examples into fully fledged deployment techniques. Here, we shall briefly discuss two possible architectural choices:

```
//ORB Init
org.OMG.CORBA.ORB orb = org.OMG.CORBA.ORB.init(args,props);
//Obtain a reference to the Factory Servant
org.OMG.CORBA.object obj = orb.get_inet_object(" romeo.sci.univr.it" ,
    5432, " FactoryServant" );
//Generate the Factory object reference from the CORBA object reference
Factory f = FactoryHelper.narrow(obj);
```

Listing 11.1 Obtaining an object reference in CORBA.

- One database client for each CORBA client
- A single database client for several CORBA clients

The first solution must be chosen when the CORBA clients run concurrently on the same data in potentially conflicting modes. In this case they need to rely on the database's own transactional system (one client per transaction).

The second solution can be adopted when either the CORBA clients are not conflicting (for instance they all run in read-only mode) or when each request coming from a CORBA client can be implemented as a complete transaction (which is valuable only when the implementation of the request involves a significant amount of data manipulation).

Conclusion

Though several well-known techniques are available for Web-based deployment of OO databases, they do not yet lend themselves to automation in the framework of the UMP process, mainly because they require additional classes to be identified and inserted at the design level to facilitate deployment. The insertion of such classes may impair design uniformity, especially when alternative choices are available (e.g., inheritance versus delegation in CORBA-based deployment).

We have discussed some of these deployment schemes and described their major drawbacks, namely the cost and complexity burden they add to the design stage, the need for manual installation and maintenance of system-wide software architectures, and their potential lack of scalability to large populations of clients and servers.

Automatic deployment should also involve finding and retrieving deployment-related classes from code repositories, and shipping those classes to the sites requiring them. Although some interesting research [Rodriguez-Martinez 2000] has been done in this area, much work still needs to be done to incorporate such capabilities in the UMP process.

Teaching Object-Oriented Database Concepts

Teaching object-oriented database management systems (OODBMSs) is not just about teaching concepts or the use of a specific system. It is also about putting current knowledge of databases, which is generally based on the relational technology, into the object-oriented context. This can be done by showing how the two technologies contrast, and by making sure that the OODBMS-specific concepts are well understood. In this chapter, we describe our experiences in teaching a subject related to OODBMSs. We focus mainly on the issues that were problematic for students, particularly the issues related to algebra and SQL. Also, we comment on the collaboration of lecture material, laboratory work, and assignment work, which was coordinated to enforce the learning of the concepts being taught. Some technical issues of the practical component of the subject are discussed. At the end of this chapter, we give some recommendations to people who are interested in teaching such a subject, based on our own experience of teaching OODBMSs for a period of three years.

For those who have already taught (or are currently teaching) this subject, we hope that this chapter contains some useful discussions on the topic, and is useful for comparing to your own experiences.

Background

This chapter is based on our teaching experiences at the Department of Computer Science of Royal Melbourne Institute of Technology (RMIT[1]). This department serves both

[1] See www.cs.rmit.edu.au.

local and international students and is one of the largest Computer Science departments in Australia. The entrance requirements to RMIT University are tough, and students need to have a tertiary entrance score of more than 85 percent in their VCE (Victorian Certificate of Education). The Department of Computer Science at RMIT has several degree programs that cover both undergraduate level (e.g., Bachelor of Applied Science in Computer Science, Bachelor of Applied Science in Software Engineering) and post-graduate degrees (e.g., Master by Course Work degree, Master by Research degree, and the PhD Degree). Our focus in this paper is on the Master by Course Work degree, where the OODBMS subject is taught within the database cluster of subjects. This cluster offers a set of subjects that provide students with appropriate technical skills and aims at developing both conceptual knowledge and practical experience in the area of the database technology. Currently, this cluster contains the following subjects:

Database engineering.[2] Covers algorithms and technologies used to implement database systems.

Multimedia information retrieval.[3] Covers basic methods of indexing and retrieval of documents including both image and speech.

Deductive databases.[4]

Distributed databases.[5] Covers the basic issues related to distributed databases, including query processing, transaction management, and replication.

There are five other clusters, including:

Distributed system cluster. For example, foundations of distributed systems, advanced client server architectures, network programming, and distributed system engineering.

Software engineering cluster. For example, software creation and maintenance, object-oriented design, software architectures, telecommunications software engineering, and usability engineering tools.

WWW cluster. For example, Web programming and digital media, multimedia information retrieval, Internet and intranet document engineering, and intelligent Web systems.

Human interaction cluster. For example, human factors in computer interaction, usability engineering, human computer interfaces, interactive 3D graphics and animation, Web technology, and digital media.

AI cluster. For example, data mining and neural networks, intelligent agents and agent-oriented systems, intelligent Web systems, and deductive databases.

Students enrolling for the Master by Course Work degree at our department must specialize in one of the available clusters. Students can choose from two paths, each taking a year and a half to complete. The Master of Applied Science is earned by completing eight subjects as well as a research thesis, and the Master of Applied Technology is

---

[2] See www.cs.rmit.edu.au/subjectguides/cs442.html.

[3] See www.cs.rmit.edu.au/subjectguides/cs444.html.

[4] See www.cs.rmit.edu.au/subjectguides/cs440.html.

[5] See www.cs.rmit.edu.au/subjectguides/cs443.html.

earned by completing twelve subjects. Students pursuing a Master of Applied Science degree must also maintain a grade point average of at least a Credit (60–70 percent).

Teaching OODBMS Concepts–A Summary

This chapter provides the details of our experiences at RMIT University in the area of teaching object-oriented database concepts to postgraduate students (that is, to those who are enrolled in a Master by Course Work, *database cluster*). The goal of this chapter is to show the difficulties encountered by students when taught concepts related to OODBMSs, such as the object-oriented data model, object-oriented algebra, object-oriented SQL (OOSQL), query processing and transaction management, and security. We will also show how we approached these concepts and used different methods of teaching to ensure that the concepts were understood.

An initial problem that was faced was the difference in student backgrounds. Many of the students already were working in software companies and were comfortable with the relational database technology. They were already familiar with relational database concepts such as the relational model, relational algebra and calculus, query processing and transaction management, as well as design methodologies such as ER models, and relational normalization theory. We soon realized that students kept using this "relational philosophy," which was making the migration to object-oriented databases very difficult for them. This was especially the case when dealing with the design of OOSQL queries, OO algebraic expressions, object storage, and transaction management. One of the last sections summarizes these problems and explains the steps we took to improve their understanding of these areas.

The second problem is what we call the "content mismatch" problem, which occurred when students attempted to map their conceptual knowledge of OODBMSs to the implementation or use of object-oriented databases. During lectures, students learned about concepts and technical solutions proposed for different aspects of OODBMSs, such as indexing, and storage and transaction management. During laboratory sessions, exercises covered the use of ObjectStore [Object Design 1996] to create applications that build and query a database. Because of the specific syntax of the system used, which is C++ based, several of the features were not as generic as those taught in the lectures. For instance, even though ObjectStore queries and indexes have underlying techniques, like the ones taught during the lectures, students had problems mainly in expressing them using a specific language (like C++). One of the last sections of this chapter describes our experiences in running laboratory sessions for postgraduate students.

The OODBMS Subject Details

The OODBMS subject deals with the understanding of the fundamental issues related to object-oriented database technology. This subject covers the extension of the relational database technology to deal with complex applications (such as multimedia), and also covers the object-oriented (OO) paradigm at different levels of a database system: data model, query language, processing, and storage management. This subject covers a few core issues of the Object-Oriented Database Management Systems, such as ODL (Object Definition Language) and OQL (Object Query Language), which were specified by ODMG (Object Database Management Group); query processing, storage structures, and access methods; and transaction management. Also, in this subject, we offer opportunities for students to learn how to design and implement object-oriented database applications using ObjectStore, a database system developed in the C++ language. At the end of this subject, our goal is for students to be able to:

- Understand the fundamental concepts related to the object-oriented paradigm, including object identity, subtyping, late binding, and so on.

- Understand the main solutions related to the main issues of OODBMSs, including query processing, strategies for storing objects, transaction management, and security.

- Design, implement, and query object-oriented databases.

From the point of view of RMIT's Planned Student Learning Experiences (PSLE), students are presented with a series of recent developments in the object-oriented database technology. The lecture materials are a compilation of papers published in well-known conferences (e.g., VLDB, SIGMOD, and ICDE) and other referred texts. Lectures are designed to cover the fundamentals of OODBMS that can help students to understand the core solutions of such systems. Exercises are provided in tutorials to improve the understanding of the students through examples. Practical exercises are provided to enable the students to put into practice the concepts and techniques learned during the lectures and tutorials. Students are required to:

- Deepen their technical knowledge in the object-oriented database area by reading research papers and books available at RMIT library and the subject's URL[6]

- Prepare for tutorial exercises prior to tutorials

- Prepare for the provided series of laboratory exercises

The planning of the content of the subject is organized over thirteen weeks, as shown in Table 12.1.

The prescribed text is the book *Object-Oriented Database Systems*, by E. Bertino & L. Martino [Bertino 1993]. Several books, including Kim's *Introduction to Object-Oriented Databases* [Kim 1992], D. Jordan's book *C++ Object-Oriented Databases: Programming with ODMG Standard* [Jordan 1997], and R.G.G. Cattell's *Object Database Standard: ODMG 2.0* [Cattell 1997] were recommended as additional documentation for different topics.

Teaching OODBMS Concepts

As mentioned earlier, most of the students have been exposed previously to relational database products or teachings. A majority of students were familiar with the concepts such as relational tables, tuples, fields, and primary keys. It is assumed that the students have not been exposed to any other database models prior to this subject. There is ample literature and mature development in relational databases, and major companies (e.g.,

---

[6] See www.cs.rmit.edu.au/~zahirt/Teaching/oodbms.html.

Table 12.1   Course Structure

WEEK	LECTURE	TUTORIAL	LABORATORY
1	Introduction to OODBMSs	No	No
2	OO data models	Relational databases	Use of ObjectStore
3	OO data models	OO data models	Schema definition
4	OO algebras	OO data models	Schema definition
5	OOSQL	OO Algebra	Querying OODBMSs
6	OOSQL	OOSQL	Querying OODBMSs
7	OOSQL	OOSQL	Indexing
8	Query processing	OOSQL	Indexing
9	Query processing	Query processing	Access control
10	Storage & Indexing	Query processing	Access control
11	Storage & Indexing	Storage & Indexing	Meta-object protocol
12	Transaction Management	Storage & Indexing	Schema versioning
13	Transaction Management	Transaction management	Schema versioning

Oracle) have created some very popular database products that have cemented the relational database model into the mainstream. It is very likely that students who had worked with databases before have done so in the context of the relational paradigm only. This had caused a tightly coupled, if not synonymous conceptualization between databases and the relational paradigm in the minds of the students.

Teaching OODBMS concepts to students who have been exposed to relational database systems was a challenge. Here, we summarize some of our experiences in different parts of the lectures. In the next section, we will deal with the problems encountered by students during laboratory exercises.

The Legacy of the Relational Area

The first lectures of the OODBMS subject covered the basics of the object-oriented paradigm. Even though students had been exposed to the object-oriented paradigm in different subjects, they had problems at the abstract level (e.g., use of polymorphic classes to increase inheritance, etc.). For some students, these problems stemmed from having learned the object-oriented paradigm from the "programming perspective." They are generally students who have done a software engineering major in their undergraduate degree. Such students use the concepts associated with the object-oriented paradigm as computational concepts (e.g., conceptual abstractions). The other group of students used object concepts as "relational" ones (e.g., thinking in terms of normalized relational schema and mapping relations to objects). Most students in this category have worked with the relational paradigm for several years.

Helping students switch from one paradigm to another was not an easy task. At first, we attempted to make the differences clear by using a conceptual model (like an Entity Relationship (ER) model). Students had to design an ER schema and later translate it into an OO design. Students seemed satisfied with the contrasts of the two models, which was a good basis for redefining their initial view of what a database is. A rule that the tutor had made was that no student was allowed to use the terms table, tuple, key, and so on unless explicitly making a comment about the relational model. They were encouraged at all times to use common OO terms such as object, attribute, and association. However, attention is needed in terms of prior knowledge of OO terminology. There are some differences in flavor when talking of OO concepts. Class attributes were also called data fields, class or object variables, and properties. It is important to settle any synonymous terms early [Borstler 1998]. All diagrams of database instances were not drawn in value tables, but in set-oriented object diagrams. This gave clarity to the role of sets and Object Identity (OID).

There are a number of contradictions between the OO model and database attributes. One particular contradiction is with the use of encapsulation. This was directly related to their implementation and the way object attributes are accessed. There were working examples in ObjectStore that allowed an application to access object attributes directly, neglecting accessor functions. Some of the more OO-knowledgeable students tried to create privately accessible attributes and public accessor functions. This, to them, seemed like good programming and is consistent with what they had been taught as good design practice. However, there was one course assignment that was centered on efficiency, requiring query execution in a database containing about 50,000 objects. An aspect of the grading centered on the execution time of the application with a standard query. Here, the design feature of encapsulation and access control suffered from the overhead of function calls, whereas direct attribute access was faster and received higher grades. This caused contention among students, who were divided between sound OO implementation and database efficiency.

Modeling and OO Schemata

The subject did not contain much detail about designing a good OO schema [Tari 1997], but did have some exercises centered on design. Angster [Angster 1998], Kelemen [Kelemen 1998], and Fernandez-Rossi [Fernandez 1998] all state the importance of teaching some modeling skills in the subjects they teach. Those subjects are designed to teach OO concepts to those who may not have had prior experiences with it. Moreira [Moreira 1998] goes as far as to say that the late introduction to modeling (in their case, toward the end of the undergraduate degree) is detrimental since it doesn't allow students to learn its full potential. This is true, but from our experience, there is a lot to cover in the context of databases alone without considering the modeling issues. Therefore, it is considered out of the scope of the subject to center on design. However, as Knudsen-Madsen [Knudsen 1988] inform, a strong conception of the theoretical aspects of OO will make programming practice in a language like C++ much easier to comprehend. Basically, the models with which the students were to work were strongly guided, with discussion about the pros and cons of different design issues, as discussed later regarding one tutorial question. Even though modeling is important, there is simply not enough time in the subject to cover it to a useful degree. Since the students knew (or should have known) C++, it is reasonable to assume that they had at least a basic knowledge of object orientation from the start.

The modeling notation used in the subject was drawn from Bertino and Martino [Bertino 1993]. Figure 12.1 gives a description of the notation used. It is quite a common notation, with the exception that set aggregates are denoted by an asterisk (*) next to the aggregate name.

Algebra for Objects

The topic of algebra for objects was taught at a measured pace. First, a reminder of the relational algebra was given (such as projection, selection, join, etc.). Later, new concepts such as schema and query graphs (for single-operand queries) were given. Finally, the generalization to multi-operand queries was detailed as an extension of the single-operand queries.

The concept of a schema graph for a given class was well received by students. After a clear definition was given, examples of how to build a schema graph were explained. The schema illustrated in Figure 12.2 was used as a basis of several examples of schema graphs given during the lectures and labs. To enforce the differences between schema graphs for related classes, the schema graph for the class Vehicle (i.e., the schema graph for those queries that have Vehicle as the target), the class Company, and the class AutoCompany were highlighted and contrasted.

One of the most frequently asked questions was about the inclusion of aggregation and inheritance hierarchies within a schema graph. For instance, the schema graph for the class Vehicle includes all of the classes that are directly or indirectly related to Vehicle, either by inheritance or aggregation relationships. This includes for example, all the subclasses of the class Vehicle as well as those of the classes Company, Employee,

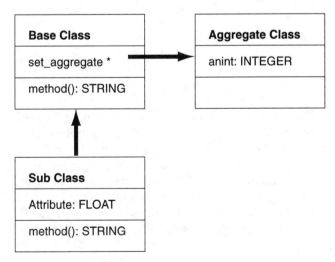

Figure 12.1   Modeling notation as used in the subject.

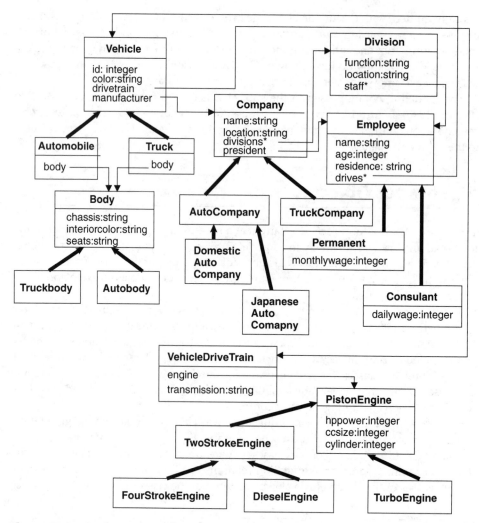

Figure 12.2 A schema example.

VehicleDriveTrain, and VehicleEngine. A few students were uncertain about the need to include such aggregation when dealing with the querying of the class Vehicle only. In fact, as mentioned earlier, the major issue was the conceptualization of the instances of the class Vehicle. Some students thought that these instances were just simple values (or tuples as in the relational model), without any link with other instances of the classes of the schema. The way we addressed this was to draw examples of instances of the class Vehicle and show that this instance is in fact a complex one (which can be pictured as a tree), and contains data from other classes along the aggregation and inheritance relationships.

When the concept of the schema graph was well understood, the second step was to explain the concept of the query graph (which is a subgraph of the schema graph and contains only those class that are in the scope of the query predicate). For instance, the query graph for the query *"Select all vehicles that are manufactured by a company whose president is 50 years old"* (Q_1) will contain the classes Vehicle, Company, and Employee as well as all their subclasses. Since this type of query graph is similar to the concept of schema graph, there were no real problems for students with regard to the new concept. However, some students struggled when the concept of query graphs became complex, such as when dealing with queries that use down-casting features. For example, with a different version of Q_1, say, Q'_1 such as *"Select all vehicles that are manufactured by a Japanese auto-companies whose president is 50 years old,"* some students struggled to model the part of the query graph relating to the class JapaneseAutoCompany. Indeed, the query graph for Q'1 should contain the classes Vehicle, JapaneseAutoCompany, and Employee as well as their subclasses. However, in this query graph, the class JapaneseAutoCompany will be extended to include all the attributes (as well as the operations) of all its superclasses (i.e., AutoCompany and Company). The problems related to the understanding of such extensions of the initial concept of the query graph were approached by clearly explaining the concept of down-casting in the context of schema graphs.

Object-Oriented SQL

It seemed that the SQL lectures were the most difficult ones for students, particularly when dealing with recursive queries and those that use down-casting operators. Before describing some of the problems in detail that the students had, let us summarize the basics of the object-oriented SQL that were taught in the subject.

Basically we used the SQL language designed by Won Kim in the context of the ORION system. This SQL was chosen for several reasons. The main reason was that ORION SQL provides "richer" facilities to express a variety of queries, including:

- Queries over aggregation hierarchies
- Queries over inheritance hierarchies
- Recursive queries
- Queries with methods

We began teaching how to express simple queries and then extended these to include more advanced selections, such as queries over aggregation hierarchies. This illustrated the complexity OOSQL queries to students, and it highlighted the differences between those queries and relational queries. We were able to clearly explain the different extensions of the relational basic SQL queries to deal with the complex queries (that is, those queries that deal with object-oriented concepts, such as inheritance and aggregation hierarchies, methods, and recursion).

Another reason we choose the ORION SQL query language was that it provides a simple syntax (similar to the relational one) and is not specific to any particular system. It extends the relational SQL to allow parts of predicates to include simple or complex paths. The gradual extension of the basic SQL syntax to deal with complex queries (e.g., queries on aggregation and inheritance hierarchies), in addition to examples, makes the concepts easier for students to understand.

Despite the details given to students about OOSQL, including examples and even articles, several of them struggled to express complex queries in OOSQL. Here, we summarize some of the problems:

Complex paths. Queries that are expressed on aggregation hierarchies are based on paths. An example of a complex path query on the schema of Figure 12.2 is: "*Find all the companies that have at least one division with at least one employee whose residence is in Rome and who drives a Ferrari*" (Q_1). This query can be expressed in several equivalent ways; however, the most suitable is one that fully uses object-oriented concepts. Even though students learned how to express such types of queries in an object-oriented way (using a specific syntax), they still kept using the "relational way" of expressing paths as a set of joins. The relational way of expressing query Q_1 is as follows:

> select   :C from Company :C, Division :D, Employee :E
> where   :D is-in :C division and :E is-in :D staff and
>   :E drives manufacturer name = "Ferrari" and
>   :E residence = "Rome"

In this SQL query, students introduced several variables to ensure that joins between the different classes could be made. In this case, abstractions (such as Company, Division, and Employee) are seen as relations and therefore the aggregation relationships are used as foreign keys to join them. During lectures and tutorials, we had demonstrated that the navigation through different classes did not require the introduction of variables. We used the following example to illustrate the navigation aspects of OOSQL queries.

> select   :C from Company :C, E: is-in :C divisions staff
> where   :E drives manufacturer name = "Ferrari" and
>   :E residence = "Rome"

Multivalued attributes. Such attributes pose some problems because a path variable involving such attributes requires the use of quantifiers, such as the use of the operators *exist* or *each*. Referring again to the example of Figure 12.2, the attribute *division* of Company is multivalued. Therefore, the specification of such an attribute with a path requires the use of a quantifier beforehand to state explicitly that either every division or at least one division needs to be considered in the predicate.

The use of such quantifiers within path variables, combined with the use of variables, has been taught both by using the syntax as well as examples. Student comprehension improved after several exercises were completed using such quantifiers.

Down-casting operator. As in previous examples, traversing different inheritance hierarchies within a schema can be done by introducing variables. For instance, if the query aims at "finding all employees who drive a car with a turbo engine of more that 100HP", then this "crosses" three different hierarchies: one with Employee as a root, the other one with Automobile as a root, and finally the last one with TurboEngine as a root. Therefore, instead of using the path that joins the three classes, students used the different variables to "control" the scope the predicate, as shown:

```
select      :E from Employee :E, Automobile :A, TurboEngine:T
where       :A is-in :E drives and :A drivetrain engine = :T
and         :T hppower > 10
```

The second variable :A is introduced to control the type of car that :E drives, and the third variable is used to control the type of engine of car :A, to make sure it is a turbo engine.

Even though there is a better way of expressing such a query (using the down-casting operator class on the predicate path, as shown next), several students still used the preceding style. As for the other aspects taught in the object-oriented database subject, we saw that their "relational culture" was still an influence in their design of query applications. Only after several examples and exercises was it possible to get them to provide a better design of OOSQL queries, such as the following:

```
select      :E from Employee :E
where       exists drives class Automobile engine
            class TurboEngine hppower > 10
```

Teaching OODBMS Programming

The theory of OODBMS was put into practice with ObjectStore, under a SPARC platform running Solaris (UNIX). The subject had a large assessment component on working applications coded by the students. However, there were the initial stumbling blocks of learning the development environment. Most students were not familiar with UNIX, the provided text editors (e.g., vi, emacs), or the compilation schemes (i.e., makefile programming). A very simple makefile was produced for the students. Initial laboratory work centered on these issues and was resolved early.

Laboratory exercises covered such things as coding a schema, creating and populating a database, creating and looking up root objects, navigating through the object graph, and creating indexes for object sets. Assignment work included a task that centered on inheritance and polymorphic behavior, and a task that centered on run-time efficiency. The latter task required students to experiment with different schemata, indexing, and query strategies to find the fastest possible implementation of a set of standard queries. We discuss these assignments in further sections.

Dealing with the ObjectStore API

The ObjectStore API was introduced with worked examples in the laboratory classes. Students were given the essential details to solve their problems. They were referred to the ObjectStore API documentation, available to them from Web page documentation, if they wanted any more details about the API. In general, the API was easy to work with. As the students were given examples of complete ObjectStore applications, they simply customized the examples to get through early practical work. Later on in the subject, more demanding problems were posed, and students asked for more examples to guide them as before. The tutor referred them to the API documentation; however, some students were not satisfied with this. It was an objective to allow the students some openness in solving the problems, so directly translatable examples were avoided. The Web-based API documentation was easy to navigate, and many students utilized the facilities of ObjectStore to a higher degree than was introduced to them. However, there were other students who asked for more elaborate examples containing more in-depth ObjectStore usage. They were referred to the documentation regardless of this type of difficulty.

ObjectStore Queries

The ObjectStore query facilities and language was radically different from that which was presented in lectures. It is a basic and incomplete query language and is not as powerful as the OOSQL presented in lectures. There was a substantial amount of practical work needing implementations of queries. Students found it difficult to map their OOSQL queries to an implementation of ObjectStore queries. This made for some disillusioned students, as they could not exercise a considerable amount of their learning in practical work.

Following is a section of the laboratory work they were to complete. Students were to write a set of queries for the database in Figure 12.3 to perform the following operations:

- Find all employees who don't make any parts.
- List all the parts that Steve makes.
- Find the employee who makes the part with part_id of 7.
- Find all employees who make parts that consist of other parts.

In this exercise, students used the os_Collection methods *query()* and *query_pick()*. An example is:

```
os_Set<Employee*> result_set;
result_set = employee_set.query ("Employee*", "emp_id == 100", db1);
```

where {emp_id == 100} is the query string of constraints. The function *os_Set.query()* returns a subset of the objects in `employee_set` and stores them by reference in `result_set`.

Generally, students who had done previous lab work had no trouble with this lab. However, the creation of the query string proved to be a tricky task. The ObjectStore documentation details how to build a query string, which is essentially a list of predicates. It is quite detailed, so rather than rewrite the documentation, the students were prompted to read the relevant sections of the ObjectStore documentation. It was still not enough for the students who were not able or willing to experiment, and there were constant requests for examples. What made writing query strings more tedious was that few syntactical errors in the string were found at compile time. This is because the string is bound in quotations and thus, the compiler treats it as a literal in a function call. Students did get proficient at writing the strings, and it was said that the mismatch between the OOSQL presented in lectures and language of the ObjectStore query string was a disappointment.

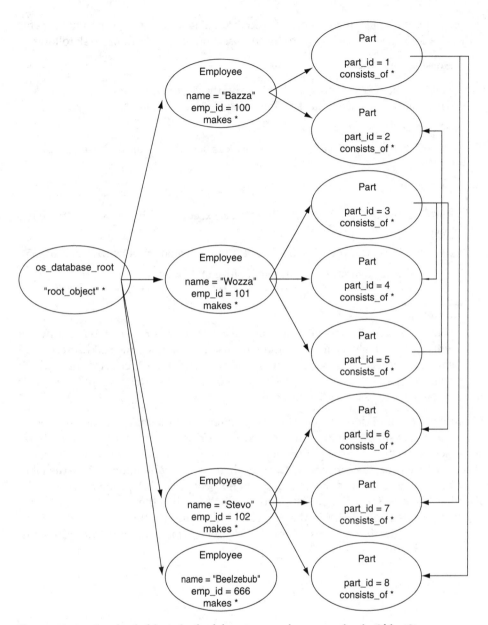

Figure 12.3   Graph of objects in the laboratory work on querying in ObjectStore.

ObjectStore Indexing

The indexing techniques of ObjectStore were quite straightforward. By the time it was introduced, the students were confident with adapting and experimenting with examples, and a lot of students were comfortable with the API documentation. Simple path and complex path indexing was introduced through laboratory work, and the benefits they have on some queries was introduced. A section of the laboratory task follows:

Work To Be Done

Running the `dbinit` program will set up the database required for this task. It will create a database to the schema in Figure 12.4 with:

- Three Employee objects
- 65536 Part objects, attached to the `makes` set in a randomly chosen Employee object
- No indexing defined

Running the `dbapp` program will time the execution of 100 runs of both the following queries:

- Find the employee who makes part number (random between 0 and 65535).
- Find a random range of parts that Steve makes.

Your Task

You are to create the indexes that will make both queries run more efficiently. You will need to create an index object, and use this to index the `makes` sets of all employee objects. Use index options to optimize query performance for both queries. Answer for yourself, "what type of index is better for what query?" If you want, discuss it with your tutor.

Students did a reasonable job at this, although once the task was understood, it was a relatively simple job to write the code for it. This is unlike the previous laboratory exercise where the concept was easy yet the implementation was difficult. In this laboratory exercise, the concept was harder than the implementation. Once the laboratory session was finished, the students did not seem to have a problem with implementing indexes in future work. This again is unlike the previous laboratory exercise. This is a good indication that the implementation in this case had reinforced the conceptual detail that the students had learned. This is the most desirable outcome of a laboratory session.

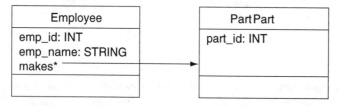

Figure 12.4   Schema of the laboratory on indexing in ObjectStore.

What the More (and Less) Successful Students Produced

In the practical work, students were generally graded on how they populated their database, the algorithms they used to access objects, and if all criteria of the assignments had been addressed. The students that performed at a high level tended to use the ObjectStore API quite well, taking advantage of its facilities to simplify their task. They created object graphs that needed a minimal of root objects and were designed for ease of navigation. However, there were some students who created a root object for every object in the database and used the find_root() operation to retrieve objects by name.

Although there was not much modeling as part of the subject, the students were still required to design their own schemata from a starting point that was given to them as part of the assignment specification. Particular attention was paid to their ability to abstract within the class hierarchies; however, their choice of attributes and methods was also important. How best to abstract these sorts of things is a very contentious issue. There are those who create elaborate class hierarchies, and those who create the bare bones of a problem. Which one is better for the problem? A more elaborate hierarchy shows the ability to think at different levels of abstraction. However, as Colbert [Colbert 1994] states:

"A developer can bog down building elaborate, "correct" class hierarchies that are unnecessary for solving a problem."

In other words, if it works with few classes, why add more? Students were introduced to the notion of reusability. This could be an argument for large class hierarchies. It is more likely that it is, as stated before, an attempt to capture as much semantics as possible in the class diagram itself. Overall, students were graded based on their ability to abstract to a *useful* level—that is, not to add classes just to pad out the diagram. There were some models that contained classes that added nothing to the design.

Queries and indexing in ObjectStore were very interrelated, as there is no benefit of indexing unless an ObjectStore query method was used, as opposed to using object graph navigation. Adding indexing to a database did not necessarily improve the performance of the database. The efficiency added by indexing was determined by the type of queries implemented. Students who did not understand this generally created indexes that were irrelevant to their queries. Non-ObjectStore provided indexing techniques; hand-coded B+tree implementations were not covered because of time constraints. There were some ways of measuring the effectiveness of indexing, but the labs were set up in such a way as to make the effects of indexing very blatant. The more successful students simply created indexing structures that satisfied their particular query implementation. The simplicity of the ObjectStore indexing provisions made the inclusion of indexes into their databases a nonissue.

Assignments

There were three assignments scheduled in the subject. Because the first one is a simple assignment, which was designed primarily for familiarization, we discuss only the two remaining ones.

Evaluating Assignments

The evaluation of the practical parts of the assignments was done in three parts:

- The students had to demonstrate the program to the tutor.
- Their programs were run and the outputs checked certain given input.
- Their written submissions and code were checked.

The first point was necessary in order to check the authenticity of the students' work. It is natural that students band together to solve problems, which can lead to submissions being no indication of a student's own knowledge or experimentation. This tactic was to find students who coded things they didn't fully understand simply because they were following what others were doing. The tutor would ask the student to explain certain aspects of the program. For example, if a program needed to attach a data object to a root object, the tutor would ask the student to find the exact line that would do this. The tutor would ask the student what lines they would change if they were asked to make a specific change to the program. There were students who knew their program well, and there were students who stumbled. A problem with this method of evaluation is that a lot of students were nervous when confronted on such a one-to-one basis. Their stumbling was accentuated by this factor. Another problem was the language barrier. Many students did not have English as their native language and questions were often misinterpreted. However, the method was successful in finding the students who were having difficulties with the subject, and often indicated which students *grouped* to solve problems. Points were generally deducted for questions unsatisfactorily answered.

The second point is a standard measure of program output. There was a standard set of test input data and a corresponding set of expected output data. Quick fixes were tried for programs that didn't compile or had other error conditions, but points were generally deducted because of them. Points were also deducted for flawed output.

For the third part, any written descriptions were read, and in conjunction with the code, the logical flow of the programs was evaluated. This was in order to check for misuse of constructs or flawed logical design. Some coding practices were scrutinized; for example, hard coding of *magic* values (literals that are meaningless by themselves) was checked and slight penalties were given for their use. This was in the hope of influencing the students to write more reusable code. In general, OO programming principles were enforced where it didn't compromise performance of the database application. Points were deducted for bad design and negligent coding in context of the assignments. Points were given for innovative design and programming as an incentive.

Generally, the assignments had highlighted the difficulties that the students had in dealing with problems they had not dealt with in laboratory work. This was the aim of testing how well the students could solve problems on their own. Many students did not speak out when having difficulties (they would rather ask a friend) and this was reflected in their performance. Essentially, this kind of task was useful in evaluating not only the students' level of understanding, but also their ability to solve open problems. At the postgraduate level, it is reasonable to expect that the students have the initiative to experiment for themselves.

The Second Assignment

In this assignment, the students were to implement a catalog system for recorded music. The preamble of the assignment specification was as follows:

"Your tutor has a considerable collection of recorded music that is a nightmare to manage. There are around 1000 of these items in the collection, and keeping track of the locality of each item is very difficult. There are people always asking to lend items, and sometimes, it is hard to remember what is in the collection. Presently, all items are listed in a crude text file, which has to be searched and modified manually. Your task is to provide a database application that provides query functions to search the database, and report information about any item, including its location."

The emphasis of the assignment was for the students to create an OO schema for the problem, which was essentially to map items to their locations, as well as to keep item information (e.g., artist name, title, track listing, etc.). There were some explicitly stated types of items with their own specific data members (e.g., vinyl, CD, cassette, video, etc.) and some explicitly stated types of locations, again with their own data members (e.g., numbered shelf, media player, borrowing friend, etc.)

The students were given a class diagram as a starting point, which featured one association between items and locations at the base class level. This was enough to allow the students to conceptualize a complete schema. It was up to the students to complete the inheritance hierarchies with classes representing the different types of items and locations.

The queries that were to be implemented were as follows:

- Given an artist, show all items in the collection by that artist. For each item, give catalog number, title, medium, and location (when more than one item fits the query, list them all).

- List all items that contain a track with a given title.

- List all items at a specified location (either player, shelf, or friend).

- List all friends, and what items they have.

There was a major misunderstanding with the wording of the third query. Students assumed that the requirement was to list all items that were at one of the three certain types of location. The intended meaning was to list all items at an actual location, that is, only one location object.

A solution to this is given in the schema diagram in Figure 12.5. It was expected that the solution included polymorphism with the *report_location()* function in the class Location and its subclasses. This would allow any location to report its specific fields, no matter what object type, with the same function call. This was an attempt to emphasize the power of the OO model. It also requires complex queries (queries that have a query path through more than one class). For example, query 2 required a query method that traverses to class Track through class Audio_medium.

Students found the task of implementing the application particularly difficult, since they had not encountered polymorphism before in practical work, even though there was a detailed example provided, including one on how to implement polymorphic behavior that was not ObjectStore specific. There was quite a lot of variance with the schemas produced, and hence the query methods that were implemented. Some students performed

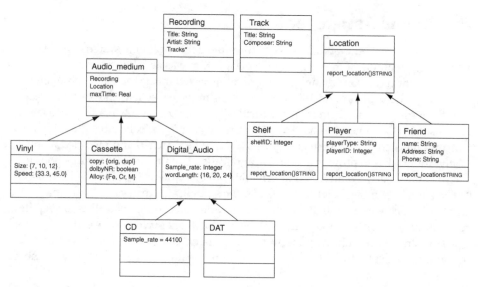

Figure 12.5 A solution schema.

a *keyword* search through the specification and created just one level of subclasses for each applicable keyword, while some abstracted further to create multiple levels. As the given starting schema showed an association at the highest level, it was clear to those that understood inheritance that no other associations were needed down the hierarchy, though one or two students did actually implement explicit associations at lower levels. A key implementation problem to solve was to be able to detect the type of an object. A common approach to the problem was to put a *type flag* in the base class to allow each object to be treated as a base class object, yet allow its type to be known by the query. It was hoped that they would use a polymorphic call to a function to get the actual class to report the type directly. On further analysis, the students were actually justified in using one inherited class attribute because it is a more efficient solution, omitting the need for another function call and the overhead it brings.

The Third Assignment

The third assignment was based on run-time efficiency. A standard database was set up based on the schema in Figure 12.6 and the students were to create a query method to run the following query:

"List all complex parts that are composed of one type of material."

The given database contained a set of employees, all of whom make one part each, which is composed of other parts. As complex parts can be composed of other complex parts as well as primitive (single component) parts, recursion is needed to solve the query. The given database contained around 50,000 objects, and each primitive part object was composed of a particular material. The meaning of the query was to return

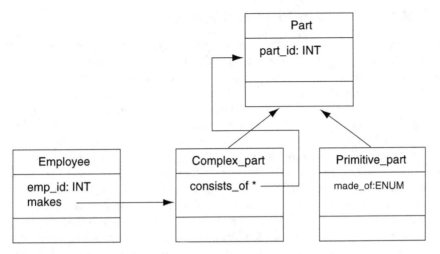

Figure 12.6   A schema example.

all *complex part* objects that are composed of other parts made of only one type of material (i.e., each primitive part connected to it was made of the same material).

The goal of this assignment was to provide an application that implements this query in the fastest time possible. Students were not allowed to change the database or the structure of the schema, although they were allowed to add methods to the schema. The emphasis on coding this query was in using a recursive query method. There was strong encouragement to experiment with different techniques to try to get the execution time of their query as low as possible. Such techniques were centered on indexing, iteration techniques, and query coding (i.e., using the ObjectStore query methods or using object navigation and manual searching).

The solution was far from what was expected. Most students tried to use recursion, but those who experimented further found that recursion was very slow because of the overheads of function calls. As the assignment was centered on run-time efficiency, an accepted solution was a very simple program based on nested loops. This would yield a low turn-around time and achieve better grades. It was not necessary to add accessor functions for object attributes since direct access was certainly much quicker.

Students found the task difficult to the degree that many were satisfied with first implementations, and few students seemed to try different techniques. However, it was somewhat obvious which students had done some experimentation, as their findings were quite reasonable. Such findings were that the omission of as many function calls as possible was beneficial, and that indexing didn't improve things much because each complex part set needed to be iterated through exhaustively. In all, students tended to use the techniques emphasized in laboratory work, without regard to those that were to the benefit of efficiency. It is here that the students learned that (at least with ObjectStore) the simple approaches are often the best. This is a direct result of the query language in ObjectStore being computationally incomplete.

Technical Problems in Practical Work

During the semester, and with the above-mentioned assignments in particular, there were some technical problems with using the ODBMS and its compilation. First, the C++ compiler used had an optimizing feature to omit any virtual function tables for classes that are not instantiated using transient *new*. This was a problem, as the application referenced existing persistent objects and never needed to create transient objects. Thus, if any overriding function in a persistent object was called, an exception was thrown saying that the *vftb* for the class was not present. After much searching, a compiler switch was found to force inclusion of every *vftb* of classes containing abstract functions. Another ODBMS-specific problem was that the database server was very volatile, and kept crashing. It seemed to have been caused by bad local configuration. The following work-around was implemented: a UNIX process was started, which performed a ping on the server every five minutes, and restarted it if it was not responding.

A major technical problem with the ODBMS was that recursive querying within the implemented query language was very flawed. Trying to write a query string that contained a function call that calls the function containing the query string itself caused a segmentation fault (not an exception) after the third recursion. This became a big issue with the third assessed project the students undertook, as recursion was a part of the assignment. The work-around to this problem was that the database given to the students was essentially a tree of objects with a depth of no more than three nodes. This allowed recursion to access the leaf nodes without causing problems, but limiting the database construction to a less interesting scope. That is, the object tree in the database was forced to be very wide with very shallow depth in order to store a sufficient number of objects on which to test queries.

Conclusion

To summarize our experience in teaching object-oriented databases, we would like to suggest some key rules that need to be adopted by the teachers and tutors as early as possible to make sure that students are on the right track and their learning is the least hindered as possible.

> **Rule 1: OO modeling first.** Covering the basic object model in one or two lectures is not at all enough for students to master some of the main issues of object-oriented databases. Students must have a full subject in object-oriented (data) modeling and design to be able to fully grasp the main concepts related to the object-oriented paradigm.

> **Rule 2: Get rid of the relational culture.** Making sure that the students switch to object data models as early as possible is the key for better learning of object-oriented databases. Students tend to use their "relational" experience in the way they see the structure of the data and the way they use data. This can induce major difficulties for them in understanding the remaining core aspects of databases, such as clustering, indexing, and transaction management.

Rule 3: Keep practice in mind. Making sure that students have enough practice with an object-oriented database system will help them bridge the gap between theory and practice. It is also very important to reinforce some of the concepts they learned during lectures.

Rule 4: Keep control of the difficulty of laboratory work. This is obvious, but as shown, it is sometimes better to have some simple laboratory exercises that are not too much of a challenge to code. The temptation is to do the opposite sometimes, especially to prepare students for assignment work. This is when detailed examples (but not reworded replicas of the assignment solution) are valuable.

CHAPTER 13

Building a Jasmine Database

This chapter is designed to be a practical demonstration of building a Jasmine database. Note that we say "database" here and not "application," since the primary focus is the construction of the back-end object database. The intention is to cover a broad range of topics as we construct all the elements of an object database, but note that space will prevent us going into real depth on any one issue. Only pertinent selections of code will be shown, but all batch files and other key constructs will be included.

We assume that you have already installed a copy of Jasmine, and selected all the options. The developer's CD-ROM contains a fully operational product, with the exception of a connection limit, and some of the esoteric backup and restore utilities. There is nothing to stop you from building and testing a fully operational pilot system.

This discussion is based on Jasmine v1.21. Where limits or other decision criteria are mentioned, it is important to verify these against the changes made in subsequent patches and releases.

Design Goals

The database we are building is a simple Timewriting database. Staff in a company record time (in hours) against project phases they are working on. Projects are divided into multiple Phases, and each Project belongs to a single Client. The Class design can be summarized as follows:

Company

Only one instance of Company will exist. It holds collection references to the current clients, projects, and staff.

PROPERTIES

companyTitle

address

staffList (a collection of Staff objects)

projectList (a collection of active Project objects)

clientList (a collection of Client objects)

METHODS

project	Retrieve instance of Project from projectList
projectCount	Methods for maintaining the projectList collection
projectAdd	
projectDelete	
client	Retrieve instance of Client from clientList
clientCount	Methods for maintaining clientList
clientAdd	
clientDelete	
staff	Retrieve instance of Staff from staffList
staffCount	Methods for maintaining staffList
staffAdd	
staffDelete	
monthReport	Monthly report for a given Project
customerInvoice	Monthly invoice of hours/costs for a Client

Client

Each client has a number of projects underway on their behalf.

PROPERTIES

name

address

projectList (a collection of Projects being worked on for this Client)

METHODS

find	Class method—retrieve a specific instance of Client

projectCount	Methods for maintaining the projectList collection
projectAdd	
projectDelete	
monthReport	Monthly report for this client

Project

A project consists of one or more Phases. Staff are assigned to each project.

PROPERTIES

name

longDescription

projectStart

estimatedFinish

ActualFinish

estimatedHours

estimatedCost

completed

staffList (collection of Staff working on this project)

phaseList (collection of Phase objects that make up this project)

client (Client object this project is for)

METHODS

find	Class method—retrieve a specific instance of Project
totalMonthHours	Hours for this project for specified month
totalMonthCosts	Matching costs
staff	Retrieve instance of Staff from staffList
staffCount	Methods for maintaining staffList
staffAdd	
phaseCount	Methods for maintaining the phaseList collection
phaseAdd	
phaseDelete	
monthReport	Monthly report for this project

Phase

Each phase is a single unit of work, with a defined beginning and end. Time is recorded by Phase.

PROPERTIES

name

longDescription

phaseStart

estimatedFinish

ActualFinish

estimatedHours

estimatedCost

completed

project (containing Project object)

METHODS

find	Class method—retrieve a specific instance of Phase
totalMonthHours	Hours for this phase for specified month
totalMonthCosts	Matching costs
monthReport	Monthly report for this project

Staff

Staff work on projects and record time to each by phase.

PROPERTIES

surname

givenName

employeeNumber

hourlyRate

projectList (collection of projects to which this person is assigned)

METHODS

find	Class method—retrieve a specific instance of Staff
projectCount	Methods for maintaining the projectList collection
projectAdd	
projectDelete	
totalDayHours	Hours for this person for specified date
totalDayCosts	Matching costs
totalMonthHours	Hours for this person for specified month
totalMonthCosts	Matching costs
totalProjectHours	Hours for this person for specified project/month
totalProjectCosts	Matching costs

Time

This class holds all the time recorded by staff on project phases each day. Time is recorded as hours and costs.

PROPERTIES

whenDone

TimeSpent

cost

phase (project phase this work was for)

staff (person who did the work)

METHODS

addTime	Add a new instance of Time
updateTime	Update a specific time instance
deleteTime	Delete a specific time instance
getTimeHours	Retrieve instance-matching specific criteria
getTimeCost	Retrieve associated costs
totalProjectHours	Retrieve total hours recorded for a specific project instance
totalProjectCosts	Same, for costs
totalPhaseHours	Retrieve total hours for a specific phase
totalPhaseCosts	Same, for costs
totalStaffHours	Hours recorded by a specific person in a month
totalClientHours	Hours charged to a client in a specific month
totalClientCosts	Cost of the above

The design is simplistic, and does have definite flaws from both an object-oriented design perspective and sheer practicality. However, it is more than enough to proceed with as a demonstration of building classes and methods in Jasmine, which is the focus here.

Physical Storage

All Jasmine commands and utilities are divided into two broad groups:

- Operating system commands (programs) that act on the database's physical file storage: backup and restore, allocating file storage, defining class families, reading and defining configuration settings, starting and stopping the database engine, connecting to the database (from a client).

- Database commands and methods that act at the class and instance level, on items stored inside the database: Object Definition Language (ODL), Object

Manipulation Language (OML), and Object Query Language (OQL). These commands can be executed only within Jasmine methods, the ODQL interpreter, or Jasmine client programs.

Both of these tend to appear under the heading of *Object Data Query Language*, or *ODQL*. However, ODQL is often used just as the programming language to write, store, and compile methods, which is how we will refer to it.

Stores and Extents

Like most server databases, we have to allocate file space explicitly for the server to work with. At this point our database design must be sufficiently advanced to determine how much space we need now, and how much we may need later on. Please note that Jasmine does not offer too many features for optimization or automation here, though future releases may provide improvements.

The basic logical unit of file allocation is the *Store*. Each Store is made up of one or more *Extents*. Each Extent can be one or more fixed length files. These have to be created by the database administrator as required. If a Store is filled before new Extents are created, then an error will occur.

Thus by using multiple Extents, a Store can span drives and be as large as the operating system permits. Optimization is achieved by placing Stores for different applications on different physical drives. Another optimization method is to place Stores on different drives to the default System Store, Work Store, and Transaction Store (the last two are specific to each session/connection between client and server).

Creating a Store is as simple as Listing 13.1.

This creates a Store that is 2000 * 8K in size, by the name of **castle_1** in the same directory as the existing Jasmine stores. The pageSize is important because this is the minimum amount that is read/written to the Store with each access.

There is one important observation to make at this point. *All* Jasmine commands (and later the entire ODQL) are case sensitive. If we had specified "**-pagesize 8**" in the preceding batch file, an error would have occurred.

```
@echo Create a store called CastleDemo01.
@echo This will consist of a single Extent 16M in size.
createStore -numberOfPages 2000 -pageSize 8 CastleDemo01
%JAS_SYSTEM%\jasmine\data\castle_1
pause


@echo Create a single class Family in this store,
@echo called castleCF01. Remember to
@echo mention that we'll always refer to it using an alias!
createCF -CFAlias castleCF castleCF01 CastleDemo01
pause


@echo Now list out all the stores and class families
@echo to show the new addition.
listStore > StoreList.txt
```

Listing 13.1   SetupStores.bat: Batch file for creating our Store and Class family.

We will discuss the Class family later, but the last command in the preceding batch file dumps a description of all Stores in the database to a file, as shown in Listing 13.2.

The information in this dump is quite useful. If you want to explore Jasmine's configuration further, use the **Jasprenv** command and the **Jasconfig** utility.

If we need to extend our Store at a later date, we can use the **extendStore** command as shown in Listing 13.3.

Here we are specifying two files for this new Extent. If we rerun listStore, then **CastleDemo01** now contains:

```
Locations:
        i:\jasmine\jasmine\data\castle_1
        i:\Jasmine\jasmine\data\castle_2a
        i:\jasmine\jasmine\data\castle_2b
```

```
===== S T O R E     C O N T E N T S
==================================
Store Name: system
Class Families:
       systemCF
Locations:
       I:\Jasmine\Jasmine\data\jas_extent_1
Page size: 8192
Total pages: 2000
Used pages: 508
===== S T O R E     C O N T E N T S
==================================
Store Name: dataStore
Class Families:
       jadelibCF1
       mediaCF1
       CAStore
       sqlCF
       WebLink
Locations:
       I:\Jasmine\Jasmine\data\jas_dataStore
Page size: 8192
Total pages: 8000
Used pages: 649
===== S T O R E     C O N T E N T S
==================================
Store Name: CastleDemo01
Class Families:
       castleCF01
Locations:
       i:\jasmine\jasmine\data\castle_1
Page size: 8192
Total pages: 2000
Used pages: 33
```

Listing 13.2   StoreList.txt: Our Jasmine database now.

```
extendStore -numberOfPages 1200 CastleDemo01
            i:\Jasmine\jasmine\data\castle_2a
            i:\jasmine\jasmine\data\castle_2b
```

Listing 13.3   SetupStores2.bat: Adding some more space.

The allocation of extents is just one reason why Jasmine, like any server database, requires careful administration. The database administrator must be aware that:

- **listStore** is currently the only command that shows how much space is in use by a database, and whether more Extents need to be allocated. It must be used regularly.

- Extents are not allocated automatically when they fill up. Jasmine will simply report an error and refuse to do anything until new extents are created using extendStore.

- There should always be some space left in the disk directory for each Store—at least 150k. This is required by the utilities for unloading, loading, and backing up data.

- In the version of Jasmine being used for this example application (v1.21), there is no control over how space is allocated within a Store, so disk striping and other advanced techniques are not possible.

- The multimedia classes that ship with Jasmine allow the programmer to store multimedia data within Stores, or separate from them. This decision will have a huge impact on storage requirements, and how you use your server's resources, and must be made as early as possible.

Class Families

The Class family is the basic logical unit within a Store. The name assigned to each Class family is unique, although there are some interesting ways to work with that.

A Class family is contained within a single Store. That is, all class definitions within that Class family and instance data for those classes is kept together. As a general rule, all classes for a single application should be kept in one Class family. The first is that classes may inherit only from classes defined within the same class family. They may contain object properties of any class type, but inheritance is strictly limited. This means that classes related to the same business process will be gathered into one Class family, but classes that are responsible for application tasks, or that you may want to reuse in other applications, will be in others. The demarcation between Class families is thus a natural one based on your object analysis and design.

The second reason has to do with *aliasing*, a technique whereby one Class family can be known by a different name while the database is running (more specifically, the name can be unique for any given session/connection). Thus, after using createCF in the batch file earlier, the following command:

```
copy local.env %JAS_ENVFILE%
```

```
bufferSize     1024
workSize       20480 10240
CF mediaCF     mediaCF1
CF jadelibCF   jadelibCF1
CF castleCF    castleCF01
```

Listing 13.4 Environment file for aliasing castleCF01.

overwrites the default Jasmine Environment file **Local.env** with a new file containing the code in Listing 13.4.

This provides for two things:

- A more colloquial name for the Class family for normal use.

- A way of creating and testing a completely separate Class family that contains a newer version of that application (classes, data, etc.) without affecting the production system. When we want to switch over, we simply change the ENV files on the client PCs to reflect the new Alias arrangement.

This way of separating Development/Testing/Production systems is common on high-end computing platforms.

Note that instances/objects in the database are specific to the real name of a Class family. Any changeover from Testing to Production may also involve a transfer of data using the Unload and Load commands. These commands can be used to create multiple copies of jadelibCF and mediaCF to better isolate multimedia data and Jasmine Studio for different applications, providing for much better backup and restore management. Both of these will be covered later.

Class families can be deleted with the command **deleteCF**. This immediately erases all the contents of the Class family (classes, instances, etc.) without pause. This is useful for cleaning up during development work, but should be used with great care otherwise. Unlike the **deleteStore** command, **deleteCF** will not prompt for confirmation from the user.

Class Definitions

Now we want to build the internals of our database, and we have two tools to use: the Database Administrator, and the ODQL Interpreter. Choosing the correct tool for each situation is very important, and impacts on our ability to administer, migrate, upgrade, and support our database.

The Database Administrator and ODQL Interpreter

The Database Administrator is part of Jasmine Studio. It is a point-and-click tool for browsing the database schema and its contents (instances of objects in the database) as well as changing the database structure (Figure 13.1).

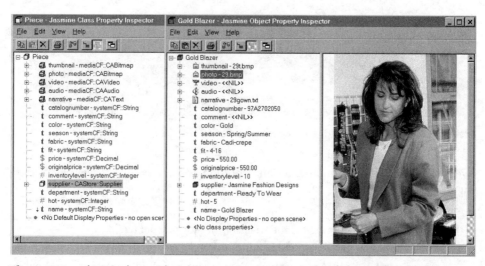

Figure13.1 The Database Administrator—Viewing class schemas and instance data.

The Database Administrator has the following advantages:

■ It is very easy to learn and to use.

■ It is the only practical way to view instances of multimedia data.

■ Drag-and-drop is a convenient way of populating data, especially multimedia types.

■ Building classes and compiling methods is a one-touch operation.

■ It is an essential party to building applications with Jasmine Studio.

The ODQL Interpreter is the antithesis of the Administrator. It is a command-line environment that accepts only ODQL language input (Figure 13.2). Although this makes the Interpreter hostile to the casual user, it is a very powerful tool. Consider it for the following:

■ It is the only way to run ODQL scripts. These could be testing code for methods, creating instances of data, or generally automating some task.

■ It is the only medium that supports the bulk creation of test data (apart from using the LOAD utility, which assumes that a database has already been created on another server).

■ It supports detailed inspection of all class attributes, instance data, and so on.

■ Using ODQL is the only way to specifically control how multimedia data are stored (Internal, Controlled, or External storage).

■ Classes defined here can select the type of collection properties they use (e.g., Array, List, Bag). The Database Administrator does not allow this.

■ You can run *any* type of test Query, including the Group By construct, which the Administrator does not support at all.

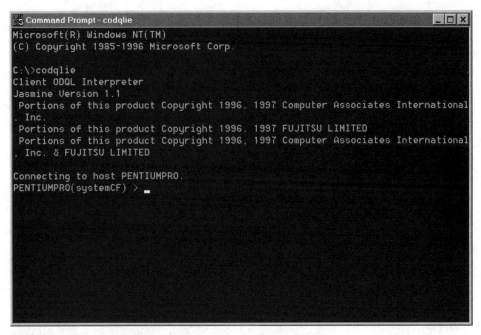

Figure 13.2   The ODQL Interpreter.

- Use the ODQL Class to help build queries, and the tuple structures required to hold the results. This can be quite difficult, and the ODQL class is a great help when writing methods. Note that this is distinct from ODQL-the-language.

- It is possible to run test scripts and capture the output to text files, thus offering a way of documenting/validating work done.

- If methods require code from C libraries to be linked-in, the Interpreter is used to do the compilation step.

As we can see, the Interpreter is used for two things: handling complex operations and writing/running ODQL scripts. The caveat is that the Interpreter is unforgiving when it comes to errors. Minor errors in case can cause long chains of messages to appear, and errors in methods can be awkward to track down.

Complexity aside, those readers who are already database administrators for relational systems will see the benefits of the ODQL Interpreter. Being able to record all database schema information, schema changes, compilation instructions, and even data unloading and loading into scripts that can be executed and reexecuted at will is a vital part of database administration. Losing a server and having to reconstruct the database from a particular point in time requires full logs of all changes, and scripts to run to bring the system up to par quickly. This is not something for which a point-and-click tool should be used.

In relational systems, these scripts consist of SQL and various stored procedures. In Jasmine, it is ODQL. Most of the following examples will be constructed using ODQL scripts and will be executed in batch format to save time and to illustrate the point about automation. Those readers familiar with C will recognize the syntax.

Class Definitions

Listing 13.5 shows the class definition script for CastleComposite, Company, and Project Classes (see Appendix 13.1 at the end of this chapter for the complete listing). Although the class structure is rather flat (inheritance is not used at all), the **Castle-Composite** Class acts as the abstract (base) class for the Class family. The reasons for this are:

- Having an abstract class means that common behavior to all classes can be added later (e.g., for error logging, audit trails, etc.) by modifying this central class.

- It provides a logical link between unrelated classes in the database. Thus anyone looking at the system later will have no doubts about which classes are part of this application.

- It provides a single class hook to use if we need to generate queries returning some data (instead of other classes in the database).

- During development and testing, a common requirement is to dump all data and reload a standard test set. Having a common abstract class makes the delete process a one-step operation. The value of this should not be underestimated.

However, perhaps the single most important class design decision is to ensure that all classes for a single application are kept in the one Class family. This is because the Unload and Load commands (or JasLoad and JasUnload) are easiest to use when whole Class families are being shifted around.

Some comments about Listing 13.5 are:

- We are defining only the basic classes (Properties), not their methods. It is sensible to keep method definitions separate; during development it is often necessary to debug, change, and recompile methods, but rarely is it necessary to change the core class structure. If we specify the Method definition here, we would have to erase the class (and all instance data) each time we reran this script. If we keep the methods separate, we can erase and redefine them without affecting the test data.

- Note that we specify the default Class family as systemCF. When running any script, it is wise not to make any assumptions about the Interpreter environment. We need to be similarly careful when using references to object properties that are in user-defined classes; for example, `List<castleCF::Project>projectList`

- We are using Lists here because it will make certain methods easier to code later. In ODQL we can specifically select the collection type to use (e.g. Array, List, Bag).

- The script file has been commented so that any maintenance programmer can go back over it later, and still understand what was being done. This is simply good coding and takes little extra time.

- We are making full use of the Description options in the Class definitions. Thus anyone viewing the class schema in the Database Administrator (or in the Interpreter) will always have some help working out what each class and property is.

- The last line is the command to build the classes. In reality we would run the entire script first to check for syntactic errors and perhaps make some corrections. After a successful run, we would issue the **buildClass** call manually.

```
/******************************************************************
File: Classes.odql
Partial Class definitions for Demonstration Timewriting Database
v1.00  March 1999
Peter Fallon
Castle Software Australia
******************************************************************/
defaultCF systemCF;
/* Class: CastleComposite
Provided in case we need to define application-wide behaviour in the
future such as error logging, audit trails, etc.
*/
defineClass castleCF::CastleComposite
  super: systemCF::Composite
  description: " Base (Abstract) class for Demonstration database."
{
};
/* Class: Company
This class is at the top of the Object Hierarchy (containing tree) for
this system. It contains the master lists of active staff, projects
and clients.
*/
defineClass castleCF::Company
  super: castleCF::CastleComposite
  description: " Principle container class for timewriting system."
{
  maxInstanceSize: 8;
  instance:
    String                  companyTitle;
    String                  address;
    List <castleCF::Staff>       staffList
      description: " List of Staff currently employed."
      default: List{};
    List <castleCF::Project>     projectList
      description: " List of active Projects being worked on."
      default: List{};
    List <castleCF::Client>      clientList
      description: " List of current clients."
      default: List{};
```

(Continues)

```
};
/*
Class: Project
A Project is the complete unit of work done for a client by the
company. It consists of one or more Phases. Time is written to Phases
of the Project by staff.
Estimates are recorded as properties while Actuals are calculated live
from methods.
*/
defineClass castleCF::Project
  super: castleCF::CastleComposite
  description: " All information about a specific project"
{
  maxInstanceSize: 4;
  instance:
    String                      name;
    String                      longDescription;
    Date                        projectStart;
    Date                        estimatedProjectFinish;
    Date                        actualProjectFinish;
    Decimal [10,2]              estimatedHours;
    Decimal [12,2]              estimatedCost;
    Boolean                     completed;
    List <castleCF::Staff>      staffList
      description: " List of Staff assigned to this project."
      default: List{};
    List <castleCF::Phase>      phaseList
      description: " List of Phases that make up this Project."
      default: List{};
    castleCF::Client            client
      description: " Client paying the bills for this project." ;
};
/* Build all classes. */
buildClass castleCF::CastleComposite
           castleCF::Company
           castleCF::Project;
```

Listing 13.5   ODQL for defining and building classes in this database (Classes.odql).

Listing 13.5 can be run at the NT Command line by

```
codqlie -execFile Classes.odql
```

If we open the Database Administrator we can see and browse these new classes as Figure 13.3 demonstrates (note that Figure 13.3 also shows an instance of the Company Class that the author of this chapter created while experimenting with test data, and the other classes not included in Listing 13.5).

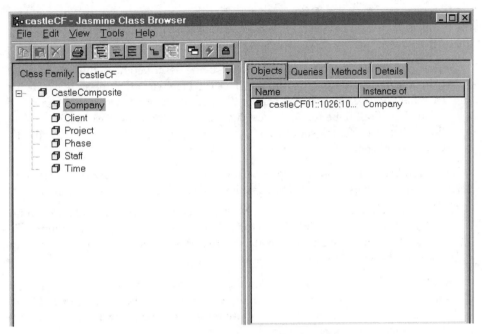

Figure 13.3   The castleCF schema after the classes are loaded.

It is necessary to explain something about defining and building Classes at this point. There are four stages in constructing Classes:

Defining the class. This is what the script in Listing 13.5 was doing. At this point the database has stored the class definitions, but we cannot create or store instances of those classes yet. Note that we can define methods here, although it is preferable not to (again, the source is recorded, but not usable).

If we make a mistake in our definition, we can correct it and rerun the define script. We do not need to delete a class definition explicitly until we have built it.

Building the class. This can be thought of as a "compile" step for the class definitions. After a successful build, we can create instances of our classes. A class cannot be built until all its superclasses have been defined (they will be built automatically if we haven't done it explicitly yet), nor can it be built unless all classes used as properties have been defined. For instance, we cannot build the preceding Staff Class until we have defined the Project Class, since Staff has a property: `List<Project> projectList`.

If we need to change the class definition after it is built, we must either **delete()** it first (this deletes all instances of the class as well), or use discrete methods such as **addProperty()**, which leave existing test data in place. There are class methods in Jasmine to edit and adjust most parts of a class definition after it is built. However, it is recommended that commented and dated scripts are written to track such changes.

One interesting note: The Database Administrator can unbuild a class, but no corresponding ability exists in ODQL. It is a sort of one step Delete and Redefine, leaving things in a state where we can make changes.

Defining methods. If you follow the process being described here, this will be done using the **addProcedure** command. This is where we define the source code for each method of each class. We can do this in any order, but we cannot compile a method until all dependent classes, types, and methods are also defined. Note that Jasmine performs some basic type and syntax checking of the method's ODQL at this point.

If we need to change the source code we must use the **removeMethod()** method to delete it first. This does not affect the class definitions or other method definitions.

Compiling methods. This invokes the Microsoft VC++ compiler in the background to compile our methods into DLLs (on NT systems). We can specify a number of options here, including ones to retain source and debugging code, linking in extra object files, compile options, and so on.

The DLLs created are placed in a method directory with the same name as the host Class family. If we want to change a method, we can use removeMethod(), redefine it, and recompile it. Note that every time we use **compileProcedure()** we are recompiling all methods for a given class.

From these steps, you can see how creating scripts to perform each task makes subsequent changes much easier to perform, control, and document. In any project you will quickly find yourself with an array of scripts performing minor tasks such as removing methods, rebuilding whole chunks of your schema, backing up changes, etc.

Loading Data

Normally the next step in construction would be to define the Methods for our Classes. However, perhaps you would like to experiment with ODQL first if you are unsure of exactly what some methods do, and you may need to practice writing queries anyway. The obvious solution is to create some test data.

Test data in a Jasmine database can be created in several ways:

Use the Database Administrator. We can create only one object at a time, however, so entering time data will be rather slow. As mentioned earlier, there is no way to log or record what has been done for later use. If the quantity of data required is small (and includes multimedia types), this is still a good choice.

Use ODQL and create a script. It is more complex initially, but it *is* a script—so it can be rerun against a fresh DB anytime. More importantly, we can write a program to generate any quantity of data we wish, which is useful if we want to create and test queries under load.

LOAD data from a previous UNLOAD file. This is excellent for loading large quantities of data, but the assumption is that it already exists in some form elsewhere. It is important to remember, however, that the LOAD file format is documented, so if we need to transfer data from another database type (say a relational database), we could write a program to output it in the Jasmine UNLOAD format.

Write a small client application and use it as a keypunching screen to enter data at will. The VB/ActiveX interface is ideal for this. The program will be a throw-away, but we may want to consider it if we need very particular test data that is not already in an electronic format somewhere.

For our present situation, the second option is the best choice, since we need to create a small number of instances for staff, projects, and clients, but *a lot* of time entries. Note that whatever method of data entry we choose, we should use JasUnload and create a backup of our test data as soon as we create it. This gives us a fast and easy method of restoring original test cases and so forth—useful later on. One of the key points to remember here is that nearly every good technique the reader has used for database system development in the past is either directly applicable with Jasmine, or has an object-oriented equivalent. At every point, you should ask yourself "What have I done with (relational) database application development before, and have I thought about applying it here?"

Listing 13.6 contains a script used to create a few instances of the Company and Project classes. The complete version can be found in Appendix 13.2 at the end of this chapter. The sample data simulates a small company operation, and is sufficient for now. We can always add more cases to this script later if required.

The script in Listing 13.6 and the next one in Listing 13.7 highlight one interesting problem with ODQL. Because this script must run inside the interpreter (in interpreted mode effectively) we are limited to strict ODQL code. However, Jasmine methods can utilize nearly anything that can be coded in C (assuming we link in the required object code). One way around this is to write our own classes, which simply provide the functionality we would like to have here (e.g., file access, certain system functions, logging operations).

```
/* File: DataEntry01.odql
Data entry script when there are no methods defined yet. Load a couple
of objects into each class.
v1.00  March 1999
Peter Fallon
Castle Software Australia
*/
defaultCF castleCF;
/* Define a Company Record */
Company oCompany;
oCompany = Company.new();
oCompany.companyTitle = " Pete's Software Emporium" ;
oCompany.address = " Melbourne, Australia" ;
/* Hold that thought, and create a couple of Project instances and add
that to the Company object
*/
Project oProject1, oProject2;
oProject1 = Project.new();
oProject1.name = " Patient Needs Trial Database" ;
oProject1.longDescription = " Touch screen based questionnaire system
for Hospital" ;
```

(Continues)

```
oProject1.completed = FALSE;
oProject1.projectStart = Date.construct(1999,3,1);
oProject1.estimatedProjectFinish = Date.construct(1999,8,30);
oProject1.estimatedHours = 250.0;
oProject1.estimatedCost = 20000.00;
oProject2 = Project.new();
oProject2.name = " Y2K Project" ;
oProject2.longDescription = " Financial System requires Y2K checking
and certification" ;
oProject2.completed = FALSE;
oProject2.projectStart = Date.construct(1998,6,1);
oProject2.estimatedProjectFinish = Date.construct(1999,10,31);
oProject2.estimatedHours = 1500.0;
oProject2.estimatedCost = 100000.00;
oCompany.directAdd(" projectList" , oProject1);
oCompany.directAdd(" projectList" , oProject2);
```

Listing 13.6   Code for creating a few instances of each class (DataEntry01.odql).

Running this script is a simple matter:

```
codqlie -execFile DataEntry01.odql
```

Or if the Interpreter was already running, we could use the line:

```
execFile DataEntry01.odql;
```

Listing 13.7 is the most interesting one because it loops around, creating time entries for each phase of each project, for each person working on them according to the start and finish time of each phase. Phases without a finish date simply have time recorded to them until the current date. We could use a random number generator to determine the hour values, but there isn't one available in ODQL, so the data have been "fudged" using the modulus operand. This routine takes a while to run, but it creates several hundred entries for the example application.

```
/* File: DataEntry02.odql
Data entry script when there are no methods defined yet.
Create a series of instances of the Time Class.
v1.00  March 1999
Peter Fallon
Castle Software Australia
*/
defaultCF castleCF;
```

```
/* Get a list of all projects */
Bag<Project> oProjects;
Project oProject;
oProjects = Project from Project;
/* For each project, get the staff and phases */
scan(oProjects, oProject){
/* For each person, create time entries for phases */
   Staff oStaff;
   List<Staff> oStaffs;
   oStaffs = oProject.staffList;
   scan( oStaffs, oStaff ) {
/* For each phase, create entries daily between Start and Completion
   Dates (or the current date if not completed) */
      Phase oPhase;
      List<Phase> oPhases;
      oPhases = oProject.phaseList;
      scan( oPhases, oPhase) {
         Integer iNumberofDays;
         Integer z;
         Time oTime;
         if(oPhase.completed) {
/* Phase is Completed - record time between the Start and Finish
   Dates*/
            iNumberofDays = oPhase.actualPhaseFinish.difference(
               oPhase.phaseStart, DAY );
         }
         else {
/* Phase is Not Completed - record time between the Start Date and
   Today*/
            iNumberofDays = Date.getCurrent().difference(
               oPhase.phaseStart, DAY );
         };
/* Just to prove we were here */
         oProject.name.print();
         oStaff.surname.print();
         oPhase.name.print();
         iNumberofDays.print();
/* For each day in this period, record hours for each person/phase.
   Make the figure arbitrary, based on the day. Don't bother accounting
   for weekends */
         z=1;
         while ( z < iNumberofDays ) {
            oTime = Time.new();
            oTime.whenDone = oPhase.phaseStart.add( z, DAY );
            oTime.timeSpent = (z % 7);
            oTime.cost =  oTime.timeSpent * oStaff.hourlyRate;
            oTime.phase = oPhase;
```

(Continues)

```
                    oTime.staff = oStaff;
                    z = z + 1;
                };
            };
        };
    };
```

Listing 13.7   Creating a lot of Time instances (DataEntry02.odql).

Experimenting with ODQL Code for Methods

The ODQL Interpreter is a rich environment for practicing our ODQL skills. We can sit at the command prompt and enter single commands a line at a time, or write scripts like the ones we have already used.

Query Syntax

Queries are the heart of most Jasmine methods. Unless classes maintain many collection properties, then they are the only way to retrieve data for reporting, editing, and maintenance.

What you may not know is that queries are far more powerful than the Database Administrator and Query Builder let us think. If we use the Query Builder to construct a query, and then examine the ODQL generated, we will have something like this:

```
Garment from Garment where Garment.season = "Summer";
```

This returns all instances of the **Garment** class (and its subclasses) where the **season** property equals the string "Summer". If we want to use the results of this query directly in Jasmine Studio or the VB/ActiveX interface, our query must always return a collection of objects as per the preceding code. But the query in ODQL can do far more, just like an SQL query does not have to return all the columns of a table each time.

To discuss the Query construct fully would require an entire chapter in itself, so we encourage you to consult the entry in the Jasref.hlp file. But a couple of important issues are:

- We can obtain a collection of atomic values, or a collection of tuples as well as objects.

- Complex expressions can be used almost anywhere (including method calls). The only restriction is that methods do not try to update data in the middle of a query.

- Queries can be based on Classes or other collections. Thus we can construct a query on the result of another. This is often done for optimization reasons.

- In ODQL, we can then use various collection methods to manipulate the results, calculate sums, join two collections into one, and so forth.

For example,

```
List<TT [String name, Bag<Person> manages, Integer seniority]> t1;
t1 = [ m.name(), m.manages(), m.seniority() ] from Manager m where m.sex
    == "F";
```

This query returns a collection of tuples. Each element contains a name, a collection of instances of the Person Class, and a numeric value. The collection contains only values for female managers in the Class Manager. Note that if we do use tuples, we have to declare them explicitly.

Group Syntax

If we think of the Query construct as the OO version of the SQL Select command, we can think of the Group construct as the OO version of using Select ... Group By ... in SQL. That is, it is a quick way of performing aggregate operations on groups of data.

Group expressions can be used on classes, or on collections, like Queries. Unlike Queries, however, Group does not support a where clause. This means that we almost always use Query and Group together, with the Group expression using the results of our Query.

The best way to elaborate is through some examples.

Experiments

The author wanted to look at his test data to check just what had been created, in broad terms. He wanted to see the Time data broken down by month/year with a total hours for each month. But the Interpreter kept rejecting the Group and Tuple definitions. Time to call up some assistance, in the form of the ODQL Class (which should not be confused with the ODQL language in general). This is a very useful feature that allows queries and Groups to be created at run time, have Jasmine describe how the output will be structured (the tuple definition), and run it if necessary.

Entering the following at the command prompt in the Interpreter:

```
defaultCF castleCF;
ODQL.prepare( "test", "group t in Time by (t.whenDone.part( YEAR ),
t.whenDone.part( MONTH ) ) with ( partition^timeSpent.sum() );");
ODQL.getOutputInfo( "test", "ODQL_STATEMENT").print();
ODQL.getOutputInfo( "test", "VARIABLE_DECLARATION", "oGroup").print();
```

produced the following result:

```
group t in Time by (t.whenDone.part( YEAR ), t.whenDone.part( MONTH ) )
with ( partition^timeSpent.sum() );
systemCF::Bag< 'oGroup'[ 'systemCF'::'Integer' 'C1',
'systemCF'::'Integer' 'C2', 'systemCF'::'Decimal'[18, 2] 'C3' ] >
'oGroup';
```

The first part, in response to "ODQL_STATEMENT" is just the original query returned. This is to ensure that there are no typing errors. In fact, the first line, ODQL.prepare() would have generated an error if the query/group syntax was incorrect in any way.

The second line of output, in response to "VARIABLE_DECLARATION", tells us how we should declare a tuple variable to hold the results of this Group construct. The format of this declaration is extremely formal, using Class family names and single quotes around all names.

To use the ODQL class, you must have version 1.21 (or greater) of Jasmine installed. Putting this to use now:

```
defaultCF castleCF;
systemCF::Bag< [ systemCF::Integer C1, systemCF::Integer C2,
                systemCF::Decimal[18, 2] C3 ] > oGroup;
String.putString("Grouping time entries by Year/Month:");
oGroup = group t in Time by (t.whenDone.part( YEAR ),
                             t.whenDone.part( MONTH ))
                    with ( partition^timeSpent.sum() );
oGroup.print();
```

Printing the result of our Group produces the following:

```
Grouping time entries by Year/Month:
Bag{
   [C1: 1998, C2: 6, C3: 255.00],
   [C1: 1998, C2: 7, C3: 279.00],
   [C1: 1998, C2: 8, C3: 285.00],
   [C1: 1998, C2: 9, C3: 261.00],
   [C1: 1998, C2: 10, C3: 288.00],
   [C1: 1998, C2: 11, C3: 270.00],
   [C1: 1998, C2: 12, C3: 531.00],
   [C1: 1999, C2: 1, C3: 567.00],
   [C1: 1999, C2: 2, C3: 252.00],
   [C1: 1999, C2: 3, C3: 421.00],
   [C1: 1999, C2: 4, C3: 75.00]
}
```

As we can see, the sample data used here was built in April 1999.

Now let us try something more ambitious and break these figures down by Project and Phase:

```
defaultCF castleCF;
systemCF::Bag< [ systemCF::Integer C1, systemCF::Integer C2,
                 systemCF::String project, systemCF::String phase,
                 systemCF::Decimal[18, 2] C3 ] > oGroup2;
String.putString ("Grouping time entries by Year/Month/Project/Phase:");
oGroup2 = group t in Time by (t.whenDone.part( YEAR ),
                              t.whenDone.part( MONTH ),
                              t.phase.project.name, t.phase.name )
                     with ( partition^timeSpent.sum() );
oGroup2.print();
```

Running this produces:

```
Grouping time entries by Year/Month/Project/Phase:
Bag{
  [C1: 1998, C2: 6, project: "Y2K Project", phase: "Client Modelling
    System", C3: 255.00],
  [C1: 1998, C2: 7, project: "Y2K Project", phase: "Client Modelling
    System", C3: 279.00],
  [C1: 1998, C2: 8, project: "Y2K Project", phase: "Client Modelling
    System", C3: 285.00],
  [C1: 1998, C2: 9, project: "Y2K Project", phase: "Client Modelling
    System", C3: 261.00],
  [C1: 1998, C2: 10, project: "Y2K Project", phase: "Client Modelling
    System", C3: 288.00],
  [C1: 1998, C2: 11, project: "Y2K Project", phase: "Client Modelling
    System", C3: 270.00],
  [C1: 1998, C2: 12, project: "Y2K Project", phase: "Client Modelling
    System", C3: 270.00],
  [C1: 1998, C2: 12, project: "Y2K Project", phase: "Internal Systems",
    C3: 261.00],
  [C1: 1999, C2: 1, project: "Y2K Project", phase: "Client Modelling
    System", C3: 279.00],
  [C1: 1999, C2: 1, project: "Y2K Project", phase: "Internal Systems",
    C3: 288.00],
  [C1: 1999, C2: 2, project: "Y2K Project", phase: "Internal Systems",
    C3: 252.00],
  [C1: 1999, C2: 3, project: "Patient Needs Trial Database", phase:
    "Analysis and Specification", C3: 85.00],
  [C1: 1999, C2: 3, project: "Patient Needs Trial Database", phase:
    "Construction", C3: 63.00],
  [C1: 1999, C2: 3, project: "Y2K Project", phase: "Internal Systems",
    C3: 273.00],
  [C1: 1999, C2: 4, project: "Patient Needs Trial Database", phase:
    "Construction", C3: 15.00],
  [C1: 1999, C2: 4, project: "Y2K Project", phase: "Internal Systems",
    C3: 60.00]
}
```

Time spent learning just what can be done with Queries and Groups is time well spent. C-Jasmine-API programmers also have access to this functionality for client applications, as do WebLink developers.

Method Definitions

To compile a method, any classes or methods on which it relies must already be defined. Thus the simplest process to take when writing methods is to start at the bottom of the dependency tree and work up. In our example application, nearly everything relies on Time, so that is the first class we need to tackle.

Listing 13.8 shows the first attempts.

```
/* File: TimeMethods.odql
Method Definitions for Time Class
v1.00  May 1999
Peter Fallon
Castle Software Australia
*/
defaultCF castleCF;
/*
Method: AddTime
Adds a new time entry. If one is there matching those keys, the hours
are added to what is there. Returns success.
Only one instance of Time exists for key combinations...
*/
addProcedure Boolean castleCF::Time::class:addTime(Staff oStaff,
Phase oPhase, Date dWhenDone, Decimal [10,2] nHours )
    description: " Adds a new time entry."
{
    $defaultCF castleCF;
    $Time oTime;
    $Bag<Time> oEntries;
    $Iterator<Time> itEntries;
/* Is there an existing entry? */
    $oEntries = Time from Time
                where Time.whenDone == dWhenDone
                    and Time.staff == oStaff
                    and Time.phase == oPhase;
    $if (oEntries.count() == 0)
    {
/* No existing entry - make one */
        $oTime = Time.new();
        $oTime.whenDone = dWhenDone;
        $oTime.timeSpent = nHours;
        $oTime.cost =  oTime.timeSpent * oStaff.hourlyRate;
        $oTime.phase = oPhase;
        $oTime.staff = oStaff;

    }
    else {
/* Retrieve the existing entry - there will only be one */
        $itEntries = oEntries.createIterator();
        $itEntries.advance();
        $oTime = itEntries.get();
/* Entry existing - add to it ... */
        $oTime.timeSpent = oTime.timeSpent + nHours;
        $oTime.cost =  oTime.timeSpent * oStaff.hourlyRate;
/* Tidy up ... */
        $itEntries.delete();
    };
    $oEntries.delete();
    $return( TRUE );
```

```
};
/* Method: UpdateTime
Creates a New time entry, replacing any existing one matching those
keys.
Use this when the external routines want to make a single update.
Only one instance of Time exists for key combinations ...
*/
addProcedure Boolean castleCF::Time::class:updateTime(Staff oStaff,
Phase oPhase, Date dWhenDone, Decimal [10,2] nHours )
    description: " Update time entry."
{
    $defaultCF castleCF;
    $Time oTime;
    $Bag<Time> oEntries;
    $Iterator<Time> itEntries;
/* Is there an existing entry? */
    $oEntries = Time from Time
                where Time.whenDone == dWhenDone
                  and Time.staff == oStaff
                  and Time.phase == oPhase;
    $if (oEntries.count() == 0)
    {
/* No existing entry - make one */
        $oTime = Time.new();
        $oTime.whenDone = dWhenDone;
        $oTime.timeSpent = nHours;
        $oTime.cost =  oTime.timeSpent * oStaff.hourlyRate;
        $oTime.phase = oPhase;
        $oTime.staff = oStaff;
    }
    else {
/* Retrieve the existing entry - there will only be one */
        $itEntries = oEntries.createIterator();
        $itEntries.advance();
        $oTime = itEntries.get();
/* Entry existing - change it ... */
        $oTime.timeSpent = nHours;
        $oTime.cost =  oTime.timeSpent * oStaff.hourlyRate;
/* Tidy up ... */
        $itEntries.delete();
    };
    $oEntries.delete();
    $return( TRUE );
};
/* Method: DeleteTime
Removes the time entry matching those keys.
Only one instance of Time exists for key combinations ...
*/
```

(Continues)

```
addProcedure Boolean castleCF::Time::class:deleteTime(Staff oStaff,
Phase oPhase, Date dWhenDone )
    description: " Delete a specific time entry."
{
    $defaultCF castleCF;
    $Time oTime;
    $Bag<Time> oEntries;
    $Iterator<Time> itEntries;
/* Is there an existing entry? (Ignore if there isn't) */
    $oEntries = Time from Time
                where Time.whenDone == dWhenDone
                  and Time.staff == oStaff
                  and Time.phase == oPhase;
    $if (oEntries.count() != 0)
    {
        $scan( oEntries, oTime )
        {
            $oTime.delete();
        };
    };
    $oEntries.delete();
    $return( TRUE );
};
/* Method: getTimeHours
Retrieves the hours recorded matching those keys.
*/
addProcedure Decimal [10,2] castleCF::Time::class:getTimeHours(Staff
oStaff, Phase oPhase, Date dWhenDone )
    description: " Retrieve hours for a specific time entry."
{
    $defaultCF castleCF;
    $Bag<Decimal [10,2]> oEntries;
    $oEntries = Time.timeSpent from Time
                where Time.whenDone == dWhenDone
                  and Time.staff == oStaff
                  and Time.phase == oPhase;
/* Is there an existing entry? */
    $if (oEntries.count() == 0)
    {
        $return(0);
    }
    else {
        $return(oEntries.sum());
    };
    $oEntries.delete();
};
/* Method: TotalStaffHours
Retrieves the hours recorded for a person in a specific iMonth.
Note: yes, my query technique could use some optimizing ...
```

```
Note: There is no matching totalStaffCosts() method, as this is simply
(totalStaffCosts() * Staff.hourlyRate )
*/
addProcedure Decimal [18,2] castleCF::Time::class:totalStaffHours(
Staff oStaff, Integer iYear, Integer iMonth )
    description: " Retrieve hours for a person/iMonth"
{
    $defaultCF castleCF;
    $Bag<Decimal [10,2]> oEntries;
    $oEntries = Time.timeSpent from Time
                where Time.whenDone.part(YEAR) == iYear
                  and Time.whenDone.part(MONTH) == iMonth
                  and Time.staff == oStaff;
/* Is there an existing entry? */
    $if (oEntries.count() == 0)
    {
        $return(0);
    }
    else {
        $return(oEntries.sum());
    };
    $oEntries.delete();
};
compileProcedure castleCF::Time;
```

Listing 13.8 Initial version of methods for Time Class (TimeMethods01.odql).

This built and compiled beautifully! Let us test it briefly in the Interpreter:

```
defaultCF castleCF;
Staff oStaff;
Bag<Staff> bagStaff;
bagStaff = Staff from Staff;
bagStaff = Staff from Staff;
scan (bagStaff, oStaff) { Time.totalStaffHours(oStaff, 1998, 11); };
```

It should be noted that there has been no attempt to optimize the code here, and no doubt some attention to indexes, reworking queries, and a few benchmarks will work wonders to prevent deadlocks and other scaling issues. But that is beyond the scope of this chapter.

Compiling and Testing

The following are obvious comments, but we need to be reminded of them from time to time.

- Build methods in small lots. Jasmine/Compiler error messages are painful to debug at present because the line number returned is the *real* line of C code that Jasmine sends to the compiler for a method, not the line of ODQL. As such, it doesn't hurt to do them a few at a time, and it certainly makes it easier to deduce where a variable declaration went wrong.

- If/When you get run-time errors, do not despair over the message Jasmine gives you. Check out the Message.txt file that is in the `%JAS_SYSTEM%\Jasmine\ Files\english` directory. If your installation is not an English one, you will find the file in one of the other parallel language subdirectories. This file contains helpful comments on the causes of each error.

- Test your queries to ensure they are returning the data you need, and check out their performance. If you think it is slow, then there are many optimization techniques you can employ.

- Perform load testing (make sure you have enough test data in key areas—this is a common failing even for relational systems). Do not be afraid to try different things.

- ReadOnly transactions will improve query speed, but these cannot be initiated within a method, so they aren't immediately relevant.

- Test methods in the interpreter as they are compiled. If nothing else, this will improve your ODQL skills.

More Methods

At this point, you will have to assume that various ODQL scripts that define and compile the methods for the remainder of this chapter have been run. To include the source here is not practical.

However, we will discuss one other set of methods. This author wanted a method that would output a monthly report. ODQL has some string handling methods, but by and large its abilities in this area are rudimentary. Obviously one of the reporting tools now available for Jasmine will be far better suited to this, but we wanted to restrict the code to pure ODQL for demonstration purposes. The result is in Listing 13.9.

ODQL as a scripting language has no real ability to get user input for parameters or other run-time variables, so it was necessary to hardwire March 1999 as the report date, and also get it to report for all Phases. This is less important than the attempt to present and format data in some fashion from Queries and Group functions. This produces the result shown in Listing 13.10.

This is sufficient information for a multiline text box in Jasmine Studio, if quick feedback is required.

Converted to an instance method of the Phase class, with variables replaced by parameters, and print() calls replaced by concatenating results to a string variable (the return value of our method), we end up with Listing 13.11.

```
/* File: TestMethods03.odql
   Sample Report of Phase activity for a Month/Year

v1.00  June 1999
Peter Fallon
Castle Software Australia
*/


defaultCF castleCF;
Integer iYear, iMonth;
Phase oPhase;
List<Phase> oPhases;
Bag<Time> bagTime;
Bag< testquery[ Staff oStaff, Decimal[18,2] nHours,
                Decimal[18, 2] nCosts ] > oPhaseActivity;
testquery[ Staff oStaff, Decimal[18,2] nHours,
                      Decimal[18, 2] nCosts ] oMonth;

iYear = 1999;
iMonth = 3;


/* Construct phase list */

oPhases = Phase from Phase;

/* For each phase - get time entries for specified Month/Year and
   then produce a report of time entries by staff */

String.putString(
   "Testing code for Report\n----------------------\n" );
Date.getCurrent().print();
String.format(
   "Reporting Time Entries for Month %2s, Year %4s" ,
   iMonth, iYear).print();

scan( oPhases, oPhase ) {
   bagTime = Time from Time
               where Time.phase == oPhase
                 and Time.whenDone.part(YEAR) == iYear
                 and Time.whenDone.part(MONTH) == iMonth;

   oPhaseActivity = group t in bagTime by (t.staff)
                  with ( partition^timeSpent.sum(),
                         partition^cost.sum() );

   String.format( " \nProject: %s, Phase: %s",
                  oPhase.project.name,
                  oPhase.name).print();
```

(Continues)

```
  if ( oPhaseActivity.count()==0) {
    String.putString(
       "No time recorded for this phase in this month.\n" );
    }
  else {
    String.putString(
       "Name                    Hours    Costs\n--------------------
-----------------\n"  );

    scan (oPhaseActivity, oMonth ) {
      String.format( " %20s %7s %8s",
                     oMonth.oStaff.surname,
                     oMonth.nHours,
                     oMonth.nCosts ).print();
      };
   };
};
```

Listing 13.9   An ASCII report (TestMethods03.odql).

```
Testing code for Report
-----------------------
07/02/1999
Reporting Time Entries for Month  3, Year 1999
Project: Patient Needs Trial Database, Phase: Analysis and
Specification
Name               Hours    Costs
-------------------------------------
           Bloggs   85.00  4675.00
Project: Patient Needs Trial Database, Phase: Construction
Name               Hours    Costs
-------------------------------------
           Bloggs   63.00  3465.00
Project: Y2K Project, Phase: Client Modelling System
No time recorded for this phase in this month.
Project: Y2K Project, Phase: Internal Systems
Name               Hours    Costs
-------------------------------------
           Bloggs   91.00  5005.00
              Doe   91.00  5460.00
            Smith   91.00  5915.00
```

Listing 13.10   The results of the TestMethods03.odql script.

```
addProcedure String castleCF::Phase::instance:monthReport( Integer
iYear, Integer iMonth )
    description: " Retrieve costs for this phase in a given month."
{
/*
    Method: monthlyReport
    Report of all activity on this phase for the given Month/year.
    Return a formatted multi-line string
*/
    $defaultCF castleCF;
    $Bag<Time> bagTime;
    $Bag< testquery[ Staff oStaff, Decimal[18,2] nHours,
                    Decimal[18, 2] nCosts ] > oPhaseActivity;
    $testquery[ Staff oStaff, Decimal[18,2] nHours,
              Decimal[18, 2] nCosts ] oMonth;
    $String sReturnValue;
    $sReturnValue = String.format(
      " Time recorded for Month: %2s, Year:%4s\n" , iMonth, iYear);
    $bagTime = Time from Time
              where Time.phase == self and
                    Time.whenDone.part(YEAR) == iYear and
                    Time.whenDone.part(MONTH) == iMonth;
    $oPhaseActivity = group t in bagTime by (t.staff)
                              with ( partition^timeSpent.sum(),
                                      partition^cost.sum() );
    $sReturnValue = sReturnValue.stringCat(
                  String.format(
                    " \nProject: %s, Phase: %s\n" ,
                    self.project.name, self.name) );
    $if (oPhaseActivity.count()==0) {
        $sReturnValue = sReturnValue.stringCat(
          " No time recorded for this phase in this month.\n" );
    }
    else {
        $sReturnValue = sReturnValue.stringCat(
          " Name   Hours    Costs\n----------------------------\n" );
        $scan (oPhaseActivity, oMonth ) {
            $sReturnValue = sReturnValue.stringCat(
                                String.format(
                                  " %20s %7s %8s" ,
                                  oMonth.oStaff.surname,
                                  oMonth.nHours,
                                  oMonth.nCosts ) );
        };
    };
    $return( sReturnValue );
```

(Continues)

```
/* Housekeeping...*/
    $oPhaseActivity.delete();
    $bagTime.delete();
};
```

Listing 13.11   Method Phase::monthReport().

The Importance of Being Scripted

We discussed earlier that a major reason to use the ODQL Interpreter for class and method development is that it provides a written record of development. This means:

- You can use source code management and version control tools to record your database schema in full.

- You have a chronological record of all changes.

- In case of failure, you can restore from backups, and then make any required schema changes simply by running the last few scripts again.

- Migrating to another (database) server is easy, so is reconstructing a database from scratch.

- The Development/Testing cycle almost always involves stripping and rebuilding a database several times. This becomes very tedious if you do not have something like Listing 13.12.

Once a database has been created, it is possible to use JasUnload (or Unload) to copy it in its entirety (with and without instance data). All the execFile commands can be replaced with a single JasLoad, assuming no other changes are required. Correctly dated and commented, this leaves a complete trail for maintenance and support to follow.

There is one further point that must be made here. While you are constructing your classes, start thinking about your backup and upgrade strategy for your database. That is, read the migration notes that come on the Jasmine CD about what to do when a new version of Jasmine is released. It is essential you know how to cope with changes to built-in Jasmine classes. The multimedia classes are the main ones affected. If you store multimedia data, then three things are vital: store all data in your own classes, do not use the Bitmap and Movie classes, and create your own subclasses such as CABitmap and CAMovie. This allows you to back them up discretely using JasUnload.

The second recommended option is to create separate copies of the Multimedia Class Family for each application and to use aliasing to point to the one required for each application. This means problems or issues with one application will not affect others. You will have to recopy the core mediaCF Class family again for any upgrade, but it means you retain complete control over the situation. Some example batch files to do this are presented later.

The other Classes most affected are Jasmine Studio (jadelibCF). Again, it is best to separate each Studio application into its own CF, and use aliasing to keep them separate.

- Start working on your batch files and scripts to do all of this as soon as your basic classes are built. Have your procedures automated and ready to go at a moment's notice. Again, source and version management tools will integrate extremely well here.

- Plan your backup strategy. Understand how you will journal and back up stores. Understand the dependencies between stores according to instance data and make sure the right files are backed up in synchronization.

- Upgrades to the database engine are something you must put a great deal of planning into when a production system is involved. Treat this just as seriously as you would upgrading a relational engine.

- Test all of these steps and retest with data, and retest as soon as you start acceptance testing (i.e., with real data). Having a strategy in place is nice, but having one that works is rather important.

Backing Up a Database

Ideally this discussion should go on to cover client application development around this database, but we do not have the space in this chapter. However, we can cover a final topic: backing up the database schema. We have deliberately picked a hard

```
@echo off
rem     Master batch file for creating the entire database, executing
rem     all scripts and batch files in the correct sequence. The only
rem     thing that needs editing is specific Class Family stuff related
rem     to Aliasing.
rem     (Assume LOCAL connection is the default one)
rem     Create stores and Class families:
call SetupStores
copy local.env %JAS_ENVFILE%
rem     Define and build all Classes
codqlie -execFile Classes.odql
rem     Construct some test data!
codqlie -execFile DataEntry01.odql
codqlie -execFile DataEntry02.odql
rem     Define and compile Methods for classes
codqlie -execFile TimeMethods2.odql
codqlie -execFile StaffMethods.odql
codqlie -execFile PhaseMethods.odql
codqlie -execFile ProjectMethods.odql
codqlie -execFile ClientMethods.odql
codqlie -execFile CompanyMethods.odql
```

Listing 13.12   Master database script (CreateEverything.bat).

topic—duplicating the Jasmine Studio Class family—to demonstrate the complexities of backing up multimedia data, and how Class family aliasing can work.

Creating Duplicates of jadelibCF and mediaCF

This was mentioned earlier, so how do we copy jadelibCF and mediaCF?

You need to read the help listings for the JasUnload and JasLoad commands carefully and understand what they are doing. But this is the batch file used (note that these commands are rather long and have been indented to make for easier reading. In the original batch file each JasUnload or JasLoad command forms a single line):

```
rem Jasmine must be running here!
jasunload %JAS_SYSTEM%\unload\jStudioBackup.uld
        -s -L %JAS_SYSTEM%\unload\jStudiomethods.lib
        -m %JAS_SYSTEM%\unload\jStudioMedia.uld
        -M mediaCF1 jadelibCF1 mediaCF1
```

This code creates three files. The class and instance data is about 675K, the methods about 1.5M, and the multimedia instances about 25M. Note that when making the initial copy, we only need the multimedia data instances that are referenced in jadelibCF, but we cannot separate those easily. So it is better to copy them all, and remove unwanted data after it has been deposited elsewhere.

This is how we can create new Class families. We have to do this manually before loading them with the Studio data:

```
rem Jasmine must be running here!
createCF jadelibCF11 CastleDemo01
createCF mediaCF11 CastleDemo01
jasload %JAS_SYSTEM%\unload\jStudioBackup.uld
        -l %JAS_SYSTEM%\unload\jStudiomethods.lib
        -m %JAS_SYSTEM%\unload\jStudioMedia.uld -M mediaCF1
        -a %JAS_SYSTEM%\jasmine\data\mmarea
            jadelibCF1=jadelibCF11 mediaCF1=mediaCF11
```

Note the jadelibCF1=jadelibCF11 mediaCF1=mediaCF11 part. This is the most important option. It tells the load routines to change all references of jadelibCF1 and mediaCF1 to jadelibCF11 and mediaCF11, respectively. It is essential to back up and restore the two Class families together to maintain object integrity throughout.

If you use multimedia data in your own database, you have to be similarly careful when unloading and loading your application. Starting with an independent mediaCF11 is a great help.

If we do a listStore now, we will see the following for the CastleDemo01 Store:

```
===== S T O R E    C O N T E N T S
=====================================
Store Name: CastleDemo01
Class Families:
```

```
        mediaCF11
        jadelibCF11
        castleCF01
Locations:
        i:\jasmine\jasmine\data\castle_1
        i:\Jasmine\jasmine\data\castle_2a
        i:\jasmine\jasmine\data\castle_2b
Page size: 8192
Total pages: 3216
Used pages: 512
```

The final step is to adjust the environment file. Currently it reads:

```
bufferSize      1024
workSize        20480 10240
CF mediaCF      mediaCF1
CF jadelibCF    jadelibCF1
CF castleCF     castleCF01
```

But we now want it to be:

```
bufferSize      1024
workSize        20480 10240
CF mediaCF      mediaCF11
CF jadelibCF    jadelibCF11
CF castleCF     castleCF01
```

If our connection uses this ENV file, any references to Jasmine Studio or the Multimedia classes will be directed to our new copies of them. If we need to go back and use the original class families at any time, we can restore the old file, or just set up a different connection to use it. The two, and their respective instance data and multimedia files, are completely independent of each other.

Figure 13.4 shows something interesting. At this point, we can see the original class families **jadelibCF1** and **mediaCF1**. If we browse them we find their references are explicitly to each other. Meanwhile our new **mediaCF11** is, of course, aliased to **mediaCF** and we cannot see a reference to the new **jadelibCF** because it is considered an internal Class family to Studio like **System**.

You may have tried the Jasmine Studio Tutorial where multimedia items are placed in certain resource classes inside the CAStore Class family. From there they can be dragged and dropped onto scenes, and Studio creates the appropriate widget for each item. Since we want to be independent of the CA samples, let us copy those classes as well and put them into our own castleCF.

First we unload them—just the class definitions this time. There aren't any methods here, but we do have to specifically name each class, as we want a portion of the CAStore Class family, not the whole lot:

```
jasunload %JAS_SYSTEM%\unload\CAStoreStuff1.uld -s -c
CAStore::Resource
        CAStore::Control CAStore::MenuItem
```

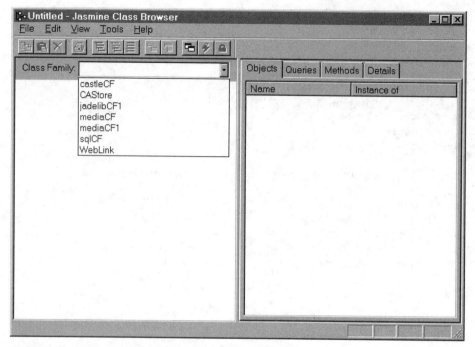

Figure 13.4 The Database Administrator after duplication.

```
                    CAStore::ActivationObject CAStore::Language
                    CAStore::Button CAStore::Label
jasunload %JAS_SYSTEM%\unload\CAStoreStuff2.uld -s -c
CAStore::Decoration
                    CAStore::Background CAStore::Pictures
                    CAStore::Sounds CAStore::Movies
```

The –c option was added so that the resulting unload files would have comments. The Top class in this hierarchy is **Resource**, but it is a subclass of CAComposite. To move it into castleCF, which doesn't have a CAComposite, we need to change the CAComposite reference in the unload file:

```
# Super Class Information
# cfname,clsname
"CAStore","CAComposite"
```

to the composite class we are using, CastleComposite:

```
# Super Class Information
# cfname,clsname
"CAStore","CastleComposite"
```

Notice that we are leaving the Class family references alone. That is because we are letting the JasLoad command take care of those for us:

```
rem Jasmine must be running here!
jasload %JAS_SYSTEM%\unload\CAStoreStuff1.uld -s CAStore=castleCF01
jasload %JAS_SYSTEM%\unload\CAStoreStuff2.uld -s CAStore=castleCF01
```

And done! Figure 13.5 shows the class hierarchy in my Class family now.
Using the preceding commands and batch files is not difficult, but familiarity with the
Jasmine documentation is highly recommended. Follow the recommendations in the
earlier section, "Importance of Being Scripted," and make sure you have backups
before, during, and after you try all of this, and plan for it as soon as possible in
development (certainly *before* any Jasmine Studio development begins).

Conclusion

To treat any one of the subjects covered in this chapter properly would require an
entire book. The purpose here was to provide a quick overview with solid examples.

Jasmine *is* an easy product to use, especially compared to other available relational
products. Your biggest hurdle may be understanding object-oriented techniques, in
analysis, design, and programming. Much of the Jasmine advertising you may have
seen focuses on client development gains provided by Jasmine Studio, and so on.
These gains are still real compared to client development with other products. They do
not describe the back-end server work simply because this cannot be scoped without
first finding out exactly what a customer requires.

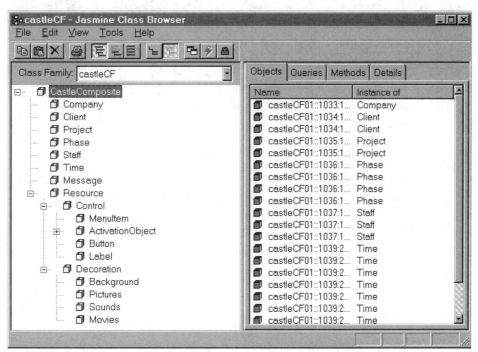

Figure 13.5 We are now set for Jasmine Studio development independent of all the CA
sample code.

Appendix 13.1 Complete ODQL for Defining and Building Classes in This Database (Classes.odql)

```
/******************************************************************
File: Classes.odql
Class definitions for Demonstration Timewriting Database
v1.00  March 1999
Peter Fallon
Castle Software Australia
******************************************************************/
defaultCF systemCF;
/* Class: CastleComposite
Provided in case I need to define application-wide behaviour in the future
such as error logging, audit trails, etc.
*/
defineClass castleCF::CastleComposite
  super: systemCF::Composite
  description: "Base (Abstract) class for Demonstration database."
{
};
/* Class: Company
This class is at the top of the object hierarchy (containing tree) for
this system. It contains the master lists of active staff, projects and
clients.
*/
defineClass castleCF::Company
  super: castleCF::CastleComposite
  description: "Principle container class for timewriting system."
{
  maxInstanceSize: 8;
  instance:
    String                  companyTitle;
    String                  address;
    List <castleCF::Staff>      staffList
      description: "List of Staff currently employed."
      default: List{};
    List <castleCF::Project>    projectList
      description: "List of active Projects being worked on."
      default: List{};
    List <castleCF::Client>     clientList
      description: "List of current clients."
      default: List{};
};
/* Class: Client
Clients of the Company. Each may have one or more projects in progress.
Note that past clients remain instances of this class, but they won't be in
the Company.ClientList{}
```

```
*/
defineClass castleCF::Client
  super: castleCF::CastleComposite
  description: "Client for whom project work is done."
{
  maxInstanceSize: 8;
  instance:
    String                    name;
    String                    address;
    List <castleCF::Project>  projectList
       description: "List of active Projects being worked on."
       default: List{};
};
/* Class: Project
A Project is the complete unit of work done for a client by the company. It
consists of one or more Phases. Time is written to Phases of the Project by
staff.
Estimates are recorded as properties while Actuals are calculated live from
methods.
*/
defineClass castleCF::Project
  super: castleCF::CastleComposite
  description: "All information about a specific project"
{
  maxInstanceSize: 4;
  instance:
    String                    name;
    String                    longDescription;
    Date                      projectStart;
    Date                      estimatedProjectFinish;
    Date                      actualProjectFinish;
    Decimal [10,2]            estimatedHours;
    Decimal [12,2]            estimatedCost;
    Boolean                   completed;
    List <castleCF::Staff>    staffList
       description: "List of Staff assigned to this project."
       default: List{};
    List <castleCF::Phase>    phaseList
       description: "List of Phases that make up this Project."
       default: List{};
    castleCF::Client          client
       description: "Client paying the bills for this project.";
};
/* Class: Phase
A Phase is a single unit of work in a project, such as Analysis or
Construction. Estimates are recorded as properties while Actuals are
calculated live from methods.
*/
defineClass castleCF::Phase
  super: castleCF::CastleComposite
  description: "Information about a specific phase of a project"
```

```
{
  maxInstanceSize: 4;
  instance:
    String                   name;
    String                   longDescription;
    Date                     phaseStart;
    Date                     estimatedPhaseFinish;
    Date                     actualPhaseFinish;
    Decimal [10,2]           estimatedHours;
    Decimal [12,2]           estimatedCost;
    Boolean                  completed;
    List <castleCF::Project>  project
      description: "Parent project for this phase.";
};
/* Class: Staff
Staff are the resources that do the work on all projects. All time
recorded is allocated to specific staff members.
*/
defineClass castleCF::Staff
  super: castleCF::CastleComposite
  description: "The people that do all the work."
{
  maxInstanceSize: 4;
  instance:
    String                   surname;
    String                   givenName;
    String [10]              employeeNumber
      mandatory:
      unique:;
    Decimal [5,2]            hourlyRate
      default: 0;
    List <castleCF::Project>  projectList
      description: "List of Projects this person is assigned to."
      default: List{};
};
/* Class: Time
These are the basic units of time recording. Instances of time are specific
to staff, project phases, and date.
*/
defineClass castleCF::Time
  super: castleCF::CastleComposite
  description: "The basic units of time recording."
{
  maxInstanceSize: 4;
  instance:
    Date                     WhenDone;
    Decimal [10,2]           timeSpent
      default: 0;
    Decimal [12,2]           cost
      default: 0
      description: "Calculated from staff's hourly rate";
```

```
      castleCF::Phase              phase
        description: "Project Phase time is recorded for";
      castleCF::Staff              staff
        description: "Who did the work";
};
/*
Build all classes. Until this command is executed, you cannot create
instances of these classes. Note that compiling methods is a separate step,
and doesn't have to be done if we just want to create instances of these
classes.
*/
buildClass castleCF::CastleComposite castleCF::Company
           castleCF::Client castleCF::Project castleCF::Phase
           castleCF::Staff castleCF::Time;
```

Appendix 13.2 Code for Creating a Few Instances of Each Class (DataEntry01.odql)

```
/* File: DataEntry01.odql
Data entry script when there are no methods defined yet. Load a couple of
objects into each class.
v1.00  March 1999
Peter Fallon
Castle Software Australia
*/
defaultCF castleCF;
/* Define a Company Record */
Company oCompany;
oCompany = Company.new();
oCompany.companyTitle = "Pete's Software Emporium";
oCompany.address = "Melbourne, Australia";
/*
Hold that thought, and create a couple of Project instances and add that to
the Company object
*/
Project oProject1, oProject2;
oProject1 = Project.new();
oProject1.name = "Patient Needs Trial Database";
oProject1.longDescription = "Touch screen based questionnaire system for
Hospital";
oProject1.completed = FALSE;
oProject1.projectStart = Date.construct(1999,3,1);
oProject1.estimatedProjectFinish = Date.construct(1999,8,30);
oProject1.estimatedHours = 250.0;
oProject1.estimatedCost = 20000.00;

oProject2 = Project.new();
oProject2.name = "Y2K Project";
```

```
oProject2.longDescription = "Financial System requires Y2K checking and
certification";
oProject2.completed = FALSE;
oProject2.projectStart = Date.construct(1998,6,1);
oProject2.estimatedProjectFinish = Date.construct(1999,10,31);
oProject2.estimatedHours = 1500.0;
oProject2.estimatedCost = 100000.00;

oCompany.directAdd("projectList", oProject1);
oCompany.directAdd("projectList", oProject2);
/* Create some Client Objects
Add Clients to Company object, respective Project objects, and Projects to
Clients
*/
Client oClient1, oClient2;
oClient1 = Client.new();
oClient1.name = "Hospital";
oClient1.address = "Somewhere Abouts, Melbourne";
oClient1.directAdd("projectList", oProject1);
oCompany.directAdd("clientList", oClient1);
oProject1.client = oClient1;

oClient2 = Client.new();
oClient2.name = "Contracting Agency";
oClient2.address = "May as well be Woop Woop";
oClient2.directAdd("projectList", oProject2);
oCompany.directAdd("clientList", oClient2);
oProject2.client = oClient2;
/* Create Staff
Add to Company, and Project instances
*/
Staff oStaff1, oStaff2, oStaff3;
oStaff1 = Staff.new( employeeNumber:="XX1234567" );
oStaff1.surname = "Bloggs";
oStaff1.givenName = "Joseph";
oStaff1.hourlyRate = 55.00;
oStaff1.directAdd("projectList", oProject1);
oStaff1.directAdd("projectList", oProject2);
oCompany.directAdd("staffList", oStaff1);
oProject1.directAdd("staffList", oStaff1);
oProject2.directAdd("staffList", oStaff1);

oStaff2 = Staff.new( employeeNumber:="YY1111111" );
oStaff2.surname = "Doe";
oStaff2.givenName = "Jaqueline";
oStaff2.hourlyRate = 60.00;
oStaff2.directAdd("projectList", oProject2);

oCompany.directAdd("staffList", oStaff2);
oProject2.directAdd("staffList", oStaff2);
```

```
oStaff3 = Staff.new( employeeNumber:="XY3333333" );
oStaff3.surname = "Smith";
oStaff3.givenName = "Anonymous";
oStaff3.hourlyRate = 65.00;
oStaff3.directAdd("projectList", oProject2);

oCompany.directAdd("staffList", oStaff3);
oProject2.directAdd("staffList", oStaff3);
/* Create Project Phase instances
Add these to the Project Instances (each phase object can only belong to a
single project)
*/
Phase oPhase11, oPhase12;
oPhase11 = Phase.new();
oPhase11.name = "Analysis and Specification";
oPhase11.longDescription = "Get user's business requirements down";
oPhase11.completed = TRUE;
oPhase11.phaseStart = Date.construct(1999,3,1);
oPhase11.estimatedPhaseFinish = Date.construct(1999,3,14);
oPhase11.actualPhaseFinish = Date.construct(1999,3,31);
oPhase11.estimatedHours = 50.0;
oPhase11.estimatedCost = 5000.00;
oPhase11.project = oProject1;

oPhase12 = Phase.new();
oPhase12.name = "Construction";
oPhase12.longDescription = "Build it - all the progamming";
oPhase12.completed = FALSE;
oPhase12.phaseStart = Date.construct(1999,3,10);
oPhase12.estimatedPhaseFinish = Date.construct(1999,8,30);
oPhase12.estimatedHours = 200.0;
oPhase12.estimatedCost = 15000.00;
oPhase12.project = oProject1;

oProject1.directAdd("phaseList", oPhase11);
oProject1.directAdd("phaseList", oPhase12);
Phase oPhase21, oPhase22;

oPhase21 = Phase.new();
oPhase21.name = "Client Modelling System";
oPhase21.longDescription = "Y2K checking and certification";
oPhase21.completed = TRUE;
oPhase21.phaseStart = Date.construct(1998,6,1);
oPhase21.estimatedPhaseFinish = Date.construct(1998,12,31);
oPhase21.actualPhaseFinish = Date.construct(1999,1,31);
oPhase21.estimatedHours = 500.0;
oPhase21.estimatedCost = 35000.00;
oPhase21.project = oProject2;

oPhase22 = Phase.new();
oPhase22.name = "Internal Systems";
```

```
oPhase22.longDescription = "Y2K checking and certification";
oPhase22.completed = FALSE;
oPhase22.phaseStart = Date.construct(1998,12,1);
oPhase22.estimatedPhaseFinish = Date.construct(1999,10,31);
oPhase22.estimatedHours = 1500.0;
oPhase22.estimatedCost = 65000.00;
oPhase22.project = oProject2;

oProject2.directAdd("phaseList", oPhase21);
oProject2.directAdd("phaseList", oPhase22);
```

CHAPTER

14

Seamlessness and Transparency in Object-Oriented Databases

A major objective motivating the development of object-oriented databases (OODBs) was smoother integration between information storage mechanisms and the applications that use them. Our experience with OODBs, however, suggests that they frequently have fallen well short of this objective. In particular, OODBs have typically lacked *seamlessness* and *transparency*. Here we describe some of the shortcomings that we have encountered in using object-oriented databases and some enhancements that we believe could lead to improved seamlessness and transparency in OODBs.

Traditional information storage mechanisms, such as files or relational database systems, fit relatively smoothly with the applications of earlier generations. When most data could appropriately be viewed as tabular, such as arrays of numerical values or rows of records, and most programming languages offered no data types more complex than arrays or records, these traditional mechanisms were quite adequate.

New generations of applications, written in modern programming languages with richer and more powerful type systems, proved much less well matched to traditional information storage mechanisms, however. In particular, the complex structure within, and complex relationships among, data whose types are defined using an object-oriented typing system are very difficult to map to files or relational database systems. This incompatibility has been termed *impedance mismatch*.

Object-oriented databases were developed specifically to overcome this impedance mismatch. As developers of object-oriented applications, we therefore hoped that OODBs would integrate very smoothly with such applications. Although they have certainly been a major improvement over traditional information storage mechanisms, our experience with OODBs suggests that they still fall well short of this goal. In particular, we have found that OODBs generally have lacked *seamlessness* and *transparency*.

Seamlessness and transparency are closely related properties, both of which have a major impact on the how easily software developers can use advanced components such as OODBs. By seamlessness, we mean the absence of evident rough edges in the integration between parts of an application. By transparency, we mean the invisibility of underlying mechanisms from the perspective of the application (or its developer). As a glaring example of the lack of seamlessness and transparency in many OODBs, consider the following.

The Object Data Management Group (ODMG), in describing the C++ binding for their Object Manipulation Language (OML), articulates the goal that "the syntax used to create, delete, identify, reference, get/set property values, and invoke operations on a persistent object should be, so far as possible, no different than that used for objects of shorter lifetimes" [Cattell 1997]. That is, they claim to be striving for seamlessness and transparency. In reality, however, a C++ reference to a transient instance of class `Person` would be of type `Person*`, whereas an OML reference to a persistent instance of class `Person` would be of type `d_Ref<Person>` [Cattell 1997]. This means that existing applications for manipulating `Person` objects must be modified in order to operate on `Person` objects retrieved from an ODMG-compliant OODB, which violates seamlessness, and that the underlying OODB is far from invisible to developers, which obviates transparency.

A few OODBs have been relatively successful at achieving seamlessness and transparency. In particular, we have had the opportunity to use the Open Object-Oriented Database (OpenOODB) developed by Texas Instruments (and later Raytheon TI Systems) under sponsorship of the Defense Advanced Research Projects Agency (DARPA) [Wells 1992]. The OpenOODB was unusually seamless and transparent with respect to use with applications written in a single language; however, it was less so when used with multilanguage software, although it was specifically developed to support such use. This led us to develop several enhancements aimed at raising OODB seamlessness and transparency to an even higher level.

In the remainder of this chapter we first briefly describe the OpenOODB and some of our experiences with it. We then focus on some areas in which the OpenOODB originally lacked seamlessness and transparency, and outline the enhancements we developed to improve on these shortcomings. We conclude by evaluating the success of our efforts, and we consider the future of OODBs, specifically with regard to the issues of seamlessness and transparency.

General Experience Using OpenOODB

Although OpenOODB can be categorized as a research prototype (in contrast to commercial OODBs, such as O2 and ObjectStore), the approach it embodies demonstrates that transparency and seamlessness can be achieved for practical object-oriented application programming interfaces (APIs). From this perspective, our experience using and extending OpenOODB has been, for the most part, extremely positive. Our work with OpenOODB has also led to some interesting discoveries and insights regarding transparency and seamlessness. In the remainder of this section, we outline our overall experience using OpenOODB and discuss its strengths and shortcomings with respect to these two critical properties.

Both the C++ and CLOS APIs that are supported by OpenOODB allow programmers to incorporate persistence into applications with minimal changes to application source. To help illustrate the OpenOODB approach, consider, for example, the C++ class definition of a `Person` (stored in a file called `Person.h`) in Figure 14.1(a). (The CLOS API is almost identical to the C++ API; however, a preprocessor, as discussed later, is not required to make CLOS objects persist.) The application in Figure 14.1(b) instantiates several `Person` objects and saves them in a database by invoking a persist operation on each object. The application in Figure 14.1(c) shows how these objects are retrieved from the database by invoking the fetch operation on the OODB object, which is defined by the OpenOODB run-time system.

To a large extent, the C++ `Person` class and the two applications in Figure 14.1 look almost identical to a C++ application that does not use the OpenOODB. One distinguishing characteristic is that OpenOODB applications must include an `OpenOODB.h` file, which must appear prior to any subsequent class definitions. Another obvious distinction is that an application must bracket all accesses to persistent objects with invocations of the `beginT()` and `commitT()` operations of the OODB object, which serves to enclose those accesses in an OpenOODB transaction. Applications must also end with a call to the `commit()` operation that closes the OODB object.

The actual accessing of persistent objects in an OpenOODB application is otherwise quite seamless and transparent. To enable the use of the `persist()` and `fetch()` operations that implement the persistence features, a preprocessor is applied to the source code. This preprocessor transparently extends classes with a special persistence class, which makes (sub) classes persistence-capable. It adds a persist operation to a persistence-capable class (as shown in Figure 14.1(b)). When invoked, the persist operation causes the object and all objects in its transitive closure to be made persistent. A fetch operation, as defined by the OODB object (as shown in Figure 14.1 (c)), is used to retrieve persistent objects. Note that a type cast must be used when retrieving persistent objects.

Although we have illustrated only (some of the) OpenOODB persistence capabilities for the C++ API, both the C++ and CLOS APIs provide transparent and seamless persistence for a majority of C++ and CLOS type constructs, respectively. In general, objects can be made to persist at any time during an object's lifetime. Furthermore, the OpenOODB does not require the explicit usage of special types or declarations for persistent objects, nor does it require special pointer types for referencing (potentially) persistent objects.

```
// Person.h
class Person {
  private:
    int      born;
    char*    name;
    Person* mother;
    Person* father;
  public:
    Person (...);
    char* getAge ();
    char* nameOf ();
    Person* motherOf ();
    Person* fatherOf ();
}
            (a)
```

```
// create.h
#include "OpenOODB.h"
#include "Person.h"
main (int argc, char *argv[]) {
  OODB oodb;
  Person* alan, *jack;
  oodb.beginT();
  alan = new Person (...);
  jack = new Person (...);
  alan->persist ("alan");
  jack->persist ("jack");
  oodb.commitT();
  oodb.commit();
}
            (b)
```

```
// fetch.h
#include "OpenOODB.h"
#include "Person.h"
main (int argc, char *argv[]) {
  OODB oodb;
  Person* any;
  oodb.beginT();
  any = (Person *) oodb.fetch("jack");
  cout << jack->nameOf();
  any = (Person *) oodb.fetch("alan");
  cout << any->nameOf();
  oodb.commitT();
  oodb.commit();
}
            (c)
```

Figure 14.1   OpenOODB C++ API.

In general, OpenOODB makes it relatively easy to incorporate persistence into both new and existing applications. Since it is a research prototype, however, it does have some limitations. For example, the C++ API does not completely support all C++ type constructions, such as certain uses of templates and array structures. The OpenOODB approach also requires availability of a source representation for classes, which may not always be practical in various situations. In addition, classes that are extended with OpenOODB persistence cannot be debugged using the standard UNIX debuggers. Thus, while persistence is relatively transparent and seamless in OpenOODB programs, the use of software engineering tools, such as debuggers, can be seamy.

Despite these limitations in the current prototype, overall the OpenOODB does a relatively good job at providing transparent and seamless persistence for two nontrivial object-oriented programming languages. Our experience using OpenOODB has, however, led us to explore several interesting issues with respect to transparency and seamlessness in OODBs.

First, we observed that the name management service provided by OpenOODB is flat, which means that managing the names for persistent objects becomes problematic for large numbers of objects. Second, we noticed that the OpenOODB name management service is segregated according to the language used to define objects. Thus, names for persistent objects defined in C++ are not visible to objects defined in CLOS, and vice versa. These two observations led us to investigate richer and more powerful name management mechanisms to use with persistent language systems. Third, although a potential strength of OpenOODB is its support for multiple APIs, OpenOODB provides little in the support for interoperability between objects defined in different languages. This raises an interesting seam in accessing persistent data from applications that are implemented in different languages, and we have worked on approaches to overcoming this seam. Finally, with the emergence of Java, we saw opportunities for an even more seamless and more transparent incorporation of persistence into a programming language with notable similarities to C++ and CLOS, and we have pursued those as well. In the next section, we report on our own experience in developing seamless approaches to name management, interoperability, and persistence as motivated by our OpenOODB experience.

Detailed Experience Extending OpenOODB

Our experience with seamless and transparent extensions to OODBs is centered on developing and experimenting with name management, interoperability, and persistence capabilities. We begin this section with a brief description of these capabilities, along with their relationship to, and importance in, OODB technology. We then describe in greater detail our experience with extending the OpenOODB along these three dimensions.

Name management is the means by which a computing system allows names to be established for objects, permits objects to be accessed using names, and controls the meaning and availability of names at any point in time in a particular computation [Kaplan 1996]. Existing approaches to name management in OODBs tend to be incommensurate with the rich type and computation models they support and are therefore, in general, neither very transparent nor very seamless. As observed by Loomis [Loomis 1995], existing OODBs are generally limited to flat naming structures, which means that names for all objects must be unique. Such limitations are examples of highly visible seams in OODBs, since programmers must develop *ad hoc* schemes to overcome this shortcoming.

Since many OODBs support multiple programming languages, seamless, and transparent approaches to interoperability play a critical role in OODBs. An OODB may contain data objects originally defined, created, and persistently stored using the capabilities provided by several distinct programming languages, and an application may need to process those data objects uniformly. We call such an OODB *polylingual* and term the corresponding interoperability problem the *polylingual access* problem. Unfortunately, today's OODBs fall far short of providing transparent and seamless polylingual access to persistent objects. Most approaches to addressing this problem have been based on the ODMG ODL standard [Cattell 1997]. Such approaches, however, inherently lack seamlessness and transparency because ODL imposes an intermediary type model that all developers must be aware of [Kaplan 1998]. Moreover, the ODL type model has some significant semantic shortcomings [Alagic 1997] that limit its usefulness for supporting interoperability.

One measure of the seamlessness and transparency provided by an OODB is the extent to which it provides those properties across multiple, distinct, programming language APIs. As noted, OpenOODB was relatively successful at achieving this for two of the most significant object-oriented languages extant when it was designed, namely C++ and CLOS. The subsequent emergence, and immediate popularity of Java offered an opportunity to further assess the extent to which the OpenOODB approach could support seamlessness and transparency. It also represented a further challenge for the name management and interoperability support available with the OpenOODB.

With sponsorship from Texas Instruments, Raytheon TI Systems, and DARPA, we have explored enhancements to OpenOODB in each of these areas. Our approach to transparent and seamless naming, interoperability, and persistence centers on a framework that we call PolySPIN, which stands for polylingual support for persistence, interoperability, and naming. The PolySPIN framework provides a uniform name management mechanism that not only offers application developers a library of useful abstractions for organizing and navigating OODBs but, as a byproduct, offers an interoperability mechanism providing transparent polylingual access to persistent objects, thus allowing applications to manipulate objects as though they were all implemented in the language of the application. In the remainder of this section, we first describe PolySPIN's approach to name management. Next we show how PolySPIN enables transparent and seamless interoperability in an OODB. We then report on our experience extending PolySPIN with support for Java. The section concludes with an overall assessment of our experience in developing and experimenting with these extensions.

Name Management

With respect to name management, OpenOODB is similar to many OODBs. In its plain, vanilla form, OpenOODB is limited to a flat-name space for persistent objects. Thus, the OpenOODB API `persist` and `fetch` operations assume that all names (for all persistent objects) must be unique. Although such schemes are simple to understand, they do not scale for large systems, which may have thousands of nameable persistent objects.

Another important characteristic of the default name management mechanism in the OpenOODB (and in OODBs in general) is that the persistent store is segregated according to the language used to define objects. For example, names for persistent C++ objects are not visible to CLOS objects and vice versa. Moreover, not only is the name space segregated, but the data space is segregated as well. For example, persistent CLOS data cannot be accessed by C++ applications, and vice versa. This latter visible seam is addressed in the section on Interoperability.

The PolySPIN framework addresses these various seams by providing a uniform, flexible, and powerful approach to name management. Although the details of its interface are beyond the scope of this chapter, the name management mechanism allows names to be assigned to objects in binding spaces (where binding spaces are collections of name-object pairs) and names for objects to be resolved in contexts (where contexts are constructed from existing binding spaces) [Kaplan 94]. In addition, binding spaces may be assigned names, resulting in the ability to organize hierarchically the name space for objects (similar to directory structures found in modern file systems). Coupled with the persistent store, this approach results in a name-based persistence mechanism where any object (and, transparently, all the objects in that object's transitive closure) bound to a name in a binding space reachable from a specially designated root binding space automatically persists. The approach is based on techniques pioneered in Galileo [Albano 1985] and Napier [Morrison 1993], where *environments* correspond to binding spaces. The name management mechanism in PolySPIN is more general, however, since it supports objects defined in multiple languages.

To participate in this mechanism, an object's class definition must inherit from a common base class, designated the `NameableObject` class. By inheriting from this class, instances of the subclass can be, among other things, named and resolved using the operations supported by the various abstractions that make up the PolySPIN name management mechanism. For example, Figure 14.2 shows a (partial) C++ definition for a `Person` class, a code fragment illustrating how a name might be assigned to an instance of `Person`, and a portion of a persistent store organization based on this approach.

This more flexible approach to naming clearly eliminates the *flat name space seam*. It allows OODBs to be organized more effectively and intuitively. Furthermore, it elimi-

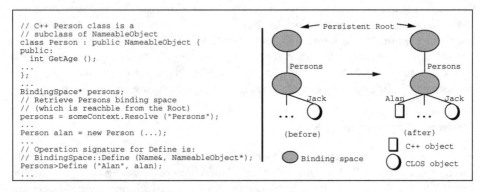

Figure 14.2   Using PolySPIN's name management mechanism.

nates the *name segregation seam* by providing uniform support for objects defined in multiple languages. Specifically, the same name management mechanism is used to manage both persistent C++ and CLOS objects. A binding space may, for instance, contain bindings to objects that have been defined in different languages. The name management mechanism is also transparent since it can be employed for all objects, independent of whether they are persistent or not. For example, an application may wish to use the name management mechanism as a means of hierarchically organizing a collection of objects. The application may also make the collection persist simply by creating a binding to the collection's root in some persistent binding space.

Interoperability

The flexible and uniform name management mechanism for the OpenOODB removed the flat, segregated name space seams. It also opened up an important opportunity to explore approaches that allow transparent and seamless access to persistent data from applications that are implemented in different languages. Most of the shortcomings in existing approaches to interoperability result from inadequate levels of abstraction. By basing higher level abstractions for OODB data object access on a general and uniform approach to name management, PolySPIN provides a suitable framework for supporting polylingual access.

As suggested, having a class inherit from `NameableObject` could, and frequently might, be done quite independently of any intention to make objects interoperate. Inheriting from `NameableObject` does, however, also enable the use of the interoperability capabilities of PolySPIN. First, having a uniform name management mechanism in place results in a language-independent method of establishing visibility paths to persistent objects (i.e., via their assigned names), regardless of the defining language of either the objects or the applications. Second, the name management mechanism serves as a useful place for capturing and recording language-specific information about objects, which can be used to support polylingual access. In particular, once an application has established an initial connection to a persistent object (via its name), the name management mechanism can provide the necessary information permitting the application to create a data path to the object. In other words, when resolving a name of some object (on behalf of some application), the name management mechanism can detect the defining language of the object and set up the necessary communication medium for manipulating the object. The features supporting this capability are hidden from application developers within the internals of the PolySPIN architecture.

Given this interoperability mechanism, what is needed is the ability to determine whether two class interfaces defined in different languages can indeed interoperate, and in the event they can, to instrument their implementations (including generating any necessary foreign function interface code) such that the interoperability features of PolySPIN can be employed. For example, Figure 14.3 shows the C++ and CLOS class definitions and implementations for the `Person` class, where the plain-face type represents the original source code and the boldface type represents the code enabling polylingual access. The details of the various operations calls are beyond the scope of this chapter, but the general idea is that a C++ application continues to use its original class interface, whereas the implementation of the class is modified so that it invokes the appropriate language. Initially, we carried out this modification manually. In other words, the code shown in boldface in Figure 14.3 was generated and inserted into the class definitions by hand. As a step toward automating our approach, however, we have developed the PolySPINner toolset, details of which can be found in [Barrett 1996].

The most important aspect of this interoperability mechanism is that applications view persistent data as if it were implemented in the language of the application itself. All the details of transparent polylingual aspect are hidden inside the name management mechanism. In addition, the implementations of methods must be instrumented with interoperability code, whereas method interfaces remain unchanged. Thus, an interface to a persistent object does not need to be changed in order to interoperate in a polylingual setting.

Persistence

To validate the seamlessness and transparency of both the OpenOODB approach to persistence and also our name management and interoperability extensions to the OpenOODB, we developed JSPIN, a Java API for the OpenOODB. The design of JSPIN is described in "Our spin on persistent Java: The JavaSpin approach." [Kaplan 1996]. Its implementation and some comparative performance studies based on the 001 benchmark are described in "Toward assessing approaches to persistence for Java" [Ridgway 1997]. Efforts to extend JSPIN further to support persistence for classes as well as for instances are described in "Toward class evolution in persistent Java" [Ridgway 1998]. Here we briefly outline our goals, our approach, and our experience with the JSPIN effort.

```
class Person : public NameableObject {
private:
  int born;
public:
  int GetAge ();
};
// GetAge member function
int Person::GetAge () {
 if (this->language == CLOS)
    return
      (__Callout_CLOS_Person_GetAge(this->tidForObject));
    else {
    int result;
    result = 1995 - born;
    return (result);
    }
}
// Foreign Function Interface Section
// Callout CLOS Person GetAge
extern "C"int __Callout_CLOS_Person_GetAge (TID this);
// Callout from CLOS into C++
extern "C" int __Callout_CPP_Person_GetAge (TID self )
{
  Person* object = (Person *) TidToCid (self);
  return (object->GetAge());
}
```

                        C++ Person Class

```
(defclass Person (NameableObject)
  ((born :accessor born
          :type Date
          :initform "MM/DD/YY")
   )
  )
;; GetAge method
(defmethod  GetAge ((this Person))
  (declare (return-values Integer))
(cond( (EQUAL (language this) CLOS)
          (- Today (born this))
      ( (EQUAL (language this) C++)
          (__Callout_CPP_Person_GetAge (tid this)))
   )
)
;; Foreign Function Interface Section
;; Callout C++ Person GetAge
(DEF-ALIEN-ROUTINE ("__Callout_CPP_Person_GetAge"
          __POLYSPIN_CPP_Person_GetAge)
  int  (self TID )
)
;; Callout from C++ into CLOS
(DEF-FOREIGN-CALLABLE
          (__Callout_CLOS_Person_GetAge
          (:language :c) (:return-type int))
      ( ( this TID) )
  (GetAge  (tid-to-cid this))
)
```

                        CLOS Person Class

Figure 14.3   Interoperating C++ and CLOS classes.

Our work on JSPIN had several goals. Among those goals, the most important was:

Seamless extension of Java. Our highest priority was to provide a set of extensions to Java in the most seamless manner possible. Seamlessness implied that our extensions should be compatible with Java and the programming style that it defines, including its type safety and security properties. The specific extensions included in the JSPIN approach are:

Persistence. JSPIN currently provides orthogonal, reachability-based (transitive) persistence for Java, in a style that is essentially identical to that provided for C++ and CLOS by the OpenOODB. It also provides a basis for the same kinds of name-based persistence capabilities for Java that our enhancements to the OpenOODB make available for C++ and CLOS.

Enhanced name management. JSPIN also provides a basis for extended name management capabilities, based on the Piccolo model [Kaplan 1995] and therefore suitable for use with Conch-style tools [Kaplan 1994]. These capabilities are independent of (that is, orthogonal to) persistence. As a result, this enhanced approach to name management can be applied uniformly to C++, CLOS, and Java objects.

Basis for polylingual interoperability among C++, CLOS, and Java. The extensions provided by JSPIN transparently incorporate the necessary information into Java objects to support polylingual interoperability among C++, CLOS, and Java [Kaplan 1996].

The JSPIN API provides basic, OpenOODB-style persistence to Java users. The API includes methods added to each class processed by JSPIN, together with several JSPIN-specific classes (in a package named `EDU.umass.cs.ccsl.JSPIN`). The appearance is that most methods are added to the `Object` class and inherited from it by every other class. In reality this is not exactly the case because of return-type restrictions. Specifically, the `fetch` method of a class is required to return an object of that class and thus must be specific to the class.[1] The JSPIN API adds the following methods to each class:

`public void persist([String name])`. When invoked on any object, this method results in that object, and all objects reachable from it, becoming persistent. The optional `name` parameter can be used to assign a name to the persistent object, by which name it can later be retrieved. If no name is assigned, the object can be retrieved only if it is referenced from some other object.

`public static class fetch(String name)`. When invoked, this method returns the persistent instance of the class corresponding to the name given by the `name` parameter. If there is no such instance in the persistent store, the `Unknown-PersistentName` exception is thrown.

---

[1] We could inherit the fetch method, but then it would have to return Object, and the programmer would be required to cast the returned Object to an object of the desired class. This remains type-safe, but is slightly unpleasant.

The JSPIN API also defines the `PersistentStore` abstract class (in the JSPIN package), which is shown in Figure 14.4. All of the methods of this class, abstract or not, may potentially throw a `PersistentStoreException`, which we have omitted from these brief descriptions.

JSPIN is implemented via modifications to the Java Developers Kit (JDK) compiler and suitably modified interfaces to the OpenOODB kernel. Importantly, JSPIN runs on an unmodified Java Virtual Machine.

As reported in the aforementioned papers ([Kaplan 1996]; [Ridgway 1997]; [Ridgway 1998]), our JSPIN effort successfully demonstrated that the goals of seamlessness and transparency could be achieved with relative ease through the combination of Java and the OpenOODB. We take this as evidence that:

- Seamlessness and transparency are reasonable and attainable objectives for OODB developers
- Both Java and the OpenOODB are particularly well-designed artifacts in their respective domains

It is our hope that our JSPIN work will inspire future OODB developers to strive for seamlessness and transparency in the systems that they produce.

Summary

We believe the work reported in this chapter represents an important extension to object-oriented database technology. Though modern OODBs often provide multiple language interfaces, interoperating among the various languages can be a cumbersome and complex process, thus limiting their overall potential. Using PolySPIN, both C++ and CLOS objects are organized under a single, unified name management mechanism. PolySPIN also provides transparent, polylingual access to objects (of compatible types), even though the objects may have been created using different programming languages. Thus, application developers are free to work in their native language without precluding the possibility of interoperating with foreign language objects or applications. Finally, our work on JSPIN illustrates the practicality and plausibility of achieving transparency and seamlessness for Java in OODBs.

```
public abstract class PersistentStore {
  public void beginTransaction();
  public void commitTransaction();
  public void abortTransaction();

  public void persist(Object obj, String name);
  public void persist(Object obj);
  public Object fetch(String name);
}
```

Figure 14.4 The JSPIN `PersistentStore` abstract class.

Conclusion

In this chapter we have related some of our experience and observations regarding seamlessness and transparency in OODBs. This account has been centered on our usage of and extensions to the Open Object-Oriented Database, which was developed by Texas Instruments (and later Raytheon TI Systems) under DARPA sponsorship. We found the OpenOODB to be unusually seamless and transparent when used with applications written in a single language, but less so when used with multilanguage software. By developing extensions to the OpenOODB to support enhanced name management, interoperability, and persistence for Java, we have attempted to raise OODB seamlessness and transparency to an even higher level.

We believe that our experience in using the OpenOODB and our extensions to it demonstrate both the feasibility and the value of seamlessness and transparency in OODBs. We hope that this account of our experience and extensions will inspire developers of future OODBs to strive for greater levels of seamlessness and transparency in the systems that they build. We note, for example, that the OMG's work on persistence services for distributed systems is attempting to provide more seamless and transparent approaches to persistence [OMG 1998]. In the meantime, we will be continuing to investigate approaches for improving OODB support for these important properties.

PART

Six

Case Studies

A common argument for using object databases instead of relational databases for some applications is that they provide better capabilities to capture the structure and behavior of objects from the problem domain. There are many examples from the financial and telecommunications industries that show this to be the case. Genetics is another domain where this technology appears to have proved itself useful. Today, many research laboratories and academic institutions exist that are actively undertaking important research into the human genome project, and some have published their experiences with object databases in the recent past. To determine whether advances in object databases over the past few years have led to improved support for genetics work, we have included Chapters 15 and 16. Chapter 15, "Experiences Using the ODMG Standard in Bioinformatics Applications" by Paton, provides a discussion and evaluation of a product that claims ODMG compliance, for modeling and analyses of the yeast genome. Chapter 16, "An Object-Oriented Database for Managing Genetic Sequences" by Bellahsene and Ripoche, provides a discussion of object and relational databases for genomic data and of how some of the limitations in a prototype using an object database were overcome.

Another area that has attracted strong interest in the use of object databases is for modeling geospatial information. Such data consist of features, such as lines and points, that can be awkward to model in a relational database, since they may contain many relationships that incur a performance overhead when trying to reconstruct topological features. Chapter 17, "The Geospatial Information Distribution System (GIDS)" by Chung et al., discusses the use of an object database for modeling multidimensional spatial data in a three-tier system, consisting of thin Java clients, CORBA in the middle-tier, and an object database on the backend. The three technologies worked very successfully together as demonstrated by a warfare simulator that is also described.

Mergers and acquisitions between organizations are commonplace today. This can be problematic when integrating their Information Technology (IT) systems since companies may use different hardware and software platforms. Chapter 18, "Architecture of the Distributed, Multitier Railway Application DaRT" by Zimmermann et al., describes a multitier distributed system that was used to integrate the two different parts of the German railway company Deutsche Bahn AG (from East and West Germany). To improve performance for users, caching was used on the various tiers of their architecture and they evaluate a number of caching policies with database clustering in mind. The experiences reported also demonstrate the benefits of using object technology, although the learning curve for those unfamiliar with this approach can be steep. The lessons reported should be very beneficial to others facing similar system integration problems.

CHAPTER 15

Experiences Using the ODMG Standard in Bioinformatics Applications

This chapter is about the use of object databases in bioinformatics, and seeks to make clear where object databases can be used effectively with biological data. There has been widespread experimentation with object databases in bioinformatics for most of the history of object databases, both in support of public information resources and for use with tightly coupled analyses. This chapter focuses principally on the use of object databases in analysis-oriented biological applications, and reports on experiences using an ODMG-compliant object database with a number of genomic information resources.

Object databases have generally been associated with challenging applications, for which relational databases were considered inappropriate because of limitations relating to their modeling facilities, programming interfaces, or performance. Scientific applications, including those that involve the storage of information relating to molecular biology, are typical of the sorts of applications for which relational systems are sometimes felt to be unsuitable.

Bioinformatics is the use of computational techniques for the storage, analysis, sharing, and presentation of information from biology, and in particular, molecular biology [Attwood 1999]. As such, the principal information sources in bioinformatics relate to DNA and protein sequences, plus associated experimental data on the structure and function of proteins. For many years there has been exponential growth in the amount of sequence information available, a trend that is continuing as the complete genome sequences of organisms have started to be produced. Complete genome sequences, and novel experimental techniques that provide insights into the biological behavior of complete cells, are making available new information resources that promise to further increase the role of bioinformatics in important areas such as drug discovery in the pharmaceutical industry.

Although bioinformatics is an information-rich discipline, being based on the storage of experimental results, database technologies have often been adopted more slowly in bioinformatics than in commercial applications. There are a number of reasons for this. For example, updates to bioinformatics sources, although ongoing, generally involve additions to data sets rather than modifications to existing data, and most programs that use bioinformatics information sources are read-only. This means that database facilities, such as effective concurrency control, seem less central to bioinformatics applications than some others. However, it is clear that an important impediment to the adoption of the relational model in bioinformatics has been the fact that biological data is often more cumbersome to model using relational structures than using some alternative approaches.

In practice, to date, most bioinformatics sources and tools have leaned heavily on the use of flat file structures, with all the associated problems with system evolution and limited access facilities that such a baseline implies. Although many of the largest and most heavily used sources now make use of relational storage systems, it is still often the case that the external representation made available to programmers is based on flat file structures. It can be anticipated that flat files will continue to be important in the foreseeable future, but that representation standards such as XML will help in the provision of less ad-hoc approaches to the organization and sharing of biological information in a distributed setting.

However, although flat file structures have persisted in bioinformatics, it is clear that there is considerable interest in the use of object-orientation. In particular, the OMG has a Life Sciences Research (LSR) group [LSR] that is developing a collection of standard definitions for describing biological objects in CORBA. The scope of the LSR activity is quite broad, including sequence analysis, genome maps, gene expression, macromolecular structure, and clinical trials. This activity, however, leaves open the question as to how the underlying data repositories should be organized and in particular whether there is a role for object databases for managing and analyzing biological data.

This chapter contains a brief overview of bioinformatics projects that have made use of object databases. This is followed by some experience reports, including some examples of biological information models, a description of how these models can be implemented in an ODMG database [Cattell 1997], and a discussion of how these databases have been populated and used. The experience presented is essentially of a genomic data warehouse, where information that is available elsewhere is replicated in an object database in order to allow efficient analyses over the data.

Object Databases in Bioinformatics

Information in bioinformatics has a number of characteristics that fit well with the facilities provided by object orientation:

Order is important. Much of the most important biological information involves ordering. For example, basic DNA or protein sequence information is intrinsically ordered. However, orderings also exist among higher level concepts, such as secondary structure elements in proteins, or genes in a chromosome. As a result, it is important that data models for biological data are able to represent ordered data directly. The fact that the relational model contains no explicit mechanism for describing ordered collections has been a significant impediment to its use in bioinformatics.

Schemas are complex. Although many biological analyses essentially involve fairly exhaustive searches over raw sequences, the description of associated structural, organizational, or functional information tends to give rise to complex schemas. For example, a schema for describing protein structure data or for describing the organization of a genome involves many object types and relationships among them. Furthermore, there are often hierarchical relationships (*part of* and *is-a*) within biological databases that can also benefit from explicit representation in data models.

Analyses are complex. Although there is a role for ad-hoc queries expressed using declarative query languages in biological databases, in practice, query language interfaces are generally less important than programming interfaces. This is because typical analysis tasks can be difficult to express using standard query language facilities, and thus applications have to be constructed using program libraries that perform complex searches and computations. This means that it is important that programming interfaces to biological data are clean and efficient.

These characteristics of bioinformatics applications have led to a number of projects that make use of object databases for different kinds of biological data. Representative projects have tackled the following tasks:

Protein structure analysis [Gray1990]. This project was perhaps the first to make use of object databases with molecular biology data, and emphasized modeling and querying of the 3D structures of proteins. Protein structure data is more normally accessed by users by way of molecular graphics packages, but is certainly also amenable to database style search and analysis.

Management of genome mapping data [Goodman 1995]. This project used a persistent C++ system to support the results of genome mapping experiments. The paper identifies a number of difficulties using early commercial object database products in a highly dynamic environment, in which the schema as well as the data changes on an ongoing basis.

Repository for transcription factors data [Ghosh 1999]. This is a WWW resource (www.ifti.org) that makes available information on proteins and interactions that are involved in the regulation of genes within a cell.

Management of genome data [Durbin 1991]. The ACeDB system is a database system developed especially to manage genome data, and has been used widely with different genomes. ACeDB databases are used as the principal repositories for several genomes, and support browsing, analysis, and visualization of genomic data. The ACeDB data model emphasizes the storage of hierarchical information representing component/subcomponent relationships.

Integration of biological databases [Kosky 1998]. OPM is an object-oriented data model designed to describe scientific experiments, and has been used for linking several sequence and genome resources. It has recently been turned into a product.

Overall, the wide variety of projects that make use of object database technology reflects the rapid development of object database systems and biological applications. Many of these projects are experimental, but the fact that ACeDB has been so widely accepted as a repository manager for genomic data demonstrates that object databases can play an important role in bioinformatics applications. The next sections provide examples of how genomic information can be managed using the facilities of the ODMG model.

Modeling Genomic Information

The genome is all the genetic material in the chromosomes of an organism. This section describes how the structural properties of genomic information can be captured using the ODMG data model. Models are described using UML [Booch 1999] class diagrams, but using only constructs that map very directly onto the ODMG model. The modeling of genome information is discussed more fully in [Paton 2000]. Although most work to date on modeling genomic information has focused on supporting the accumulation of experimental data during the genome sequencing process, this section presents models that describe fully sequenced genomes, and not the experimental results that are combined to produce the complete genome sequence.

Figure 15.1 presents a class diagram for genome sequence data in UML. Where the full sequence of an organism is known, the genome consists of several chromosomes, each of which is essentially a long sequence of DNA. This sequence, however, consists of a sequence of chromosome fragments, each of which is either a transcribed or a nontranscribed region. The process by which a protein is produced that conforms to the information described in a length of DNA has two principal phases. First, the DNA is rewritten as RNA, a process known as transcription, and second this RNA sequence is translated into a protein sequence. The lengths of sequence that are converted into RNA are represented in Figure 15.1 by the class transcribed. The nontranscribed regions are either associated with regulation of gene expression or have some structural role within the chromosome. The regulation of gene expression is the process by which the amount of a protein in a cell is controlled; the amount of a protein required within a cell at any time depends on the environment of the cell, and determines the way in which the cell behaves. The precise purpose of much of the nontranscribed DNA is unknown.

The diagram in Figure 15.1 includes a number of the modeling features we just discussed, which are less than straightforward to support in the relational model. In particular, the chromosome consists of an ordered list of chromosome fragments, and there are several different kinds of nontranscribed regions in an inheritance hierarchy.

Figure 15.2 provides more details on the way that a transcribed region of the chromosome is modeled, along with an illustration of what is happening in terms of the sequence. A transcribed region consists of an ordered collection of primary transcripts. Each of these in turn is either an intron, which is not transcribed into RNA, or a spliced transcript component, which eventually is. In essence, the model has to represent the fact that the introns are removed from the transcribed region, and that the spliced transcript components that result are combined to form spliced transcripts. Furthermore, there is more than one way in which a collection of spliced transcript components may

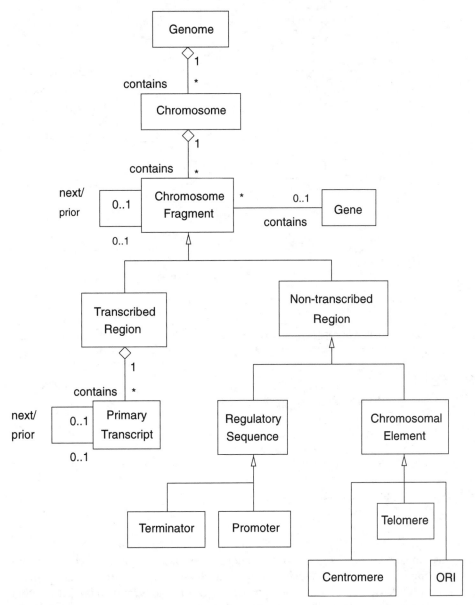

Figure 15.1   Class diagram for genome sequence data.

be assembled to form a spliced transcript. These spliced transcripts represent some form of RNA. The different kinds of RNA have different roles; for the purpose of this chapter, it is probably most relevant to note that mRNA is in turn translated into protein.

This section has provided some details on how genomic information can be modeled using object-modeling techniques. The purpose of the section is to illustrate that the

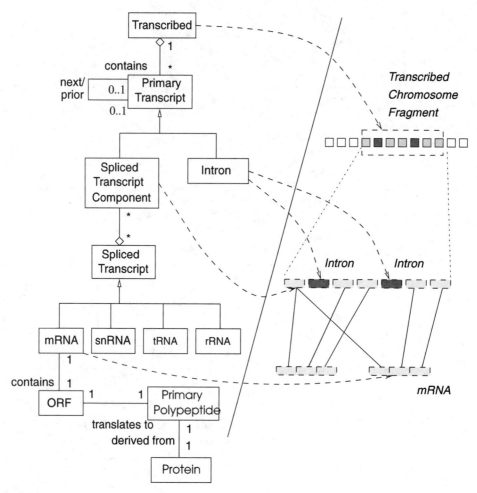

Figure 15.2 Transcribed region.

information models can become quite complex. In fact, the basic genome sequence information is related to a significant number of other information resources, for example describing protein structures, similarities between sequences, patterns in sequences, levels of mRNA in a cell in different environmental conditions, and so on. These other sources of information must themselves be modeled within a database if it is to be straightforward to perform analyses over the data. Thus genomic data should be seen as presenting significant modeling and management challenges for databases, at least some of which can be addressed using object database techniques.

Application Development

Most bioinformatics applications are analysis oriented. Although there are regular and ongoing updates to information sources, these tend to be monotonic, with only periodic changes to existing data entries, and only very occasional deletions. Thus although there are applications that modify information repositories, most applications read from but do not write to the main information sources. In the GIMS project [Moussouni 1999]; [Eilbeck 1999], information is either replicated from other sources or computed using bioinformatics tools, prior to replication in an object database for subsequent analysis.

Figure 15.3 illustrates the architecture of the GIMS system, the components of which are described in the rest of this section.

Implementing the Object Model

Mapping the class diagrams into the constructs of the ODMG model for implementation is straightforward. Each class, its attributes and relationships, can be represented

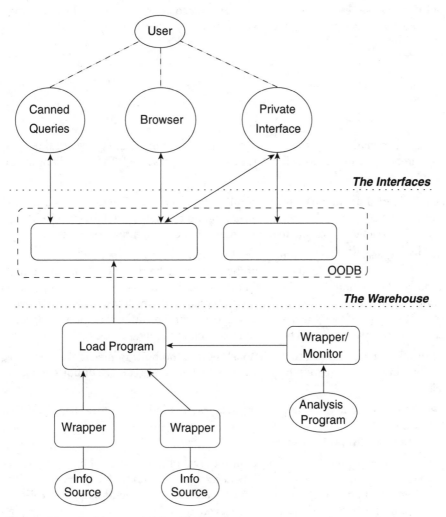

Figure 15.3   Architecture of the GIMS system.

using the object definition language (ODL) of the ODMG standard [Cattell 1997]. For example, the class Genome can be implemented in ODL as follows:

```
class Genome
(       extent genomes)
{       attribute string name;
        relationship list<Chromosome> contains
        inverse Chromosome hasGenome;
        ...
}
```

However, by no means do all products that offer some measure of ODMG compliance provide ODL compilers, and in the product we are using (Poet), there is not an ODL compiler that generates definitions for use in the ODMG Java binding [Cattell 1997]. However, Poet does provide comprehensive support for the ODMG Java binding, and UML classes can be mapped fairly directly to classes using the Java binding. For example, the class Genome can be represented as follows:

```
class Genome
{
    public String name;
    public ListOfObject contains;
}
```

Direct implementation of ODMG constructs using only the language features of Java leaves a number of features from the ODL schema unrepresented. These are handled in Poet as follows:

Extents. As well as the basic Java definition for every persistent class, a separate options file contains additional information on the data in databases. Using this file, it is possible to indicate that an extent is to be maintained for a class.

Collection types. The ODMG model makes extensive use of parameterized collection types—for example, the type of the *contains* attribute on Genome in the preceding ODL definition above is *list<Chromosome>*. However, as Java does not support parameterized types, this is represented using the less precise *ListOfObject* in Poet. Again, in Poet, the developer can use a configuration file option to specify the types of values that can be stored in collection-valued attributes.

Inverses. Java provides directed relationships, and no built-in mechanism for supporting inverses. There are three ways in which inverses can be supported in Java bindings:

- Inverses are maintained by the database behind the scenes, based on the ODL definition or on entries in a configuration file—this is the best option, but is not supported in Poet.

- An index is used to provide rapid retrieval of the inverse of a stored value. This is a satisfactory solution, which can be exploited by the query optimizer in evaluation of OQL queries, but is sure to lead to vendor-specific calls in applications when inverses are retrieved.

- Methods are used to maintain the inverse relationship between classes. This is a somewhat cumbersome manual process that hides inverse relationships from the query optimizer, but avoids vendor-specific index accesses in applications.

To summarize, mapping from UML class diagrams to ODMG schemas for implementation is straightforward, with complications arising only where the ODMG specification is less than precise in terms of the constructs and semantics of the Java binding. It is also the case that the ODMG specification encourages an emphasis on a structural rather than a behavioral view of the data, and thus the initial modeling process tends to view classes principally in terms of their attributes rather than their operations.

Populating the Database

In GIMS, there are two principal categories of data to be handled:

Experimental Data. Most of the data described in the UML models earlier in this chapter are experimental data, from what can be considered primary information resources. Thus the data are essentially facts that have been obtained as results of experimental activities. Most bioinformatics data falls into this category, including sequence data, protein structure data, and molecular interaction data.

Derived Data. Experience shows, however, that data derived using bioinformatics techniques from experimental data can be useful in forming associations between experimental results and in identifying recurring patterns in experimental data. For example, the comparison of sequences using homology programs is perhaps the most common task undertaken in bioinformatics, and the identification of patterns, or motifs, in sequences can also be useful in associating sequences with possible functions.

The GIMS database contains information from both categories, but there are significant differences in the ways in which the data are obtained. In fact, populating object databases is by no means always straightforward. Unlike relational tables, the complex network of objects that is the extent of an object database schema lacks a straightforward representation in textual form. As a result, constructing load files or load programs for use with object databases is often quite a time-consuming task. In GIMS, experimental data in text files is parsed by a load program, which makes calls to create new objects, and to create links from the new objects to those already in the database. In practice, creating links to new objects requires the execution of queries that retrieve existing objects. Overall, this process tends to be significantly more cumbersome than the loading of textual data in a relational setting. Although the ODMG provides a notation for describing database objects in a textual form, the Object Interchange Format (OIF), this doesn't appear to be widely used for database loading.

The population of the database with derived data involves calls being made to analyze facilities, which may exist locally, or remotely on the WWW—examples are described in *Introduction to Bioinformatics* [Attwood 1999]. Since most bioinformatics resources are made publicly available as WWW pages, calling them from programs involves cumbersome activities like parsing HTML result pages. Although in the longer term, results are likely to be made available using XML or CORBA, currently, much practical bioinformatics involves programs connecting with information resources that were designed for interactive rather than programmatic use. The current practice in the GIMS project is to wrap the bioinformatics sources using Java, and for Java to communicate with the underlying WWW resource using `Java.net.URLConnection`. This is essentially client-side object-oriented wrapping, in that each source is seen as a factory class that manufactures instances in response to parameterized requests. We would rather be benefiting from CORBA wrapping, but the provision of CORBA servers requires action on behalf of the resource providers, rather than users.

Developing User Interfaces

There are three principal ways in which databases are accessed by biologists:

Browsers. Browser interfaces essentially provide object-at-a-time exploration of the database, where objects are retrieved on the basis of simple conditions, as instances of a chosen class, or based upon the location of an object in a visual representation. In the current version of GIMS, the main browser is driven from the schema diagram—the schema diagram is drawn as shown in Figure 15.1, and selecting a class leads to the instances of the class being presented in a browser. These can then be stepped through or navigated between, as illustrated in Figure 15.4.

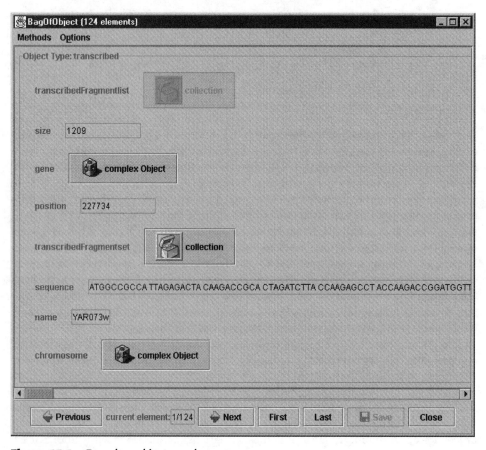

Figure 15.4   Form-based instance browser.

Canned Queries. A canned query is a straightforward interface, normally a form, which allows the user to specify the parameters of a query. This query may or may not be complex; the way in which the information is retrieved is not explicit in the form. For example, a simple canned query might compute the GC content (essentially the percentage of one pair of nucleic acids compared with another) of a length of sequence within a chromosome. Such a query presents the user with a list of the available genomes and chromosomes, and prompts for start and end positions. A list of typical canned queries is included in Figure 15.5, including the GC content example mentioned previously, and a straightforward query to retrieve the introns in a given chromosome. Assuming that this latter query is selected, the interface in Figure 15.6 is displayed, so that the user can select from an offered list of chromosome numbers.

Visualizations. Many bioinformatics concepts have one or more standard visual representations (e.g., this is true of protein structures or genome maps), which users expect to see supported from databases. Relationships between concepts in novel biological data sets can be difficult to understand, so several researchers are actively involved in developing novel ways of visualizing biological concepts (e.g., [Basalaj 1999]). From a database standpoint, the tight coupling of Java programs with object databases eases the programming of visual interfaces, although caution is required in addressing issues such as how much information should be cached and which computations should be performed on the client rather than the server.

There are two issues with respect to user interfaces upon which it is perhaps worth remarking. The first is that it is quite unusual for end users to make use of query languages for carrying out straightforward analysis tasks in bioinformatics. This is, at least in part, because many bioinformatics sources have traditionally been supported by platforms that do not have query languages. However, even where sources are supported by relational databases, it is unusual for end-users to be provided with access to an SQL interface. One reason for this is the ease with which users can express complex requests that place a heavy load on database servers, and another is that many biologists are reluctant to learn textual query languages. As a result, although some use is

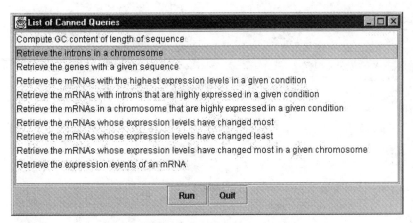

Figure 15.5 Canned query selection interface.

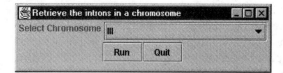

Figure 15.6 Simple intron retrieval canned query.

made of OQL in the implementation of canned queries in GIMS, OQL is not visible to users through the standard interfaces to GIMS.

An example of the use of embedded OQL for implementing a canned query is given in Listing 15.1, which makes use of the ODMG Java binding, as implemented in Poet. The variable query is first declared to be of type OQLQuery, and is initialized with a new instance of OQLQuery associated with the transaction txn. The new query object is then associated with the string of the OQL query that is to be evaluated. The query string references $1, which is the input parameter to the query. A value is associated with $1 by the later call to bind. The variable vec is used to refer to the values supplied by the user through the canned query form in Figure 15.6. The invocation of the execute() method on query returns a collection of objects as a result. The collection can then be examined using standard Java language facilities. The query includes a path expression, which navigates from the intron to the TranscribedRegion and then the Chromosome of which it is part.

An additional issue that is relevant to interface construction in the ODMG setting is the need to be able to construct interfaces that act over any database from any domain. For example, a form-based instance browser, as illustrated in Figure 15.4, should be usable on a genome database or a spatial database, for example. This involves writing programs that access database objects using low-level, generic application programming interfaces, rather than the higher level language bindings specified in the ODMG standard. Poet provides a low-level API for C++ but not for Java, so the browser illustrated in Figure 15.4 uses Java introspection to interrogate objects about their structure and operations.

```
OQLQuery query = new OQLQuery(txn);

query.create("SELECT * " +
  "FROM intron IN intronExtent " +
  "WHERE intron.transcribedRegion.chromosome.number = $1");

String number = (String)vec.elementAt(1);
query.bind(number);

Object result = query.execute();
```

Listing 15.1 Embedded OQL for intron canned query.

Conclusion

This chapter has described and illustrated the use of object databases in bioinformatics applications. It has been argued that object databases contain a range of modeling and programming facilities that makes them suitable for use with complex biological data.

The two principal weaknesses of the relational model—limited modeling facilities and impedance mismatch-prone programming—have limited its uptake in bioinformatics, in particular for use in systems that deal with the more complex data sets or that support sophisticated analyses. The recent extensions to the relational model, in particular to support abstract data types (also known as data blades or cartridges), allow certain bioinformatics tasks to be supported much more effectively in the database than was previously the case. For example, it is possible to envisage a data type sequence for storing protein sequences that supports homology-based sequence comparisons, searching for motifs, and construction of alignments. Support for such facilities within the database would allow sequence analysis and other retrieval tasks to be conducted in a much more integrated environment than has traditionally been the case.

However, the ODMG standard also provides facilities that fit well with current trends in bioinformatics. In particular, object-orientation in general is well suited for use with bioinformatics applications; in fact, all of object-oriented design, programming, and middleware are now prominent in research and development activities. The close relationship between the ODMG model and models for design, programming, and interoperation of software systems means that ODMG databases can fit in well with existing technologies.

To date, a significant proportion of the object database activity in bioinformatics has made use of homegrown object models and systems [Gray 1990]; [Durbin 1991]; [Kosky 1998]. This has limited reuse of ideas, software, interfaces, and experience across the different platforms, and has prevented bioinformatics activities from benefiting from the performance and scalability benefits of commercial products. Although several industrial and research projects have made use of commercial object databases, such activities are quite thinly spread over organizations and problems. However, the success of ACeDB as a repository for genomic data indicates that object database technology can have a significant impact in bioinformatics. Furthermore, the rapidly changing face of bioinformatics, with new kinds of data and analyses in the post-genome sequencing phase, means that the data management challenges presented by bioinformatics applications are by no means on the wane.

The GIMS object database is currently being used at Manchester University in the UK for conducting analyses over the yeast genome, in particular for relating core sequence data, as described in this chapter, with information on protein-protein interactions [Eilbeck 1999] and transcription levels [Paton 2000]. Ongoing work will increase the range of analyses being carried out, and will extend the system to support different kinds of functional genomic data and data relating to organisms other than yeast. A public interface to GIMS will be made available in due course from http://img.cs.man.ac.uk/gims.

CHAPTER 16

An Object-Oriented Database for Managing Genetic Sequences

Genome projects provide huge quantities of data and the current learning systems are not adequate to handle these data. Database technology is needed to store and manage genetic sequences. Furthermore, biological databases need to store some static kind of information on sequences, and also dynamic information that is computed from the static one. This computed information is used to detect patterns in intron-exon junctions [Dunham 1994] and structural patterns in proteins, and to speed up or facilitate queries. Object-oriented database systems provide more ability to represent complex data and to take into account the dynamic aspect.

This chapter covers the management of queries and learned functions produced by a learning system in an object-oriented database, to provide a computer-aided tool for the investigation of genetic sequences.

The information on genetic sequences can be divided into two parts:

- Knowledge acquired by biologists experimenting on biological data (in vivo experiments)

- Additional knowledge obtained from the previous kind of knowledge that results from computation with machine learning techniques (in silico experiments)

The Learning Environment

An environment for the management of genetic information should not only store biological and learned knowledge but also offer the possibility of revising this knowledge in order to improve the performance of the system by progressive refinement.

A possible environment is described in Figure 16.1.

A learning system receives examples and counter-examples and produces learned functions. These functions are used in queries to select sequences according to some biological property. If the result is poor, that is, if the sequences selected by the function are not interesting from a biological point of view, the user has to refine the function through cycles until he or she is satisfied. When a biologist thinks of a conjecture on a set of sequences, he or she can formulate a query. The conjecture is a pair (query, expected result). The result of the query is an experimental proof (refutation) of the conjecture. If the result is good, the query may be refined into several subsequent queries that will help cross-validate or simply explicit the results of the query. This allows a

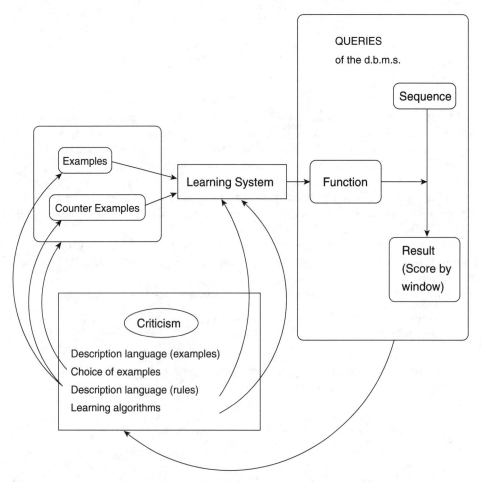

Figure 16.1 A sample learning environment.

data-driven and empirical approach to learning. A formal approach to learning by queries can be found in [Angluin 1988]. Learned functions may be refined in order to fit a general or specific biological concept. The improvement of the function is due to the choice of the examples and counter-examples, and also to the choice of the learning algorithms and the tuning of their parameters.

The proof that the learned function fits the biological concept is still given by experimentation via queries. The interpretation of a query may be ambiguous: If the result differs from the expected result, this difference may be caused either by the biological data or by the learned functions.

On a larger scale, the learning system itself could be improved by optimizing the description language used for the examples (counter-examples) and the functions. This is close to schema evolution problems.

The cycle of knowledge revision is detailed in Figure 16.2.

Biological knowledge can be refined externally by biologists whereas queries help refine biological knowledge or learned functions. The schema (i.e., the structures of the data) evolves when the structure of biological data or functions evolves.

In this chapter, we are interested in the management of queries and learned functions in an object-oriented database to provide a computer-aided tool for the investigation of genetic sequences. This experiment has been undertaken in our laboratory [Sallantin 1986] with the object-oriented database management system (OODBMS), O2 [Bancilhon 1992].

Other problems arise if we consider that biological information is not purely genetic. A cell is divided into several compartments by membranes, and the distribution of molecules between these compartments represents some kind of information. In the same way, an organism is divided into numerous cells. In an organism, all the cells contain the same genetic information, but the "programs" executed may differ. The structural arrangement of the cells, the distribution of molecules in the cells and in the extra-cellular space, is another example of nongenetic information.

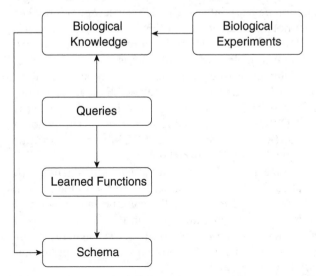

Figure 16.2   The cycle of knowledge revision in our environment.

Hopefully, we need not know and understand all the information. The knowledge of a specific part, corresponding to the genetic information on some disease, is quite relevant in itself. In the future, the aim of an investigation in this field might be to understand the biological programs well enough to create programs that can interfere with existing ones, for example, to specifically stop or replace a defective program.

To describe the complexity of the genome challenge, we can follow K.A. Frenkel [Frenkel 1991] and compare genomic data to the data stored on a tape. This tape would be very large and would contain both data and application programs. Most of the content of the tape would be unknown. The information on some particular program or data would be dispersed throughout the tape. Part of the tape may contain no useful information at all. The knowledge we have on the CPU of the computer that could run such programs is ill-defined and continuously evolving. The code itself uses sophisticated self-modifying techniques. The information stored on the tape is a hypothetical reconstruction that results from the study of different cells in different individuals, and may not work for any real living being.

The rest of this chapter is organized as follows. First we review several databases used in similar biological applications. We compare the relational and object-oriented data models and then describe our prototype and examples of queries.

Related Work

Biologists often use data banks to store genetic information into a computer. Data simply are stored in text files. Usually, one text file represents one gene or one protein. Reviews about data banks can be found in "Genome Databases" [Courteau 1991] and "The human genome project and informatics" [Frenkel 1991]. Databases often import data from these data banks. The first drawback of using text files is that the application programs that read these files must know precisely the structure of the files. The second drawback lies in the fact that data are split into numerous files, whereas a Database System (DBMS) stores information efficiently and independently of the physical storage. Ultimately, they are not suitable for data update and maintenance operations. For instance interactive modification is not possible [Frishman 1998]. Furthermore, normalization rules of the relational model avoid redundancy and ensure integrity constraints.

Established in 1980, the EMBL nucleotide sequence database is primarily a collection of nucleotide sequences maintained at the European Bioinformatics Institute (EBI). Nucleotide sequences are stored and managed in an ORACLE database system [EMBL 2000] and are accessible via the Web. Work reported in [Kanehisa 1984] describes one use of a relational DBMS for storing biopolymer data. The genome Sequence Database (GSDB) based on Sybase DBMS provides SQL interface for manipulating genetic sequences [Harger 1998]. There is a special field where relational DBMS has received much attention: the storage of 3D macromolecular data [Huysmans 1991].

An object-oriented database, called OOTFD (Object-Oriented Transcription Factors Database), was developed for modeling and managing the complicated network of relationships between transcriptions factor polypeptides [Ghosh 1998].

Recently, object-relational DBMSs have been used for storing genetic sequences. For example, the SYSTERS protein sequence cluster set is a protein sequences application developed on a PostgresSQL DBMS [Krause 1999].

The first types of genetic databases have been built for storing genes and information about their location on chromosomes. Data banks are not sufficient because they do not allow you to store and manage complex information with many cross references. Besides, the graphical visualization of this type of data requires hypertext-like tools. Furthermore, the schema of these databases evolves frequently. An example of this type of database is the ACeDB system [Dunham 1994], which is currently in use to represent the genetic information of a worm, *Cænorhabditis elegans*, and other species. This database is freely available and widely used in sequencing projects. However, the data model is not standard: it is a kind of object-oriented model that does not support inheritance—objects have a tree-like structure. The graphical interface allows the computation and display of complex genetic maps. In fact, the data model of ACeDB can be considered as the one of the first semistructured data models [McHugh 1997].

Databases are also used for learning from biological sequences. This is close to the problem of data mining; in other words, the extraction of knowledge from a large set of real-world data with machine learning techniques. But in this case the schema of the database usually can be chosen according to the problem that has to be solved.

C. Sander and R. Schneider conceived HSSP [Sander 1991] as a data bank of aligned sequences. The sequences are aligned using information on their two-dimensional and three-dimensional structures.

T. Blundel [Blundel 1987]; [Blundel 1988] built a relational database for protein modeling including crystallographic information. Part of the content of the database is computed to speed up the access.

G.J.L. Kemp [Kemp 1991] used an OODBMS (P/FDM, an extension of the functional data model) to store information about protein structures. The Daplex language is used for definition and for querying the database. The underlying system is written in Prolog; this allows complex queries that cannot be expressed directly in Daplex to be written in Prolog.

This review shows that biological databases need to store a static kind of information on sequences and also on dynamic information that is computed from the static one. This computed information is used to detect patterns (intron-exon junctions [Dunham 1994]) and structural patterns in proteins [Kemp 1991], and to speed up or facilitate queries.

Our database stores computed information in two forms: function result and query result. The originality of our work is in the management of dynamic knowledge.

Relational versus Object-Oriented Databases

Genome applications provide huge quantities of data, which are shared by many users who have various requirements. Databases provide flexible access to the data. Furthermore, the solution of managing genome data with a database system promotes standardization and validation of the data. Many other features are provided by a database system:

- Persistence of data: data persist beyond program execution.
- Security presents many aspects:
  - Control of data access: a user should not necessarily have access to all data. Each user should have his or her own view of the database.

■ Crash protection and recovery: database systems are able to rebuild the database in the event of hardware or software problems.

■ Query languages.

Storing data in a database system requires describing the data according to some data model. Each database system has a specific data model. A brief review of data models should begin with the first record-oriented models—the hierarchical and network models—and go on with the development of the relational model [Codd 1970], which is closer to the end-user in terms of modeling power and ease of use. Semantic data models provide a high abstraction level for representing data and their relationships.

Object-oriented models, issued from object-oriented languages, have been proposed [Atkinson 1989]. Their approach combines the organizational features of semantic data models with the operational features of object-oriented programming languages. The main features of object-oriented databases are discussed in [Atkinson 1989]; [Kim 1990].

Whether genomic databases should be relational or object-oriented is currently under debate [Frenkel 1991]. We will compare some features of the two models.

Relational Data Model

The relational model is based on mathematical set-theory. An entity of the real world is represented by a relation that is a subset of the cartesian product of domains. A domain is a set of atomic values. Individual facts are represented as tuples of values of these domains.

Relational Database Management Systems (RDBMSs) have focused on business processing applications, and many researchers have highlighted their inadequacies for broader classes of applications using more complex data.

Usually, biologists find it difficult to store many kinds of basic data like DNA sequences because relational databases cannot handle sequential information and deal instead with (unordered) sets. One of the disadvantages of relational DBMSs is that hierarchical data structures are not directly supported. Relational models have been successful for databanks that require schemas of limited complexity. The database design based on object-oriented models allows decomposition of a large database into components that involve methods into the data structures themselves, and permit the building of complex hierarchical data structures.

Impedance Mismatch

The second drawback concerns the query language: SQL is too weak to support complex queries. Application programs written in C, FORTRAN, or COBOL often contain embedded SQL statements. This solution is not very satisfactory since it presents the impedance mismatch problem: the granularity of the data in an application program and in a SQL statement is different because SQL deals with sets of tuples.

The object-oriented programming paradigm may help the development of a new generation of database technology by offering facilities for the management of complex data and procedures. Furthermore, it avoids the impedance mismatch by providing an integrated data programming language like O2C [O2Technology 1992].

Besides, the complexity of genomic data will require much more than a pure SQL interface to a relational database if biologists are to use it effectively.

We used the O2 database management system, which provides a query language called O2query. This query language is an object-oriented SQL that offers the ability to call methods within the query language. This last feature is very useful for our application for modeling the behavior of genetic sequences and learning functions.

Object-Oriented Database Management Systems

An object-oriented data model is based on the notion of objects and classes. Objects are used to model real-world entities; they have an identity. A class can be used to define a set of objects. Objects of the same class have the same data structure and the same operations, called methods. Classes are organized in a class hierarchy and constitute the database schema.

Object-oriented database management systems (ODBMSs) are more suitable to build systems in new fields such as CAD and multimedia. Typically, objects in a genomic database have a dynamic nature. In the following *Prototype* section, we address part of this problem. Some OODBMSs provide schema evolution facilities [Kim 1990], but they seldom support automatic propagation to the instances. A survey of the schema evolution problem can be found in [Zicari 1991].

In summary, we can conclude that OODBMSs provide the ability to represent complex data (composite objects, list of objects) and to build efficiently advanced applications such as genomic information systems.

In this chapter, we present an approach using an object-oriented database management system to store and manage genetic sequences. We will show some limitations of these systems due to a lack of flexibility. This particularly concerns dynamic propagation of update operations. To overcome the last limitation, we introduced a mechanism inspired from Smalltalk [Goldberg 1983] that dynamically propagates update operations on objects.

Prototype

In this section, we describe the structure of the database and the operations that can be applied on objects. We store sequences, queries, functions predicting properties about sequences, and the results of the application of these functions on the sequences. Therefore, the schema of our object-oriented database consists of four main classes: Sequence, Function, Result, and Query.

Application Requirements

In our application, we needed to store data as lists and matrices, the treatment on the sequences, learning functions, and results of certain queries. Our study began with the use of an RDBMS, but we found it inadequate for modeling our data, and the SQL language was not powerful enough to express the treatment on the sequences and the learning functions. The main benefit of using an OODBMS lies in the possibility of the embodiment of methods in the data structures themselves. Besides, in an OODBMS these methods can be triggered in queries. We have intensively used this capability in our implementation.

Learning techniques may be used at the level of DNA, for example, to search the sequences coding for genes. However, one of the main challenges in this field is the prediction of protein structures from their amino-acid sequence. Only a few hundred proteins have a known three-dimensional structure. The structures of these proteins are stored in a database and used for reference to facilitate the search of the structure of other proteins by using an alignment algorithm. An alignment consists of searching similar patterns of two sequences with a dynamic programming algorithm like [Needleman 1970]. This is called *homology modeling*. Our prototype allows coupling the OODBMS O2 with a 1D alignment program developed by J. Gracy [Gracy 1991], which can be triggered through a method [Ripoche 1995]. Furthermore, it is possible to store alignments as objects and then to pose queries on them and on the way they were obtained. An alignment allows a matrix to be built [Gribskof 1987], which is itself a query that can be invoked to retrieve sequences close to example sequences that have been used in the alignment process. This allows us to automate the production of consensus motifs and their exploitation with an object-oriented query language like OQL.

Modeling Genetic Sequences

A genome sequence consists of two parts:

- A nucleic sequence (succession of nucleic acids)
- A proteic sequence (succession of amino acids)

In a cell, the proteic sequence is the result of the translation from the nucleic sequence. A proteic sequence can be viewed, in fact, according to three aspects:

- Primary structure, which is actually the succession of amino acids
- Secondary structure, which is a succession of more elaborated structures (alpha-helix or beta-sheet)
- Tertiary structure, where the position of each amino acid in space is known

We need to model these sequences because genome projects provide large amounts of data. They are difficult to model because they can be viewed according to several aspects.

Nucleic sequences are coded by four letters (CGUA for RNA and CGTA for DNA). Proteic sequences consist of a sequence of amino acids coded by an alphabet of twenty letters. Six letters are excluded: B, J, O, U, X, and Z. Each sequence is represented as a string. Examples of sequences are:

Sequence 0   ACHGKLMPACERVATR

Sequence 1   ERTACDEAPMLKNVCWCFAA

Class Sequence

In our application, we are interested in protein sequences, which are coded by a string. This represents the primary structure of proteins. This basic kind of information is linear. Furthermore, proteins may be represented in two other ways more relevant to biologists: The secondary structure is a list of blocks having a known structure and the tertiary structure describes the atomic coordinates of each element of the protein. This information is richer because the shape of the protein is directly related to its biological function. Class Sequence contains only simple information about the sequence of amino-acids in a protein (e.g., its name and the string corresponding to the primary structure).

Class Pdb is a subclass of class Sequence. It contains information about the spatial structure of proteins. The data of this class Pdb are imported from a biological data bank, the Protein Data Bank [Bernstein 1977]. Other data banks could be modeled in the future by adding other subclasses to class Sequence.

Listing 16.1 is an example showing the definition of class Pdb. To understand this definition, you should remember the following points:

- Class Pdb *inherits* class Sequence.

- In the schema definition language of O2, an object is usually defined as a tuple of items. The items of the tuple have the same meaning as instance variables in traditional object-oriented languages.

```
class Pdb
   inherit Sequence
   type tuple(code: string,
             date: string,
             revdate: string,
             source: string,
             authors: string,
             reference: Text,
             comment: Text,
             resolution: real,
             s2: /* Secondary structure */
             list(tuple(type: string,
                        num: integer,
                        first: string,
                        firstRank: integer,
                        last: string,
                        lastRank: integer))
          s3: /* Tertiary structure */
             list(tuple(atomNum: integer,
                        atomName: string,
                        x: real,
                        y: real,
                        z: real)))
   end;
```

Listing 16.1   Class Pdb using the O2 data description language.

- Each item of a tuple has a name and a type.
- This definition contains type declarations (string, integer, real), class declarations (Pdb, Sequence), and type constructors (tuple, list) that allow the use of complex types.

Figure 16.3 shows an instance of the class Pdb with the O2 query language.

Modeling the Behavior of Sequences

In this section we discuss the Result and Query Classes, how we manage Dynamic Updates, and some comments on the Query Language.

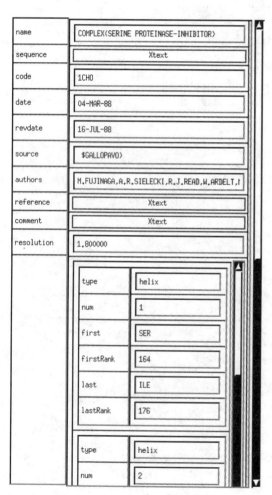

name	COMPLEX(SERINE PROTEINASE-INHIBITOR)
sequence	Xtext
code	1CHO
date	04-MAR-88
revdate	16-JUL-88
source	$GALLOPAVO)
authors	M.FUJINAGA,A.R.SIELECKI,R.J.READ,W.ARDELT,I
reference	Xtext
comment	Xtext
resolution	1.800000

type	helix
num	1
first	SER
firstRank	164
last	ILE
lastRank	176

| type | helix |
| num | 2 |

Figure 16.3   An example of a sequence.

Class Result

This class deals with the results of the application of the functions to the sequences. In this kind of application, it is necessary to store the results, because previous results must be compared to the new results.

This comparison is essential to check that the quality of the new functions is increasing through time.

Class Query

Queries can also be stored as objects in the database. This class has two fields: the query (in text form) and its result. A method triggers the evaluation of the query and the update of its result.

A query is used to select sequences of the database. The sequences can be selected according to the value of their attributes or the value returned by the methods. Some methods are used to apply learned functions on sequences; they are called decision methods. Initially, we thought that the learned functions could be modeled directly as methods of our object-oriented database. However, it appeared later that the handling of the learned functions would be much more convenient if they were considered as objects instead of methods. One of the advantages is the ability to query the learned functions. So, we decided to define a Function class in the schema.

In our system, a function is an object produced by machine learning techniques. It can be used in queries as a filter that selects sequences according to some biological property. This class has two subclasses, NumericFunction and SymbolicFunction.

The first kind of function is numeric. These functions are produced by the learning system of J. Gracy [Gracy 1993]. They consist mainly of a set of matrices. The numbers of a matrix are the weights of a neural network. These functions are used to predict properties on amino-acid sequences: secondary structure and solvent interaction.

Another type of function is symbolic. These functions are produced by the learning system LEGAL of E. Mephu Nguifo [Mephu 1993], which is based on Galois Lattices. This kind of function consists of a set of rules:

Rule 0 : XX[A,C,G]X[T,R,D]M

Rule 1 : [R,G,H]AC[L,M,P]XM

For example, Rule 0 selects sequences such that:

- amino-acid number 1 is of any type (X)
- amino-acid number 2 is of any type (X)
- amino-acid number 3 may be either A, or C, or G
- And so on

The result of the application of a function on a part of the sequence is the number of rules that are checked. When a function is applied on a biological sequence, the sequence is divided into fragments of fixed size (windows). In this way, each sequence yields to a set of numeric values (each window gives one value). This value represents the "attraction" of the function for this window.

However, this approach has a serious drawback: we lose the functional aspect and these objects cannot be applied to sequences to check some property. So we decided to define an "apply" method in each class of functions. This method interprets the value of a functional object as code that can be applied to check the presence of a property in a sequence.

An example of a functional object is given in Figure 16.4.

This is only a tradeoff, and an ideal system should be able to handle programs as well as data. Other languages avoid the mismatch problem between static objects and functions. Smalltalk [Goldberg 1993] offers better integration because methods themselves are considered as objects (the text of a method can be compiled dynamically, and the resulting code itself is an object). In Frame languages, procedures and attribute values are both stored at the instance level.

Dynamic Updates

Objects that represent the result of the application of a function must be updated when the function is modified.

We have chosen a mechanism inspired from Smalltalk that dynamically maintains dependence links between objects. From each object, a list of dependent objects can be accessed. As soon as an object is modified, the list of its dependent objects is run through and each dependent object is sent an update message. This mechanism uses method calls in an object-oriented database and is similar to the triggers of some relational databases. The notion of reflex of Frame languages would be very useful here to propagate the modifications.

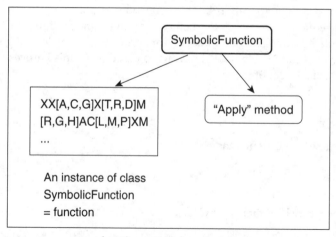

function->apply(sequence)
is used within queries and computes the value of a sequence.

Figure 16.4   An example of a functional object.

Query Language

We used O2query, the query language of the O2 system [Bancilhon 1992]. This language is close to the standard SQL, but offers some additional (object-oriented) features of which we took advantage. The main feature according to our application is the ability to call methods from within the query language.

For example, let us consider a subset of the set of all sequences, for instance the sequences of the Globin family, and a subset of functions having a property P1. What is the average value of the functions applied on the selected sequences? The following query gives the answer:

```
Avg(select windows.score
    from sequences in Sequences,
         function in Functions
         windows in function->apply(sequence)
    where sequence->name like "*GLOBIN*"
    and "P1" in function->keywords)
```

In this query, *sequences* stands for the set of all sequences available in the database, and functions stands for the set of all the functions.

Function -> apply(sequence) splits sequence into overlapping windows on which function is applied; the result of this expression is a set of tuples having two fields, the window string and its score.

Now, suppose we want to select the parts of the sequences that can be detected by some functions: The result given by the application of the function on the part of the sequence must be greater than a given threshold. This threshold may be chosen according to the result of the previous query: This is an example of the use of a query for knowledge refinement.

```
Select tuple(sequence: sequence,
             function: function,
             windows: select window
                      from window in function->apply(sequence)
                      where window.score > 70)
from sequence in Sequences,
     function in Functions
where sequence->name like "*GLOBIN*"
and "P1" in function->keywords;
```

Furthermore, it has been possible to extend the standard string function for use with genetic sequences. OQL has a reserved keyword "like" to select the strings that match a given pattern (for example, xx* matches both xxa and xxb). This is not convenient to match strings representing genetic sequences. Since the query language allows the use of methods in a query, it has been possible to define our own string-matching method. This method uses a dynamic programming algorithm [Needleman 1970] to measure a distance between two strings. This permits us to search a sequence that is close to another sequence (close here means having the minimal number of insertions, deletions, or substitutions). This feature would not be possible with a relational DBMS due to the impedance mismatch problem.

Conclusion

In this chapter, we have presented an approach using an object-oriented database management system to store and manage genetic data. We discussed the benefits of using DBMS and show that an object-oriented DBMS is more appropriate than the relational DBMS.

We have implemented a system capable of storing, in an object-oriented database, data and knowledge learned from genetic sequences (functions, queries, and their results) produced by a learning system. This experiment has been undertaken with the object-oriented database system, O2.

Our system is also able to apply this knowledge to detect interesting properties in sequences. Furthermore, using an object-oriented database system made possible the following two features:

- Modeling genetic sequences as complex objects provides more powerful possibilities for querying than data banks storing sequences as text files.

- The inheritance mechanism of the object model enables computing processes to be triggered according to data type (i.e., sequences family).

Finally, this study gave us better knowledge of the differences between the object and relational models in a real application. Object-oriented database systems provide better support for representing complex data and aid the efficient building of advanced applications such as genomic information systems. However, we also found some limitations, particularly concerning dynamic propagation of update operations. To overcome this limitation, we introduced a mechanism inspired from the Smalltalk language [Goldberg 1983] that dynamically propagates update operations on objects.

The need for interoperability is very important in the Biological domain. Indeed, many databases provide links to other resources. An attempt to build a federated database has been made [Robbins 1994]. However, this solution met with difficulties due to the extreme semantic heterogeneity. An alternative solution providing the interoperability is the middleware approach that allows remote retrieval from external databases. Several CORBA-based applications have been developed to provide access to a set of biological databases [Achard 1997]. For instance, the European Community supports a project to provide CORBA access to public databases like EMBL, SWISS-PROT, and several others.

CHAPTER 17

The Geospatial Information Distribution System (GIDS)

The widespread use of computers has fostered a progression of mapping from the form of paper charts, maps, and satellite photos to the digital format. The National Imagery and Mapping Agency (NIMA), bearing the sole responsibility for developing mapping information for the Department of Defense, embarked on a program to transform their traditional paper mapping products into digital format. To accomplish this goal, in the 1980s, NIMA designed the Vector Product Format (VPF) as its database specification. VPF was developed as a relational data model. As the VPF products were reviewed and used, however, it became apparent that the relational format was not suited to the complexity of spatial mapping data. For example, the use of many tables to represent spatial topology of one feature resulted in referential integrity problems during an update process.

The Naval Research Laboratory's (NRL) Digital Mapping, Charting, and Geodesy Analysis Program (DMAP) at Stennis Space Center in Mississippi proposed a possible solution to some of the VPF problems. An alternate data model using object-oriented technology seemed to accommodate the complexity of spatial data. In 1994, the DMAP team was able to successfully prototype the first object-oriented application using one of NIMA's VPF products, the Digital Nautical Chart (DNC). The prototype showed the reusability and rapid-prototyping that resulted from use of object-oriented technology. Consequently, DMAP expanded the object-oriented data model to integrate the other VPF products with the DNC into an object-oriented VPF (OVPF). These additional VPF products are Digital Topographic Data (DTOP), Vector Map (VMAP), Urban Vector Map (UVMAP), World Vector Shoreline (WVS), and Foundation Feature Data (FFD). DMAP has continued to advance OVPF to include other NIMA data types such as Raster Product Format (RPF), which is the basic format for raster products such as satellite imageries and scanned charts; and Text Product Standard (TPS), which uses SGML-based standard for textual information such as sailing directions.

Having demonstrated that object-oriented technology easily accommodates the complexity of the spatial data, the next milestone for NIMA and DMAP was to provide a vehicle for distribution. As the Web technology began to advance with the rise of the Java programming language and object-oriented standard committees such as the Object Management Group (OMG), DMAP was able to prototype spatial information distribution over the Web. This was through an area-of-interest (AOI) application called the Geospatial Information Distribution System (GIDS). The GIDS provides all available information over the specified AOI independent of the data type. Some of the more diverse data types handled by the GIDS include ESRI's shape file format, video clips, audio clips, and other industry standards such as tiff, gif, and jpeg. Adding these to the GIDS was relatively simple due to the object-oriented nature of the data model.

Much of the work to date has been the database design to accommodate the multiple spatial data types, the development of a Web applet for map display, and the implementation of query mechanisms. While this work has concentrated on two-dimensional mapping, the need for the three-dimensional representation of some geographic entities to support mission preparation and rehearsal especially in an urban setting is also present. Thus DMAP, in conjunction with the University of New Orleans, proceeded to research and design a 3D spatial data model, called *VPF+*.

This chapter describes the overall system and database design. As an example, an actual experimental situation, the March 1999 Urban Warrior Experiment (UWE), is used to demonstrate the use of GIDS. Furthermore, the VPF+ data model, as well as its applicability in the UWE, is presented.

Use of Object-Oriented Technology and ODBMS

Object-oriented technology was chosen to handle the complexity of spatial data. Some spatial data such as VPF produced by NIMA already is designed as relational data. A minimum of nine tables is used to define one point feature; at minimum, sixteen tables are used to define one polygon feature. Rather than considering a feature as rows of nine to sixteen tables, an object-oriented approach allows data manipulation and management at a feature level. An analogous point feature object would have the same values that are defined from the rows of nine tables, as an example, for a specific feature; however, instead of having to access feature information from different rows of different tables for a given feature, a single access to a feature object would provide all the information for that given feature.

The complexity of spatial data is also due to the stored topology (i.e., immediate neighbor information). When the geometry of a feature changes in any manner, this requires the stored topology to be recomputed. Recomputation implies a change to table columns for a certain row. Due to the dependency on other related tables, recomputation may require several tables to be changed. Recomputation may also affect adjacent feature information. Tables related to the adjacent feature may also be modified. Such a rippling effect of feature updates makes the manipulation and management of spatial data in relational format error-prone. Maintenance of referential integrity during these updates of multiple features is an additional concern. On the other hand, for feature objects, a change is localized to that feature object only. Thus, a change is applied by accessing the feature object. Likewise, topology recomputation requires those adjacent feature objects to be accessed and modified accordingly.

As the volume of data increased and the need for multi-user access developed, the need to have true database functionalities such as persistent storage, controlled access to the data, and backup and recovery capabilities, among others, became important. Object-oriented database management systems (ODBMS) provide these functionalities specifically for objects.

The distinction between persistent and transient objects is somewhat less clear for ODBMSs than RDBMSs, due to the tightly coupled nature of the object-oriented database with the application. Transient objects are defined as those objects that exist in the computer's memory only during execution of the application, whereas persistent objects exist even when there is no application program running. Transient and persistent objects can coexist within a running process. Persistent data accessed from the database can be assigned to a transient object. It is important for application programs to manage both transient and persistent data in consistent ways so updates to persistent data are made when needed, and data that should remain transient are not inadvertently made persistent.

A natural extension to the decision of using object-oriented technology and an ODBMS was the utilization of the Common Object Request Broker Architecture (CORBA). CORBA allows interoperability among different programming languages as well as different hardware platforms. For example, this project demonstrated interoperability between Smalltalk and Java, and from a Solaris platform to Windows NT using CORBA infrastructure. Since the ODBMS selected provided an Object Request Broker (ORB) directly interfaced to the ODBMS, the data access was achieved at the repository level. Thus, multi-user access was provided through different clients such as applets, which enabled direct Web browser interaction with the ODBMS.

2D GIDS Design

The GIDS has a client/server architecture. It is composed of server, interface, and client modules as shown in Figure 17.1.

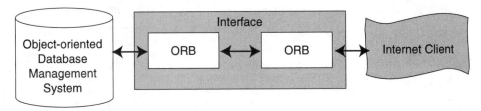

Figure 17.1   GIDS system components.

Server

A commercial, off-the-shelf object-oriented database management system, GemStone, is used as an object server that stores, manipulates, and processes objects referenced by each client. The server consists of two functional modules: data storage and data manipulation or processing. Based on the request from each client, the GemStone server searches and retrieves only those objects that meet the requested criteria. Data search for retrieval is performed mostly on the server.

A server maintains a class hierarchy as shown in Figure 17.2. The MapObject class is the super class or parent to all the spatial classes. Each database has its subclasses. For example, Figure 17.3 shows the class hierarchy for VPFDatabase and MMDatabase.

Each subclass of MapObject has a global variable, Databases, which maintains a collection of all its instances. The VPFDatabase class is the superset of all VPF data, and has a class variable or a global dictionary called Databases that contains all instances of the VPFDatabase class. A root entry to any feature access begins with the Databases dictionary. Likewise, other classes such as ShapeDatabase has a global variable called Databases. The MMDatabase class, however, does not have a global variable that maintains a collection of all its instances. This is because the other database classes have a complex data structure such as the complex hierarchical grouping as well as metadata information. This can be seen in Figure 17.4.

For MMDatabase instances, however, each instance is a multimedia object such as a JPEG object. Thus, rather than maintaining a global variable called Database to hold all the instances, another global variable is used, MMmanager.

The MMmanager is an instance of VPFSpatialDataManager class. The GIDS has implemented a quadtree based on a minimum-bounding rectangle to index all spatial objects. This is based on the regular recursive subdivision of blocks of spatial data into four equal-sized cells, or quadrants. Cells are successively subdivided until some criterion is met, usually either that each cell contains homogeneous data, or that a preset number of decomposition iterations have been performed. Thus, the cells of a quadtree are of a standard size (in powers of two) and are nonoverlapping in terms of actual representation. This can be seen in Figure 17.5.

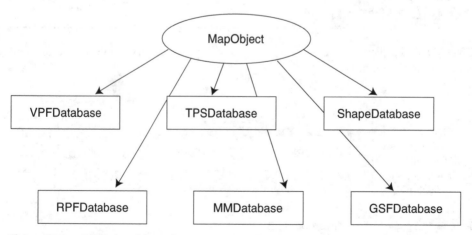

Figure 17.2 GIDS class hierarchy.

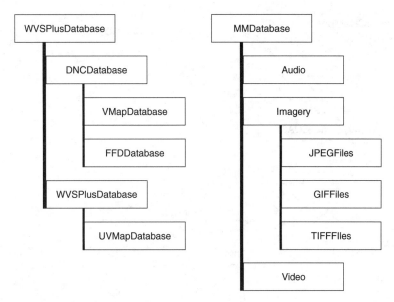

Figure 17.3 GIDS subclass hierarchy.

This spatial indexing scheme is the key to the spatial data integration. All data are spatially indexed into a quadtree. Each database maintains its own quadtree, which allows independent spatial indexing of each common data set. A global spatial integration of all objects in the ODBMS is achieved by addressing all the quadtree instances in the ODBMS. This is how the AOI request is accomplished; the spatial integration enables users to find all information available at the specified AOI. In other words, if, for example, two different data sets from different sources provide information over at San Francisco, California, the GIDS would let the user know that there is information about San Francisco, California from two different data sets that are different in format and contents. This basically achieves the AOI-driven search capability in the GIDS.

Interface

An object request broker (ORB) functions as an interface to the server and client. A server has to have its own broker and a client has to have its own broker. GemORB is a CORBA 2.0-compliant object request broker used by the server. GemORB provides an interface for the Smalltalk programming language. GemORB interfaces directly to the ODBMS. Clients use VisiBroker as their CORBA 2.0 compliant brokers. VisiBroker provides an interface for the Java programming language.

GemORB establishes a connection between the client broker, VisiBroker, to the object server, GemStone, through CORBA compliant communication. See the works by Thomas Mowbray et al., [Mowbray 1997a], the OMG [OMG 1996], and Jon Siegel [Siegel 1996] for information on CORBA. An Interface Definition Language (IDL) file defines a correct mapping of objects between the client and the server. An IDL file also defines operations or methods that are available for clients to invoke on the server.

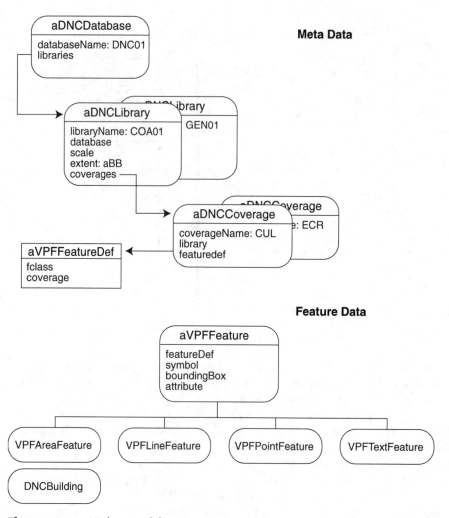

Figure 17.4 VPF data model.

Since GemORB and VisiBroker are based on CORBA, all the benefits of interoperability among programming languages and platforms apply.

An IDL is essential for communication between different programming languages. An IDL file must be created to allow for correct mappings of objects from one application to another; it is the means by which potential clients determine what operations are available and how they should be invoked. In our system, our IDL file defines all of the objects that are common to both client and server, as well as methods that can be invoked to perform certain operations on the server, as shown in Listing 17.1.

The first object that is utilized by both the Java client and the GIDS server is a bounding box for the AOI, an instance of the BoundingBox class. To define our BoundingBox object, we use a `struct` data type that allows related items to be grouped together. For example, `struct Point {float x,y; };` defines a point to be made up of two float

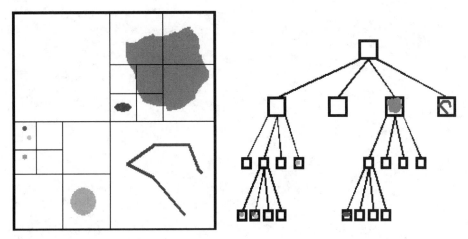

Figure 17.5 Example of a quadtree.

values, x and y. Similarly, our BoundingBox is defined to be composed of two points, an origin and a corner: `struct BoundingBox {Point origin; Point corner;};`. We then defined an interface called `GIDBsyms`, which contains the methods on the server that are invoked by the client. An interface is the most important aspect of IDL, since it provides all the information needed for a client to be able to interact with an object on the server.

Note that the interface contains the method names with their parameters, as well as the data type of the returned object. The most complex structure defined in our IDL is the struct VectorFeature.

The Smalltalk application has an object class called VPFFeature from which our VectorFeature is derived. The Smalltalk VPFFeature class is more complex. The VPFFeature objects have geometry, as well as attributes. The geometry information basically provides the footprint of the object in pairs of latitude and longitude. Attribute information consists of meta-data and actual properties or characteristics of the object. The meta-data provides information about the data, such as VPF specification relevant information as well as information like the originator, security. VPFFeature objects are richly attributed; for example, a DNCBuilding has attributes such as bfc, which is building function code, and hgt, for the height of a building. For our Internet applet, though, only those attributes that are needed for display and user queries are defined as shown here.

Our IDL contains another structure that defines Attribute: `struct Attribute {string name, value;};`. The Attribute structure is used as part of the VectorFeature structure and gives attribute names and values for a given feature instance. For example, a given building may have an attribute name "Structure Shape of Roof" with attribute value "Gabled."

The final data type included in our IDL file is a *sequence*, which is similar to a one-dimensional array, but does not have a fixed length. We use sequences to reduce the number of messages passed from server to client. The size of each sequence is determined dynamically on both the server and the client.

```
module GIDBmodule {
    struct Point    {float x,y;};
    struct BoundingBox {Point origin,
    struct Attribute {string name,

    typedef sequence<Attribute>
    typedef sequence<Point> Coordinates;
    typedef sequence<string> StringColl;

    struct VectorFeature {
        string          featname;
        long            type;
        AttributeColl   attributes
        Coordinates     cords
        BoundingBox     boundingBox;};

    struct MediaFeature {
        string          objectType;
        string          description;
        string          filename;
        BoundingBox     boundingBox;};

    typedef sequence<VectorFeature>
    typedef sequence<MediaFeature>

    interface GIDBsyms {
        StringColl ReturnDatabasesForAOI (in BoundingBox
        StringColl ReturnCovsAndFeatsForAOI (in BoundingBox aBB, in
                dbname, in string libname);
        FeatureColl ReturnFeats (in StringColl featColl, in aBB
        MediaColl ReturnMediaFeats (in BoundingBox aBB);
    };
}
```

Listing 17.1   IDL used by GIDS.

This IDL file must be compiled on both the client and the server. On the server, the IDL is filed, bindings to objects are made appropriately, and new methods are created. On the Java client, the process is similarly performed via an IDL to Java mapping. Objects defined in the IDL can then be referenced and used in both the client and server code.

Client

A client request for information expects the object server to search and completely process the information. A client therefore receives fully processed information that can be used readily. Fully processed implies that the data are in a useful format by the clients. Once the client receives the requested data, these data are cached on the client for performance enhancement. Thus, any functionalities that need to be performed using the data, such as spatial query, are all performed on the client.

Clients have an online access to geospatial data such as raster images and vector features over the Internet. These geospatial objects would be retrieved from a GemStone server. Communication between the server and a client is accomplished using CORBA-compliant vendor ORBs. The use of VisiBroker on the client side and GemORB for the database server is completely transparent to anyone accessing the applet. Figure 17.6 shows the basic architecture of our system. A Web-based client has the capability to display, select, and query objects interactively.

The retrieval of features from the GIDS is based on the concept of area of interest (AOI). The first screen of the applet displays a world map from which the user can select a location graphically through the use of a rectangle (bounding box), as shown in Figure 17.7. The user also has the option of entering the coordinates for the AOI manually, or selecting a predetermined region. From the user input, a bounding box of the AOI is transmitted from the applet via CORBA to the Smalltalk server.

The server responds with a set of database and library names for which data are available in that region. NIMA provides VPF data in databases, and each database contains one or more libraries. The user then selects a database and library, resulting in a list of coverages and feature classes being returned from the server through another CORBA request. Finally, the user selects the feature classes of interest and submits a request for them to be displayed, as shown in Figure 17.8. This request results in further CORBA communication, and the server returns a set of all of the features of the requested classes that are located in the given AOI. These features that are returned are complex objects with both geometric (coordinate) and attribute information. The applet can then display, select, and query on the returned features.

The underlying motivation for having a Web-based Java client access our OO mapping database is to give end users the ability to access and use NIMA data quickly and efficiently. At the present time, users of NIMA data must have software to view the data resident on their own computer systems, and must obtain the data primarily on CD-ROM or other storage media with limited Web interaction available for the user. Our Java applet allows any user with a Java-enabled Web browser to access our GIDB

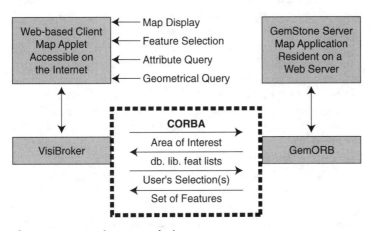

Figure 17.6 Basic system design.

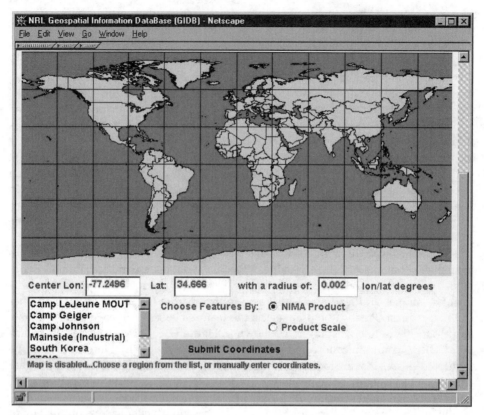

Figure 17.7   GIDS applet map display.

over the Internet and to display map data available in their area of interest. In addition to display of map objects, we have extended the functionality of the Java client to include simple queries, individual feature selection, zoom capabilities, attribute queries, geometrical queries, and updates of attribute values.

After the selected features in a user's AOI have been returned to the Java client and displayed as shown in Figure 17.9, the user can change the colors of the features to distinguish between the feature classes retrieved. A color key is shown providing the color, feature class, and number of those features in the given AOI. The user also has the ability to change the color of the background. Zoom capabilities are provided, allowing the user to zoom in, zoom out, or zoom to a user-specified area in the AOI. An individual feature may be selected by clicking on it in the map pane, resulting in the display of that feature's attributes.

Clicking on the Query button below the map pane performs a simple query. This query lists all of the features in the map pane and gives the user access to each feature's attribute information. More advanced queries can be performed by clicking on the Adv. Query button below the map pane. The advanced query screen allows users to display new feature classes in the AOI. The user can also perform attribute-level queries. For example, the user can highlight all of the four-lane roads, or all buildings

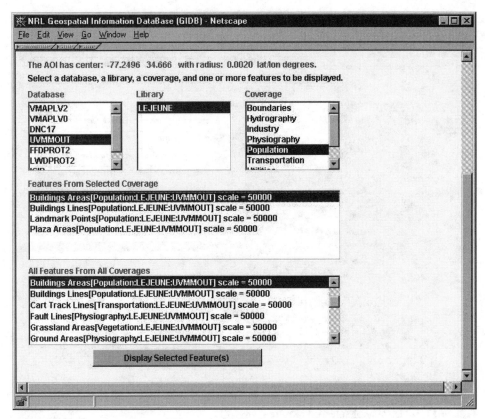

Figure 17.8   User selection window.

that function as government buildings. Users can also perform geometrical queries, such as "find all buildings that are greater than 50 feet from the road," or "find all homes that are within 20 meters of the Embassy."

Update of feature attributes is also possible with the Java client. For example, a newly paved road could have its attribute for surface type updated from "gravel" to "concrete." This function of the applet must be password protected so that only users with authorization can change data in the database.

Another function available in our Web applet includes the ability to perform Internet queries based on our AOI. A user can perform an Internet query by selecting the Internet Query button, and then selecting "Weather," "News," "Yellow Pages," or "Other Maps." For example, if a user decides to find out the weather for the current AOI and selects appropriately, the GIDS server will locate the nearest city to the user's AOI and will open a Web page with that city's local weather forecast.

Our existing Smalltalk mapping application has been extended to the Web utilizing a Java interface via CORBA. The success of our effort is exhibited in the current functionalities of our Java applet on the Web. We have several ongoing projects to improve our Web application, including the display of raster data. We are investigating ways to move to a truly distributed database. Additionally, we want to give users the ability to

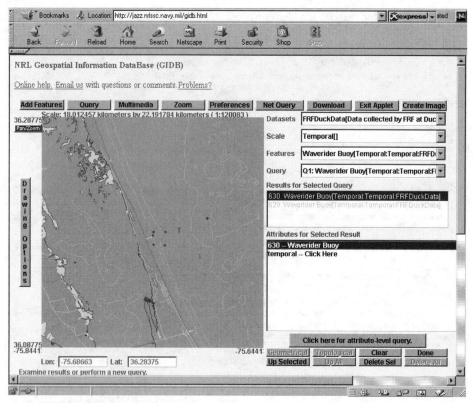

Figure 17.9 Display of selected features.

download data over the Internet from our Java interface to expedite the distribution of mapping data. Another extension to our Java interface is the ability to display the features in our map pane in 3D utilizing VRML. We anticipate the user being able to click on a "Render in 3D" button to obtain a VRML generated 3D model of the features in the current AOI. The open standard of VRML 2.0 is an excellent format for 3D modeling of land and underwater terrain, natural features, and man-made features. We will generate 3D models using gridded, TIN (Triangulated Irregular Network), and vector data. Our VRML models will provide additional information about the AOI by immersing the viewer into and allowing interaction with a virtual world.

Once these tasks are accomplished, users interested in a wide variety of mapping data will be able to access and benefit from our GIDS over the Internet from any platform using a Java-enabled Web browser. This will allow the functionality of more powerful server machines to be exhibited on less capable client machines. It will also give users faster access to mapping data. Our migration to a Web-based mapping client is a revolutionary way of allowing clients with modest computing resources user-friendly access to state-of-the-art mapping data and software.

2D GIDS Application

In this section we discuss the 2D GIDS Application. We begin with a discussion of Urban Warrior and present the IMMACCS Architecture in Figure 17.10.

Urban Warrior

In the post–cold-war era there has been more focus on urban warfare. The presence of civilians, urban infrastructures, and open space with obstructed views are some of the complications present in urban warfare. In preparation for potential urban warfare, the Marine Corps Warfighting Lab (MCWL) has performed an experiment and demonstration on how to conduct combat in urban settings using the latest technology. In 1997, an exercise called Hunter Warrior took place with the focus on fighting smarter, using less physical force, and relying more on microchips [CNN 1997].

Since many military operations take place via a chain of command, MCWL focused on the command and control activity within the Enhanced Combat Operations Center (ECOC). A specific requirement was imposed in supporting the experiment; the overall system was required to be object-oriented. MCWL believed that an object-oriented system would better meet the overall objective in effectively controlling the urban warfare. The Integrated Marine Corps Multi-Agent Command and Control System (IMMACCS) consists of a number of different components. A real-time display was required to visualize the common tactical picture by officers in the ECOC as activities took place in the "battle space." Stanford Research Institute (SRI) developed and pro-

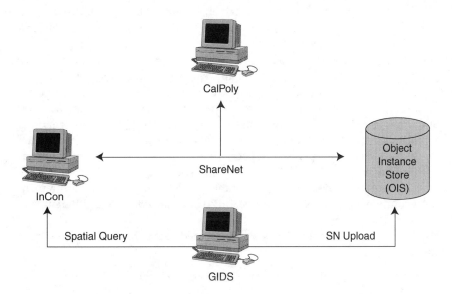

Figure 17.10   IMMACCS architecture.

vided the two-dimensional (2D) view of the urban battle space. Jet Propulsion Laboratory (JPL) provided a backbone (ShareNet) for all communication among the IMMACCS participants. Common Object Request Broker Architecture (CORBA) was the underlying medium that was used to exchange information among different components of the IMMACCS. California Polytechnic Institute (CalPoly) developed and provided the intelligent "software" agents to assist in the decision making process at the ECOC. SPAWAR's Multi-C4I Systems IMMACCS Translator (MCSIT) ingested all track information from legacy command and control systems such as Joint Maritime Command Information System (JMCIS) and translated it into object-oriented format for the IMMACCS components to access and use. SRI's 2D viewer (InCon) as well as CalPoly's agents required the urban infrastructure to provide a visualization of the battle space as well as a capability to reason about the surroundings.

Both the intelligent agents and the display had two categories of information: static and dynamic. Static information is geospatial information that encompasses physical and built-up environments, man-made structures (e.g., buildings, facilities, and infrastructure), and natural structures (e.g., topography, vegetation, coastlines). Dynamic information deals with tracking the movements of troops, tanks, helicopters and a company of marines, and is based upon the urban infrastructure in terms of its position, mobility, and operation. It is the static information contained in maps that provides much of the strategic and tactical basis for any military operation. Since NIMA's mapping products provide mapping data in relational form and MCWL specifically required the overall system to be object-oriented, DMAP provided the conversion to object-oriented format through the GIDS. The GIDS was used as the geospatial component of the IMMACCS system.

Dynamic as well as static urban infrastructure objects were persisted in the Object Instance Store (OIS) maintained by ShareNet. All objects must be in the OIS to be accessible by each system component. The OIS stores only the attributes of urban infrastructure objects, not the positional information. Since the InCon 2D viewer did not support vector maps for the infrastructure objects, an image was used as a reference map. Therefore, InCon needed to query the GIDS to determine which objects were available in the area of interest (AOI). Both the GIDS and the OIS maintained a global identification of each infrastructure object. When the GIDS provided the global identification of the objects to InCon, InCon then in turn requested OIS for other information. This two-step query process was implemented because the attributes of the infrastructure objects as provided by NIMA are a subset of the attributes defined for each infrastructure object in the IMMACCS object model (IOM). The OIS provides more information relevant to the IMMACCS environment. Due to the imposed requirement of using object-oriented systems, CORBA readily was realized among different systems to create an integrated system.

The following list of GIDS capabilities were provided to the IMMACCS as a part of the integrated system:

- Transform the relational vector map information to object-oriented format
- Upload the urban infrastructure objects to the ShareNet's Object Instance Store via CORBA
- Allow InCon to perform spatial query via CORBA

Figure 17.10 shows the overall IMMACCS and the GIDS support within the IMMACCS.

Additional functionality was tested during the Urban Warrior. An online spatial data updating took place from Bethesda, Maryland, to San Diego, California. This was a valuable test, which demonstrated that the object-oriented technology allows ease of updating complex data, such as spatial data. This work is discussed in detail in [Chung 1999].

3D GIDS

Mapping has been the chief means of geospatial data visualization provided by traditional Geospatial Information Systems (GIS). A GIS can produce a highly accurate digital map for a given area of interest, using well-recognized symbols to represent such features as mountains, forests, buildings and transportation networks. Although this flat view of the world provides an excellent means of orienting the user to the general nature and location of the features for a given area, it fails to provide the full experience that comes from viewing a three-dimensional (3D) environment. To address this shortcoming, NRL's DMAP, in conjunction with the University of New Orleans' Computer Science department, has investigated the development of a 3D-GIS that would assist the U.S. Marine Corps with mission preparation and rehearsal and also provide on-site awareness during actual field operations in urban areas.

We designed our 3D-GIS to supplement NIMA's traditional 2D digital-mapping output with a 3D synthetic environment counterpart. The map output remains useful for general orientation and query functions. The 3D output addresses the targeted application area. Instead of merely applying photo-textures to highly simplified geometric shapes, we include detailed, 3D, natural and man-made features such as buildings, roads, streetlights, and so on. We maximize the user's experience in this synthetic environment by providing for movement within and interaction with the environment consistent with the types of interactions expected of marines during anticipated urban operations. We construct the environment such that the user can *walk* or *fly* across terrain and can *walk* into buildings through doorways or *climb* through open windows. Since we construct synthetic buildings that conform to their real world floor plans, direct *line of sight* into and out of buildings through open doorways and windows is available. Additionally, once inside a building, the user can walk through interior rooms via interior doorways and climb stairs to different floors.

Our 3D synthetic environment is constructed using an extension of the NIMA's Vector Product Format (VPF) [DoD 1996] designed by DMAP and the University of New Orleans. The extended VPF, referred to as *VPF+* [Abdelguerfi 1998], makes use of a nonmanifold data structure for modeling 3D synthetic environments. The data structure uses a boundary representation (B-rep) method. B-rep models 3D objects by describing them in terms of their bounding entities and by topologically orienting them in a manner that enables the distinction between the object's interior and exterior. Consistent with B-rep, the representational scheme of the proposed data structure includes both topologic and geometric information. The topologic information encompasses the adjacencies involved in 3D manifold and nonmanifold objects, and is described using a new, extended Winged-Edge data structure. This data structure is referred to as "Non-Manifold 3D Winged-Edge Topology."

VPF+

The data structure relationships of the Non-Manifold 3D Winged-Edge Topology are summarized in the object model shown in Figure 17.11. References to geometry are omitted for clarity.

There are five main VPF+ primitives:

Entity node. Used to represent isolated features.

Connected node. Used as endpoints to define edges.

Edge. An arc used to represent linear features or borders of faces.

Face. A two-dimensional primitive used to represent a facet of a three-dimensional object such as the wall of a building, or to represent a two-dimensional area feature such as a lake.

Eface. Describes a use of a face by an edge.

Inside the primitive directory, a mandatory Minimum Bounding Box (MBB) table (not shown in Figure 17.11) is associated with each edge and face primitive. Because of its simple shape, an MBB is easier to handle than its corresponding primitive. The primitives shown in Figure 17.11, except for the eface, have an optional spatial index. The spatial index is based on an adaptive-grid–based 3D binary tree, which reduces searching for a primitive down to binary search. Due to its variable length records, the connected node table has a mandatory associated variable length index.

The ring table identifies the ring forming the outer boundary and all internal rings of a face primitive. This table allows (along with the face table) the extraction of all of the edges that form the outer boundary and that form the internal rings of a face prim-

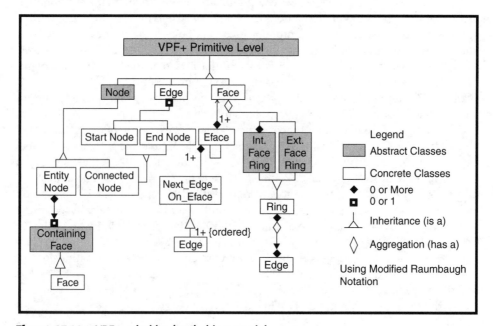

Figure 17.11 VPF+ primitive level object model.

itive. The entity node and the internal and external rings are not essential to the understanding of the VPF+ data structure, and as such, will not be discussed further.

The eface is a new structure that is introduced in VPF+ to resolve some of the ambiguities resulting from the absence of a fixed number of faces adjacent to an edge. Efaces describe the use of a face by an edge and allow maintenance of the adjacency relationships between an edge and zero, one, two, or more faces incident to an edge. This is accomplished by linking each edge to all faces connected along the edge through a circular linked list of efaces. As shown in Figure 17.12, each eface in the list identifies the face with which it is associated, the next eface in the list, and the "next" edge about the face with which the eface is associated. Efaces are also radially ordered in the linked list in a clockwise direction about the edge. The purpose for the ordering is to make traversal from one face to the radially closest adjacent face a simple list operation.

Additionally, VPF's Connected Node Table is modified to allow for nonmanifold nodes. This requires that a node point to one edge in each object connected solely through the node and to each dangling edge. This allows the retrieval of all edges and all faces in each object, and the retrieval of all dangling edges connected to the nonmanifold node.

Unlike traditional VPF's Level 3 topology, the "universe face" is absent in VPF+'s full 3D topology since VPF+ is intended primarily for 3D modeling. Additionally, since 3D modeling is intended, faces may be one- or two-sided. A two-sided face, for example, might be used to represent the wall of a building with one side used for the outside of the building and the other side for the inside of the building. Feature attribute information would be used to render the two different surface textures and color. A one-sided face might be used to represent a portion of a terrain surface. Orientation of the interior and exterior of 3D objects is organized in relation to the normal vector of faces forming the surface boundary of closed objects. Faces may also be embedded within a 3D object.

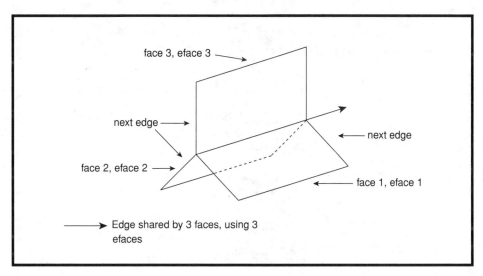

Figure 17.12 Relationship of a shared edge to its faces, efaces, and next edge about each face.

3D GIDS System Overview

Figure 17.13 shows the flow chart of the steps taken to develop the VPF+ database for the United States Public Service Health Hospital in Presidio, California for the Urban Warrior project. Flat floor plans of the building were the only required inputs to this process. These plans provided detailed information about the building such as floor layouts, dimensions, and means of entry. One of the VPF+ tools we have developed is an on-screen digitizer that allows a user to interface with scanned floor plans to extract 3D geometric data and automate production. This allows accurate definition of the overall exterior of the building and also accurate placement of interior rooms, windows, and doorways by defining the nodes, edges, and faces that form the three-dimensional structure of the building. Using this tool and scanned floor plans of the hospital, 3D data were gathered for the building and populated the VPF+ database.

An example of the result of this process is shown in Figure 17.14. Figure 17.14(a) illustrates an example of a typical 2D representation of the building as might be found in a traditional VPF database. Figures 17.14(b) and 17.14(c), on the other hand, show detailed VPF+ object models.

An example of the user interface is shown in Figure 17.15. User interaction is through a Web browser equipped with a 3D graphic plug-in such as Cosmo Player, and an application applet. Interactions with the 3D virtual world include the ability to walk into the building through doorways or climb through open windows, to look through open doorways and windows either from outside or inside the building, and to enter rooms through interior doorways and climb stairs to different floors. A 2D map of the hospital is displayed adjacent to the 3D counterpart in order to provide general orientation.

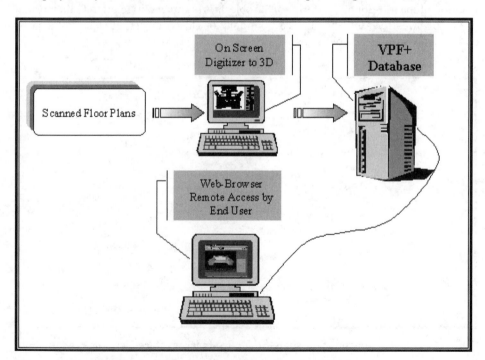

Figure 17.13   Flowchart of 3D model generation for Urban Warrior.

The USPS Hospital is a complex building consisting of nine floors and hundreds of rooms. To provide general orientation to marines inside the building, the 3D model is supplemented with a 2D map of the building. A pointer on the 2D map shows the user's location within the building and the direction in which he or she is heading. This can be seen in Figure 17.16. As the user moves between floors, the 2D map is updated automatically to show the level the user is on.

Experience Report

Through the experience of using an ODBMS and object-oriented technology, we have learned that memory management, input/output (IO) processing, data structure requirements, and utilization of fundamental object-oriented design all play a significant role in the overall performance of the ODBMS. During the development phase of our system, we encountered multiple instances that highlight the importance of giving attention to each of these factors. In this section, we will provide several of our experiences with these factors and will describe what we did to improve our system performance.

Memory management for data storage is a mandatory task because the storage requirement for objects can be significantly greater compared to the relational format. Objects require more storage for NIMA formats because of the requirement to export the updated data back into the original source format. To accomplish this, some of the source information or the relational formats are captured in the object definition to ensure the capability to export. This adds to the increase in the storage requirement. We believe that the storage increase would reduce if the relational information were

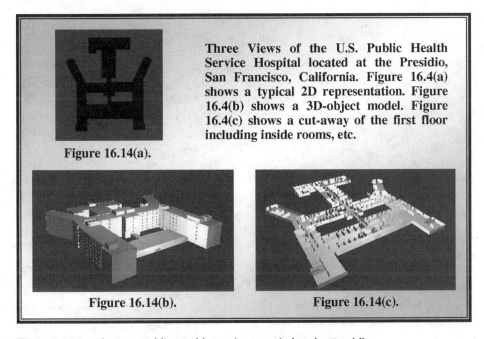

Three Views of the U.S. Public Health Service Hospital located at the Presidio, San Francisco, California. Figure 16.4(a) shows a typical 2D representation. Figure 16.4(b) shows a 3D-object model. Figure 16.4(c) shows a cut-away of the first floor including inside rooms, etc.

Figure 16.14(a).

Figure 16.14(b).   Figure 16.14(c).

Figure 17.14   The U.S. Public Health Service Hospital at the Presidio.

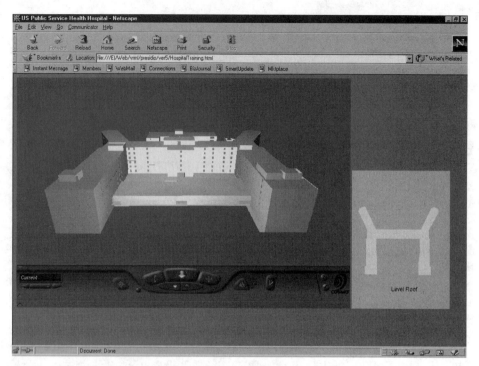

Figure 17.15 Sample user interface to the USPS Hospital.

dropped from the object definition, but our requirement for export capability prevents us from doing so. Consequently, we focus on other ways to minimize storage requirements. The most dramatic improvement in the size of the database occurred when we did not predefine the size of collections. Previously we would use "OrderedCollection new: 200" with the thought that it would be faster to populate the collection if its size were preset. However, the ODBMS would utilize the space for the collection even if only a few objects were actually placed in it. When we changed to using the command "OrderedCollection new" instead, the database size decreased dramatically (over tenfold) with no major degradation of performance.

Memory management in terms of RAM is also extremely important for increased performance. While testing the initialization of new datasets in our database, we noticed that performance tended to degrade with time; the first few objects initialized quickly, but as more objects were initialized the longer it took for individual object initialization. We concluded that this was due to an increasing number of objects to be managed by RAM before being persisted in the database repository. To resolve this performance degradation, we decided to commit or persist the objects in the database repository during the initialization periodically rather than all at once at the end of initialization. We chose to persist 100 objects at a time, which eliminated this performance problem.

Because network-based client-server applications have inherently poorer performance than single-system applications, we sought to fine-tune the application performance to make the network hit less noticeable. Since IO processing is the most expensive processor

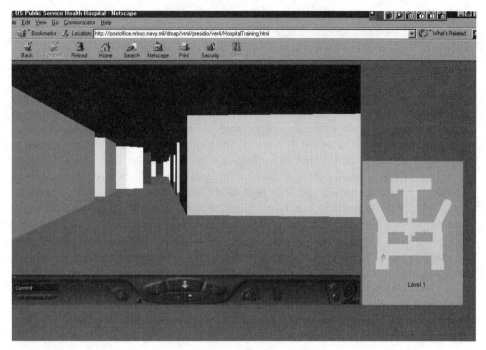

Figure 17.16   Tracking a marine inside the USPS Hospital.

operation, performance in transforming the relational into object format took a significant amount of time. This performance drawback was due primarily to the file open and close operations. Performance improved tremendously when we revised the procedure to read all the contents of a file at one time, storing the data in memory as a dictionary or collection for subsequent use. This memory is released once the data have been used for object creation.

In addition to IO performance tuning, we realized performance improvements after targeting three other areas for revision:

- Reimplementing duplicate, lower-level methods as a single method in a common superclass

- Storing intermediate results in local variables, rather than having repeated message sends

- Reducing the reliance on collections and dictionaries

Because the application was incrementally expanded to handle additional data types, reuse of existing code was not always optimal. This was due largely to the fact that the size of the application made it difficult for developers to "see the forest for the trees." When the time was found to take a broad-based view of the design, it was found that many methods were significantly overlapping in functionality. Merging these methods from the class hierarchy into one method at the superclass level resulted in significant performance improvement. With regard to the second area of performance improvement, we found that often within the same method, message sends were being repeated to compute the same results multiple times. Performance improved when local variables were used to store intermediate results rather than repeating the message sends.

Finally, the use of collections and dictionaries was dramatically decreased. A great performance degradation was noticed when a dictionary size increased from 1000 to 1001 and thereafter. This is due to the Smalltalk hashing functionality. When an item has to be added to a full dictionary, the dictionary is split into two. A new dictionary is created that is 150 percent of the size of the original dictionary. The contents of the dictionary are then copied to a new dictionary. The performance of this process began to degrade significantly as the size of a dictionary reached over 1000. Thus, we have implemented a large dictionary that basically maintains a collection of dictionaries of size 1000. A new dictionary of size 1000 is created each time a new dictionary is needed.

In our ODBMS, each object is assigned a unique object identifier known as an object-oriented pointer (oop). The oop can be used to access any object in the database quickly. We make extensive use of the oop for our Web interface. Our Web interface is a Java applet embedded in an html document and accessible over the Web. The applet communicates with the ODBMS using CORBA. Users of our Web interface want to obtain our data over the Web quickly. To accomplish this, objects in the ODBMS are accessed by the applet through utilization of the object oop. In this manner, we take advantage of the oop to obtain the information that we need from the database, thus quickly providing data to the user.

Conclusion

In this chapter, we have shown how a Web-based distributed system for retrieval and updating of mapping objects has implemented the GIDS. The GIDS architecture relies heavily upon object technology and includes a Smalltalk server application interfaced to a GemStone ODBMS, Java/applet-based client applications, and CORBA middleware in the forms of VisiBroker and GemORB. The GIDS was the realization of our goal to have NIMA data available for electronic information distribution and updating, and played a significant role in the Marine Corps' Warfighting Lab's Urban Warrior Advanced Warfighting Experiment. The architectural components of the system worked well together; using Smalltalk as the server development environment allowed us to prototype new capabilities quickly, while Java provided the Web-based capabilities for the user interface. CORBA proved an excellent choice to serve as a bridge between the two.

A description and prototype of a 3D synthetic environment using VPF+ was also discussed. The 3D developments demonstrated how marines could utilize this technology for an improved situational awareness and mission planning. Users have the ability to view the environment in a more realistic manner. VPF+ is the vehicle that allowed the synthetic environment to be constructed with topology intact. Furthermore, such 3D visualization is Web-enabled through the Web browser plugins. Future directions consist of bridging the gap between the 2D and 3D by allowing 3D rendering from the GIDS's 2D display.

CHAPTER 18

Architecture of the Distributed, Multitier Railway Application DaRT

In the beginning of the 1990s, the German railway company Deutsche Bahn AG had two software environments: one from the Eastern Deutsche Reichsbahn and one from Western Deutsche Bundesbahn. Both were based on classical mainframes, and the data could not be up-to-date. Therefore, the fully object-oriented system DaRT (DaRT is the abbreviation for the German expression Datenbank für Reisezugwagen und Trieb-fahrzeuge) for management of carriages and locomotives was designed by sd&m and developed by a mixed team with Deutsche Bahn AG. The data model for vehicles is deeply structured with more than 230 properties, and additionally it is required that end-users have the ability to add new properties at run time. Because DaRT users are spread all over Germany, a three-tier architecture is built to minimize the communication costs, and various caching mechanisms are used at each tier. Four caching alternatives for the application servers are evaluated and it is explained how the caching policy of the application servers can be matched efficiently with database clustering. Finally the end-user client is presented with its own cache and an optimistic synchronization between the heterogeneous object request brokers; in other words, the objects of the end-user client are implemented with Distributed Smalltalk and the corresponding objects of the application servers are implemented with ORBIX/C++.

Introduction and Motivation

In 1990, Deutsche Reichsbahn (East Germany) and Deutsche Bundesbahn (West Germany) merged. The challenging integration had to focus on both organizational and technical aspects like the set of all vehicles, the routes, and the data processing infrastructure. Especially the management of all vehicles was a nontrivial issue to provide an optimized utilization and implementation of railway traffic. Therefore, it is indispensable to have up-to-date data about the current usage of all vehicles, their location and technical condition and, finally, correlation with maintenance scheduling.

Therefore, in 1993 the DaRT project was set up to develop a system that covered both the management and the maintenance scheduling of the locomotives and passenger vehicles of the Deutsche Bahn AG—the cargo wagons being handled by a separate system. The DaRT system was designed and implemented by sd&m and Deutsche Bahn in a joint project. In 1996, the first release of the DaRT system was deployed and it was labeled with the "Object Application Award" of the OMG in the category "Best Use of Object Technology within Enterprise or Large Systems Environment." Today DaRT manages 12,000 locomotives and 17,000 carriages, including maintenance scheduling. Furthermore, multiple export and import interfaces to neighbor systems are available to provide current data and to avoid redundant data management.

The DaRT system has a three-tier architecture using CORBA with a central database. More than 800 end-users are working with DaRT and their cardinality is expected to grow beyond 1000. The end-users are located all over Germany so that DaRT is a wide-distributed CORBA application using object technology in all tiers.

The next section describes the application domain and the data model for the various vehicles. Then the three-tier architecture and the according software platform are presented. In the next step the database clustering is described, which is very important for the object-oriented database management system ObjectStore. Next, the middle-tier application servers are characterized from a performance point of view. After this, various caching alternatives are described and evaluated. Finally the end-user tier is discussed and caching is again stressed due to the communication costs in a wide-distributed application.

The Application Domain

The data describing the deep structure of vehicles (locomotives and carriages) are organized in objects referencing subobjects. In total, a vehicle is composed of more than 250 fixed attributes and quite a number of flexible attributes that are composed of various subobjects (more than 20 classes). Figure 18.1 presents a small subset of an instance diagram. Each vehicle is associated with a so-called model; for example, the model with the identifier 478 describes all dining cars with steam and electronic heating, but without air conditioning. This model is referenced by 13 other application objects. Additionally there are variants for each model so that there is a one-to-many relationship between the objects of class Model and objects of class ModelVariant. Each variant has an identifier that is unique relative to the model; that is, to identify a model variant the identifiers for the model (e.g., 478) and the variant (e.g., 3) are required. A model variant contains a description that makes sense only together with the description of the model. The main reason to have a model variant is to comprise the default equipment, the main information, and additional information.

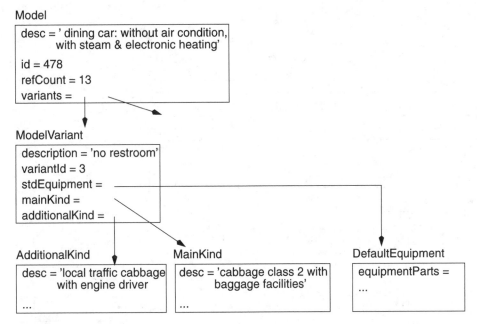

Figure 18.1 Instance diagram for a subset of DaRT.

The attributes of the vehicles are divided up into 20 hierarchical classes. In 1995, a serious requirement for the DaRT system was to handle end-user clients even if the available bandwidth was only 9600 Baud. Therefore, the set of more than 230 vehicle attributes is organized hierarchically in small classes, each forming a logical unit. A subset is presented in Figure 18.2. A vehicle consists of, for example, the model variant, the modified equipment, and the data sheet. The model variant aggregates the default equipment, the main information, and the additional information as discussed before, and the data sheet consists of some descriptions—for example, the brakes, baggage facilities, and the measurement such as length.

When a vehicle is put into operation for the first time, the model variant including the standard equipment is defined. During the vehicle's lifecycle, parts have to be repaired or even exchanged. These actions are logged in the object of class ModifiedEquipment; that is, the DefaultEquipment preserves the data about the original equipment during the whole lifecycle. This information is essential for periodic maintenance.

Three-Tier Architecture

DaRT is based on a three-tier architecture as shown in Figure 18.3, and supports clients that are distributed all over Germany. Due to the wide distribution of the clients, the architecture is focused on reducing the transmission times, which have a tremendous impact on the throughput and response time of the system. The end-user clients are running on Windows PCs and provide a graphical user interface based on Smalltalk.

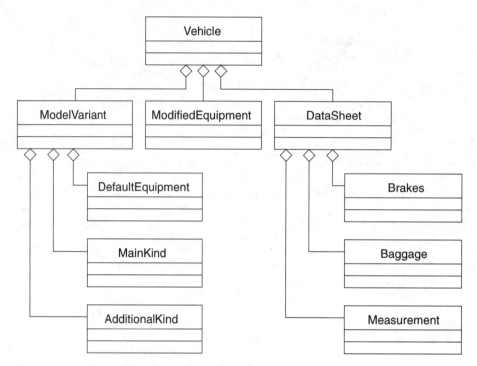

Figure 18.2 Class diagram for a subset of DaRT.

The main business logic is realized by the application servers and implemented in C++ using ORBIX to communicate with the end-user clients. The database backend is responsible only for storing the persistent objects in an ObjectStore database. Because of the use of object technology in each tier, there is no semantic gap in the application.

As Figure 18.3 shows, there is more than one application server running in Berlin. The overall application logic is divided in three categories. Typically an end-user wants to select one dedicated object out of a set of objects with only a rough idea about the values of the interesting object. For instance, to select a carriage, the selection dialog provides the vehicle and model number of the carriages and some additional information. The values for such a selection dialog are shipped by a *selection server*.

Once the end-user has selected an interesting object, an *update server* transmits the full-fledged object to the client, and the values are visualized in the according dialog where the user can modify the object if the required access permissions are granted. When the dialog is closed the modified objects are sent back to the update server and finally stored in the database.

The *query servers* execute complex and long-running queries like «Give me all carriages with a length between 20.50m and 26.70m, with red doors, with head form "Wittenberg" and belonging to the branch Frankfurt». The end-user can interactively compose a query out of the 250 attributes specifying various conditions and sort criteria. Such a query expression is transmitted to a query server, which retrieves the matching vehicles and sends them back to the client.

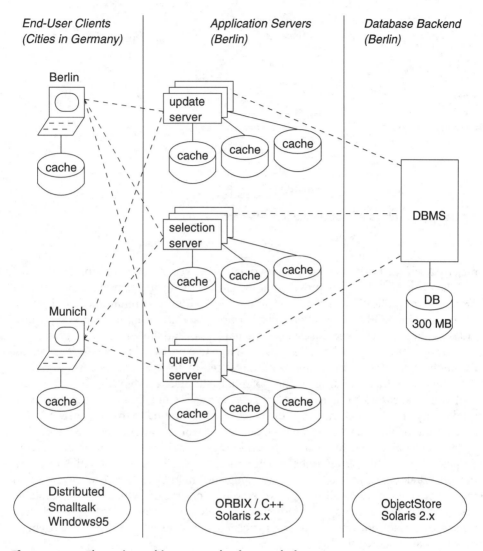

Figure 18.3 Three-tier architecture and software platform.

To reduce read and update locks, the selection and query servers use the ObjectStore mechanism MVCC (multiversion concurrency control). In this mode the last transactional state (before the start of the MVCC transaction) can be read from the database without requiring a read lock. The MVCC mode provides data that are consistent in terms of transaction boundaries, which is totally different from dirty reads. A high throughput of multiple application servers running concurrently can be achieved by using the MVCC mode.

Layered architectures are a well-established principle for mainframe and client/server applications. Typical layers focus on presentation, business logic, and database access. Such a functional separation is also applied for DaRT as shown in Figure 18.4: The

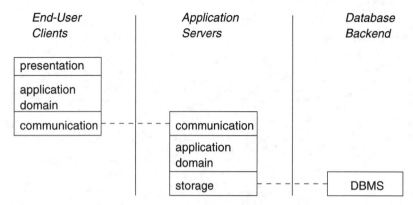

Figure 18.4 Software layers in the three-tier architecture.

major part of the business logic and the database access is realized at the server side, and the presentation logic is provided at the client side. In addition to mainframe and client/server applications, a three-tier application requires a communication layer to encapsulate the CORBA invocations. Furthermore the DaRT communication layer provides the mapping between the clients' Smalltalk types and the servers' C++ types.

The application logic in DaRT is separated into two parts: the main part, realized by the application servers; and a minor part, realized by the end-user clients. To reduce the network traffic according to the potentially limited bandwidth, the clients are buffering the server objects by smart proxies. Let us assume that an end-user tries to modify any object and all values of the object are transmitted to the server by clicking an OK button. Now the server can check the values for consistency before the modifications are stored in the database. The end-users would not accept such a behavior, because of the late consistency check. The end-users prefer checks immediately after a field in a dialog is completed. However, doing such field-based consistency checks on the server side would result in an increasing network traffic, which is not acceptable due to the potentially limited bandwidth. Therefore, simple plausibility checks are done on the client side; for example, syntax checks for vehicle identifiers or verifying a date for maintenance scheduling.

Clustering in the Database

The architecture of the ObjectStore database server is page-based and therefore strongly dependent on a well-designed clustering. Clustering means the physical placement of the persistent objects inside the database when the objects are created. From now on the location is fixed until the object is deleted and the placement cannot be changed. Therefore, defining a good clustering policy is the main design task for an ObjectStore database. Using the important and/or dominating use cases is a good starting point to determine the clustering. ObjectStore has three granularities for clustering: databases, segments, and ObjectStore clusters. Coarse-level clustering is done by selecting one of several databases as a persistent storage for a new object. For instance there can be one database for unchangeable master data and a second database for changeable data.

The next granules for clustering are segments that can be compared with table spaces in Oracle, for example, and are the most important clustering unit. There are some rules of thumb to design the segmentation: the number of segments per database should be less than 1000 and the size of a segment should be less than 50MB. These values are determined by the internal architecture of ObjectStore, which was totally changed in release 6.0 in 1999. From now on the upper boundary of 50MB is not as critical as it was until release 5.1.

Figure 18.5 presents a subset of the segmentation of the DaRT database. The singleton vehicle manager is located in a dedicated segment together with other manager objects. The vehicle manager is responsible for creating, deleting, and querying vehicles; that is, locomotives and carriages that are stored in separate segments. The more than 230 attributes of a locomotive or carriage are grouped together in full-fledged objects as previously mentioned. Some of these objects have a significant size so that a distinct segment is required due to the page-server architecture of ObjectStore. For instance, there are data describing the planned and the actual home station to which a locomotive belongs. These data shall not be transmitted over the network each time a client accesses a locomotive object. Therefore, there is one segment for the data of the actual home stations of a locomotive and one for the planned home stations. The home data of the carriages are separated in the same way.

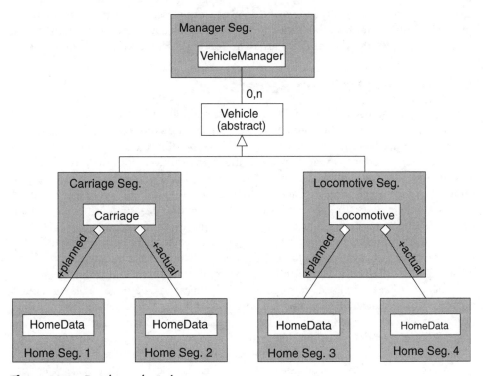

Figure 18.5 Database clustering.

The main patterns used in DaRT are the factory pattern and the partitioning pattern. New objects have to be created according to the right segmentation policy. Therefore, manager objects like the `VehicleManager` are responsible for object creation and allocation. The factories are the general interface to the end-user clients and are implemented as singletons so that there is only one factory instance per class. Additionally all queries like «give me all carriages with the model 062» are handled by the factory, too.

Large objects like vehicles having more than 230 attributes are separated in several objects as discussed earlier. As shown in Figure 18.5, there are some vehicle attributes that are more important than others. Since ObjectStore is based on a page-server architecture, the less important attributes like those encapsulated in `HomeData` are stored in separate segments so that the more important objects are stored closely together—ideally on the same disk pages.

Designing the Application Servers

As shown in Figure 18.4, the application servers provide the application logic and the according business objects. To process the client requests, the application server operates on persistent objects. If these objects must be constructed for each transaction, the application server must submit a lot of database requests to retrieve the persistent values for the business objects. Designing the application servers for good throughput and short response times is a key issue in designing a three-tier architecture, and server-side caches drastically reduce the database requests and thus the response times and overall throughput. In this section four alternatives about the server architecture are presented. In DaRT the fourth alternative, "dialog-oriented servers," was chosen.

Alternative 1: Uniform Servers

In the first prototype of DaRT only uniform servers were implemented; that is, all server types (update, selection, and query server) had the same executable as shown in Figure 18.6. Since the application servers are also ObjectStore clients there is only one update server in order to avoid locking conflicts. In addition, both the three selection servers and the three query servers were running in MVCC mode. Therefore, the implementation of the first prototype was pessimistic, but could guarantee that no locking conflict will occur. Of course such an architectural design does not scale at all, and there are serious performance issues regarding the overall throughput.

Using uniform servers for the first prototype led to early availability so that the functionality of the new system could be validated early and the implementation efforts were reasonable. The only configuration of the application servers addressed their local ObjectStore cache. Each ObjectStore client has its own cache where the pages containing the objects of the current transaction are buffered. At the end of an ObjectStore transaction the page locks are released, but the pages still remain in the client cache. If the ObjectStore server detects a conflict with another concurrent database client, then the server calls those pages back that are residing in the cache after the commit of a transaction and that were not accessed later on. This technique is called *callback locking*.

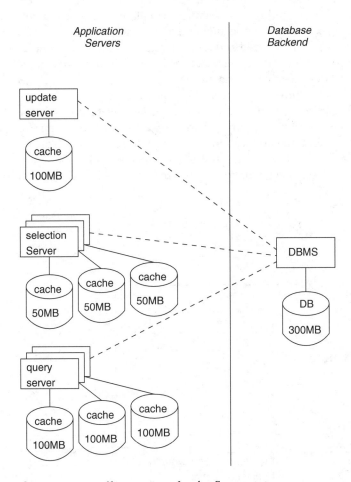

Figure 18.6 Uniform servers for the first prototype.

The single update server and the three query servers have a local cache of 100MB, respectively. This cache size is large enough to capture all objects for a sequence of transactions, so that cache eviction can be avoided because objects of an older transaction are still in the cache due to the callback locking mechanism. However, such a configuration of the caches does not scale well with database size.

Alternative 2: Multithreaded Servers

Since alternative 1 is useful only for prototyping and does not scale, the design has to be improved. The single update server obviously is a bottleneck regarding the overall throughput. Therefore, a multithreaded update server would overcome this restriction as illustrated in Figure 18.7. Concurrent threads in a single process could handle the concurrent incoming client requests. Consequently, the selection and the query servers could also be implemented as multithreaded servers so that the same executable would still be possible. The existence of a selection and a query server is still helpful because their access profile is still unchanged and they can still run as MVCC clients of the ObjectStore database so that locking conflicts between the multithreaded update server and the selection and query servers cannot occur.

Since ObjectStore was far from providing true multithreaded transactions when the DaRT project was started in 1995, the update server would be responsible for isolating persistent objects in different threads. In addition there should be a single commit for all concurrent threads. Therefore, the application server cannot accept new requests after a global commit is announced. When the last thread finishes its job the global commit can occur. To avoid a blocking situation during the potentially long commit

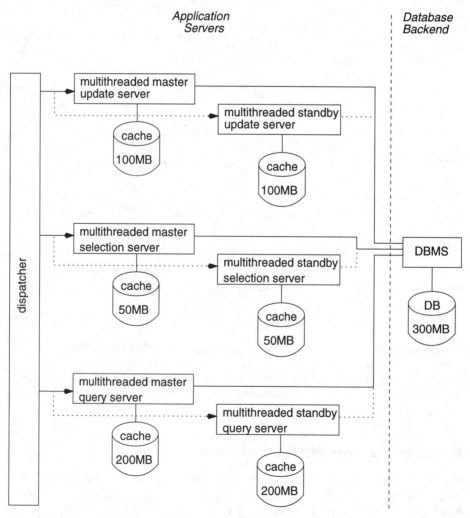

Figure 18.7 Multithreaded servers with standby facilities.

phase a standby server will be activated, which accepts the new requests of the clients. When the commit is done the first server will become the standby server and will be activated when the other server prepares for commit.

Several issues have to be considered when servers are implemented in a multithreaded way. First of all the code has to be thread-safe; this is not trivial at all. Furthermore the code maintenance becomes harder because bug fixing in multithreaded code is much more difficult and debuggers normally do not help significantly.

Alternative 3: Data-Specific Servers

To avoid the problems with multithreading and to improve the throughput, the third alternative considers parallel processes working on distinct object sets. Figure 18.8 shows the process organization of such data-specific servers for locomotives, carriages, their models, workshop scheduling, access control, etc. Since each application server operates on its own set of persistent objects and since these sets are nonoverlapping, the concurrent update servers cannot block each other because lock conflicts cannot occur.

Identifying the nonoverlapping object sets is a challenging design task. As mentioned, an ObjectStore database consists of nonoverlapping segments. Thus the data-specific servers should be designed so that each server is responsible for a set of clusters, and the objects in a cluster are accessible by only one application server. Therefore, the caches of the database clients match with the database clustering and good cache utilization can be expected. Additionally the ObjectStore cache of each application server for a database client can be configured so that all addressed clusters fit into the cache; that is, the application servers will provide a *main memory database*. As indicated in Figure 18.8, the cache sizes may vary depending on the accessible object sets. For instance, an application server for carriages needs a larger cache than an application server that provides the model data (see Figure 18.1) for carriages and locomotives.

Not only the update servers, but also the selection and query servers can be adapted to specific object sets. The access profiles of selection servers are similar to the access profiles of the update servers. Therefore, the partitioning of the selection servers can be done analogously; that is, there will be selection servers for locomotives, carriages, their models, workshop scheduling, access control, and so on. The partitioning for query servers is much simpler because the end-users are unlimited in composing queries interactively. Basically there are three query types: queries on locomotives, queries on carriages, and queries on all vehicles. Therefore, three types of query servers are available, and for each type there are multiple instances; for example, there are four query servers for locomotives and three query servers for all vehicles.

The data-specific servers will scale to some extent. More concurrent application servers can be provided by addressing smaller sets of database clusters, and blocking of servers or even deadlocks are still avoided because locking conflicts cannot occur. However, the dispatcher requires more coding efforts to reflect the data separation between the various application servers. Additionally, the end-users' requirements and/or access profile might change so that the database clustering must be adapted. Such an adaptation will also affect the dispatcher because its code is closely related to database clustering.

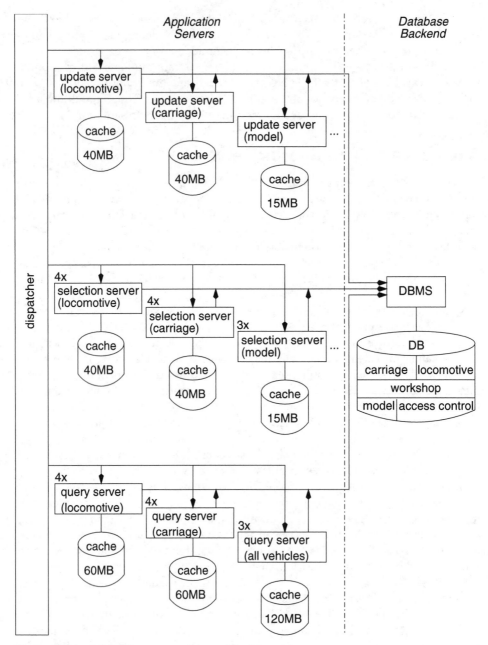

Figure 18.8   Application servers for specific data sets.

Alternative 4: Dialog-Oriented Servers

The design principle of this alternative is also partitioning, but a partitioning from the end-user perspective and not from a database perspective. The goal is to group the dialogs in categories that are related together; that is, when an end-user is working with dialog A and normally then moves to dialog B, both dialogs belong to the same dialog category. For instance, there will be dialogs for maintaining the locomotive data, the carriage data, their model data, the maintenance schedules, the access control, etc., so that application servers for exactly these categories are required. If an end-user maintains the data of locomotives he or she also might want to read some data of the according locomotive model. Therefore, the locomotive application server has to access some data that are mainly controlled by the model application server. This is the principal difference to data-specific servers: dialogue-oriented servers access overlapping object sets.

If the object sets of the application servers are overlapping, locking conflicts in the concurrent database transactions can occur so that an application server might be blocked or, in the case of a deadlock, might even be reset. Therefore, the application server program has to consider that a transaction can be aborted due to a deadlock detected by the database server. This is routine work for a programmer.

A more challenging task than handling deadlocks is to reduce the likelihood that the application servers' transaction can be blocked or even aborted. If the dialog categories are defined carefully then only a small subset of the persistent objects can be accessed via different dialog categories. Figure 18.9 illustrates the partitioning of the DaRT application servers according to different dialog groups. As mentioned for the data-specific servers, each dialog-oriented server has its own ObjectStore cache with an adjusted size. For instance the locomotive application server requires a cache size of 40MB, and the application server for the model data requires only 15MB.

The selection and query servers can also be adapted to various dialog categories. The selection servers are partitioned in the same way as the update servers, so that there are selection servers, for example, for locomotives, carriages, model data, maintenance schedules, and access control. According to the access profiles there are different numbers of selection servers for each selection category. For instance, four selection servers for locomotives are required for good throughput, but only three selection servers for model data. The partitioning of the query servers is the same as for data-specific servers; that is, different query servers handle queries on locomotives, on carriages, and on all vehicles.

Dialog-oriented servers consider overlapping object sets from the very beginning because they are designed with the assumption that the dialogs and therefore the accessed persistent objects will overlap. This design issue is promising for future requirements. If new or changed requirements have to be taken into account in a new DaRT release then the according dialogs might access objects that are already addressed by another dialog. However, there will be no problem because locking conflicts of concurrent transactions were already considered. The only design issue is to examine the amount of objects in the overlapping object set and to ensure that there will be a reasonable size in the intersection.

Comparison and Evaluation

Comparing the four alternatives for DaRT, obviously the uniform servers were a reasonable choice for the first prototype, but they do not scale at all. To guarantee the required response time the cache size has to be the same as the database size in order to avoid periodic cache overflows resulting in periodic cache evictions. Thus the

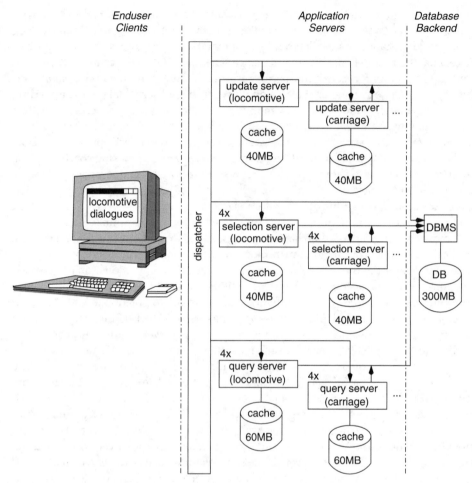

Figure 18.9 Servers for dialog categories.

response times will be significantly longer when the cache size is too small. Therefore, the alternative with uniform servers cannot be considered seriously.

Scalability can be improved by having multithreaded servers and concurrent client requests will be handled in parallel so that a good throughput can be provided. However, maintaining multithreaded C++ code is not a simple job. Finding and fixing bugs can be a very challenging task because the debuggers are not well suited for handling multithreaded programs. This consideration was the knockout criteria for multi-threaded DaRT servers.

The third alternative of data-specific servers is separating the objects in nonoverlapping sets. Specialized servers can handle concurrent client requests in a multiprocess environment (i.e., without multithreading). Due to multiple concurrent server processes the required scalability and throughput can be ensured. The servers can access and modify objects concurrently and will not block if the objects are in different data sets. If the database size will grow, additional application servers operating on smaller object sets can still provide the necessary throughput. However, such a design requires a correspondence of the database clustering and the specialized servers. As soon as there are changed user requirements and/or access profiles the database clustering might be changed and consequently the data-specific servers and their dispatcher process have to be adapted to the new clustering strategy. From a maintenance point of view the data-specific servers are not very promising.

The last alternative focuses on dialog-oriented servers that also can handle concurrent client requests in a multiprocess environment. The required scalability and throughput will be provided in the same way as for data-specific servers of the third alternative, but the code complexity and maintenance is simpler. When new or different end-user requirements arise there might be overlapping accesses of concurrent servers that sometimes might cause a blocking situation. The dialog-oriented servers take care of blocking and deadlocks from the very beginning because they were designed with the basic assumption that overlapping accesses will occur. Therefore, the DaRT system is realized with dialog-oriented servers.

Selecting the right server architecture is the most challenging task for a multitier application. The various aspects and arguments regarding DaRT are summarized in Table 18.1.

Designing the End-User Client

This section discusses caching on the client side to preserve the read objects on the client side as long as possible in order to avoid network communication. However, distributed caches on the client side require a mechanism to ensure cache consistency. DaRT handles distributed cache consistency by implementing optimistic synchronization, and each object is enhanced with a version number. When a client sends a modified object back to the server the (unchanged) version number of the modified object is compared with the current version number attached to the persistent object. If there is a difference between the version numbers, a concurrent end user caused an update conflict, and the modification is rejected. If there is no update conflict the version number is incremented and the modifications are stored in the database.

The communication layer presented earlier is also responsible for the clients' cache management. The typical tasks are handling the smart proxies, invoking remote methods, preparing the data structures for network transport, and incrementing the version

Table 18.1   Characterization of Alternative Server Architectures

	UNIFORM SERVERS	MULTI-THREADED SERVERS	DATA-SPECIFIC SERVERS	DIALOG-ORIENTED SERVERS
Scalability	–	+	+	+
Performance	–	+	+	+
Code maintenance	+	–	–	+

numbers. There are two implementation alternatives to organize the clients' caches. In the first alternative the cache of a single client is controlled on the class level of the objects. The second alternative maintains the cache implicitly and exhausts the garbage collection facility of the programming language. In DaRT the second alternative, implicit caching, was chosen.

Alternative 1: Class-Based Caching

The data model of DaRT considers the WAN of the Deutsche Bahn AG so that objects are adjusted for the clients' dialogs and the according network transfer. If the client preserves the objects as long as possible, that is, until their values are outdated, the client cache might significantly grow and the cache organization might become a bottleneck. Therefore, alternative 1 provides a dictionary for each class to access the cached objects.

This approach is illustrated in the scenario of Figure 18.10. Objects of the application domain are locomotives (class LocomotiveDom), and carriages (class CarriageDom) were requested by the client because their maintenance has to be scheduled. The maintenance will take place in a workshop that is presented in a dialog (class WorkshopPres) and provides the values of the cached domain objects. Each domain object has a reference to a so-called communication object (e.g., class LocomotiveComm), which handles the communication with the application server; that is, the invocation of remote methods and the mapping between Smalltalk and C++ types. The communication object is a singleton because the domain objects just delegate the remote method invocations and the type mapping. Only one class-level attribute is required for a communication object, namely a reference to the dictionary that manages all domain objects of the same class. For instance the singleton of class LocomotiveComm has a reference to the dictionary managing all objects of class LocomotiveDom. The keys of such a dictionary are the domain objects, and the according values are references to objects of class CachedObject. An instance of CachedObject encapsulates the data for the cache organization and for optimistic synchronization:

- version number, which will be incremented when the domain object is modified in a client transaction

- dirtyFlag, which is set when a modification takes place

- cacheState, which indicates whether the attribute values of the domain object are still valid or not

- remoteRef, which is the remote reference to the ORBIX domain object on the server side, which again references the so-called TIE-object (ORBIX 2.3 provides two implementation techniques: the BOA approach, which uses inheritance, and the TIE approach, which uses delegation)

Using dictionaries and administrative objects of the Comm classes and of CachedObject, the values of the cached domain objects are provided transparently via the communication layer. Therefore, the GUI programmers can realize the dialogs and just access the domain objects. It is not required that they are aware of the CORBA communication and the caching technique.

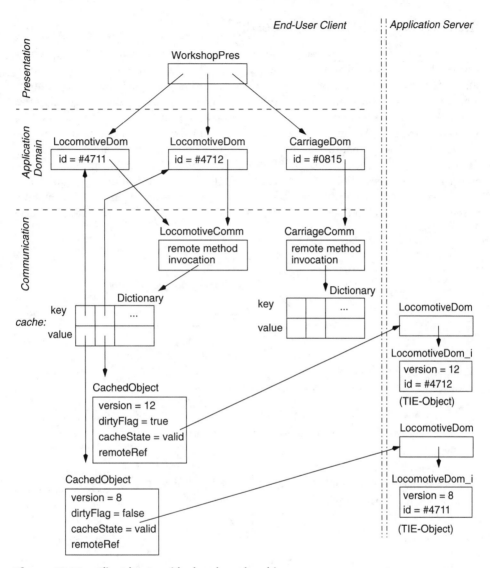

Figure 18.10 Client layers with class-based caching.

The presented cache organization addresses scalability because there is one dictionary for each application domain object. However, these dictionaries will grow as soon as the client requests another domain object. Therefore, a strategy is required to evict a cached object. A simple implementation might be to limit the items in the dictionary, and in an overflow situation an LRU algorithm, for example, can select the objects to be evicted. Another approach can tolerate variable-sized dictionaries. Then the eviction will be more sophisticated because, for example, the access time and/or the frequency of accesses will be considered. In any case scalability and cache eviction requires an additional, nontrivial implementation effort.

Alternative 2: Implicit Caching

The second alternative is to cache the objects implicitly: each object transparently knows about its administrative caching information. In Figure 18.11, a scenario is shown for how a graphical presentation object accesses the objects of the application domain. A workshop for maintenance of locomotives and carriages is presented in the dialog `WorkshopPres` and references domain objects of the classes `LocomotiveDom` and `CarriageDom`. The attribute set of each domain class is extended with administrative attributes to handle caching and optimistic synchronization: `version`, `dirtyFlag`, `cacheState`, and `remoteRef`. Last, but not least the attribute `comm` references the communication object where the CORBA communication is encapsulated as in alternative 1. All administrative attributes are inherited from the Frammento framework of sd&m so that the technical information is implicitly provided for each domain object.

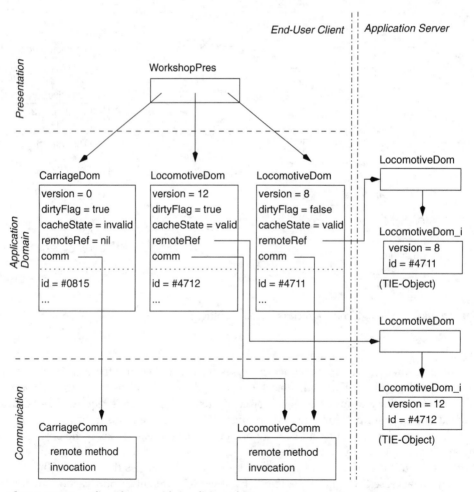

Figure 18.11 Client layers with implicit caching.

The caching information is spread implicitly over all domain objects. An object is evicted from the cache when the domain object is removed due to the automatic garbage collection of Smalltalk. Thus no implementation of a cache eviction algorithm is required. An object is cached as long as it is in the scope of the client, that is, as long as a dialog references a domain object so that all cached domain objects are up-to-date, and the required memory for the object cache is pretty small.

Comparison and Evaluation

The two approaches for caching on the client side are looking promising in terms of performance. The domain objects can be cached and accessed efficiently. However, they differ in the implementation technique by using delegation or inheritance. The delegation approach of class-based caching has a dictionary for each domain class and can thus provide global information about all cached objects. However, handling a large cache and managing cache eviction is an open issue that requires sophisticated algorithms.

The inheritance approach of implicit caching does not require algorithms for cache eviction because the automatic garbage collection of the programming language Smalltalk is exhausted; an implementation with Java would be analogous. A minor disadvantage is that there is no global cache information so that a separate cache component cannot be available. Considering the pros and cons that are summarized in Table 18.2, the DaRT clients are implemented with implicit caching, and not with class-based caching.

Conclusion

First of all, DaRT is deployed and more than 800 end-users are working with the widely distributed system. Although in 1995 a small bandwidth of 9600 Baud had to be considered, the design of the three-tier architecture had to ensure good throughput and short response times. Due to object technology in each tier, the communication between the development teams was made easy because everybody was talking about the same classes and objects. There was no misunderstanding because of any semantic gaps between different tiers or layers. Another benefit of thorough usage of object technology was that a mapping layer between the objects of the application domain and flat relational tables, for example, was not required.

Table 18.2   Characterization of Caching Options at the Client Side

	CLASS-BASED CACHING	IMPLICIT CACHING
Concept	delegation	inheritance
Performance	+	+
Algorithmic simplicity	–	+–
Cache as component	+	+–

However, using pure object technology in each tier required new technology and products when the implementation started in 1995: the object-oriented programming languages C++ and Smalltalk, the heterogeneous CORBA products ORBIX and Distributed Smalltalk, and the object-oriented database system ObjectStore. Looking back there are pros and cons regarding these technologies. A couple of years ago Smalltalk definitely was the best object-oriented environment for graphical user interfaces, and it was easy to learn even if project members had no experience in object-orientation. However, the Java wave blocked the further development and spread of Smalltalk.

The future of object-oriented database systems looked promising in the middle of the 1990s. However, the breakthrough is still to occur, and the (object-) relational database systems are dominating the market. Because the vendors' growth was staying behind the expectations, some initial limitations of the products are still there. If an ObjectStore application has to be adapted to new requirements there is no tool to add new indexes or to change the clustering. Therefore, DaRT required a home-grown implementation of a dump-and-load utility to dump the whole database into ASCII files and reload them with the new indexes and/or changed clustering. Furthermore, the DaRT dump-and-load utility helped to overcome the schema evolution of Object-Store, which was error prone. Serious problems are the limited query language and index support; for example:

- It is not possible to have one index for a combination of attributes.
- The result of a query cannot be sorted as it would be possible with the ORDER BY clause of SQL.

On the other hand, in the production environment ObjectStore was absolutely stable and very fast. Hence using an object-oriented database for a new project should be considered very carefully. There is no guarantee how the vendors evolve. It is hard to compare object-orientation and relational tables considering the implementation and maintenance effort. Each technology has its drawbacks resulting in additional efforts that have to be scheduled for the project plan.

None of the DaRT developers were familiar with the CORBA technology in 1995, when the project started. Therefore, it was no surprise that technical difficulties arose in the very beginning. Furthermore the two heterogeneous products ORBIX and Distributed Smalltalk were new and immature when the development started. The interactions with the vendors were very helpful and all upcoming difficulties could be solved in a sufficient manner.

The development of DaRT required an effort of more than 60 person years. In such a large project the object technologies have been proved good both for the initial implementation and the succeeding maintenance.

PART

Seven

Conclusions

The chapters in this book have come from a wide range of application domains and uses, and we hope that we have provided you with many interesting examples on the use of Object Data Management. Overall, the experiences reported have been positive. Technological trends have meant that many pure object database vendors have had to respond to market forces in order to compete and survive, and some have moved quickly into EJB and XML (even to the point of changing the company name in one case). The pure vendors continue to provide solutions to some problems and we would expect this to continue. However, it seems that the major object-relational vendors slowly are coming into their own now and starting to offer strong support for object-orientation within their products. For many relational users, this provides an easier upgrade path, allowing them to build upon their existing investment and skills.

As far as standards are concerned, the ODMG effort appears to have settled into care and maintenance for C++ and Smalltalk, and the focus now has shifted entirely to Java. It is disappointing that many vendors have not implemented ODMG-compliant language bindings. Perhaps part of the reason for this has been that the standard suffers from a number of major technical problems and there have been no compliance-checking test suites to validate vendor claims. For performance benchmarking, a number of papers showed the importance of understanding object database product architectures and the trade-offs between alternative implementation techniques. This is also an important area for object-relational database vendors, as they continue to offer support for richer data and stronger object-oriented features.

CHAPTER
19

Conclusion

The object database research and development field reached its peek in the late 1980s. At that time object databases were positioned in the market as an alternative to classical relational database systems. People using object databases at that time were pioneers or more appropriately, early adopters.

Almost a decade later, the situation has changed radically. It is clear that object databases did not replace classical relational databases. Several real applications have been developed using object database and/or a variation of the object/relational database, or others. The distinction between a "pure" object database and an hybrid combination of relational and object databases has blurred. Companies come and go, change name and position in the market. The market and ultimately the customers dictate which technologies succeed for solving real business problems. It has become evident that classical business applications are still developed using conventional database systems, such as relational. Moreover, tons of legacy software will not go away that rapidly.

The market for object database systems have changed dramatically since the early days of their introduction. With the advent of the Web and the push of the Internet, new technologies have been proposed where databases find an important role. This is turning out to be a very important new market for object and object/relational databases. In particular the so called Web Application Servers market, where databases (both object and object/relational) are playing an increasingly important role. Web Application Servers are complex programs that "sit" in-between a Web application and a Web-server. For Web-applications such as On-line catalogs, B-To-B market places, Web Portals, to name a few, storing and retrieving complex multimedia information is vital. This is the kind of data object/relational databases handle well. For such applications, scalability and robustness is also crucial. As an example, Yahoo! has of today over 145 million subscribed users, hitting the Yahoo! site several times a day.

XML and the need to store XML documents in the Web, as already discussed in this book, is another important market. XML promises to be a very important technology for the Web. Object/relational databases are well suited to store and handle such documents. Since accessing the right information at the right time and delivering it to the right person is key on the Web, this is potentially a huge market.

Other technologies to watch are those that make business mobile. Here the idea is to bring the business anywhere you need it, as opposed to constrain business activities to the locations where office infrastructure exist. In a not so distant future it is likely that anyplace (be a waiting room of an airport or a freeway, etc.) could be networked and become part of the "virtual" cyber office.

If you then add the trend towards the Application Services Providers (ASP), that is, programs that can be rented from the Web, the equation is perfect. No need for an office, no need for software programs. All you is need is a device to access the Internet. There you'll find everything: a cyber office desk, software programs, and tools to be rented on demand.

But one thing will not go away, the need to access information! Since our society is basically built around information, and the Web/Internet is a powerful media to make information even more widely distributed, databases that handle complex, structured, and linked data do have a future. Perhaps databases will become commodity and you'll find them embedded in your "fridge" next time you buy one.

This market is so rapidly changing that it is difficult to keep up with all the evolutions. We would be delighted to hear from you, the reader. If you know of any new interesting advances in the field of object /relational database systems, in particular in relation with the Web, please write us at: Zicari@ltt.de and akmal@soi.city.ac.uk. We will appreciate receiving your input.

References

[Abdelguerfi 1998] Abdelguerfi, M., R. Ladner, K.B. Shaw, M.J. Chung, and R. Wilson. "VPF+: A Vector Product Format Extension Suitable for Three-Dimensional Modeling and Simulation." Technical Report NRL/FR/7441–98–9683. Stennis Space Center Mississippi: Naval Research Laboratory, 1998.

[Abiteboul 1991] Abiteboul, S., and A. Bonner. "Objects and Views." In *Proceedings of the ACM SIGMOD International Conference on Management of Data*, (Boulder, Colorado: ACM Press, May 1991), 238–247.

[Abiteboul 1998] Abiteboul, S., J. Widom, and T. Lahiri. "A Unified Approach for Querying Structured Data and XML." www.w3.org/TandS/QL/QL98/pp/serge/html.

[Abola 1987] Abola, E., F.C. Bernstein, S.H. Bryant, T.F. Koetzle, and J. Weng. "Protein Data Bank in Crystallographic Databases." *Information Content, Software Systems, Scientific Applications* (1987): 107–132.

[Agarwal 1995] Agarwal, S., C. Keene, and A.M. Keller. "Architecting Object Applications for High Performance with Relational Databases." *Proceedings of the OOPSLA 95 Workshop on Object Database Behavior, Benchmarks, and Performance*, Austin, Texas, October 1995.

[Agesen 1997] Agesen, O., S.N. Freund, and J.C. Mitchell. "Adding Type Parameterization to the Java Language." In *Proceedings of the ACM International Conference on Object-Oriented Programming Systems, Languages, and Applications (OOPSLA 97)*, (Atlanta, Georgia: ACM Press, October 1997), 49–65.

[Alagic 1997] Alagic, S. "The ODMG Object Model: Does it Make Sense?" In *Proceedings of the ACM International Conference on Object-Oriented Programming Systems,*

Languages, and Applications (OOPSLA 97), (Atlanta, Georgia: ACM Press, October 1997), 253–270.

[Albano 1985] Albano, A., L. Cardelli, and R. Orsini. "Galileo: A Strongly-Typed, Interactive Conceptual Language." *ACM Transactions on Database Systems (TODS)* 10,2 (1985): 230–260.

[Allen 1987] Allen, F.H., G. Bergerhoff, and R. Sievers. *Data Commission of the International Union of Crystallography*, Bonn/Cambridge/Chester: (1987): 107–132.

[Alpern 1999] Alpern, B., A. Cocchi, D. Lieber, M. Mergen, and V. Sarkar. "Jalapeno—a Compiler-Supported Java Virtual Machine for Servers." *ACM SIGPLAN 1999 Workshop on Compiler Support for System Software (WCSSS 99)*, Atlanta, Georgia, May 1999.

[Anderson 1990] Anderson, T.L., A.J. Berre, M. Mallison, H.H. Porter, and B. Schneider. "The HyperModel Benchmark." In *Proceedings of the European Conference on Extending Database Technology (EDBT 90)*, (Venice, Italy: Springer, March 1990), 317–333.

[Andrews 1987] Andrews, T., and H. Harris. "Combining Language and Database Advances in an Object-Oriented Development Environment." In *Proceedings of the ACM International Conference on Object-Oriented Programming Systems, Languages, and Applications (OOPSLA 87)*, (Orlando, Florida: ACM Press, October 1987), 430–440.

[Anfindsen 1999] Anfindsen O.J., and A. Danielsen. "Java Databases: an Evaluation." Telenor Research Report TR-1999–18. Kjeller, Norway: Telenor Research & Development, 1999.

[Angluin 1988] Angluin, D. "Queries and Concept Learning." *Machine Learning* 2 (1988): 319–342.

[Angster 1998] Angster, E. "Teaching Concepts in the Object-Oriented Field." In *Proceedings of the ECOOP 98 Workshop on Learning and Teaching Objects Successfully* (Brussels, Belgium: Springer, July 1998), 335–339.

[ANSI SQLJ] ANSI Specification X3.135.10–1998. "Information Technology—Database Languages—SQL—Part 10—Object Language Bindings (SQL/OLB)." www.ansi.org.

[Apostrophe 1996] Apostrophe Software. "Apostrophe Software Reviews." Apostrophe Software, Canada. www.aposoft.com/Reviews.html.

[Atkinson 1989] Atkinson, M., F. Bancilhon, D. DeWitt, K. Dittrich, D. Maier, and S. Zdonik. "The Object-Oriented Database System Manifesto." In *Proceedings of the First International Conference on Deductive and Object-Oriented Databases*, Kyoto, Japan: North-Holland/Elsevier Science Publishers, 1989.

[Atkinson 1995] Atkinson, M.P., and R. Morrison. "Orthogonally Persistent Systems." *The VLDB Journal* 4,3 (1995): 319–402.

[Atkinson 1996] Atkinson M.P., M.J. Jordan, L. Daynés, and S. Spence. "Design Issues for Persistent Java: A Type-Safe, Object-Oriented Orthogonally Persistent System." In *Proceedings of the International Workshop on Persistent Object Systems (POS-7)*, (Cape May, New Jersey: Morgan Kaufmann Publishers, May 1996), 33–47.

[Attwood 1999] Attwood, T.K., and D.J. Parry-Smith. *Introduction to Bioinformatics*, Harlow: Addison-Wesley Longman, 1999.

[Australian Bureau of Statistics] Australian Bureau of Statistics. www.abs.gov.au.

[Baker 1997] Baker, S. *CORBA Distributed Objects*, Reading, Massachusetts: Addison-Wesley, 1997.

[Bancilhon 1992] Bancilhon, F., C. Delobel, and P. Kanellakis (eds.). *Building an Object-Oriented Database System: The Story of O2*, San Mateo, California: Morgan Kaufmann Publishers, 1992.

[Barrett 1996] Barrett, D.J., A. Kaplan, and J.C. Wileden. "Automated Support for Seamless Inter-Operability in Polylingual Software Systems." *The Fourth Symposium on the Foundations of Software Engineering*, San Francisco, California, October 1996.

[Barry 1998] Barry, D., and S. Torsten. "Solving the Java Object Storage Problem." *IEEE Computer* 31,11 (1998): 33–40.

[Barsalou 1990] Barsalou, T., and G. Wiederhold. "Complex Objects for Relational Databases." *Computer Aided Design* 22,8 (1990).

[Barsalou 1991] Barsalou, T., N. Siambela, A.M. Keller, and G. Wiederhold. "Updating Relational Databases through Object-Based Views." In *Proceedings of the ACM SIGMOD International Conference on Management of Data* (Denver, COLORADO: ACM Press, May 1991), 248–257.

[Basalaj 1999] Basalaj, W., and K. Eilbeck. "Straight-Line Drawings of Protein Interactions." In *Proceedings of Graph Drawing 99*, 1999.

[Basu 1997a] Basu, J., A.M. Keller, and M. Poess. "Centralized versus Distributed Index Management in a Page Server OODBMS." In *Proceedings of the First East-European Symposium on Advances in Databases and Information Systems (ADBIS 97)*, (St. Petersburg, Russia,September 1997), 162–169.

[Basu 1997b] Basu, J., A.M. Keller, and M. Poess. "Performance Evaluation of Centralized and Distributed Index Schemes for a Page Server OODBMS." Technical Note, CS-TN-97–55. Stanford University: Computer Science Department, March 1997.

[Basu 1997c] Basu, J., M. Poess, and A.M. Keller. "High Performance and Scalability through Associative Client-Side Caching." *Seventh International Workshop on High Performance Transaction Systems*, Pacific Grove, California, September 1997.

[Basu 1997d] Basu, J., M. Poess, and A.M. Keller. "Performance Analysis of an Associative Caching Scheme for Client-Server Databases." Technical Note, STAN-CS-TN-97–61. Stanford University: Computer Science Department, September 1997.

[Batory 1979] Batory, D.S. "On Searching Transposed Files." *ACM Transactions on Database Systems (TODS)* 4,4 (1979): 531–544.

[Bernstein 1977] Bernstein, F.C., T.F. Koetzle, G.J.B. Williams, E.F. Meyer Jr., M.D. Brice, J.R. Rodgers, O. Kennard, T. Shimanouchi, and M. Tasumi. "The Protein Data Bank: A Computer-Based Archival File for Macromolecular Structures." *Journal of Molecular Biology* 112 (1977): 535–542.

[Bertino 1993] Bertino, E., and L. Martino. *Object-Oriented Database Systems: Concepts and Architectures*, Wokingham: Addison-Wesley, 1993.

[Bjørge 1999] Bjørge, E. "Transition from Relational DBMS to Object DBMS: A Research of DBMS Performance, Advantages and Transition Costs." Master's Degree Thesis. University of Bergen, Norway: Department of Information Science, March 1999. (In Norwegian)

[Blackburn 1998] Blackburn, S.M. "Persistent Store Interface: A Foundation for Scalable Persistent System Design." Ph.D. Thesis. Canberra, Australia: Australian National University, 1998.

[Blackburn 1998a] Blackburn, S.M., and J.N. Zigman. "Concurrency—The Fly in the Ointment?" *Advances in Persistent Object Systems: Third International Workshop on Persistence and Java*, Tiburon, California, September 1998.

[Blake 1994] Blake, G.E., M.P. Consens, P. Kilpeläinen, P. Larson, T. Snider, and F.Wm. Tompa. "Text / Relational Database Management Systems: Harmonizing SQL and SGML." In *Proceedings of First International Conference on Applications of Databases (ADB 94)*, (Vadstena, Sweden: Springer, June 1994), 267–280.

[Blakeley 1989] Blakeley, J.A., N. Coburn, and P. Larson. "Updating Derived Relations: Detecting Irrelevant and Autonomously Computable Updates." *ACM Transactions on Database Systems (TODS)* 14,3 (1989): 369–400.

[Blundell 1987] Blundell, T.L., B.L. Sibanda, M.J.E. Sternberg, and J.M. Thornton,. "Knowledge-Based Prediction of Protein Structures and the Design of Novel Molecules." *Nature* 326,6111 (1987): 347–352.

[Blundell 1988] Blundell, T., D. Carney, S. Gardner, F. Hayes, B. Howlin, T. Hubbard, J. Overington, D.A. Singh, B.L. Sibanda, and M. Sutcliffe, "Knowledge-Based Protein Modelling and Design." *European Journal of Biochemistry*172 (1988): 513–520.

[Böcker 1990] Böcker, H.-D., and J. Herczeg. "What Tracers Are Made of." In *Proceedings of ACM International Conference on Object-Oriented Programming Systems, Languages, and Applications (OOPSLA 90)*, (Ottawa, Canada: ACM Press, October 1990), 88–99.

[Böhm 1997] Böhm, K., K. Aberer, E.J. Neuhold, and X. Yang. "Structured Document Storage and Refined Declarative and Navigational Access Mechanisms in HyperStorM." *The VLDB Journal* 6,4 (1997): 296–311.

[Bokowski 1998] Bokowski, B., and M. Dahm. "Poor Man's Genericity for Java." *Proceedings of JIT '98*, Frankfurt am Main, Germany: Springer, November 1998.

[Booch 1991] Booch, G. *Object-Oriented Design with Applications*, Redwood City, California: Benjamin/Cummings, 1991.

[Booch 1999] Booch, G., J. Rumbaugh, and I. Jacobson. *The Unified Modeling Language User Guide*, Reading, Massachusetts: Addison-Wesley, 1999.

[Borstler 1998] Borstler, J. "Learning and Teaching Objects Successfully—Workshop Summary." In *Proceedings of the ECOOP 98 Workshop on Learning and Teaching Objects Successfully* (Brussels, Belgium: Springer, July 1998), 333–334.

[Bray 1998] Bray, T., J. Paoli, and S. Sperberg-McQueen. "Extensible Markup Language (XML) 1.0." W3C Recommendation, 1998.

[Bretl 1989] Bretl, R., D. Maier, A. Otis, J. Penney, B. Schuchardt, J. Stein, E. Williams, and M. Williams. "The GemStone Data Management System." *Object-Oriented Concepts, Databases and Applications*, W. Kim and F. Lochovsky (eds.). New York: ACM Press, 1989.

[Brodsky 2000] Brodsky, S. "XMI Production of XML Schema RFP." OMG Public Documents, 2000.

[Brown 1996] Brown, K.P., M.J. Carey, and M. Livny. "Goal-Oriented Buffer Management Revisited." In *Proceedings of the ACM SIGMOD International Conference on Management of Data* (Montreal, Quebec, Canada: ACM Press, June 1996), 353–364.

[Brown 1998] Brown, L.J., M.P. Consens, I.J. Davis, C.R. Palmer, and F.Wm. Tompa. "A Structured Text ADT for Object-Relational Databases." *Journal on Theory and Practice of Object Systems* 4,4 (1998): 227–244.

[Burkhardt 1995] Burkhardt. R. *UML – Unified Modeling Language*. Bonn: Addison-Wesley, 1995.

[Burkowski 1991] Burkowski, F.J. "An Algebra for Hierarchically Organized Text-Dominated Databases." University of Waterloo, Canada: Department of Computer Science, 1991.

[Cao 1997] Cao, P., and S. Irani. "Cost-Aware WWW Proxy Caching Algorithms." In *Proceedings of the 1997 USENIX Symposium on Internet Technology and Systems* (December 1997): 193–206.

[Carey 1991] Carey, M., M. Franklin, M. Livny, and E. Shekita. "Data Caching Tradeoffs in Client-Server DBMS Architecture." In *Proceedings of the ACM SIGMOD International Conference on Management of Data* (Denver, COLORADO: ACM Press, May 1991), 357–366.

[Carey 1993] Carey, M.J., D.J. DeWitt, and J.F. Naughton. "The 007 Benchmark." In *Proceedings of the ACM SIGMOD International Conference on Management of Data* (Washington, DC: ACM Press, May 1993), 12–21.

[Carey 1994] Carey, M.J., M.J. Franklin, and M. Zaharioudakis. "Fine-Grained Sharing in a Page Server OODBMS." In *Proceedings of the ACM SIGMOD International Conference on Management of Data* (Washington, DC: ACM Press, May 1994), 359–370.

[Carey 1994a] Carey, M.J., D.J. DeWitt, M.J. Franklin, N.E. Hall, M.L. McAuliffe, J.F. Naughton, D.T. Schuh, M.H. Solomon, C.K. Tan, O.G. Tsatalos, and S.J. White. "Shoring up Persistent Applications." In *Proceedings on the ACM SIGMOD International Conference on Management of Data* (Minneapolis, Minnesota: ACM Press, May 1994), 383–394.

[Carey 1996] Carey, M.J., and D.J DeWitt. "Of Objects and Databases: A Decade of Turmoil." In *Proceedings of the International Conference on Very Large Data Bases (VLDB 96)*, (Mumbai, India: Morgan Kaufmann Publishers, September 1996), 3–14.

[Cattell 1991] Cattell, R.G.G. *Object Data Management: Object- Oriented and Extended Relational Systems.* Reading, Massachusetts: Addison-Wesley, 1991.

[Cattell 1994] Cattell, R.G.G. *Object Data Management: Object- Oriented and Extended Relational Systems.* Reading, Massachusetts: Addison-Wesley, 1994.

[Cattell 1996] Cattell, R.G.G. (ed.). *The Object Database Standard: ODMG-93.* San Francisco, California: Morgan Kaufmann Publishers, 1996.

[Cattell 1997] Cattell R.G.G., D. Barry, D. Bartels, M. Berler, J. Eastman, S. Gamerman, D. Jordan, A. Springer, H. Strickland, and D. Wade. *The Object Database Standard: ODMG 2.0,* San Francisco, California: Morgan Kaufmann Publishers, 1997.

[Cattell 1999] Cattell, R.G.G. (ed.). *The Object Data Standard: ODMG 3.0.,* San Francisco, California: Morgan Kaufmann Publishers, 1999.

[Cattell 2000] Cattell, R.G.G. (ed.). *The Object Data Standard: ODMG 3.0, ,* San Francisco, California: Morgan Kaufmann Publishers, 2000.

[Chamberlin 1975] Chamberlin, D.D., J.N. Gray, and I.L. Traiger. "Views, Authorization, and Locking in a Relational Data Base System." In *Proceedings of the National Computer Conference 1975* 44, AFIPS Press (1975): 425–430.

[Chang 1989] Chang, E.E. "Effective Clustering and Buffering in an Object-Oriented Database System." Ph.D. Thesis. UCB/CSD 89/515. University of California. Berkley, California: Department of Electrical Engineering and Computer Science, 1989.

[Chaudhri 1995] Chaudhri, A.B. "An Annotated Bibliography of Benchmarks for Object Databases." *SIGMOD Record* 24,1 (1995): 50–57.

[Cheung 1994] Cheung S.C., J. Kramer. "An Integrated Method for Effective Behavior Analysis of Distributed Systems." In *Proceedings of the 16th International Conference on*

Software Engineering (Sorrento, Italy: IEEE Computer Society Press, May 1994), 309–320.

[Chung 1999] Chung, M., R. Wilson, K. Shaw, and M. Cobb. "Distributing Mapping Objects with the Geospatial Information Database." In *Proceedings of the First International Symposium on Distributed Objects and Applications* (September 1999): 77–87.

[CIM] "CIM standards." Distributed Management Task Force (DMTF), www.dmtf.org/spec/cims.html.

[Clark 1990] Clark, D.A., G.J. Barton, and C.J. Rawlings. "A Knowledge-Based Architecture for Protein Analysis and Structure Prediction." *Journal of Molecular Graphics* 8 (1990): 94–107.

[Coad 1991] Coad, P., and E. Yourdon. *Object-Oriented Analysis*, Englewood Cliffs, New Jersey: Yourdon Press, Computing Series, Prentice Hall, 1991.

[Codd 1970] Codd, E.F. "A Relational Model for Large Shared Databanks." *Communications of the ACM* 13,6 (1970): 377–387.

[Colbert 1994] Colbert, E. "Abstract Better and Enjoy Life." *Journal of Object-Oriented Programming*, 7,1 (1994).

[Cooper 1997] Cooper, R. *Object databases: An ODMG Approach*, International Thomson Computer Press, 1997.

[Courteau 1991] Courteau, J. "Genome Databases." *Science* 254 (1991): 201–215.

[CSE494DB 2000] CSE494DB Course Web Site. Arizona State University: Department of Computer Science and Engineering, Spring 2000. www.eas.asu.edu/-cse494db.

[Danielsen 1999] Danielsen, A. "An Evaluation of Two Strategies on Object Persistence; Evaluating PJama and Versant." M.Sc. Thesis, University of Oslo, Norway: Department of Informatics, 1999.

[De Ferreira Rezende 1998] De Ferreira Rezende, F., and K. Hergula. "The Heterogeneity Problem and Middleware Technology: Experiments with and Performance of Database Gateways." In *Proceedings of the International Conference on Very Large Data Bases (VLDB 98)*, (New York, New York: Morgan Kaufmann Publishers, August 1998), 146–157.

[Delis 1992] Delis, A., and N. Roussopoulos. "Performance and Scalability of Client-Server Database Architectures." In *Proceedings of the International Conference on Very Large Data Bases (VLDB 92)*, (Vancouver, British Columbia, Canada: Morgan Kaufmann Publishers, August 1992), 610–623.

[DeWitt 1990] DeWitt, D.J., D. Maier, P. Futtersack, and F. Velez. "A Study of Three Alternative Workstation-Server Architectures for Object-Oriented Database Systems." In *Proceedings of the International Conference on Very Large Data Bases (VLDB 90)*, Brisbane, Australia: Morgan Kaufmann Publishers, August 1990.

[DoD 1996] Department of Defense. "Interface Standard for Vector Product Format." MIL-STD 2407, 28 June 1996.

[DOOR Esprit Project 1998] DOOR Esprit Project. "Lessons Learned." www.dbis.informatik.uni-frankfurt.de/~door.

[Duhl 1988] Duhl, J., and C. Damon. "A Performance Comparison of Object and Relational Databases Using the Sun Benchmark." In *Proceedings of the ACM International Conference on Object-Oriented Programming Systems, Languages, and Applications (OOPSLA 88)*, (San Diego, California: ACM Press, September 1988), 153–163.

[Dunham 1994] Dunham, I., R. Durbin, J.T. Mieg, and D.R. Bentley. "Physical Mapping Projects and ACEDB." *Guide to Human Genome Computing*, M.J. Bishop (ed.). Academic Press, 1994.

[Durbin 1991] Durbin, R., and J.T. Mieg. "A C.elegans Database." 1991. www.sanger.ac.uk/Software/Acedb.

[Eilbeck 1999] Eilbeck, K., A. Brass, N.W. Paton, and C. Hodgman. "INTERACT: An Object-Oriented Protein Interaction Database." In *Proceedings of the 7th International Conference on Intelligent Systems for Molecular Biology (ISMB)*, AAAI Press (1999): 87–94.

[Elmasri 1989] Elmasri, R., and S.B. Navathe. *Fundamentals of Database Systems*. Redwood City, California: Benjamin/Cummings, 1989.

[Elmasri 2000] Elmasri, R., and S. Navathe. *Fundamentals of Database Systems*. 3rd Edition. Redwood City, California: Benjamin/Cummings, 2000.

[EMBL 2000] www.ebi.ac.uk/embl/index.html.

[Embley 1997] Embley, D. *Object Database Development: Concepts and Principles*, Reading, Massachusetts: Addison-Wesley, 1997.

[Fernandez 1998] Fernandez, A., and G. Rossi. "An Effective Approach to Learning Object-Oriented Technology." In *Proceedings of the ECOOP 98 Workshop on Learning and Teaching Objects Successfully* (Brussels, Belgium: Springer, July 1998), 344–349.

[Ferrandina 1995] Ferrandina, F., T. Meyer, R. Zicari, G. Ferran, and J. Madec. "Schema and Database Evolution in the O_2 Object Database System." In *Proceedings of the International Conference on Very Large Data Bases (VLDB 95)*, (Zurich, Switzerland: Morgan Kaufmann Publishers, September 1995), 170–181.

[Fishman 1989] Fishman, D., *et al.* "Overview of the Iris DBMS." *Object-Oriented Concepts, Databases and Applications*, W. Kim and F. Lochovsky (eds.). New York: ACM Press, 1989.

[Flatscher 2000] Flatscher, R. "Metamodeling in EIA/CDIF – Meta-Metamodel and Metamodels." *Information ModelModeling in the New Millennium*, M. Rossi and K. Siau (eds.). Idea Group Publishing, 2000.

[Florescu] Florescu, D., G. Gardarin, H. Laude, C. Campanaro, F. Sha. MIRO-WEB (EP 25208) Deliverable (D6–1/1): JAVA API Specification.

[Fortier 1999] Fortier, P. *SQL 3. Implementing the SQL Foundation Standard*, New York: McGraw Hill, 1999.

[Fowler 1997] Fowler, M., and K. Scott. *UML Distilled: Applying the Standard Object Modeling Language,* Harlow: Addison-Wesley, 1997.

[Frank 1997] Frank H., and J. Eder. "Integration of Behavior Models." In *Proceedings of the ER97 Workshop on Behavioral Models and Design Transformations: Issues and Opportunities in Conceptual ModelModeling*, Los Angeles, California, November 1997.

[Franklin 1993] Franklin, M.J., M.J. Carey, and M. Livny. "Local Disk Caching for Client-Server Database Systems." In *Proceedings of the International Conference on Very Large Data Bases (VLDB 93)*, (Dublin, Ireland: Morgan Kaufmann Publishers, August 1993), 641–654.

[Frederiks 1997] Frederiks P.J.M., A.H.M. ter Hofstede, and E. Lippe. "A Unifying Framework for Conceptual Data Modelmodeling Concepts." *International Journal of Information and Software Technology* 39,1 (1997): 15–25.

[Frenkel 1991] Frenkel, K.A. "The Human Genome Project and Informatics." *Communication of the ACM* 34,11 (1991): 40–51.

[Frishman 1998] Frishman, D., K. Heumann, A. Lesk, and H. Mewes. "Comprehensive, Comprehensible, Distributed, and Intelligent Databases: Current Status." *Bioinformatics* 14,7 (1998): 551–561.

[Futtersack 1997] Futtersack, P., C. Espert, and D. Bolf. "Good Performances for an SGML Object Database System." In *Proceedings of the SGML 97 Conference*, Boston, Massachusetts, 1997.

[Gancarski 1995] Gancarski, S., G. Jomier, and M. Zamfiroiu. "A Framework for the Manipulation of a Multiversion Database." In *Proceedings of the DEXA 95 Workshop* (San Mateo, California: OMNIPRESS, 1995), 247–256.

[Garcia-Molina 1997] Garcia-Molina H., Y. Papakonstantinou, D. Quass, A. Rajaraman, Y. Sagiv, J. Ullman, V. Vassalos, and J. Widom. "The TSIMMIS Approach to Mediation: Data Models and Languages." *Journal of Intelligent Information Systems* 8,2 (March/April 1997): 117–132.

[Gasarch 1992] Gasarch, W.I., and C.H. Smith. "Learning via Queries." *Journal of the ACM* 39,3 (1992): 649–674.

[GeoKnowledge 2000] www.geoknowledge.com/.

[Georgalas 1998] Georgalas N. "Enterprise Data and Knowledge Integration Using Repository Technology." M.Phil. Thesis. UMIST, Manchester, UK: Information System Engineering Group, Department of Computation, 1998. www.labs.bt.com/people/georgan.

[Georgalas 1999a] Georgalas N. "A Framework That Uses Repositories for Information Systems and Knowledge Integration." In *Proceedings of the ASSET 99 Symposium on Application-Specific Systems and Software Engineering Technology*, Dallas, Texas: IEEE Computer Society Press, March 1999.

[Georgalas 1999b] Georgalas N. "The Role of Repositories in Integrating Information Systems and Enterprise Knowledge." In *Proceedings of the UKAIS 99 Conference of the UK Academy for Information Systems in "Information Systems: The Next Generation"*, York, UK: McGraw Hill, April 1999.

[Georgalas 1999c] Georgalas N. "Policy-Driven Customisation of Personalised Services." In *Proceedings of Policy Workshop 1999*, Bristol, UK: HP-Laboratories, November 1999. www-dse.doc.ic.ac.uk/policy-99/program.html.

[Georgalas 2000] Georgalas N. "An Information Management Environment Based on the Model of Object Primitives." *Information ModelModeling in the New Millennium*, M. Rossi and K. Siau (eds.). Idea Group Publishing, 2000.

[Ghosh 1998] Ghosh, D. "OOTFD (Object-Oriented Transcription Factors Database): An Object-Oriented Successor to TFD." *Nucleic Acids Research* 26 (1998): 360–362.

[Ghosh 1999] Ghosh, D. "Object-Oriented Transcription Factors Database (ooTFD)." *Nucleic Acids Research* 27,1 (1999): 315–317.

[Girow 1997] Girow, A. "Limitations of Object Data Models." *Object Currents* 2,1. (1997).

[Goldberg 1992] Goldberg, A., and D. Robson. *Smalltalk-80: The Language and Its Implementation*, Reading, Massachusetts: Addison-Wesley, 1983.

[Goldman 1999] , R., J. McHugh, and J. Widom. "From Semistructured Data to XML: Migrating the Lore Data Model and Query Language." In *Proceedings of WebDB* (1999): 25–30.

[Goodman 1995] Goodman, N. "An Object-Oriented DBMS War Story: Developing a Genome Mapping Database in C++." *Modern Database Systems*, W. Kim (ed.). Reading, Massachusetts: Addison-Wesley, 1995.

[Gracy 1991] Gracy, J., E. Mephu Nguifo, L. Chiche, and J. Sallantin. "New Methods for Alignment of Weakly Homologous Proteins. Part I: Improved Alignment Using Structural Information," In *Proceedings of Pred. and Exp. 3D Struct. of Hom. Prot.*, Braunschweig, Germany, 1991.

[Gracy 1993] Gracy, J., L. Chiche, and J. Sallantin. "A Modular Learning Environment for Protein Modeling." In *Proceedings of the First International Conference on Intelligent Systems for Molecular Biology*, AAAI Press (1993): 145–153.

[Gray 1990] Gray, P.M.D., N.W. Paton, G.J.L. Kemp, and J.E. Fothergill. "An Object-Oriented Database for Protein Structure Analysis." *Protein Engineering* 4,3 (1990): 235–243.

[Gray 1993] Gray, J., and A. Reuter. *Transaction Processing: Concepts and Techniques*, San Francisco, California: Morgan Kaufmann Publishers, 1993.

[Gribskov 1987] Gribskov, M., A.D McLachlan, and D. Eisenberg, "Profile Analysis: Detection of Distantly Related Protein." In *Proceedings of National Academic Sciences*, USA, 1987.

[Griffioen 1994] Griffioen, J., and R. Appleton. "Reducing File System Latency Using a Predictive Approach." *USENIX, Summer 1994*, 197–207.

[Grimes 1998] Grimes, S. "Modeling Object/Relational Databases." *DBMS Magazine*, April 1998.

[Gupta 1993] Gupta, A., I.S. Mumick, and V.S. Subrahmanian. "Maintaining Views Incrementally." In *Proceedings of the ACM SIGMOD International Conference on Management of Data* (Washington, DC: ACM Press, May 1993), 157–166.

[Hammer 1997] Hammer, J., M. Breunig, H. Garcia-Molina, S. Nestorov, V. Vassalos, and R. Yerneni. "Template-Based Wrappers in the TSIMMIS System." In *Proceedings of the ACM SIGMOD International Conference on Management of Data* (Tucson, AZ: ACM Press, May 1997), 532–535.

[Hammer 1997a] Hammer, J., J. McHugh, and H. Garcia-Molina. "Semistructured Data: The TSIMMIS Experience." In *Proceedings of the First East-European Symposium on Advances in Databases and Information Systems (ADBIS 97)* (St. Petersburg, Russia, September 1997), 1–8.

[Härder 1983] Härder, T., and A. Reuter. "Principles of Transaction-Oriented Database Recovery." *ACM Computing Surveys* 15,4 (1983): 287–317.

[Harger 1998] Harger, C., *et al.* "The Genome DataBase (GSDB): Improving Data Quality and Data Access." *Nucleic Acids Research* 26(1998): 21–26.

[Hayes-Roth 1984] Hayes-Roth, B. "BB1: An Architecture for Blackboard Systems That Control, Explain and Learn about Their Own Behavior." Technical Report STAN-CS-84–1034 Stanford University, 1984.

[Hohenstein 1997] Hohenstein, U., V. Plesser, and R. Heller. "Evaluating the Performance of Object-Oriented Database Systems by Means of a Concrete Application." In *Proceedings of the DEXA 97 Workshop on Object-Oriented Database Systems* (Toulouse Cedex, France, September 1997), 496–501.

[Hohlfeld 1998] Hohlfeld, M., and B. Yee. "How to Migrate Agents." Technical Report, University of California at San Diego, 1998.

[Hosking 1998] Hosking, A., N. Nystrom, Q. Cutts, and K. Brahnmath. "Optimizing the Read and Write Barriers for Orthogonal Persistence." In *Advances in Persistent Object Systems: Proceedings of the International Workshop on Persistent Object Systems (POS 8)*, (Tiburon, California: Morgan Kaufmann Publishers, August-September 1998), 37–50.

[Huck 1999] Huck, G., and I. Macherius. "GMD-IPSI XQL Engine V 1.0.2." http://xml.darmstadt.gmd.de/xql/.

[Huysmans 1991] Huysmans, M., J. Richelle, and S.J. Wodak. "SESAM: A Relational Database for Structure and Sequence of Macromolecules." *Proteins* 11 (1991): 59–76.

[IETF] "Active IETF Working Groups: Policy Framework (Policy) – Charter." www.ietf.org/html.charters/policy-charter.html.

[INRIA 1999] INRIA. "Object Driver, an Open Object Wrapper Dedicated to Relational Databases." www.inria.fr/cermics/dbteam/ObjectDriver

[JDBC Spec] JDBC 1.2 API Specification. http://java.sun.com/products/jdbc/.

[JDBC20 Ext] JDBC 2.0 API Specification. http://java.sun.com/products/jdbc/.

[Jordan 1997] Jordan, D. *C++ Object-Oriented Databases: Programming with ODMG Standard*, Reading, Massachusetts: Addison-Wesley, 1997.

[Kanehisa 1984] Kanehisa, M., J.W. Fickett, and W.B. Goad. "A Relational Database System for the Maintenance and Verification of the Alamos Sequences Library." *Nucleic Acids Research* 12,1 (1984): 149–158.

[Kanne 1999] Kanne, C.-C., and G. Moerkotte. "Efficient Storage of XML Data." Unpublished manuscript. University of Mannheim, 1999.

[Kaplan 1994] Kaplan, A., and J. Wileden. "Conch: Experimenting with Enhanced Name Management for Persistent Object Systems." In *Proceedings of the International Workshop on Persistent Object Systems (POS 6)*, (Tarascon, Provence, France, September 1994), 318–331.

[Kaplan 1995] Kaplan, A., and J.C. Wileden. "Formalization and Application of a Unifying Model for Name Management." In *The Third Symposium on the Foundations of Software Engineering*, Washington DC, September 1995.

[Kaplan 1996a] Kaplan, A., and J.C. Wileden. "Toward Painless Polylingual Persistence." In *Proceedings of the International Workshop on Persistent Object Systems (POS 7)*, (Cape May, New Jersey: Morgan Kaufmann Publishers, May 1996), 11–22.

[Kaplan 1996b] Kaplan, A., G.A. Myrestrand, J.V.E. Ridgway, and J.C. Wileden. "Our Spin on Persistent Java: The JavaSpin Approach." In *Proceedings of the First International Workshop on Persistence and Java*, , Scotland: Drymen, September 1996.

[Kaplan 1996c] Kaplan, A. "Name Management: Models, Mechanisms and Applications." Ph.D. Thesis, University of Massachusetts. Amherst, Massachusetts, May 1996.

[Kaplan 1998] Kaplan, A., J.V.E. Ridgway, and J.C. Wileden. "Why IDLs Are Not Ideal." In *Proceedings of the 9th IEEE International Workshop on Software Specification and Design*, Japan: Ise-Shima, April 1998.

[Kato 1992] Kato, K., and T. Masuda. "Persistent Caching: An Implementation Technique for Complex Objects with Object Identity." *IEEE Transactions on Software Engineering* 18,7 (1992): 631–645.

[Katz 1987] Katz, R.H., R. Bhateja, E. Chang, D. Gedye, and V. Trijanto. "Design Version Management." *IEEE DESIGN and TEST* (1987): 12–22.

[Kelemen 1998] Kelemen, B. "A Newcomer's Thoughts about Responsibility Distribution." In *Proceedings of the ECOOP 98 Workshop on Learning and Teaching Objects Successfully* (Brussels, Belgium: Springer, July 1998), 340–343.

[Keller 1986] Keller, A.M. "Choosing a View Update Translator by Dialog at View Definition Time." In *Proceedings of the International Conference on Very Large Data Bases (VLDB 86)*, Kyoto, Japan: Morgan Kaufmann Publishers, August 1986.

[Keller 1993] Keller, A.M., and C. Hamon. "A C++ Binding for Penguin: A System for Data Sharing among Heterogeneous Object Models." In *Proceedings of the 4th International Conference on Foundations of Data Organization and Algorithms* (Evanston, IL, October 1993), 215–230.

[Keller 1993a] Keller, A.M., R. Jensen, and S. Agarwal. "Persistence Software: Bridging Object-Oriented Programming and Relational Databases." In *Proceedings of the ACM SIGMOD International Conference on Management of Data* (Washington DC: ACM Press, May 1993), 523–528.

[Keller 1995] Keller, A.M., and P. Turner. "Migrating to Object Data Management." In *Proceedings of the OOPSLA 95 Workshop on Legacy Systems and Object Technology*, Austin, Texas: October 1995.

[Keller 1996] Keller, A.M., and J. Basu. "A Predicate-Based Caching Scheme for Client-Server Database Architectures." *The VLDB Journal* 5,1 (1996): 35–47.

[Kemp 1991] Kemp, G.J.L. "Protein Modelling: A Design Application of an Object-Oriented Database." Research Report AUCS/TR9102, University of Aberdeen, Scotland, 1991.

[Kemper 1993] Kemper, A., and D. Kossmann. "Adaptable Pointer Swizzling Strategies in Object Bases." In *Proceedings of the International Conference on Data Engineering (ICDE 93)*, (Vienna, Austria: IEEE Computer Society Press, April 1993), 152–162.

[Kent 1989] Kent, W. "An Overview of the Versioning Problem." In *Proceedings of the ACM SIGMOD International Conference on Management of Data* (Portland, OR: ACM Press, May-June 1989), 5–7.

[Kim 1990] Kim, W. *Introduction to Object-Oriented Databases*. Cambridge, Massachusetts: MIT Press, 1990.

[Kim 1992] Kim, W. *Introduction to Object-Oriented Databases*. Cambridge, Massachusetts: MIT Press, 1992.

[Kim 1994]: Kim, W. "Observations on the ODMG-93 Proposal for an Object-Oriented Database Language." www.acm.org/sigmod/record/issues/9403/Kim.txt.

[Knudsen 1988] Knudsen, J.~L., and O. Lehrmann Madsen. "Teaching Object-Oriented Programming is More Than Teaching Object-Oriented Programming Languages." In *Proceedings of the European Conference on Object-Oriented Programming (ECOOP 88)*, (Oslo, Norway: Springer, August 1988), 21–40.

[Kosky 1998] Kosky, A., I.M.A. Chen, V.M. Markowitz, and E. Szeto. "Exploring Heterogeneous Biological Databases: Tools and Applications." In *Proceedings of the International Conference on Extending Database Technology (EDBT 98)*, (Valencia, Spain: Springer, March 1998), 499–513.

[Krause 1999] Krause, A., P. Nicodème, E. Bornberg-Bauer, M. Rehmsmeier, and M. Vingron. "WWW Access to the SYSTERS Protein Sequence Cluster Set." *Bioinformatics* 15,3 (1999): 262–263.

[Kutlu 1998] Kutlu, G., J. Eliot, and B Moss. "Exploiting Reflection to Add Persistence and Query Optimization to a Statically Typed Object-Oriented Language." In

Advances in Persistent Object Systems: Proceedings of the International Workshop on Persistent Object Systems (POS 8), (Tiburon, California: Morgan Kaufmann Publishers, August-September 1998), 123–135.

[Lamb 1991] Lamb, C., G. Landis, J. Orenstein, and D. Weinreb. "The ObjectStore Database System." *Communications of the ACM* 34,10 (1991): 34–49.

[Larsen 1992] Larsen, A.B. "A Test Evaluation Procedure for Object-Oriented and Relation Database Management Systems." Master's Degree Thesis. Institute of Informatics, University of Oslo, Norway, 1992.

[Lausen 1997] Lausen G., and G. Vossen. *Models and Languages of Object-Oriented Databases*, Addison-Wesley, 1998.

[Law 1990] Law, K.H., G. Wiederhold, T. Barsalou, N. Sambela, W. Sujansky, and D. Zingmond. "Managing Design Objects in a Sharable Relational Framework." *ASME Meeting*, Boston, Massachusetts, August 1990.

[Lee 1994] Lee, B.S., and G. Wiederhold. "Efficiently Instantiating View-Objects from Remote Relational Databases." *The VLDB Journal* 3,3 (1994): 289–323.

[Lee 1999] Lee, S.-W., and H.-J. Kim. "Object Versioning in an ODMG-Compliant Object Database System." *Software Practice and Experience* 5,29 (1999): 479–500.

[Lieuwen 1999] Lieuwen, D., and N. Gehani. "Versions in ODE: Implementation and Experiences." *Software Practice and Experience* 5,29 (1999): 397–416.

[Lippman 1991] Lippman, S.B. *The C++ Primer*. Reading, Massachusetts: Addison-Wesley, 1991.

[Lobo 1999] Lobo, J., R. Bhatia, and S. Naqvi. "A Policy Description Language." In *Proceedings of AAAI 99 Conference* (Orlando, Florida: AAAI Press, July 1999), 291–298.

[Loomis 1995] Loomis, M.E.S. *Object databases: The Essentials*, Reading, Massachusetts: Addison-Wesley, 1995.

[Maier 1997] Maier, C. "Component Event Diagram a Hierarchical Dynamic Technique to Model Distributed Systems." December 1997. www.fast.de/Projekte/forsoft/component/componentDiagramMain.html.

[Maier 1998] Maier, D. "Database Desiderata for an XML Query Language." www.w3.org/TandS/QL/QL98/pp/maier.html.

[Manola 1994] Manola, F. "An Evaluation of Object-Oriented DBMS Developments." Technical Report No. TR-0263–08–94–165. Waltham, Massachusetts: GTE Laboratories Inc., 1994.

[Marquez 2000] Marquez, A., J.N. Zigman, and S.M. Blackburn. "Fast Portable Orthogonally Persistent Java." *Software Practice and Experience*. To appear.

[Marriot 1997] Marriott, D.A. "Policy Service for Distributed Systems." Ph.D. Thesis, Dept of Computing, Imperial College, London, UK, June 1997.

[Matthes 1996] Matthes, F., R. Müller, and J.W. Schmidt. "Towards a Unified Model of Untyped Object Stores: Experiences with the Tycoon Store Protocol." In *Proceedings of the Third International Workshop on Advances in Databases and Information Systems (ADBIS 96)*, (Moscow, Russia, 1996), 1–9.

[Mattos 1996] Mattos, N. "An Overview of the SQL3 Standard." San Jose: Database Technology Institute, IBM Santa Teresa Laboratory, 1996.

[McAuliffe 1998] McAuliffe, M.L., M.J. Carey, and M.H. Solomon. "VClusters: A Flexible, Fine-Grained Object Clustering Mechanism." In *Proceedings of the ACM International Conference on Object-Oriented Programming Systems, Languages, and*

Applications (OOPSLA 98), (Vancouver, British Columbia, Canada: ACM Press, October 1998), 230–243.

[McBrien 1998] McBrien, P., A. Poulovassilis. "A Formalisation of Semantic Schema Integration." *Information Systems Journal* 23,5 (1998): 307–334.

[McHugh 1997] McHugh, J., S. Abiteboul, Q.D. Goldman, and J. Widom. "Lore: A Database Management System for Semistructured Data." *SIGMOD Record* 26,3 (1997): 54–66.

[Mephu 1993] Mephu Nguifo, E., and J. Sallantin. "Prediction of Primate Splice Junction Gene Sequences with a Cooperative Knowledge Acquisition system." In *Proceedings of the First International Conference on Intelligent Systems for Molecular Biology*, AAAI Press (1993): 292–300.

[Moerkotte 1999] Moerkotte, G. "Building Query Compiler." EDBT Summer School. La Baule Les Pins, France, 1999.

[Moreira 1998] Moreira, A.M.D. "Teaching Objects: The Case for Modelling." In *Proceedings of the ECOOP 98 Workshop on Learning and Teaching Objects Successfully* (Brussels, Belgium: Springer, July 1998), 350–354.

[Morrison 1993] Morrison, R., F. Brown, R. Connor, Q. Cutts, A. Dearle, G. Kirby, and D. Munro. "The Napier88 Reference Manual (Release 2.0)." University of St. Andrews, Scotland, November 1993 (CS/93/15).

[Moss 1992] Moss, J E B. "Working with Persistent Objects: To Swizzle or not to Swizzle." *IEEE Transactions on Software Engineering* 18,8 (1992): 657–673.

[Moussouni 1999] Moussouni, F., N.W. Paton, A. Hayes, S. Oliver, C.A. Goble, and A. Brass. "Database Challenges for Genome Information in the Post Sequencing Phase." In *Proceedings of the International Conference on Database and Expert Systems Applications (DEXA 99)*, (Florence, Italy: Springer, August-September 1999), 540–549.

[Mowbray 1997] Mowbray, T.J., and R.C. Malveau. *Corba Design Patterns*, New York, New York: John Wiley & Sons, 1997.

[Mowbray 1997a] Mowbray, T.J., and W.A. Ruh. *Inside CORBA: Distributed Object Standards and Applications*, Reading, Massachusetts: Addison-Wesley, 1997.

[Munro 1994] Munro, D.S., R.C.H. Connor, R. Morrison, S. Scheuerl, and D.W. Stemple. "Concurrent Shadow Paging in the Flask Architecture." In *Proceedings of the International Workshop on Persistent Object Systems (POS 6)*, Tarascon, Provence, France: Springer, September 1994.

[Mylopoulos 1990] Mylopoulos J., A. Borgida, M. Jarke, and M. Koubarakis. "Telos: Representing Knowledge About Information Systems." *ACM Transactions on Information Systems* 8,4 (1990): 325–362.

[Navathe 1986] Navathe, S.B., R. Elmasri, and J.A. Larson. "Integrating User Views in Database Design." *IEEE Computer* 19,1 (1986): 50–62.

[Needleman 1970] Needleman, S.B., and C.D. Wunsch. "A General Method Applicable for the Search for Similarities in the Amino Acid Sequences of Two Proteins." *Journal of Molecular Biology* 48 (1970): 443–453.

[O'Neil 1993] O'Neil, E.J., P.E. O'Neil, and G. Weikum. "The LRU-K Page Replacement Algorithm for Database Disk Buffering." In *Proceedings of the ACM SIGMOD International Conference on Management of Data* (Washington DC: ACM Press, May 1993), 297–306.

[O2 Technology 1992] O2 Reference Manual, *O2 Technology*, 1992.

[Object Design 1996] Object Design. "ObjectStore C++ API Reference." Release 4.0.1, May 1996.

[Object Design 1999] Object Design. "An XML Data Server for Building Enterprise Web Applications." White Paper, 1999.

[Object Design 1999a] Object Design. "ObjectStore Java API User Guide (ObjectStore 6.0)." 1999.

[Objectivity 1995] Objectivity. "Database Development of Objectivity/DB Version 3." Mountain View, California, 1995.

[Objectivity 1998] Objectivity. "Getting Started." www.objectivity.com/Products/Java/JavaGettingStarted.html.

[ODI 1999] Object Design. "Excelon—the EBusiness Information Server." White Paper, 1999.

[ODMG 1994] Object Data Management Group. "Response to the March 1994 ODMG-93 Commentary." www.acm.org/sigs/sigmod/record/issues/9409/ODMG.txt.

[ODMG 1996] Object Data Management Group *The Object Database Standard: ODMG-93*, Release 1.2, R.G.G. Cattell (ed.). San Francisco, California: Morgan Kaufmann Publishers, 1996.

[ODMG 1997] Object Data Management Group. "Object Database Standard: ODMG 2.0." San Francisco, California: Morgan Kaufmann Publishers, 1997.

[ODMG 1998] Cattell, R.G.G., D. Barry, D. Bartels, M. Berler, J. Eastman, S. Gamerman, D. Jordan, A. Springer, H. Strickland, and D. Wade. *The Object Database Standard: ODMG 2.0,* , San Francisco, California: Morgan Kaufmann Publishers, 1998.

[OMG] LSR. "OMG Life Sciences Research." www.omg.org/homepages/lsr/.

[OMG 1996] Object Management Group. "The Common Object Request Broker: Architecture and Specification." X/Open Company Ltd., UK.

[OMG 1998] Object Management Group. "CORBAservices: Common Object Services Specification." Chapter 5, Object Management Group. Cambridge, Massachusetts: December 1998.

[OMG 1999] Object Management Group. www.omg.org.

[ONTOS 1995] ONTOS. "ONTOS DB 3.1 Versioning Guide." 1995.

[Oracle 1999] Oracle Corporation. "XML Support in Oracle8i and Beyond." White Paper, 1999.

[Oracle 1999a] Oracle Corporation. "Oracle 8 Reference Manual, Release 8.0." 1999.

[Oracle JDBC Doc] Oracle Corporation. "JDBC Developer's Guide and Reference." Release 8.1.6. December 1999.

[Oracle JPub Doc] Oracle Corporation. "JPublisher Developer's Guide and Reference." Release 8.1.6. December 1999.

[Oracle SQLJ Doc] Oracle Corporation. "SQLJ Developer's Guide and Reference." Release 8.1.6. December 1999.

[Papakonstantinou 1995] Papakonstantinou, Y., H. Garcia-Molina, and J. Widom. "Object Exchange Across Heterogeneous Information Sources." In *Proceedings of the International Conference on Data Engineering (ICDE 95)*, IEEE Computer Society Press (March 1995): 257–260.

[Papazoglou 1994] Papazoglou M.P., B.J. Kramer, and A. Bouguettaya. "On the Representation of Objects with Polymorphic Shape and Behavior." In *Proceedings of the ER 94 Conference* (Manchester, UK: Springer, December 1994), 223–240.

[Parent 1992] Parent C., and S. Spaccapietra. "ERC+: An Object-Based Entity Relationship Approach." *Conceptual Modeling, Databases and CASE: An Integrated View of Information System Development*, P. Loucopoulos and R. Zicari (eds.). New York: John Wiley & Sons, 1992.

[Paton 1999] Paton, N.W., S.A. Khan, A. Hayes, F. Moussouni, A. Brass, K. Eilbeck, C.A. Goble, S. Hubbard, and S.G. Oliver. "Conceptual Modelling of Genomic Information." Submitted for publication, 1999.

[Poet] Poet Software. www.poet.com/.

[Poet 1999] Poet Software. "POET 6.0 User Guide." 1999.

[Poulovassilis 1998] Poulovassilis A., and P.A. McBrien. "General Framework for Schema Transformation." *Data and Knowledge Engineering* 28,1 (1998): 47–71.

[Quass 1996] Quass, D., J. Widom, R. Goldman, K. Haas, Q. Luo, J. McHugh, S. Nestorov, A. Rajaraman, H. Rivero, S. Abiteboul, J.D. Ullman, and J.L. Wiener. "LORE: A Lightweight Object Repository for Semistructured Data." In *Proceedings of the ACM SIGMOD International Conference on Management of Data* (Montreal, Quebec, Canada: ACM Press, June 1996), 549.

[Quass 1997] Quass, D., and J. Widom. "On-Line Warehouse View Maintenance for Batch Updates." In *Proceedings of the ACM SIGMOD International Conference on Management of Data* (Tucson, AZ: ACM Press, May 1997), 393–404.

[Rational 1998] Rational Software Corporation. "Rational Rose 98: Using Rational Rose/Oracle 8." 1998.

[Ridgway 1997] Ridgway, J.V.E., C. Thrall, and J.C. Wileden. "Toward Assessing Approaches to Persistence for Java." In *Proceedings of the Second International Workshop on Persistence and Java*, Half Moon Bay, California, August 1997.

[Ridgway 1998] Ridgway, J.V.E., and J.C. Wileden. "Toward Class Evolution in Persistent Java." In *Proceedings of the Third International Workshop on Persistence and Java* (Tiburon, California, September 1998), 353–362.

[Ripoche 95] Ripoche, H. "Une Construction Interactive d'Interpretations de Données, Applications aux Bases de Données de Séquences Génétiques". Ph.D. Thesis of University Montpellier II, December 1995.

[Rizzo 1999] Rizzo M. "Policies for Context-Aware Session Control." In *Proceedings of Policy Workshop 1999*, , Bristol, UK: HP-Laboratories, November 1999. www-dse.doc.ic.ac.uk/policy-99/program.html.

[Rodriguez-Martinez 2000] Rodriguez-Martinez, M., and N. Roussopoulos. "Automatic Deployment of Application-Specific Metadata and Code in MOCHA." In *Proceedings of International Conference on Extending Database Technology (EDBT 2000)*, (Konstanz, Germany: Springer, March 2000), 69–85.

[Rumbaugh 1991] Rumbaugh, M., M. Blaha, W. Premerlani, F. Eddy, and W. Lorensen. *Object-Oriented Modeling and Design*, , Englewood Cliffs, New Jersey: Prentice Hall, 1991.

[Sacki 1996] Sacki M. "A Meta-Model for Method Integration." *International Journal of Information and Software Technology* 38,14–15 (1998): 925–932.

[Sallantin 1986] Sallantin, J., *et al.* "Artificial Intelligence and Genetic Sequence Analysis: Toward an Intelligent Workstation, the BIOSTATION." Cube report for CEE BAP-0136F, 1986.

[Saltor 1997] Saltor, F., and E. Rodriguez. "On Intelligent Access to Heterogeneous Information." In *Proceedings of the 4th Workshop KRDB-97*, Athens, Greece, , August 1997. CEUR Workshop Proceedings, Volume 8, 15.1–15.7.

[Sander 1991] Sander, C., and R. Schneider. "Database of Homology-Derived Protein Structures and the Structural Meaning of Sequence Alignment." *Proteins* 9 (1991): 56–68.

[Schenck 1994] Schenck, D., and P. Wilson. *Information Modeling the EXPRESS Way*, Oxford: Oxford University Press, 1994.

[Schreiber 1994] Schreiber, H. "JUSTITIA: a Generic Benchmark for the OODBMS Selection." In *Proceedings of the Fourth International conference on Data and Knowledge Systems in Manufacturing and Engineering*, Hong Kong (1994): 324–331.

[Shaw 1999] Shaw, P., B. Becker, J. Klein, M. Hapner, G. Clossman, and R. Pledereder. "SQLJ: Java and Relational Databases." Tutorial, 1999. www.sqlj.org/.

[Shilling 1989] Shilling, J.J., and P.F. Sweeney. "Three Steps to Views: Extending the Object-Oriented Paradigm." In *Proceedings of ACM International Conference on Object-Oriented Programming Systems, Languages, and Applications (OOPSLA 89)*, (New Orleans, LA: ACM Press, October 1989), 353–361.

[Siegel 1996] Siegel, J. *CORBA Fundamentals and Programming*, New York: John Wiley & Sons, 1996.

[Singhal 1992] Singhal V, S.V. Kakkad, and P.R. Wilson. "Texas: An Efficient, Portable Persistent Store." In *Proceedings of the International Workshop on Persistent Object Systems (POS-5)*, San Miniato (Pisa), Italy: Springer, September 1992, 11–33.

[Sjolin 1994] Sjolin, M.A. "WWW Front End to an OODBMS." In Proceedings of *the 2nd International Conference on the World-Wide Web*, Chicago, IL, October 1994.

[Skarra 1987] Skarra, A., and S. Zdonik. "Type Evolution in an Object-Oriented Database." *Research Directions in Object-Oriented Programming*, Cambridge, Massachusetts: MIT Press, 1987.

[Sloman] Sloman, M., N. Dulay, and B. Nuseibeh. "EPSRC Grant GR/l 96103–SecPol: Specification and Analysis of Security Policy for Distributed Systems." Imperial College, Department of Computing, www.dse.doc.ic.ac.uk/projects/secpol/SecPol-overview.html.

[Software AG 1999] Software AG. "Tamino Information Server for Electronic Business." White Paper, 1999.

[SQLJ Home] www.sqlj.org/.

[Steel 1980] Steel, Jr., T.B. "Status Report on ISO/TC97/SC5/WG3–Data Base Management Systems." In *Proceedings of the International Conference on Very Large Data Bases (VLDB 6)*, (IEEE Computer Society Press, October 1980), 321–325.

[Stonebraker 1990] Stonebraker, M., L.A. Rowe, B. Lindsay, J. Gray, M.J. Carey, M.L. Brodie, P.A. Bernstein, and D. Beech. "Third-Generation Database System Manifesto—The Committee for Advanced DBMS Function." *SIGMOD Record* 19,3 (1990): 31–44.

[Stonebraker 1996] Stonebraker, M. and D. Moore. *Object Relational DBMSs: The Next Great Wave*, San Francisco, California: Morgan Kaufmann Publishers, 1996.

[Stroustrup 1986] Stroustrup, B. *The C++ Programming Language*, Reading, Massachusetts: Addison-Wesley, 1986.

[Summerville 1997] Summerville, I., and P. Sawyer. *Requirements Engineering*, Chichester, England: John Wiley & Sons, 1997.

[Sun Microsystems 1997] Sun Microsystems. "JavaBeans." Technical Report. Sun Microsystems, Inc. 2550 Garcia Avenue, Mountain View, California 94043.

[Sun Microsystems 1999] Sun Microsystems. "Java Data Objects Specification, JSR-12." Technical Report. Sun Microsystems, Inc. 2550 Garcia Avenue, Mountain View, California 94043.

[Tapia 1999] Tapia, P. "An Application of Object-Relational Concepts Using Oracle 8 and Java." Undergraduate Independent Study Report. Department of Computer Science and Engineering, Arizona State University. Summer 1999.

[Tari 1997] Tari, Z., J. Stokes, and S. Spaccapietra. "Object Normal Forms and Dependency Constraints for Object-Oriented Schemata." *ACM Transactions on Database Systems (TODS)* 22,4 (1997): 513–569.

[Teitelman 1984] Teitelman, W., and L. Masinter. "The Interlisp Programming Environment." *Computer* 14,4 (1981).

[Tjahjadi 1997] Tjahjadi, M. "The Design and Implementation of an EXPRESS to Oracle 8 Mapping." M.S. Thesis. Department of Computer Science and Engineering, Arizona State University. Summer 1997.

[TM-language 1996] TM-language. "OODM; Object Oriented Database Models." University of Twente, Department of Computer Science. 1996. http://wwwis.cs .utwente.nl:8080/oodm.html.

[Tsalgatidou 1991] Tsalgatidou A., and P. Loucopoulos. "Rule-Based Behavior ModelModeling: Specification and Verification of Information Systems Dynamics." *Journal of Information and Software Technology* 33,6 (1991).

[Tsichritzis 1988] Tsichritzis, D., and O. Nierstrasz. "Fitting Round Objects into Square Databases." In *Proceedings of the European Conference on Object-Oriented Programming (ECOOP 88)*, (Oslo, Norway: Springer, August 1988), 283–299.

[Turner 1995] Turner, P., and A.M. Keller. "Reflections on Object-Relational Applications." In *Proceedings of the OOPSLA 95 Workshop on Object and Relational Databases*, Austin, Texas: October 1995.

[Ullman 1988] Ullman, J.D. *Principles of Database and Knowledge-base Systems, Volume 1: Classical Database Systems*, Rockville: Computer Science Press, 1988.

[UML] "UML Resource Centre, Unified ModelModeling Language, Standard Software Notation." Rational Software Corporation. www.rational.com/uml/index.jtmpl.

[Urban 2000] Urban, S., M. Tjahjadi, J. Shah, J. Schafer, E. Harter, T. Bluhm, and B. Hartman. "A Case Study in Mapping Conceptual Designs to Object-Relational Schemas." To appear in the *Theory and Practice of Object Systems Section* of *Concurrency: Practice and Experience*, John Wiley & Sons, 2000.

[Vauttier 1999] Vauttier S., M. Magnan, and C. Oussalah. "Extended Specification of Composite Objects in UML." *Journal of Object Oriented Programming*, May 1999.

[Versant 1998] Versant. "Database Scalability and Clustering." Versant Object Technology. www.versant.com/us/whitepaper/scalability.pdf

[W3C 1998] W3C. 1998. "Document Object Model (DOM) Level 1 Specification." www.w3c.org/TR/REC-DOM-Level-1.

[W3C 1998a] W3C. "XML-Data." January 1998. www.w3.org/TR/1998/NOTE-XML-data-0105/Overview.html.

[Wade 1998] Wade, A.E. "Hitting the Relational Wall." Objectivity White Paper, 1998.

[Wang 1991] Wang, Y., and L.A. Rowe. "Cache Consistency and Concurrency Control in a Client-Server DBMS Architecture." In *Proceedings of the ACM SIGMOD International Conference on Management of Data* (Denver, Colorado: ACM Press, May 1991), 367–376.

[Wasserman 1998] Wasserman, T. "Features of UML Tools." In *Proceedings of the Technology of Object-Oriented Languages and Systems (TOOLS 98)*, IEEE Digital Library, 1998.

[Wells 1992] Wells, D.L., J.A. Blakeley, and C.W. Thompson. "Architecture of an Open Object-Oriented Management System." *IEEE Computer* 25,10 (1992): 74–82.

[White 1992] White, S.J., and D.J. DeWitt. "A Performance Study of Alternative Object Faulting and Pointer Swizzling Strategies." In *Proceedings of the International Conference on Very Large Data Bases (VLDB 92)*, (Vancouver, Canada: Morgan Kaufmann Publishers, August 1992), 419–431.

[White 1994] White, S J. "Pointer Swizzling Techniques for Object-Oriented Database Systems." Technical Report CS-94–1242, University of Wisconsin, Department of Computer Science, 1994.

[Wiederhold 1980] Wiederhold, G., and R. Elmasri. "The Structural Model for Database Design." *Entity-Relationship Approach to System Analysis and Design*, North-Holland (1980): 237–258.

[Wiederhold 1986] Wiederhold, G. "Views, Objects and Databases." *IEEE Computer* 19,2 (1986): 37–44.

[Wiederhold 1987] Wiederhold, G. *File Organization for Database Design*, New York: McGraw-Hill, 1987.

[Wisconsin, 1999] Wisconsin. "Lambda-DB." http://lambda.uta.edu/lambda-DB/manual.

[Wood 1998] Wood, L., (ed.). "Document Object Model (DOM) Level 1." W3C Recommendation. 1998.

[Woodfield 1997] Woodfield, S. "The Impedance Mismatch between Conceptual Models and Implementation Environments." In *Proceedings of the ER97 Conference*, Berlin, Germany: 1997.

[Young 1994] Young, N.E. "The k-Server Dual and Loose Competitiveness for Paging." *Algorithmica* 11,6 (1994): 525–541.

[Zicari 1991] Zicari, R. "A Framework for Schema Updates in an Object-Oriented Database." In *Proceedings of the International Conference on Data Engineering (ICDE 91)*, (Kobe, Japan: IEEE Computer Society Press, April 1991), 2–13.

[Zou 1998] Zou, C., B. Salzberg, and R. Ladin. "Back to the Future: Dynamic Hierarchical Clustering." In *Proceedings of the International Conference on Data Engineering (ICDE 98)*, (Orlando, Florida: IEEE Computer Society Press, February 1998), 578–587.

About the Contributors

Akmal B. Chaudhri is a Senior Architect with the Chief Technology Office at Informix Software. He has been working in the area of Object Databases both academically and commercially for nearly 10 years. He has been a regular presenter at a number of international conferences, such as OOPSLA and Object World. He has also co-edited the book *Object Databases in Practice*, Prentice-Hall, 1998. He holds a B.Sc. in Computing & Information Systems, an M.Sc. in Business Systems Analysis & Design and a Ph.D. in Computer Science. He likes to think that he is not an evangelist.

Roberto Zicari is full professor of computer science at the Johann Wolfgang Goethe University in Frankfurt, Germany. Previously he was an associate professor at Politecnico di Milano, Italy; visiting scientist at IBM Almaden Research Center and UC Berkeley; visiting professor at EPFL (Lausanne, Switzerland) and National University of Mexico City. Professor Zicari is the editor-in-chief of Theory and Practice of Object Systems (John Wiley). He is an internationally recognized expert in the field of object database systems. He has consulted and lectured in Europe, North America and Japan. Roberto Zicari holds a doctor of engineering degree from Politrecnico di Milano.

Chapter 1: OODBMS History and Concepts

Elisa Bertino is full professor of computer science in the Department of Computer Science of the University of Milan. She has been a visiting researcher at the IBM Research Laboratory (now Almaden) in San Jose, at the Microelectronics and Computer Technology Corporation in Austin, Texas, and at Purdue University. She is or has been on the editorial board of the following scientific journals: *ACM Transactions on Information* and *Systems Security, IEEE Transactions on Knowledge and Data Engineering, Theory and Practice of Object Systems Journal, Journal of Computer Security, Very Large Database Systems Journal, Parallel and Distributed Database,* and the *International Journal of Information Technology.* She is currently serving as Program chair of ECOOP 2000. Professor Bertino can be reached at bertino@dsi.unimi.it.

Giovanna Guerrini is an assistant professor at the Department of Computer and Information Sciences of the University of Genova. She received the MS and PhD degrees in Computer Science from the University of Genova, Italy, in 1993 and 1998, respectively. Her research interests include object-oriented, active, deductive and temporal databases, and the management of semi-structured information. She coorganized the "Objects and Databases" workshops associated with the ECOOP conference in '99 and 2000. Dr. Guerrini can be reached at guerrini@disi.unige.it.

Chapter 2: Mapping UML Diagrams to Object-Relational Schemas in Oracle 8

Susan D. Urban is an associate professor in the Department of Computer Science and Engineering at Arizona State University. She received the BS, MS, and PhD degrees in computer science from the University of Southwestern Louisiana. Her research interests include object-oriented data modeling, active rule processing in centralized and distributed environments, engineering databases, and distributed object computing. She is currently investigating the use of active rules in distributed environments for the interconnection of distributed database/software components. Urban is a member of the Association for Computing Machinery, the IEEE Computer Society, and the Phi Kappa Phi Honor Society. Dr. Urban can be reached at s.urban@asu.edu.

Suzanne W. Dietrich is an associate professor in the Department of Computer Science and Engineering at Arizona State University. Dr. Dietrich received the BS degree in computer science and applied mathematics in 1983 from the State University of New York at Stony Brook, and as the recipient of an Office of Naval Research Graduate Fellowship, earned her PhD degree in computer science at Stony Brook in 1987. Dr. Dietrich's areas of teaching and research include the educational, theoretical, and practical aspects of databases. Her current research focuses on the integration of active, object-oriented and deductive/declarative databases, and the application of this technology. Currently, her research is investigating the design of an integration rule language and the development of a middle-tier, rule-processing framework for the integration of distributed, black-box components. Dr. Dietrich is a member of the Association for Computing Machinery and IEEE Computer Society. Dr. Dietrich can be reached at dietrich@asu.edu.

Pablo Tapia works in the Department of Computer Science and Engineering at Arizona State University. Tapia received his BS degree in computer science from Arizona State University. During his senior year he did extensive research and study on object-oriented data modeling and fault analysis. His areas of interest are object-oriented technology, cellular networks and design patterns. He is currently working at Motorola in the CDMA Systems Division. He is a member of the IEEE Computer Society. Pablo Tapia can be reached at pt@asu.edu.

Chapter 3: SQLJ and JDBC: Database Access in Java

Julie Basu is presently a Development Manager in the Java Platform Group at Oracle and formerly was the project lead for Oracle's SQLJ product. She has over 10 years of design and hands-on development experience at Oracle and has worked on various projects relating to database programming. Julie holds a Master's and a PhD degree in Computer Science from Stanford University, and a Master's Degree from Indian Institute of Science, Bangalore. She has published several papers in database conferences and journals—details are available on her home page: www-db.stanford.edu/~basu/index.html. Julie can be reached at jbasu@us.oracle.com.

Chapter 4: Penguin: Objects for Programs, Relations for Persistence

Dr. Arthur M. Keller is Managing Partner and co-founder of Minerva Consulting, and consults for several high-tech e-commerce startups. Dr. Keller is co-founder and Chief Technical Advisor of ccRewards.com, an e-commerce startup offering online promotion products and services to Internet-based sellers and purchase management services to consumers. Dr. Keller served as Chief Technical Advisor for Persistence Software, starting with them shortly after their founding and continuing through their IPO in June 1999. During part of this period, he served on their Board of Directors. He also lead their Technical Advisory Board. Dr. Keller helped with the conceptual design of Persistence's PowerTier, the Engine for E-Commerce. Dr. Keller was also a co-founder of Mergent Systems (previously known as Epistemics), which was acquired by Commerce One in January 2000. Dr. Keller left Stanford University in 1999 after almost 12 years of research management in the Computer Science Department with the title of Senior Research Scientist. He served as project manager for Stanford's Center for Information Technology, and managed research and development work on integration of heterogeneous distributed databases and electronic commerce. He also managed Stanford's participation on CommerceNet, a consortium that pioneered electronic commerce on the internet, where his focus was on product information exchange. Dr. Keller can be reached at arthur@minervaconsulting.com.

Gio Wiederhold is a professor of Computer Science at Stanford University, with courtesy appointments in Medicine and Electrical Engineering. Wiederhold has authored and coauthored more than 250 publications and reports on computing and medicine. Current research includes privacy protection in collaborative settings, large-scale software composition, access to simulations to augment decision-making capabilities for information systems, and developing an algebra over ontologies. His early education was in Holland, he obtained a PhD in Medical Information Science from the University of California at San Francisco in 1976, after working 16 years in the software industry. He has been elected fellow of the ACMI, the IEEE, and the ACM. Gio's web page is http://www-db.stanford.edu/people/gio.html.

Chapter 5: A New Stage in ODBMS Normalization: Myth or Reality?

Sylvain Guennou is a senior consultant at the computer science R&D department of Caisse des Depots Group. With a theoretical and practical background of 15 years in Database Systems, his interests concern advanced database technologies like object, object-relational, deductive, time series or semi structured databases. Sylvain Guennou can be reached at sylvain.guennou@icdc.caissedesdepots.fr.

Chapter 6: PDOM: Lightweight Persistency Support

Gerald Huck is a member of research staff of GMD's Institute for Integrated Publication and Information Systems (IPSI) in Darmstadt, Germany. His research interests are methods and technologies for processing and managing semi-structured data, and their application in XML-middleware. Mr. Huck received an M.Sc. from Technical University Darmstadt in 1992 and is participating in European research projects as well as in W3C activities. Mr. Huck can be reached at huck@darmstadt.gmd.de.

Ingo Macherius is a member of research staff of GMD's Institute for Integrated Publication and Information Systems (IPSI) in Darmstadt, Germany. His research interests are focused on distributed, autonomous and heterogeneous information systems and their application in mediated e-commerce. Mr. Macherius received an M.Sc. from Clausthal University in 1998 and is participating in several W3C activities, including the XML Query working group. Mr. Macherius can be reached at macherius@gmd.de.

Peter Fankhauser is senior researcher and director of the XML Competence Center at the GMD Institute for Integrated Publication and Information Systems (IPSI). His main research and development interests lie in information brokering and transaction brokering. He has been the technical leader in the development of tools for unified access to information retrieval systems, document structure recognition, and the integration of heterogeneous databases. He is member of the W3C XML Query working group, and is one of the editors of the W3C XML-Query Requirements. He has received a PhD in computer science from the Technical University of Vienna in 1997, and has published several reviewed papers and book-chapters on document structure recognition, heterogeneous database integration, and robust transaction protocols for mediated e-commerce. Dr. Fankhauser can be reached at fankhaus@darmstadt.gmd.de.

Chapter 7: The Model of Object Primitives (MOP)

Nektarios Georgalas is a Research Engineer for British Telecommunications PLC. He received his Diploma in Electrical and Computer Engineering from the University of Patras, Greece in 1996 and his MPhil in Information Systems Engineering from the Department of Computation, UMIST, Manchester UK in 1998. He is currently working at British Telecommunications PLC (BT) conducting research in the areas of Data Management and Distributed Information Systems. He also pursues his BT-sponsored PhD studying the area of heterogeneous data management systems at the Department of Computer Science, Birkbeck College, University of London. His interests cover the areas of internet technologies (Java, XML), middleware, software components, modelling and integration of heterogeneous data. He is a member of the ACM SIGMOD. He can be reached at Nektarios.Georgalas@bt.com.

Chapter 8: A Performance Comparison of Object and Relational Databases for Complex Objects

Erlend Bjørge is a Senior Software Engineer in mogul.com Norway, formerly Numerica-Taskon. His focus is on Web/XML development with DBMS and is currently developing Web solutions with the ODBMS Jasmine ii. Bjørge graduated from Department of Information Science, University of Bergen, in March 1999 and can be reached at erlend@bjorge.net.

Chapter 9: Object Databases and Java Architectural Issues

Asbjørn Danielsen is an Assistant Professor at Narvik Institute of Technology (Høgskolen i Narvik) where he teaches in distributed systems, modern databases, and algorithms and datastructures. He has been working with databases for 12 years and computer science for 20 years. The last three years he has been working with object databases. He holds an MSc. degree in informatics from University of Oslo, Department of Informatics. He can be reached at asd@hin.no.

Chapter 10: Addressing Complexity and Scale in a High Performance Object Server

Alonso Marquez has a PhD in Computer Sciences from Paris XI University, France (1988). His major research interests include Orthogonal Persistence, Compilation, Dynamic program transformation, Database query optimization, Object Oriented Databases and Multidimensional Databases. This research activity has generated more than twenty publications in journals and proceedings. Dr. Marquez has 5 years of commercial experience in database and web server technologies including the complete design and development of a Web Site Manager System. In July 1998 he joined the Department of Computer Science at the Australian National University. He is now a Sun fellow and the project leader of the Upside project. This project is run by the CRC for Advanced Computational Systems. He can be reached at alonso@cs.anu.edu.au.

Steve Blackburn has a PhD in Computer Science from the Australian National University, where his primary research focus was on high performance persistent systems. He was leader of the Upside project at the ANU before leaving for the University of Massachusetts. His current research is focussed on scalable JVM design and implementation. Dr. Blackburn can be reached at steveb@cs.umass.edu.

Chapter 11: The Unified Modeling Process in Web-Deployed, Object-Oriented Database Systems

Terry Janssen received a PhD from George Mason University's School of Information Technology and Engineering and a Master of Science Degree from Boston University. Over the past 20 years has been involved with research and development, and systems engineering, of information systems. Until recently he was with University of Chicago's Argonne National Laboratory where he was a Scientist and Program Manager in the Decision and Information Sciences Division. In 1998 he formed a startup company, Expert Decision Systems, Inc. (www.exds.com). He is currently the President and CEO of EXDS and an Adjunct Professor at GMU, where he is currently conducting research and teaching in the Computer Science Department. During the writing of this Chapter he was teaching a graduate course on object-oriented database management systems.

David Rine is Professor of Computer Science and Professor of Information and Software Engineering at George Mason University. His research interests include improving software reuse practices, reusable software architectures, reusable components and adapters in distributed systems, quality assurance of distributed systems, and object-oriented modeling and design. He has held research grants from NSF and NASA. He obtained a PhD from the University of Iowa in 1970 and is a member of the ACM and IEEE.

Dr. Ernesto Damiani is a tenured Assistant Professor at the University of Milan's campus located in Crema, Italy, and a Visiting Senior Lecturer at the Computer Science Department of LaTrobe University, Melbourne, Australia. He is currently a Visiting Assistant Professor at the Computer Science Department of George Mason University. Dr. Damiani has published more than 60 papers in the fields of network-oriented software engineering, semi-structured information processing and soft computing. He is one of the authors of the XML-GL query language. He can be reached at edamiani@cs.gmu.edu.

Chapter 12: Teaching Object-Oriented Database Concepts

Dr. Zahir Tari is an Associate Professor at RMIT University in Melbourne, Australia. Currently, Dr. Tari is leading the DOK project which aims at designing and implementing federated services on a CORBA platform. Dr. Tari has been active in the international community, where he has acted as the PC co-chair of several international conferences (e.g. IFIP Working Conference on Database Semantics in 1998, IFIP Working Conference on Database Security in 2000, International Conference on Distributed Objects and Applications in 1999 and 2000). More details about Dr. Tari can be found at www.cs.rmit.edu.au/~zahirt.

Dr. Bukhres is an Associate Professor, Purdue University at Indianapolis, Indiana. Prior to joining Purdue University at Indianapolis, he was visiting associate professor on the faculty of Purdue University, West Lafayette, Indiana. His research interests include data mining and warehousing, integration of heterogeneous database systems, distributed transaction, multimedia databases, mobile and client server computing. Currently, Dr. Bukhres is the co-principal investigator of the Large Scale Distributed Computing and Multimedia Laboratory, Purdue University at Indianapolis. The purpose of this laboratory is to conduct both theoretical and experimental research in distributed multimedia information systems. The research projects are being conducted in close collaboration with the multimedia laboratory at Purdue University, West Lafayette campus. The current research focus is in two areas: (I) database management systems for multimedia data, and (II) seamless integration of the distributed multimedia databases. He has served on the program committees of various IEEE database conferences, SIGMOD, VLDB, ICDE, RIDE and EDBT. He has co-authored over 70 articles, 15 book chapters and two books on object-oriented multidatabases and distributed object management. He is a member of the ACM IEEE/CS, and SIGMOD/ACM. Dr. Bukhres can be reached at bukhres@cs.iupui.edu.

Gregory Craske completed his computer science undergraduate degree with honors in 1997. He is currently conducting his PhD research on the CORBA Trading Service and has published in conferences (ICDCS, DOA) and a journal (IEICE). He has been a sessional tutor and laboratory instructor for four years in undergraduate and postgraduate subjects. He has taught subjects in the areas of programming, software engineering, and databases, all within the context of object orientation. He can be reached at craske@cs.rmit.edu.au.

Chapter 13: Building a Jasmine Database

Peter Fallon is the director of Castle Software Australia Pty Ltd, a company providing custom software development, training and consulting. He has been developing and supporting PC database applications since 1986, ranging from small business systems to large corporate installations. Peter has spoken on topics covering programming, project management, object-oriented techniques and Jasmine at many CA conferences from Technicon 1992 to CA-World 99. Currently Peter is working on a number of Jasmine products and training services as well as various CA-Visual Objects, Visual Basic and Access development projects. He can be reached at peterfallon@castlesoftware .com.au.

Chapter 14: Seamlessness and Transparency in Object-Oriented Databases

Dr. Alan Kaplan is an Assistant Professor in the Department of Computer Science at Clemson University in Clemson, South Carolina. Dr. Kaplan received the B.S. degree in computer science from Duke University, Durham, NC, and the M.S. and Ph.D. degrees in computer science from the University of Massachusetts at Amherst. His research interests include tools and techniques supporting software development, object-oriented databases, and interoperability. He can be reached at kaplan@cs.clemson.edu.

Jack C. Wileden is a Professor in the Department of Computer Science at the University of Massachusetts at Amherst and Director of the Convergent Computing Systems

Laboratory there. Dr. Wileden received a degree in mathematics and the MS and PhD degrees in computer and communications sciences from the University of Michigan, Ann Arbor. His current research interests center on tools and techniques supporting seamless integration of advanced capabilities into computing systems. Professor Wileden can be reached at wileden@cs.umass.edu.

Chapter 15: Experiences Using the ODMG Standard in Bioinformatics Applications

Norman W. Paton is a Professor of Computer Science at the University of Manchester, where he co-leads the Information Management Group. He obtained a BSc in Computing Science from Aberdeen University in 1986, and a PhD from the same institution in 1989. From 1989 to 1996, he worked as a lecturer at Heriot-Watt University. His research interests have mainly related to object databases, including work on deductive, active and spatial facilities, and user interfaces to data intensive systems. He is currently also working on bioinformatics, including systems for supporting querying over distributed bioinformatics resources. He can be reached at norm@cs.man.ac.uk.

Chapter 16: An Object-Oriented Database for Managing Genetic Sequences

Zohra Bellahsene is an Assistant Professor in Computer Science at the University of Montpellier II France, since 1987. She received her PhD degree in Computer Science from the University of Paris VI, in 1982, and her Habilitation à Diriger des Recherches from the University of Montpellier II, in 2000. She has devoted her recent research to object-oriented database views and view adaptation in data warehousing systems. Dr. Bellahsene can be reached at bella@lirmm.fr.

Hugues Ripoche has a PhD from Montpellier University / LIRMM laboratory. His interests include object-oriented databases, genetic sequence analysis, and data mining. He currently works at Fi SYSTEM, a group specialized in providing global internet/intranet solutions for dot coms and other companies. Dr. Ripoche can be reached at hugues.ripoche@fisystem.fr.

Chapter 17: The Geospatial Information Distribution System (GIDS)

Miyi Chung has been technically leading the development of the Geospatial Information Database System at Naval Research Laboratory. Her research interests are in spatial data management, spatial data mining in object-oriented database, and spatio-temporal data modeling. She received her BSEE from University of Maryland in College Park in 1985, MSEE from George Washington University in 1991, and pursuing PhD at Tulane University in Computer Science. She can be reached at chung@nrlssc.navy.mil.

Ruth Wilson is a mathematician for the Naval Research Laboratory. Her research interests include object-oriented programming, mathematical techniques to improve digital mapping, and distributed communication of mapping data between servers and users in real time. Wilson received a BS in mathematics from the University of Southern Mississippi and an MS in mathematics from McNeese State University. She can be reached at ruth.wilson@nrlssc.navy.mil.

Roy Ladner is a computer scientist at the Naval Research Laboratory at Stennis Space Center, Mississippi where he is engaged in research in the generation of 3D synthetic environments. He holds a Master's Degree in Computer Science, and he is currently a PhD candidate in Engineering and Applied Sciences at the University of New Orleans. He can be reached at rladner@nrlssc.navy.mil.

Todd Lovitt is a computer scientist and mathematician with Planning Systems Incorporated. He has been working with the Naval Research Laboratory on the design and development of object-oriented databases of digital mapping data. His research interests include realistic 3-D visualization of urban areas, and distributed techniques for integration and display of disparate geospatial data types across the internet. He received a BS in mathematics and computer science from Mississippi State University. He can be reached at todd.lovitt@psislidell.com.

Maria A. Cobb is an assistant professor in the Department of Computer Science & Statistics at the University of Southern Mississippi in Hattiesburg, MS. Dr. Cobb received a PhD in Computer Science from Tulane University in 1995. She is currently an assistant professor of computer science at the University of Southern Mississippi, and was previously employed by the Naval Research Laboratory as a computer scientist. Her primary research interests are spatial data modeling, including techniques for modeling and reasoning about spatial data under uncertainty, and distributed object-oriented systems. Dr. Cobb can be reached at maria.cobb@usm.edu.

Mahdi Abdelguerfi is chair of the Computer Science Department at the University of New Orleans. His research interests include databases, 3D synthetic environments, and GIS systems. He can be reached at mahdi@cs.uno.edu.

Kevin B. Shaw leads a Naval Research Laboratory R&D team that focuses on advanced geospatial modeling and database design and implementation for improved Naval mapping. Mr. Shaw received a BS in Electrical Engineering from Mississippi State University in 1984, an MS in Computer Science from the University of Southern Mississippi in 1987, and a MEE in Electrical Engineering from Mississippi State University in 1988. Mr. Shaw can be reached at shaw@nrlssc.navy.mil.

Chapter 18: Architecture of the Distributed, Multitier Railway Application DaRT

Juergen Zimmermann is a recognized expert in object technology and in particular in database systems and middleware. As a researcher he was involved in many research projects. For instance he co-operated with the labs of Texas Instruments, Dallas, in the Open OODB project sponsored by DARPA. Between 1996 and 1998 Zimmermann set up the consulting group for Object Design, Germany. In 1998 he joined sd&m as a senior consultant for large-scale projects. His main focus is on software architectures and IT strategies.

Heiko Wilhelm is senior executive at sd&m. He is/was manager of several software projects, especially for the German Railway Company, and consultant for Audi and DaimlerChrysler. He focuses on object-oriented technology. Dr. Wilhelm studied mechanical engineering and received his Ph.D. from the Technical University of Chemnitz. After three years in the technique department at the Wismut AG, he joined sd&m in 1992. Dr. Wilhelm can be reached at heiko.wilhelm@sdm.de.

Marcus Zander is a senior consultant at sd&m AG, a software company based in Munich. He is specialized in client/server architectures and has been the technical designer for several software projects, including the DaRT system.

Also contributing to this chapter is **Manfred Lange**.

Index